A Long Short Life

By

Merle W. Mc Morrow

Also by Merle W. Mc Morrow

Remembrance of Things Past

From Breckenridge to Bastogne

From Rome to Berlin via Bastogne

A Long Short Life

The Trials, Tribulations, Travels, and Trivia of an 88 Year Old Kid

MERLE W. McMORROW

Order this book online at www.trafford.com
or email orders@trafford.com

Most Trafford titles are also available at major online book retailers.

Printed in the United States of America.

ISBN: 978-1-4269-4938-8 (sc)
ISBN: 978-1-4269-4939-5 (e)

Trafford rev 12/06/2010

 www.trafford.com

North America & international
toll-free: 1 888 232 4444 (USA & Canada)
phone: 250 383 6864 ♦ fax: 812 355 4082

To my two wonderful sons

Tom Mc Morrow
Mark Mc Morrow

CHAPTERS

Foreword

I am 88 years old and I recognize that I have passed the life expectancy figure used to establish what constitutes a life span. I lived in a period that went from outhouses to outer space; from kerosene lamps and kerosene stoves to electric ovens and microwaves; from simple hand-operated adding machines and typewriters .to I-pods, Blackberries, cell phones and computers.

Before my final day arrives, I would like to leave behind some information that proves I really did exist. I don't want my life to be a mystery such as my dad's life was to me and to my brothers and sisters. We know very little about things that may have happened in his 65 years of life between the period 1891 and 1956. I wished he had had lived long enough to experience some the exciting things that I have had the opportunity to see and enjoy.

This book is not a story of my life per se but merely events and happenings that occurred and are documented to the extent possible, in a sequential order of time. I would have preferred to create an interesting, exciting story of my life. However, after the death of my parents what little I knew about events that happened in their lives, I felt it was more important for me to make this a documentary rather than a story.

A number of chapters, such as my sons' scouting years and memories of the times spent at Otter Tail Lake in Minnesota, are chapters that can stand alone and may cover events over a long period of time. I tried, to the extent possible; to keep events that happened to me in an orderly listing by years. I found that items relating to a specific subject, such as medical problems, were best handled in one chapter even though they took place over many years.

I believe I became aware one day in 1956,while sitting on the bank of Otter Tail Lake in Minnesota, how little I really knew about my parents. I realized then that in order to fill the gap between generations, information must be shared and made available to bridge that gap. This can only be done by leaving an oral or written record of events that related to the family and members of the family. By doing so it provides the only means of establishing a direct link between the past and the present.

As I sat there above the lake shore watching my two young sons playing the sand, I realized it seemed as though it hadn't been, too many years since my brother Bob and I were that age. We played in a sandpit adjacent to the Otter Tail River on the north end of 10th Street in Breckenridge, Minnesota. A fellow named Ray Lambert scooped out an area adjacent to the river. He then built a wooden chute next to the scooped out pit. A large pump attached to a 12-inch diameter hose would provide a vacuum as the hose was dropped into the river. The pump would convey sand-laden water to the pit. The sand would settle out of the water in the scooped out area. When the area was filled with water the water would overflow and return to the river via a constructed channel. Soon the dished out area was filled with sand.

We had built castles and constructed roads in the sand at Lambert's pit as the two young brothers were now doing at the lakeshore. As a father watching and listening to them I realized how little I knew about my parents. At their age I probably showed no more interest in anything beyond the moment at hand. As I sat there I thought of many things I needed to ask my parents. However, there would always be time to ask those questions after the more important things were taken care of. Later that year on a cold November 6th day my father died.

Now the questions I had in my mind would never be answered. How simple it would have been to spend short periods of time with my dad and let him reminisce and share with me some of his most memorable events in his life. I knew nothing in detail about his family or his early life. How simple it would have been to occasionally ask him about his early days of growing up on the farm. What were his brothers and sisters like? What were his memories of his military life in Texas during World War I? How did he and my mother meet? I would like to have had him share with me what their early dreams and expectations were as far as sharing a life together. Now many of the items relating to my parents were from my memory of events as a child or obtained through research or by word of mouth from others that knew them. Nothing would be a first-hand account conveyed by them to me.

My parents separated about the time I graduated from high school. After that I had very little contact with my mother prior to her death in 1968. I was bitter and blamed her for destruction of our family. Never would the family, as a total unit, share in celebrations such as holidays, graduations, weddings, christenings and reunions. I now wish I could have recognized that it must have been an agonizing decision that she had to make before leaving. She evidently had a good reason for leaving because she must have recognized that it would totally destroy the family.

Our only contact following her decision to leave was an exchange of letters while I was in Bremerton, Washington during 1942. I spent 9 months working in the Puget Sound Navy Yard. She indicated to me she was going to seek a divorce and I responded by pleading that she reconsider her action. She followed up with a letter indicating she had given it considerable thought and was going to proceed. That then was the end of our communication for a number of years.

I wish I could delay the publishing of this book as long as possible to eliminate the need for subsequent editions. I don't think I will be granted that wish.

What follows are, to the best of my knowledge, events in my life that I reminisce about when I reflect back on the years that have come and gone. I hope it will help explain who I am and why.

Introduction

Initially I intended to start telling the story of my life by beginning with my birth and continuing from that point year by year. As I got into the first chapter it became readily apparent that that approach wouldn't be practical or possible. The need to backtrack to certain material became obvious. Also it seemed logical to handle specific material in separate sections or chapters unrelated to other events that may have happened during the same time period. I am hoping I may be able to have each chapter stand-alone and cover one part or event of my life. A summary or synopsis of the lives of my parents and brothers and sisters is set out separately in the book. However, as I begin to relate my story they naturally become interwoven with other things that happened to me.

It is surprising how many things come to mind as one begins to reminisce. I am certain by the time I finish with this writing many things will have been overlooked. That was the case with the first book that I had written about my military activities. I produced a 2nd and 3rd edition with each having additional material included. The latest version relating to my military time is titled

From Rome to Berlin via Bastogne and is available from Amazon.com and BookSurge.com. Even more could be added after visiting the battlefields of France during their 65th anniversary celebration in August 2009. They call August 15th Liberation Day. My wife Mardy and I met so many wonderful people who are second and third generation and so totally grateful for our sacrifices during World War II. They celebrate with parades, food, dancing and the wine flows freely. For three days we feel like 20 year olds again and we are welcomed as conquering heroes.

Having lived through what was termed the Great Depression, World War II and the Cold War many events that took place during those three periods in time provided some unforgettable memories.

The Cold War began almost immediately after conclusion of World War II in 1945 and wasn't over until the 1990s. I was in Berlin on occupation duty for five months at the end of the war. The city was broken into four zones-American, French, British and Russian. Tensions were strained right from the start. An arms race began. President Roosevelt had hoped and believed that if the bomb being developed by the Manhattan Project was successful it would perpetuate the wartime alliance with the Soviet Union and force it into cooperation in the post-war years. However, the President didn't live to see the successful testing of the bomb in the New Mexico desert on July 16, 1945 nor the successful use of the bomb against Japan on two occasions in August 1945.

During the Potsdam meeting, held by the Big Three on July 24, 1945, Truman had approached Stalin with contrived casualness as the dictator was leaving the conference room. Truman had said the United States "had a new weapon of unusual destructive force." Stalin simply nodded his thanks and left the room. Spies had already provided Stalin with the information. Truman used scare tactics which he thought would hold the

Soviets in check for many years into the future. He and his new secretary of state James Byrnes had devised a scheme of "atomic diplomacy" to wield the bomb as a cudgel to keep the Soviets in line in the post war years. However, the scientific community and the intelligent services believed the Soviets would have a comparable bomb by no later than the mid-1950s. Today in a little over 50 years nine nations have the capability of nuclear retaliation.

By 1955 the consensus of a few leaders at the top had become the consensus of the nation. We needed the intercontinental ballistic missiles (ICBM) to prevent Russia from a preemptive strike. Many things have happened since then.

Also many wonderful developments became available in my time. I saw the invention of radio, the first use of electricity in many of our appliances of today. Television, electric typewriters and calculators, computers, air travel, space travel, automatic washers and dryers, electric stoves, air conditioners, microwave, cell phones, ipods and a host of other electronic gadgets are available to those living today. Those using these items see nothing special about their availability. I still marvel at many of conveniences we have today.

I will delay publishing this book in an attempt to eliminate the need for subsequent editions. This will permit me to add items and material as things come to mind.

As mentioned earlier, I at the age of 87 assume I will not be blessed with too much time to ponder on what I may have missed and failed to include in my writing. However, it will give me an opportunity to reminisce as I review the events that happened during a long short life.

Preface

As mentioned earlier, it is hoped this book will not only help the reader to better understand who I am but with a little family background also why I am as I am.

Both my parents were intelligent, but not the type of intelligence recognized and measured by diplomas and awards, but in the ways of life. They weren't ignorant of the importance of an education but they never had the opportunities nor did they ever believe their children would ever have the opportunity of an education beyond high school.

I remember many evenings when the whole family would sit and listen to my mother read. It wasn't Shakespeare or other great literary works. Rather than books or magazines containing intellectual content, it was True Story, Saturday Evening Post or other comparable magazines that were published more to entertain rather than to inform.

They left no record of their lives in words other than legal documents required by law such as marriage license, birth certificates, baptism certificates and other such requirements. I wished I had asked my parents more questions about their early lives and the lives of their parents. It didn't seem important at the time when I had the opportunity and suddenly one day it was too late.

As I watched those two young brothers playing in the sand, I realized they were unaware of the past and unconcerned about the future. I decided that warm afternoon by the lake that I needed to document everything I could remember about my life. This would not only put some continuity to the events that I remembered which seemed important to me but it would also help my family and siblings understand and appreciate the hardships and difficulties their ancestors encountered to make a better life for themselves. They would be more appreciative of the things they have been blessed with in their lifetime.

My life has not been what would be considered exciting and notable to others. However, I have experienced things that can only be achieved by existing over a long period of time. Two major events in my life that helped to shape what I would become and who I am today were the Great Depression and World War II. I was born in 1923 just six years before the crash on Wall Street. In those six years production of consumer goods was unbelievable. Desirable new products such as radios, electric refrigerators and faster cars were in great demand. Free radio home entertainment resulted in 600 million dollars in radio sales in a very short time when they came on the market. Wilbur B. Foshay dedicated his 32 story Foshay Tower in August 1929. Two months later his Empire crashed. Many years later during Minnesota trips our family always made a trip to the top of the Foshay Tower to look out over the city of Minneapolis.

After six years of wonderful prosperity the stock market crashed on what became known as Black Thursday (October 24, 1929). By October 29th stock prices had dropped to unprecedented lows and people began making runs on their banks to draw out what little savings they had in the bank. My Uncle Charley and Aunt Adeline Spreckles lost $2,700 in a bank failure in Hankinson, North Dakota. That was a huge sum of money when you consider an annual salary at that time for the average person was $1,000 or less. Other family members had always considered them wealthy and suddenly they had nothing.

Years later during the mid-1930s when I visited my grandparents in Hankinson I would also spend some time at the Spreckles. Charley had a flourmill on the north end of Main Street in Hankinson. He ground wheat into flour for the State of North Dakota. It was sold under the name Dakota Maid and the flour sacks had a picture of an Indian maid on the front. Many of these sacks were made into dresses for young girls. Charley had a beat-up pickup and we would go at breakneck speed from the house to the mill. I would hang on and scream as we went around the corners on the two-track dirt roads.

It was great at their place at mealtime. There were huge plates of fried chicken and all kinds of side dishes with apple pie for dessert. They had an apple orchard on the north side of the house so apple dumplings, apple crisp and other kinds of apple delight were always available at various times of the day.

I was 6 years old at the time of the crash and starting in my first grade of school. Although there were over 3 million unemployed in the country, my dad, who had been employed four years earlier by the Great Northern Railroad, had steady work. I am fairly certain my parents worried about the economic times. Many in the larger cities were selling apples on street corners for five cents each. The freight trains rolling west carried human cargo in addition to freight. Many thought the opportunity for work in the orchards out west would provide some income. The majority of those individuals going west were either single or men who had left their families behind in hopes of finding work.

Although my dad's net useable income was reduced considerably because of cost relating to medical needs, we were much better off financially than many others were. My brother Bob, my sister Mavis and I saw no difference in our pre-depression and post-depression lifestyle. We never went to bed hungry and always seemed to have adequate clothing for the type of weather we experienced. We had everything but money. We didn't know we were poor but I am certain our parents knew it. At my age I now know hard times come and go and the Bible tells us the poor will always be with us.

One proposal to alleviate some of the hardship being experienced by many in the country was the immediate payment of a "bonus" to World War I veterans. Soldiers would receive $1 for each day of service served stateside and $1.25 for each day overseas. However, even though the bonus bill had passed in 1924, President Hoover was opposed to its passage because of its cost. The cost was estimated to be 4 billion dollars. People on relief in New York City cost the city government a little over $8.00 per month.

In the summer of 1932 up to 25,000 World War I soldiers began arriving in Washington, DC. Known as the "Bonus Expeditionary Force" the men began setting up encampments on the Capitol grounds. When the group was told to leave the grounds violence erupted and General Douglas Mc Arthur, along with DC police, were ordered to clear the area. I remember my parents discussing this matter at the dinner table since my dad was eligible for bonus money and they were very interested as to the outcome of the legislation. The House passed the bill but it was defeated in the Senate.

A self-named Bonus Expeditionary Force of 17,000 World War I veterans marched on Washington, DC and set up camp in the Anacostia flats. The war veterans, many who had been out of work since the beginning of the Great Depression, demanded immediate payment of the cash promised them eight years earlier via the Adjusted Service Certificate Law of 1924.

President Hoover ordered the Army to clear out the area and have the shelters and belongings of the veterans burned. General Douglas Mac Arthur was the Army officer in charge and was the ordered to clear the area.

After Franklin Roosevelt was elected president, his wife Eleanor urged members of the Bonus Army to apply for work with the Works Progress Administration building the Overseas Highway to Key West. Several hundred veterans were later killed in the September 1935 hurricane. We have driven that highway a number of times.

Congress overrode a Roosevelt veto in 1936 to give the veterans their bonus.

I heard no more about bonus money until 1937 when my dad told me to go down to the Post Office and pick up his bonus check. It was over $1,300. I was so proud that he had selected me to go and get the money for him. I showed the check to a number of people on my way home. I couldn't wait to get home and show it to my dad. I don't know if he was aware of the amount or not but to me that seemed like an astronomical amount.

After Franklin D. Roosevelt defeated Herbert Hoover for the Presidency in 1932, he instituted many make-work programs during his first term in office. Our newly elected president (Barack Obama) is in a similar situation to that of President Roosevelt. The country is in shambles economically and its citizens have placed their hopes in the new president to solve the many problems the country faces. Like 1929 many people lost a great part of their savings in 2008.

Our country struggled through the 1930s and into the early '40s. Economic times began changing about the time the country realized war was on the horizon and the country was woefully unprepared.

The other event that drastically changed the course of my early life was the attack on Pearl Harbor and the beginning of World War II. After being attacked by the Japanese on December 7, 1941 the country went to a war production mode. The depression no longer existed. War production almost eliminated unemployment. Jobs were available to everyone that wanted to work and most wages jumped fourfold.

CHAPTER 1

FAMILY BACKGROUND

My paternal great-grandparents originated in Canada of French ancestry. My great-grandmother, Mrs. Laura (Le Bonte) Le Mieux was born in Quebec, Canada on June 8, 1846. When she was nine years old, she came to the United States with her parents. They settled near Ashkum, Illinois. She married Thomas Le Mieux in 1866. They moved to Wisconsin the following year and in 1877 they moved to Morris, Minnesota to live. They had four daughters and one son. The oldest daughter, Adeline Agnes Louise, born in 1866, became my grandmother.

Anna, born in 1869, never married, and died at the age of 84 in Morris. Mary married Jim Hanlon and had two sons: one born in 1912 and the other in 1917. Josephine died at the age of 14 of influenza. Abraham was 20 years when he was killed near Campbell, Minnesota while working for the Great Northern Railroad. With the exception of my grandmother, all are buried in the Catholic Cemetery in Morris. My grandmother is buried in the Catholic Cemetery south of Hankinson, North Dakota.

Thomas Le Mieux, my great grandfather, was listed in the church records as being 82 years old at the time of his death in 1915. That would indicate he was born in 1833. If an article on his death can be found, it may clear up some of the confusion regarding the date of his birth.

My paternal grandfather, Henry Benjamin McMorrow, was born in County Cork, Ireland in 1850 and died in Hankinson North Dakota on March 12, 1906. When he was in his 20's, he immigrated to this country. He settled near Askum, Illinois. He married a woman named Annie, and they had three children, a daughter and two sons. This marriage ended in the late 1870's with the death of his wife. He then moved to western Minnesota where he met my grandmother, Adeline Agnes Louise Le Mieux. They were probably married in 1882 or early 1883. The first of thirteen children, William Henry McMorrow, was born on December 13, 1883. He died at the age of 14. Two other children died as infants (Laura) in 1898 and (Unnamed) 1899. The last of the 13 children born of this marriage died in the nursing home in Wahpeton, North Dakota, in 1989.

Henry McMorrow, my grandfather, came to the Hankinson, North Dakota area and homesteaded 160 acres in Greendale Township located about five miles southeast of town. He worked for R.H. Hankinson for two years in order to support his family and to buy a team of oxen. My grandmother often told her children of how she lived in fear of the Indians coming while their father was in town at work. Many times in the winter, their tiny 3-room shanty was completely buried under snow. The sod house had 16-inch thick walls and was warm in the winter and cool in the summer. The floor was compacted as hard as concrete from the constant foot traffic. Six-inch diameter cottonwood timbers overlain with prairie sod provided the roof support. At night, she could hear the coyotes and fox on the roof of the house.

My dad (Robert) was sixth in order of birth. Four brothers, William, Joseph, Frank, Phillip, and one sister, Adeline, were born at Wahpeton. My dad was born at the farm southeast of Hankinson on March 20, 1891. The other children, Leonard, Benjamin, Josephine, Laura, Infant, Margaret and Edward were also born in Hankinson.

My paternal grandfather died on March 12, 1906, leaving my grandmother with 10 children, the youngest a boy of 14 months. My paternal grandmother died eight years later in 1914 at the age of 48. She had been troubled with a goiter problem for many years, and complications associated with this problem caused her death. My dad and his two brothers, Frank and Phil, were harvesting grain in Canada and could not be located at the time of death, and therefore, missed their mother's funeral.

My maternal great grandparents, August Kath and Louise Held, were born in Germany. They married and had seven sons. In order to escape hardship and poverty in West Prussia, the family immigrated to the United States in 1893. After landing in Quebec, Canada, they traveled up the St. Lawrence River by boat to Minnesota. They then traveled over land to Dundas, a small town near Faribault, Minnesota. They came to Richland County, North Dakota a short time later in search of a better life and homesteaded in Duerr Township. Their children, Carl, John and Gustave, who were grown by this time, also came to live in the Hankinson area. Their oldest son, Albert, stayed near Faribault. Herman became a section foreman for the Great Northern Railroad in Glendive, Montana. William graduated from Lutheran Seminary in St. Paul, Minnesota, and became a parochial school teacher.

My maternal grandfather John Kath was born in Penkuhl, West Prussia, Germany on April 15, 1875. He was working in the Martin Luther Coal Mine at the time he left Germany. He was 17 years old when he left with his parents for America.

My maternal grandmother, Martha Kolterman, also came to America from Germany with her parents when she was two years old. They arrived here in 1884 and settled in the Faribault area.

John and Martha Kath were married in 1901 and settled on a farm outside of Faribault. They continued farming until 1909 when Martha was stricken with polio shortly before the birth of Edward. They gave up farming and moved to Hankinson, North Dakota.

Seven children were born during their stay in Minnesota. These were Hattie, my mother Clara, William, George, Edward Elizabeth and Arthur. There were six additional children born in Hankinson after their move to North Dakota.

Because of my grandmother's polio, her young son, Edward was left behind in Minnesota with Martha's mother, Mrs. Kolterman. She continued to raise him. One of the six children (Dorothy) born in Hankinson is alive today (2010). Dorothy lives in Hankinson. Esther died in Faribault, Minnesota on February 1, 1994 at the age of 79. Gladys died in Faribault on July 8, 1996 at the age of 74. Robert died in Minneapolis on December 30, 1999 at the age of 69. Reuben died in Wahpeton, North Dakota on September 14, 2008 at the age of 83.

My mother was born in the Faribault, Minnesota area on June 27, 1903 and moved to Hankinson with her parents during her teen-age years. She died of a heart attack at the age of 65 on August 11, 1968 while she was visiting her sister Hattie in Chisago City, Minnesota.

My father was born on March 20, 1891 on a farm located approximately five miles southeast of Hankinson North Dakota in Richland County. Hankinson is a small town in the southeast corner of the State and had a population of approximately 1,400 people at the time of my father's birth. The Minneapolis, St. Paul & Sault Ste Marie Railroad (Soo Line) bisected the town and served as it principal means for the movement of goods and transportation of its people.

My dad was 15 years old when his father died in 1906 and he was 23 years old at the time of his mother's death in 1914. He was unaware of her death until after he returned from farm work in Canada. My father also died of a heart attack at the age of 65 on November 6, 1956.

My parents were married in May 1922, and lived in Hankinson until 1925. They then moved to Breckenridge, Minnesota, where my father had been offered a job with the Great Northern Railroad.

Breckenridge was larger than Hankinson and had a population of 3,800. It is located at the junction of three rivers---Bois de Sioux comes from the south and intersects the Ottertail River coming from the east. This union forms the famous Red River of the North that flows north into Lake Winnepeg in Canada. The town is at the southern end of the Red River Valley that at one time was the bottom of glacial Lake Aggassiz. It is a very rich agricultural area. The town was named for John Cabell Breckenridge, Vice President from 1856 to 1860. The first settlement in the area that would become the town site was made in 1857. The town was destroyed during the Sioux uprising of 1862.

The move my parents made from Hankinson to Breckenridge, a distance of 27 miles, was made with a hayrack and team of horses. A part of the two-lane graveled road they traveled to get to Breckenridge is 4-lane Interstate Highway I-29 today. They moved all their worldly possessions in that hayrack. My father worked with the railroad for 31 years, retiring during the summer of 1956.

My mother and father began divorce proceedings the year after my graduation from high school in 1941. The decree became final in June 1943. My mother remarried in 1945 and lived in a number of places before returning to Breckenridge.

My parents were both born into poverty and were never able to rise above it. The Great Depression of the 1930's caused many to give up hope. Poor health, as a result of diabetes plagued my father most of his life. However, he was a hard worker and never complained that he may have been shortchanged when the qualities of life were distributed. Both parents set standards for their children to follow and they both desired more out of life for their children then than they were able to achieve for themselves. However, their period of life was short and I don't know if they were able to appreciate or were aware that their example of hard work, honesty, and love of country was instilled in their children. My father had been in World War I and I remember, as a small kid, he always removed his hat when the flag passed by. It didn't matter how far he was from the flag. If he could see the flag, he showed his respect.

Seven children were born of the first marriage. Four were boys and three were girls. A daughter (JoAnn) was born in 1945 during my mother's second marriage. Two of my brothers died at an early age. Kenneth died at two months of age in 1929 and Darrell at four years in 1937. A sister, Mavis, died in 1975 at the age of 48. My brother Bob was born in 1925 and the other two sisters were born in 1931 (Betty) and 1941 (Judith). I, Merle, was born April 22, 1923.

CHAPTER 2

MY PARENTS

There is some repetition of material among the chapters in order to cover family background and then expand on some of those individuals mentioned and identified in that background.

My dad, Robert Emmet Mc Morrow, was born March 20, 1891 on a farm in Richland County, North Dakota, approximately 4 miles southeast of Hankinson. Since all records of his birth were lost in the State Capitol fire at Bismarck, North Dakota on December 28, 1930, his birth date had to be reestablished through affidavits and other sworn statements by relatives. He didn't have this done until later in life when he needed the information to meet the necessary requirements for railroad retirement and other matters requiring proof as to date of his birth.

The farm was located in Greendale Township and buildings were constructed of prairie sod. The treeless prairie provided very little in the way of lumber for use in construction. The thick sod walls provided warmth in the winter and a cool interior in the summer.

Some of the early settlers were the Clarks, Haydens, Adams, Bresnahans, McMorrows, Nadeaus, Gowens, Waterhouses, and a number of single individuals. The big event of the year was the July 4th celebration. This event was usually held at some farm home in the area. There was music throughout the day by a band and the usual firecrackers, ice cream, and Cracker Jack. Ball games were held and much visiting was done, since in those days the neighbors living five or six miles away were not seen too often. About 6:00 P.M., some members of the family would have to go home to do the chores. While they were gone, others would prepare a makeshift type of dance floor for an evening dance. Those doing the chores would return after completing their work for an evening of festivities and dance.

Another important day for the early settlers was the Sunday school picnic. It was usually held at someone's farm that had a large yard and plenty of shade trees. The day started with an outdoor church services at 10:30. The seats were planks that had been brought out from town the day before. These planks were laid over nail kegs or wood blocks that were cut from logs the previous winter and saved for this purpose. A picnic lunch was served at noon.

Members of the Sunday school sold ice cream and pop during the afternoon. Softball diamonds were laid out in the pasture, and a number of games were played at the same time. Many of the older people would just sit and visit, thankful for a day of rest, and enjoyed watching the activities.

Greendale Township had its sorrows as well as its joys. Severe winters and especially the blizzards on the prairie caused real hardships before improved roads, tree belts and the many comforts we enjoy today became available.

My Dad had never related any stories about any incidents that had happened to members of his family while he was growing up. I gathered from fragments of information related by others that his father was a tough taskmaster. He and his brothers were worked hard on the farm, and his father demanded strict obedience to all instructions. Never once do I recall my Dad making reference to his father, good or bad. It was as though his father had never existed.

Since the farm was located only four miles from Hankinson, it was only natural that my dad and his brothers desired to go into town after the work was completed for the day. However, permission to leave the farm was required, and the fear of refusal made it difficult to muster the necessary courage to request permission.

My Uncle Frank conveyed to me in a letter dated November 25, 1956, that, on one occasion, my dad was selected to seek the necessary permission to leave. My dad was seven years old at the time, so I assume that Frank thought that his age might work to their advantage. They weren't successful and the letter gives some indication of the amount of fear generated just by the thought of asking for permission or the right to leave for the evening. My Uncle wrote:

"One evening as the sun was beginning to set, Joe and I decided we would like to go to town. We knew we would have to ask our father first, but we were both afraid to tackle the job. We could see him in the field nearby, so we persuaded Rob to go ask him. Rob started down the field to where my father was working on a harrow. Rob stood there fully ten minutes and we assumed he was pleading our cause. Instead he never mentioned our request to our father at all. Then he came back up the hill to where Joe and I were patiently awaiting his reply. He told us that father said we would have to come down and ask for ourselves. So Joe asked me to go down and ask him. So I thought as long as Rob broke the ice, the rest would be easy for me. I ran down the hill and as I got there, I almost became speechless with fear. After a long silence, I almost whispered, "Can we'?

Dad shouted, "Can we what'?

Shaking with fear in my voice, I said, "Go to town to spend the evening".

He said, "Go to bed."

That took place more than 58 years ago, but it is still fresh in my memory".

I concluded from pieces of information gathered at home during the period I was growing up that my dad had something less than six years of education. Considering the attitude of his father, I'm sure he had them enrolled in school no longer than was absolutely necessary by law. Most farm families during that period looked on sons as a source of labor.

We received a number of letters from my Uncle Frank over the years. We always had to wait until my dad came home from work before the letter was opened. The excitement would build all afternoon. When we finished eating, the dishes had to be done. We would then sit in the living room and my mother would open the letter and read aloud as we all listened. It is surprising now what joy and excitement the arrival of a letter would bring. It had come from that faraway placed called Chicago.

As indicated earlier, my dad was 15 years old when his father died in 1906. His father was 56 years old. He and his brothers continued to help their mother operate the farm until her death eight years later in 1914. She was 48 years old. My dad was 23 years old at the time of his mother's death and, as mentioned earlier, was working in Canada and missed her funeral.

Lack of steady work, I suspect, was one of the primary reasons men deferred marriage until they were in their '30's. Prior to that age they were probably fearful of assuming a responsibility of that magnitude, preferring to be responsible only for their own wellbeing.

Three years later, on May 17, 1917, at the age of 26, my dad enlisted in the United States Army. He was sent to Jefferson Barracks, Missouri, and was assigned to Company A, 1st Engineers. On June 25, 1917 he was assigned to 9th Engineers Train. His Grade was Wagoner, and he was stationed at Ft. Bliss, Texas, located near El Paso. My dad had a camera that permitted him to set the camera and then take photos of himself. He compiled pictures of his military training in a leather bound photo album. Evidently he must have loved dogs because many of his pictures contain dogs sitting up beside him with a U.S. flag in their mouths. I believe one of my sons has the album. He was discharged at Camp Dodge, Iowa on September 27, 1919, and returned to Hankinson. His Serial Number was 1142222.

Three years later he married my mother on May 16, 1922. On October 11, 1922 the State of North Dakota paid a bonus to veterans of World War II. Based on service time my dad was eligible to receive 725 dollars. That was equivalent to 9 months salary at the time It must have been welcome news to a newly married couple to hear they were scheduled to receive this large sum of money.

Approximately one year later I was born, and it became necessary to plan for the future. My dad needed to find work that assured the family of a steady income.

Two years after my birth, the family moved to Breckenridge in 1925. My dad began a steady job with the Great Northern Railroad, unloading boxcar loads of coal. The coal was burned in the furnaces used to operate the roundhouse. The workweek consisted 6 days and 10 hours per day. Pay was 80 dollars per month. Our family members back in Hankinson envied him because of the high paying job and the steady work he had.

About 1927 my dad developed a recently discovered disease called diabetes. He continued to suffer from that and the side effects of diabetes until his death about 30 years later. I remember he was continually checking his blood sugar using a Bunson Burner, test tubes, his urine and litmus paper. I was too young to understand the procedure he was using but I remember the color of the paper indicated a blood sugar reading and if it was too high it took some action on his part. Today it takes about 20 seconds to come up a digital reading. Prick the finger with a small needle, touch a small paper strip in the blood and insert the strip into small hand-held unit. The blood sugar reading registers on the face of the unit. Some units give you the reading orally.

Insulin had been discovered a couple of years earlier but prior to its discovery the disease was fatal. Insulin was expensive and about a fourth of his monthly salary was needed for the purchase of this medication.

My father and mother were separated in 1941 and their divorce was finalized in June 1943. I was in military service at this time but my brother Bob was still home. However, he spent almost all of his time on a farm northeast of town.

During the latter part of the 1940's, after his divorce, my dad began sharing time with a widow named Edith McLellan from Andrews Avenue in Breckenridge. She came over after the completion of her work each day at the hospital and prepared their evening meal. I felt better knowing she was there. His meals were better balanced nutritionally and someone was around in case he had an insulin reaction. His reactions had become a more frequent occurrence during his later years. I don't know if this was a result of his irregular eating habits or whether his diabetes had worsened, and he failed to adjust his insulin intake accordingly. Drastic consequences could result if action wasn't taken immediately to counteract the surplus sugar in his system. For this reason, it was reassuring to know there was someone there that knew he had a problem. However, he related to me after I returned from service in World War II that he had had an insulin reaction on his way home from work. He passed out and was lying on the boulevard. The police came by and assumed he was intoxicated. They put him in jail for the night. He could have died.

His vision continued to deteriorate during the early 1940's. Laser treatments and some of the other commonly known practices used today to minimize the effects of eye problems of the diabetic were unknown and unavailable at that time.

He retired during the summer of 1956 and died four months later during a short hospital stay. His body was worn down during the previous 29 years from the ravages of the disease contracted in 1927

My brother Bob talked to a lady who was visiting a patient that shared a room with my dad. She was present at the time of my dad's death and she indicated to Bob that she thought his death was due to the actions of the nurse on duty. The nurse had come in to awaken him for the evening meal. After she left, my dad fell asleep again. When the nurse returned and found him asleep, she roughly shook him and, in a loud voice, so startled him that shortly after sitting up he fell sideways on the bed and died. Cause of death was listed as a heart attack.

Services were held in the Immanual Lutheran Church in Wahpeton, North Dakota. A few days later his body was placed on a train and shipped to St. Paul, Minnesota. He had told me a number of times after the divorce that he wanted to be buried in Ft. Snelling where he was certain his gravesite would be maintained. His children and Edith McLellan were at the depot that cold November evening when his body was loaded on the baggage car at the Wahpeton, North Dakota depot. As the train headed east toward the Minnesota border, I thought that our shared time that I could remember was less than 30 years. It had seemed like such a long time between first grade and graduation. Twelve years now seems like such a short period of time. Now I would never be able to ask the many questions I thought of over the years but never bothered to ask. Reality that someone won't be around forever is given no thought at the time.

He is buried at Ft. Snelling Military Cemetery in St. Paul, Minnesota, in Grave 129 of Section F-2 adjacent to one of the roads that traverses through the Cemetery area.

My dad was a lonely man during the later years of his life. I remember stopping by on Christmas Eve to wish him holiday greetings. My wife and two young sons were with me. As we approached his home we thought he might be gone. There were no lights on in the house. However I knocked on the door and a light in the corner of the room came on so quickly that it almost seemed as though he had the switch in his hands. He had been sitting in the dark. I often wondered what his thoughts were as he sat there in the darkness on Christmas Eve. Had he been reliving his life and thinking of all the tragedies and unhappiness he had experienced in the previous 33 years. Since our family was spending Christmas at the home of my wife's parents, I have often wondered many times why we didn't invite him over there for Christmas Eve. His grandchildren were three and six years old and he would have loved to watch them open their gifts that evening.

It was obvious that he never stopped loving my mother, since he always inquired as to her well-being and never spoke badly of her. It is sad that they couldn't have spent their final years together. Those years might have provided sufficient happiness to erase some of the unhappiness experienced in earlier years. It may also have contributed to a longer life span for each of them. However, it is too late to speculate on what might have been.

My mother, Clara Louise, was born on a farm outside of Faribault, Minnesota on June 27, 1903. She was the second child in a family of thirteen children. At the age of 15, she moved to Hankinson with her parents. Her education also involved something less than eight grades. Four years after coming to Hankinson, she married my dad. They lived in Hankinson on the opposite side of the town from her parents. The marriage didn't exactly have the blessings of her parents since it was a case of the German Lutheran girl marrying the Irish Roman Catholic boy. However, in time, the strong objections mellowed.

My mother had a beautiful disposition and made friends easily. If she had any faults, it was her ability to be easily manipulated. She could be readily influenced because of her need to please and accommodate people. During the period her children were growing up, she was more of a friend than a disciplining mother. She was never too busy to listen or take time to resolve problems, regardless of how trivial or minor they might have been. At times we children would attempt to maneuver her into a situation where she might have to show favorites. She usually saw through our ruse.

Although her life during the '20's and '30's was not easy, her friends and relatives considered her to be relatively well off, with a stable marriage and a steady income.

Following the divorce in 1943, she lived in Breckenridge for a short time and then moved to South St. Paul, Minnesota. Later she moved to St. Paul, and then in 1946, she returned to Hankinson.

On July 5, 1947, John L. Mindea, Justice of the Peace, married her to Alfred Matheson in Sisseton, South Dakota. My sister Mavis and her husband Ollie Gagnier, Jr. of 182 E. Indiana in St. Paul were witnesses.

From Hankinson she moved to Kent, Minnesota for a short time and then back to Breckenridge. She bought a house from Mrs. Ovida Ladwig for 3,800 dollars on December 1, 1956 at 5.5% interest. Her payments were 50 dollars per month, and the last payment was made on September 1, 1964. Her monthly payment was always on time.

Cancer was discovered shortly after I returned from Service, and my mother had a radical mastectomy. Subsequent checkups confirmed that all the cancerous material had been removed.

In her later years, when her life should have been enjoyable, it was nothing but a series of harassment from attorneys and collection agencies about non-payment or late payment of bills. This made it necessary for her to work during the later years of her life. She never complained and, although inwardly she must have had many worries and concerns, outwardly her pleasant disposition conveyed nothing but happiness. Hopefully, she is now experiencing some of the joys and happiness that seemed to continually escape her on this earth.

A child, Jo Ann, was born to my mother and Alfred Matheson, her second husband, on August 27, 1945. She lives in Oregon. Alfred lived beyond the age of 100.

My mother was visiting her sister, Hattie, in Chisago City, Minnesota, when she died of a heart attack on August 11, 1968. Services were held in the Grace Lutheran Church in Breckenridge at 2:00 P.M. on Tuesday, August 13th and burial was at Fairview Cemetery. Her son-in-law, Art Azure, was soloist. Pallbearers were her grandsons and nephews consisting of Lyle Kath, Jack Murphy, Bruce Murphy, Thomas McMorrow, Mark McMorrow, and Louis Peterschick.

Two sons, Kenneth and Darrell, her first husband, Robert, and one brother and one sister preceded her in death.

Her two sons and a daughter, Mavis, are buried near her in the Fairview Cemetery on 11th Street North in Wahpeton, North Dakota.

CHAPTER 3

MY PARENTS' CHILDREN

I was the first born on April 22, 1923, and was two years old at the time my family moved to Breckenridge. There were three brothers, three sisters and one half-sister born during a twenty-year period between the years 1925 and 1945.

I believe the major item affecting all my brothers and sisters was the divorce of our parents. Children of divorce suffer tremendous emotional turmoil. They must cope with immediate stresses of a disrupted family and altered lifestyle and with the long-termed effects which may last into adulthood. I know in my case my bitterness toward my mother continued long after the decree was finalized by the judge. Since we never had an extended group discussion on the effects the others may have experienced, I don't know how much and to what extent each of the others may have suffered and for what period of time.

The reader may determine by events covered in each of our lives how the divorce influenced those events.

ROBERT LEE

Bob was born in Breckenridge, Minnesota on September 5, 1925, at 6 p.m. He grew up in the city and attended grade and high school in Breckenridge. He was team trainer during the time I played basketball and after I graduated he was involved in both basketball and football. During his high school days he spent much of his time at a second home; the Clark Hanson farm located about two miles northeast of town. After graduation, Bob headed for the West Coast with Jim Cahill. He bought his train ticket with part of the money he received for the car I left with him when I entered Military Service. All trains at that time were crowded with military personnel and one slept wherever one could find a spot. Bob went into the Smoker Car and as he lay on his side to catch some sleep his billfold in his hip pocket was exposed. When he awoke the billfold was gone and so was all of his money. He arrived in Seattle with 3 cents in his pocket. He found a discarded newspaper and looked for a room-for-rent in the want ads. He told the lady he checked with on a room about what had happened to him on the train. The old salesmanship must have come through because she gave him a room on credit until he could find a job and get himself established. The lady's husband worked at the Seattle-Tacoma Shipyards and Bob applied there for work. In those days, you got work wherever you applied. The lady also fed him on credit and, when he received his first check, he reimbursed her.

Later in the summer, Bob enlisted in the Merchant Marine because he said the pay was so high. I don't know if he realized it at the time but the pay was high in 1943 because the casualty rate was high. Very few ships were getting through due to the German submarine packs operating in the Atlantic between the United States and the British Isles. Before the Merchant Marine called him up for duty, the Army drafted him. He returned home to Minnesota in December and married Iva Mae Boren from Fergus Falls, Minnesota on December 19, 1943. He was 18 years old, and she was 17 and a senior in high school. Robert Colbert and my sister, Mavis, were attendants at the wedding.

Bob went into the Army almost immediately on December 27, 1943. He had been married a little more than a week when he considered going AWOL. On New Year's Day, he went down to the Greyhound Bus Depot in Minneapolis with the intention of getting on a bus and returning to Fergus. However, when he got there, the depot was filled with Military Police who were checking passes. It was obvious to Bob he would never be able to pull it off and he decided against following through on his earlier intentions.

He took his basic training at Camp Maxy near Paris, Texas (Serial Number 37583341). He was interested in the Army Paratroops and requested a transfer a number of times. However, his commanding officer kept trying to discourage him from doing it telling him "it was too dangerous for him to consider it". Eventually enough time passed where it was no longer possible to have the transfer considered. He was in the 758th Field Artillery Battalion and shipped overseas in May 1944. I also shipped over that very same month. However he was on a much faster ship.

He spent three days on the high seas and made the crossing on the Queen Mary. He was seasick during the entire trip across the Atlantic. At the end of the third day, he stepped on to the soil of Scotland. From Scotland he went to Wales, England, Southern France, back to England, and then to South Hampton where he left for France, Holland, Belgium, and Germany. He was a part of General Alexander Montgomery's 9th Army. From January 2 to February 2, 1945, he lived in the same foxhole in the Hurtgen Forest, Belgium during the Battle of the Bulge.

Bob and I were within 50 miles of each other during our time in Belgium in December 1944. Had we known that at the time, I am certain there would have been an opportunity to get together. That would have been great.

After surviving two earlier situations where he nearly drown, followed by an occurrence that happened in Service, Bob was convinced that he was not destined to die by accident. He was in charge of a 50 caliber machine-gun squad during the Battle of the Bulge. Usually he let the squad go for chow while he manned the gun. This particular time, for some unknown reason, they all went to chow together. After being about 50 yards from the gun, an 88-mm shell landed within feet of their position, completely destroying the gun and all equipment within the general area.

He returned home and was discharged on March 26, 1946. He worked for a year in Ray's Electric and Appliance Store. He once sold some woman an appliance and she wasn't too satisfied. She came back to the store to talk to him about it and let him know she was very unhappy. All she could say was "I'm just sick about it. I'm just sick about it." Bob and I use that same phrase today when we are not too happy about something.

He worked as a fireman for the Great Northern Railroad for a year or so and would stop to see us in Fargo when he was required to remain over in Fargo for the night. It was then that I tried to talk him into going to college but railroading was paying about three times what graduating engineers were getting at that time. I could never convince him school was where he belonged.

He moved to Fergus Falls in 1948 and worked for a dairy. He lived in Saulk Centre from 1951 to 1956 and worked for North American Creamery. In 1956, he moved back to Fergus Falls and worked with Town and

Country Dairy for a year before he became a salesman with Worner Auto Sales. He has been in sales since that time and became one of the top auto salesmen in the State of Minnesota. In 1990, he received a national award for achievement in sales, which only five others received.

His only child Sandy was born on December 12, 1947. She grew up in Fergus Falls, graduated from high school in 1965, and attended Fergus Falls Community College, University of Minnesota, and Concordia College in Moorhead. Sandy married Paul Peterson, an executive at the time with Control Data Corporation. They have two sons, Matthew, born June 29, 1976, and John, born March 13, 1978. They live in the Minneapolis-St. Paul area.

Bob's wife Terry (Iva) died on June 2, 1986, after an eight-year fight with cancer. On November 22, 1986, he married Evelene Oswald in Minneapolis and they now live at Wall Lake approximately four miles east of Fergus Falls.

MAVIS ELAINE

My sister Mavis was born on May 17, 1927, in the house on North 10th Street in Breckenridge, Minnesota. The house was demolished a number of years ago. She attended grade school and was ready to enter high school at the time of my parents' divorce. She was 15 years old at the time of the divorce and was probably more drastically affected than anyone else in the family. This is not to say the others didn't suffer but the rest of the children were either younger or older. Mavis was at that age that was just as difficult in those days as it is today. She didn't have the strong influence of a home environment when she needed it the most. My mother, wanting to be a good parent to those children that were placed with her by the Court, was probably more lax in her disciplinary actions than she might have been under other circumstances. As a result, Mavis was permitted to drop out of school because she wanted to. This was at a time when the war was beginning to change everyone's style of life. A training school for sailors was established at the State School of Science at Wahpeton. The free time Mavis had became too abundant for a 15-year-old. As my sister Betty described it, "She was dating too much and too soon.

Later in the year, she and four of her cousins went out to the State of Washington to work in an aircraft factory. She was entirely too young to be out on her own as an unsupervised teenager. My sister Betty also remarked regarding this situation that, "she should be home going to high school and being excited about going to a Junior-Senior Prom."

At the conclusion of the war, Mavis returned to St. Paul where my mother and other sisters were living. Shortly after returning, she married an Oliver Gagnier. In February 1946 they had a son, which almost ended in Mavis' death during childbirth.

Oliver was not reliable. His excessive drinking and poor work habits resulted in frequent job changes. The marriage got off to a poor start and continued to deteriorate as time went on. The unhappy marriage was dissolved in 1947. Mavis and Oliver Jr. (Butch) moved in with my mother and her family, who were now living in Hankinson, North Dakota.

Within a short period of time Mavis married again. Joe Peterschieck, a local fellow who had similar habits to those of the Oliver she had divorced, was a poor choice for a second marriage. I don't know if Mavis frequented the wrong places or whether she was attracted to the wrong type of people. Pete also had a drinking problem and had difficulty finding and holding a full-time job. Mavis' life continued to be one of giving explanations to bill collectors, dreading old cars that continually broke down and moving from one place to another.

She eventually ended up in a remote, uninteresting town named New Castle, Wyoming. The town was far enough from Breckenridge that her visits became very infrequent. The costs made it prohibitive and when they were able to get the money together, the trip was dangerous because of the condition of the car in which they were traveling. I know my dad sent her money to come home once after she told him how lonesome she was. They corresponded quite frequently and my dad always looked forward to her letters. I am almost certain she probably corresponded with him more than his other children.

Mavis wrote interesting and humorous letters. She especially missed her mother, who I am certain was her best friend. The distance between them and the inability to come home left Mavis lonely most of the time. Christmas time was very difficult for her. Her loneliness conveyed by her Christmas message from Helena, Montana, was obvious:

MOM

Tho' there's many miles between us
On this Holy Night
I'm thinking of you, as always
And praying things are right
I can picture you at home there
Around the Christmas tree
And tho' you're smiling and laughing
I know that you're thinking of me.

I hope that you're well and you're happy
And the New Year will treat you right
For God gave me a wonderful Mother
And I thank Him for it each night.

The marriage to Peterschieck also ended in divorce. He spent the later years of his life in Montana and that is where he was living at the time of his death.

On June 24, 1974, Mavis married Willard Treitline. He was a very responsible person, very devoted, and had steady employment that gave Mavis the first sense of security that she had probably ever known. Her last few years were undoubtedly the only happy adult years she had ever experienced. Their trips were in new or late model autos that eliminated the fear of breakdowns. They could afford to stay at the better motels and eat in decent restaurants. A trip to Hawaii was being planned when Mavis got a report in the spring of 1975 that she had lung cancer. During the summer, the cancer spread to other parts of her body. I called her from work each morning and her spirits were always high, even though she realized she only had a few months to live. Not once did she ever convey that maybe she had been shortchanged when family happiness was distributed.

All the brothers and sisters, along with some of the other relatives living in the area, spent a Sunday afternoon (June 29,1975) with her. I think it was apparent to most of us that this would probably be the last time we would see our sister alive. It was a joyous afternoon, with everyone wisecracking and recalling crazy things that had happened in the past. My Uncle Reuben showed up in shirt, tie and bib overalls. Mavis was her usual humorous self, but she must have also known more so than the rest of us, that she was saying good-bye for the last time. She died on August 11, exactly 7 years later to the day that our mother had died.

I often wondered how Mavis' life might have been had she traveled a different path. She was witty, likable, and made friends easily. She liked to write poetry and wrote this poem following her mother's death and then followed each year with a poem on the anniversary of our mother's death:

THE WATCHER

She always leaned to watch us
Anxious if we were late.
In winter by the window
In summer by the gate

And tho' we mocked her tenderly
Who had such foolish care?
The long way home would seem more safe
Because she waited there

Her thoughts were all so full of us
She never could forget
And so that I think where she is
She must be watching yet.

1969

A year ago today, Mom
The Lord took you away.
So quietly and peacefully
He called you on that day.
You left a lot of memories
When you joined Him up above
Of good times shared together
And your aboundless love.
And tho' you're missed by all of us
We know you're happy there,
To be with Him in heaven
Away from earthly care.

1970

Two long years it's been, dear Mom
Since I've seen your smiling face
Or heard your voice from across the room
While having coffee at your place.
I thought the passing of the years

Would ease the loss of you
And I do forget, for a little while
But never all day through
It's the "selfish me" that wants you back
Tho' I know you're happy there
To be with God in heaven
And in His loving care.

1971

Your Father came to get you
Three years ago today
And led you gently home with Him
And wiped your tears away.
You finally found the peace you sought
And so my tears were dried
And tho' you're still remembered Mom
It's now with loving pride.
God bless you.

1972

My heart was filled with sorrow
The day you passed away
But four years has helped to ease the pain
And the tears I shed that day
So may the time be hastened?
When all the pain and grief depart
And memories of happy times
Will live within my heart
God bless you, Mom.

1973

I can close my eyes and still recall
The day we said "goodbye"
I helped you on the train that day
And our hearts were filled with joy
For you'd be gone just one week
To relax and have some fun.

Little did we realize
Your life on earth was done.
So in the quiet of the night,
And your memory lingers still
I say a prayer for you, dear Mom
And I know it was God's will.
Loved and remembered.

1974
I had no time to say goodbye
That day you went away
For God called you unexpectedly
Upon that day
Had I known you'd be gone
And your life on earth was done
I'd have told you one last time
How much I love you, Mom.
And tho' it's been six years now
There are moments in my day
I think of you with loneliness
And pause a bit to pray
May you rest in peace, Mom.

In reading Mavis' last poem, you can almost feel a
desire on her part to leave all her earthly unhappiness
and join her mother in heavenly peace. It is so sad that
someone who brought humor and joy to the lives of
others could not have experienced more in her own.

1975
The time is drawing near, Mom
When we will be meeting face to face
For I feel myself drawn closer
In His enfolding grace
I had a mental picture
That came to me tonight
Of two figures on a hillside

Their arms raised toward the light.
And as I drew much close
And came within clear sight
You were on my left side
And Jesus on my right.

Sadly missed

Mavis died later that year and I often wondered whether she willed herself to die on the same day her mother had died (August 11).

Her first husband, Oliver, was killed in an automobile accident in the early 1950's. Her second husband, Joe, suffered a severe heart attack and died in Montana. Her third husband, Willard, married a woman from Fergus Falls that had been introduced to him by my brother Bob. He died of a heart attack in Fargo in the early 1980's. Mavis' son, Butch, married, had two sons, lived in Bismarck for a short time and worked as a barber. He joined the Army and has served in Germany and Korea. He and his wife were divorced in 1985. Shortly after their divorce, Butch resigned from the Army, moved to Sacramento, California and died in 2004.

KENNETH DEWAYNE

My second brother Kenneth Dewayne was born in Breckenridge at 810 North 10th Street on March 24, 1929. He had medical problems from the day he was born but no one could diagnose the problem. Periodically he would have convulsions but the reason for the affliction could not be determined. He suffered every day of his short life.

My mother always kept a large pan sitting on the reservoir of the cook stove. By placing him in warm water during his seizures, it seemed to help him. I was having breakfast one morning while my mother was hanging out her morning wash. The baby was in a basket next to me at the table. I could see him turning blue and I ran out the door and yelled to my mother, "Come quick". She came in and placed him in the pan of water. He continued to shake and then suddenly became very still. As I looked up at my mother and saw the tears streaming down her face I said, "He is dead, isn't he". She nodded in the affirmative. Although I wasn't quite six years old, I felt very sorry for my mother. She went out to finish hanging her clothes and then came in and sat at the kitchen table. She took my hand in hers and then started crying. She kept saying, "He was so little and there was nothing I could do to help him".

Later that day about six o'clock she began walking down the dirt road where she would meet my father coming home from work. I asked her if I should come along. She told me I should stay and take care of Mavis and Bob. I think she wanted some private time to think about how she would tell my dad about what had happened earlier in the day. From a distance I could see the two facing each other and having a discussion. Then there was an embrace before they turned and holding hands slowly began walking toward home

Kenneth was buried in Wahpeton, North Dakota, on May 1929, at Fairview Cemetery. His brother (Darrell), sister (Mavis) and his mother are buried just north of him in the same cemetery. His father is buried in the Fort Snelling National Cemetery in St. Paul, Minnesota.

BETTY JEAN

Betty Jean was born on November 14, 1931 at 229 North Ninth Street. We had moved into town from the house out on North 10th Street earlier in the year, so we always maintained Betty started life with all the luxuries, such as indoor running water and indoor plumbing.

As she grew older, I was assigned the job of being her baby sitter. In order not to be deprived of being outside when the weather was nice, I would take her along in an old wicker, large wheel, spring mounted, baby buggy I had gotten somewhere. We would bounce through ditches and across vacant lots at full speed. Betty would hang on to each side of the buggy and scream. I assumed the screaming was in delight because she never cried, and when I stopped for a rest she would began rocking the buggy from side to side. I realized it was her way of telling me that we should get going again.

In 1934, we moved to 329 North Eleventh Street. By this time she was almost three years old, but still needed a nap each day. We had an old rocker that had a tendency to creep across the floor as you rocked. By the time we had traversed the distance across the room with the rocker, either Betty or I was asleep.

In 1937 the family moved to the first house to the south which had been built on the vacant lot and our new address was 327 North Eleventh Street. She lived there until 1942 when the separation of our parents took place. She then moved with her mother to a small, upstairs apartment on the south side of town.

After Betty completed the sixth grade, the family moved to South St. Paul to what she describes as a terrible apartment. They had no money and no furniture. The kitchen table was a door set on apple boxes. However, her mother, who seemed to possess a talent for being able to make things out of nothing, soon had the apartment fixed in a comfortable manner.

Although her stepfather treated her well, she didn't want someone trying to take her father's place. She didn't want him sleeping with her mom so just about every night for quite some time she would park herself on the foot of their bed. They never said anything, and, in time, she gave up the ritual.

After one year, she moved from South St. Paul to 327 Isabell Street in St. Paul. It was an upstairs apartment in a better neighborhood. She was directly across the street from Roosevelt Junior High School, which she attended. She developed some good friends there, and her social activities consisted of picnics, school dances, roller skating parties, and, in the winter, ice skating almost every night. When she got home, there was hot chocolate and toast waiting for her.

While she was in St. Paul, her dad invited her on a trip to Chicago. He was going to visit his brother Frank. They stayed at the Sheraton Hotel, which she described as a fairy tale come true. Her dad and Uncle Frank took her to the Brookfield Zoo, the Chicago Board of Trade, a planetarium and shopping. From Chicago, they went to Mansfield, Ohio, to visit Uncle Phil and Aunt Lu. Betty's comments regarding the trip were "It was a great trip. It was nice being with dad and I hope he enjoyed my company. I think dad was a pretty lonely man. I don't think he ever quit loving my mom, and he never said anything against her. He never failed to ask how she was or if she was happy. He always spoke kindly of her."

After completing the ninth grade, the family moved to Hankinson, North Dakota. The move was difficult for Betty because she had made so many friends in St. Paul.

She graduated from high school in the spring of 1949. My wife Kay and I took our one-month-old son and attended her graduation exercises. Shortly after that the family moved again to Kent, Minnesota, and a year later moved back to Breckenridge.

Betty worked at Sears-Roebuck Catalog Office in Wahpeton from 1949 to 1956. It was during this period that I bought my Browning Shotgun for the low price of $98.50. She was office manager at the age of twenty-two, the youngest manager Sears had ever had.

In 1954, she met Don Petron, who was band director at Abercrombie and also was a telegraph operator for the Great Northern Railroad. They were married on August 20, 1955, at St. Joseph's Catholic Church in Wahpeton.

In 1957, they moved to Williston. Don retired from the railroad in 1985. They have seven talented children: Rebecca, Daniel, Julie, David, Jennifer, Joan, and Don, Jr. All are married with families and are scattered all over the country.

In September 1982, Betty began doing title work with the various oil companies associated with oil development in the Williston Basin. Although the oil exploration work has decreased in recent years, she continued to work periodically until the boom was over. Today (2008) however, drilling for oil in the Basin is a 24-hour operation.

Betty and her husband Don now live in The Villages, Florida. Despite some of the sorrows, I believe Betty has had a very enjoyable and happy life. In her words she says, "We have been so blessed! We have good health, good children, faith, love, joy and peace that only God can give."

DARRELL

My brother Darrell was born on August 28, 1933, at 229 North 9th Street. To Bob and I, Darrell seemed like a replacement for Kenneth who had died four years earlier. We had never had a younger brother to play with and, as Darrell got older, he was a great joy to both of us. He was always laughing and, unlike many younger brothers whom were a real pain to have around, we enjoyed taking Darrell everywhere with us. He was everyone's friend in the neighborhood, and the service people such as the milkman, iceman and the postman all know him by name. He would meet the postman a couple of blocks from our house and walk with him on his route until he got a couple of blocks past our house.

He loved to go fishing with me and always rode double on my bike. He was always barefoot in the summer, and during one of our rides, he got his foot caught in the front wheel of the bike. The spoke cut his heel quite severely. With tears in his eyes, he told me it didn't hurt too much. He was fearful that if he made too much of a fuss, I may not let him ride with me again. I felt so sorry for him. About all we could do was bandage it but the injury really should have had stitches to pull the wide gash together. We didn't want to tell our parents about it.

During the summer of 1937, Darrell complained about his side hurting. Our parents' only comment to him when he brought it up was, "Don't run so much". In those depression years you only went to the doctor as a last resort and close to death.

Finally, he got a fever and it was obvious there was something seriously wrong. His side ache was the first warning of appendicitis and that by the time he was taken to the hospital it had already ruptured. Since none of the modern drugs available today to fight infection were available in those days, all they could do was place tubes through his nose into his stomach and attempt to siphon out the poison. It was very pathetic to see him lying there suffering and not being able to help him in any way. I had never seen his face without a smile on it. Now it was mask of pain.

After approximately a week of suffering, he died. Bob was up at the hospital when the doctor pulled the sheet over his face. He knew immediately what that meant. He began to cry and then ran home. It was Wednesday, September 1, 1937. The date in the newspaper article is not correct.

One of his favorite friends, Durst the Postman, wrote the following poem and had it published in the local newspaper before the funeral:

The Breckenridge Gazette Telegram carried the following story:

IN MEMORY OF DARRELL MC MORROW

Mail Carrier turns poet: Writes poem in memory of Darrell McMorrow who died Thursday, September 2, 1937. The following poem is from the pen of R.S. Durst, City mail carrier. The McMorrow home was on his route, and his daily calls caused a strong friendship to develop between he and little Darrell McMorrow who died last Thursday.

MY BUDDY
I always called you buddy
'Cause I hadn't learned your name
And you never told me otherwise
Nor ever would complain
Altho' it hardly seemed to fit
With me a man full grown
And you a little mite of a boy
The name seemed best I own
We didn't care who saw us stop
To talk or walk together
The only thing that could stop us
Was cold and rainy weather
When I approached your neighborhood
I seldom saw it fail
You didn't patter up to me
And ask if you had mail
Whether you had mail or not
Didn't matter to you I know
Your little hand sought mine
And just a ways we'd go
A little trip it always was
But few stops you ever made
Then turned to patter back again
Your respects had well been paid
You never knew how bright you made

That little trip for me
I only hope that you will wait
The mail from o'er the sea

A related story in another section of the
Gazette-Telegram carried the following story:

NEIGHBORHOOD MOURNS YOUTH

Four-year old Darrell McMorrow, born August 28, 1933, died of a ruptured appendix on September 2, 1937. No death in years caused more sorrow than the passing of little Darrell McMorrow, 4 year old son of Mr. and Mrs. Rob't McMorrow. Darrell had been looking forward to his fourth birthday when he was stricken and rushed to the hospital. An operation was ordered at once, and it was then discovered he had a ruptured appendix. After 10 days in the hospital, he died at 9:44 last Thursday morning (Sept. 2). The little fellow spent his last birthday in a hospital bed surrounded by doctors and nurses that did everything possible to save the life of the little fellow they had learned to love. Neighbors mourned his loss very much. As one lady said, "He was the sweetest young one you could hope to see."

Darrell was born in Breckenridge. Besides his parents, he is survived by two sisters, Mavis and Betty, and two brothers, Merle and Rob't Jr. Kenneth Duane preceded him in death. Services were conducted at the residence at 327-11th Street North at 1:30, Sat. Sept 4th (afternoon) and at 2:00 from the German Lutheran Church with Rev. Becker officiating. Pallbearers were boys of the neighborhood - Wilfred Schwankl, Loren and Donald Hanson and Robert Becker of Wahpeton. The Gazette-Telegram joins the people of the city in extending heartfelt sympathy to the McMorrow family during their hour of sorrow.

Darrell's casket rested in the corner of our living room for three days while people came to express condolences. I am happy that practice is no longer continued because it makes for a very trying period. I had terrible dreams at night after going to bed and thinking about Darrell lying there in the corner of the next room. On Saturday, September 4th, at 3:05, he was buried near his brother in the Fairview Cemetery at Wahpeton. The minister was R.J. Becker, and the pallbearers were Loren and Donald Hanson, Robert Becker and Wilfred Schwankl. I had not only lost another brother, but in this case, a very good friend and companion.

JUDITH DIANE

Judy was born on August 21, 1941 in Breckenridge. Shortly after this, her parents were separated and divorced. She never had the opportunity to share in the family activities enjoyed by the six brothers and sisters that preceded her birth. She was reading parts of an earlier book I had written that included shared experiences about family life.

Naturally she would have little recollection of the things Betty remembered during the period from 1942 through 1945. Her first memories began about 1945 when Jo Ann was born. She moved to Hankinson in 1946, first to an apartment and then a little house on the corner. They had no indoor plumbing and their drinking water was hauled from the neighbors (Ernst) across the street. She recalls the big laundry tub that was set out in the middle of the kitchen floor for the weekly bath.

One year at Easter Judy and Jo Ann were given baby chicks as gifts. They built a pen and by fall these chicks were full-grown chickens and ready for butchering. As the chickens hopped around the yard minus their heads, Judy and Jo Ann were crying about the loss of their pets.

Judy and Jo Ann spent a considerable amount of time playing with their cousins, Bruce and Jack Murphy. They also had a nephew, Butch, living with them now.

Mavis divorced her husband and moved back in with the family. This continued until she married Joe Peterschieck, and they moved to New Castle, Montana.

She has pleasant memories of the threshing season on her Uncle Bill's farm located a few miles northeast of Hankinson. The women would cook all day for the threshers, and the kids would play in the haystacks and ride the plow horses.

Judy started first grade in Hankinson in 1947. There were 4 girls named Judy in the grade, Judy the intelligent one, Judy the Brat, Judy the Beauty and Judy the Quiet One. You would never believe today that my sister was the Quiet One.

Based on a letter I received in 1996, she also had a number of unhappy moments in her youth. She had begun reading my first book Remembrance of Things Past and I quote some excerpts from her letter.

She says, "Your book is great. I am experiencing a full range of emotions. While I read the first part of it, I have a sense of warmth for the family, a sense of sadness and even a little jealousy for the years of family life you, Bob Mavis and Betty had with a mother and father even though they were limited. My memories of growing up with a stepfather who virtually hated me and a mother, who was always working, always tired and worried about bill collectors. There were always arguments and occasional fight. Betty and Don's home in Williston was always a happy summer retreat for me. I wished I had been born sooner and had some of the memories you four have. I always seem to be that extra link that really doesn't fit or belong anywhere. Maybe that's why I'm most content when I am all alone."

She moved to Kent when she was in the second grade. Kent is located about 13 miles north of Breckenridge. She remembers Kent as being one of the most boring places in the world. The highlight of the week was going to an outdoor movie. This was not your normal outdoor movie, but one set up along the railroad tracks. There was a portable screen and the seats consisted of planks or benches. Every time a train came through town the projector was shut off until the train passed.

When she was in the third grade, they moved back to Breckenridge and rented a house on South 9th Street. This had been the best house she had ever lived in. She said that it came complete with heat, lights, running water, indoor plumbing, and no leaks in the roof. She shared a bedroom with Betty and Jo Ann until Betty married Don and moved out.

Although Judy visited her father from time to time, they never did become well acquainted. I remember one time I was standing on the sidewalk with my Dad watching a parade go by. The Breckenridge Band went by, and he asked me which one was Judith. When I pointed her out, he mumbled something I couldn't understand. When I asked him what he had said, he turned toward me with tears in his eyes and said, "I said, "Isn't it a shame when you don't even know your own daughter". Neither one of us talked after that until the parade was over. I thought better than to invade the privacy of his thoughts.

He died when Judy was in her sophomore year in school. She told me she had only visited him a few times and was usually with Betty when she did. She always got a hug when they left. She received a confirmation card and a book marked with Bible passages. Years after his death she realized she should have visited more often and gotten to know him. She admitted she was a self-centered teenager and at the time was only concerned about things that directly affected her. She was sorry she never got to know him better.

The next move Judy made was to the house on Oregon Avenue. This is where her mother started her construction work in earnest. She knocked out the living room and dining room walls. The bathroom was relocated and the second story was removed. The house appearance was changed to resemble a ranch style design. You had to admire her courage in tackling some of these construction jobs. Either she was knowledgeable enough to determine where the bearing walls existed, or she didn't know and didn't care. The house burned to the ground in 1985 and may have been a result of some electrical wiring work she also undertook.

Judy met a young man named Arthur Azure in her senior year at school and began going steady. Following her graduation from Breckenridge High School in 1959, she enrolled at St. Luke's School of Nursing that fall and completed her training in 1962. I recall having to speak to the Engineers' Club at North Dakota State University during this period, and I took her to the Gardner Hotel for dinner. I remember some of the looks I got with people thinking what is this leech doing with that young, beautiful, 21-year old chick. I felt like standing up and making the announcement that this is my sister.

Following graduation, Art and Judy were married on May 12, 1962. Art attended college and then worked for the Federal Milk Market Commission. Three children were born: Steven on June 21, 1963, Janna on February 13, 1967, and John, September 20, 1971.

The family moved to the West Coast in 1969, living first in Portland and then in Seattle. They moved back to Fargo in 1977.

Steve graduated in Engineering at North Dakota State University in 1986 and worked with the Boeing Company in Seattle. He married Linda Berg and they have three children.

Janna graduated with an engineering degree from NDSU in 1990. She married Michael Davies and they have four children.

John is also an engineering graduate of NDSU and is not married. He works for Toro in Minneapolis.

Judy and Art separated in 1986. However, the divorce was amicable and both are available at family gatherings for celebrations, holidays and other family activities. They bought a lake home together on Otter Tail Lake. The two cannot live with each other and they cannot live without each other. In the letter mentioned above, Judy commented that "I always seem to be that extra link that really doesn't fit or belong anywhere. Maybe that is why I am most content when I am all alone."

Judy worked at St. Ansgar Hospital and was there for approximately ten years; working between medical-surgical and the intermediate care units. She transferred to a Civil Service job in mid July 1987, and worked in the Veterans Hospital at Fargo until her retirement in 2004. Art was owner of Murphy Electric Co. and was involved in the installation of city street lighting and other electrical work until he sold the business in 2004

Judy' and Art's goal was to see that each child got through college and had a good start toward achieving a productive and happy life. This they accomplished and their greatest joy now comes from watching and sharing in the activities of their grandchildren.

JO ANN

Jo Ann was born after the divorce of my parents and is a child of my mother and Alfred Matheson. She was born August 27, 1945, and spent her adolescent years in the same locations as mentioned above for Judy. She was nicknamed "Stormy" during her early years because of her red hair and stormy disposition. She graduated in 1963 from Breckenridge High School, and then attended Glamour Beauty Academy in Minneapolis for one year.

She married Warren Haddock in 1965. They lived in Fargo for one year and then moved to Santa Rosa, California, in 1966. They now live in Mc Minnvile, Oregon.

While in Fargo, Jo Ann worked as a stylist, and Warren was an auto body repairman. Two children were born: Michael on December 13, 1967, and daughter Lisa on December 14, 1970.

In 1974, the Haddocks moved to the Medford, Oregon area. Jo Ann worked in the Graphics Arts Department for Northwest Printed Circuits. Warren is in auto body repair in Medford.

Their son Michael was in the United States Air Force and was stationed at the Grand Forks Air Force Base in 1988.

Michael married Aimee Cardenus on May 16, 1987. They have a son Anthony Michael born June 26, 1988. He is in the Air Force in the State of Washington. Two daughters were born; Adrea, born March 31, 1991 and Hailey born March 1, 1995.

Jo Ann's daughter Lisa has two sons, Hunter and Clayton.

CHAPTER 4

MY EARLY LIFE

As I mentioned earlier, I was born on April 22, 1923 on the north side of the tracks in Hankinson, North Dakota. Since I have very little factual data relating to family activities occurring prior to my birth, all the following material is based on information told to me by others or things I remember from about the age of four.

Young people today would just laugh if they were told of some of the things we accepted without question.

I would like to document things that happened to my parents or me. My parents never drove any of us to school. In fact our parents never owned an automobile or a telephone. Milk was delivered to the house in glass bottles and boys delivered the newspapers. Later I will reveal my work in the newspaper field. Kids have no idea we once had to have our arms out an open car window to signal which way we were going to turn. Dimmer switches for the headlights were on the floor. Coffee shops had jukeboxes on the sides of the table. Movie stars kissed with their mouths shut. At least in the movies they did. There were no movie ratings because all the movies were responsibly produced for everyone to enjoy viewing without profanity or violence. Love scenes faded out and it was left to your imagination as to what was happening. There are many other things that could be mentioned that would be difficult for today's generation to understand or accept.

Our family left Hankinson in 1925 with all our worldly possessions in a hayrack pulled by a team of horses. We took the graveled State Highway 11 and Federal Highway 81 (now I-29). The trip to Breckenridge, Minnesota took most of the day and covered a distance of approximately 27 miles. The trip today by auto over Interstate Highway and bituminous roads takes less than a half-hour.

Our first place in town was a small house on the south side at Second Street and Dakota Avenue near the railroad roundhouse. Breckenridge was a Division Point for the Great Northern Railroad and switch engines were continuing moving boxcars around to put together a freight train that could leave town. These steam engines continually belched smoke and all the switching seemed to take place in front of our place.

My mother hated that place because she no sooner got her sheets on the clothes line on Monday morning and a steam engine would go by. The belching smoke contained all kinds of soot particles. It meant she always had to run the clothes through the wash for a second time. It wasn't long before they able to rent a small house on the north side of town and adjacent to the Ottertail River. In addition to the house, a small chicken coop was situated approximately 50 yards to the northeast and an outhouse 50 yards to the east. That walk to the outhouse always seemed like a long trip to a four-year-old. A 36-inch corrugated pipe with a large wooden cover was our well and was located about halfway between the house and the chicken coop. The lot on which the house sat was large and my parents had use of a lot to the south and two lots to the north. They used these empty lots for raising food for our use and canning the surplus for the winter. Sweet corn was taken to town and sold along the street to interested customers.

The town of Breckenridge is located at the junction of three rivers---the Bois de Sioux comes from the south and meets the Ottertail flowing from the east. This union forms the Red River of the North and flows north to Lake Winnipeg located in Canada. The town site is in the valley of what was once the bottom of the great glacial Lake Agassiz covering many, many square miles of what is now rich agricultural land. The town had a population of 3,800 and most of the activities and the economy was related to the Great Northern Railroad. The Empire Builder was the name of the passenger train that provided transportation between St. Paul, Minnesota and Seattle, Washington. As mentioned earlier Breckenridge was a Division Point where the steam engines were serviced in a large roundhouse and took on coal and water in nearby in the railroad yard.

I know practically nothing about the adolescence years of my parents. It was a mere 18 years between her birth and the year my mother was married. My dad had a span of 31 years between his birth in 1891 and when he married my mother on May 17, 1922. I am certain something of interest happened during those intervening years, but we never asked and they never revealed any events of their childhood. They probably realized we really were not interested at that time. The sad part is that when you are interested they are no longer around.

My dad never discussed his father or mother, at least in our presence. He was only 15 years old when his dad died and it may be that he didn't remember too much about him. To me, details of my dad's life started about the time World War I started: at least that is about as far back in his life as he ever went in any discussions I recall.

The United States entered World War I on April 17, 1917. Approximately one month later, on May 15th, my dad enlisted in the US Army at Fargo, North Dakota. He was twenty-five years old, 5'6" in height, with brown eyes and brown hair. His complexion was ruddy in color. . This information was contained on his enlistment papers. That was about all that had to be known in those days to become a soldier. His Army Serial Number was 1142222.

He was initially sent to Jefferson Barracks, Missouri, and served in Company A, 1st Engineers until June 25, 1917. He was then sent to Ft. Bliss, Texas and remained with the 9th Engineer's Train until discharge. Ft. Bliss was a remount station near El Paso, Texas. His title became Waggoneer, and the training related to preparing horses and mules for use in military operations. A remount station usually provided replacement animals for cavalry units. He spent his entire military career at Ft. Bliss and received his discharge on September 27, 1919, at Camp Dodge, Iowa.

He assembled a leather-bound photo album of his military time in service. Many photos were of a little dog that sat up and held an American flag in his mouth. He also had numerous photos of the horses he carried for and based on this I believed he loved animals. I don't know what happened to the album but I assume one of my sons took it when I sold the house in Bismarck the summer of 2000.

I remember, as an eight year old kid, the friendly argument that was continually waged between my dad and John Cimbura, a neighbor who lived across the street and who also worked for the Great Northern Railroad. John had been in the trenches of France during the First World War and continually threw this up to my dad. John was also a member of the Veterans of Foreign Wars, and my dad was a member of the American Legion. My dad told John, "I could join the Veterans of Foreign Wars if I really wanted to."

John said, "You're not eligible to join; it requires foreign duty".

My dad replied, "I have Foreign Service ".

This argument went on for what seemed like years to a young kid. Finally, my dad bet John a sum of money that he could join if he really wanted to. The bet was made, and my dad started the necessary paper work moving. In due time he received the necessary information to show that he had been involved in foreign service for his country and was eligible to join the VFW, if he so desired. This eligibility was based on the following:

Madero, who was elected Mexican President in 1911, was not very forceful in putting an end to the political and military strife existing in the country. Rebel leaders such as Emiliano Zapata and Pancho Villa refused to submit to Madero's authority. Madero's army, conspiring with rebel leaders, seized control and had Madero murdered in 1913. Ambitions of rival military leaders continued and the area remained in turmoil. Intervention by foreign governments seeking to protect the interests of their nationals added to the confusion. Eventually Villa committed atrocities against American nationals and went so far as to lead a raid on Columbia, New Mexico. As a result of the raid, an American force was sent into Mexico to pursue Pancho Villa. A skirmish with Villa took place on June 15, 16, and 17, 1919 and, since my dad was involved, this constituted Foreign Service for him. However, the force saw little action because of the evasive maneuvers by Villa. He continued to disrupt the Mexican countryside near the US border for a number of years and later retired to an estate in Durango.

After my dad's discharge in September 1919, he worked at odd jobs and there is evidence he followed the harvest season as it progressed from North Dakota into Canada. A letter from the Extension Service in Fessenden, North Dakota, dated 1921, indicates he and three other fellows were working in that area doing harvest work. The letter gives a good recommendation for their use in Canada if they were going seek employment up there.

He was considered a good, honest hard worker and never had trouble finding work even though it may not have been permanent.

My mother continued her schooling through the sixth grade and then began working after that at various jobs until her marriage seven years later. She also was a hard and willing worker.

My parents were married on May 17, 1922. My mother was eighteen years old, and my dad was thirty-one years old. Witnesses at the wedding were August H. Kuehl and Mrs. Esther Kuehl. Because of the age and religious differences, my mother's parents were not too happy about the marriage. My dad was Irish Catholic, and my mother was German Lutheran. Nothing could have been further apart at that time. My mother's father was a stubborn, hardheaded German from the old country and set in his ways.

After the wedding, my parents moved into a small 12'X20' house in the northwest part of Hankinson. The small house consisted of a bedroom, combination dining and living room and a small kitchen. The house was not insulated or very poorly insulated because it was very cold and drafty during the winter. Everyone stacked straw or other material around the bottom of their houses in those days to keep the strong drafts from coming up through the floor. The location of the house made it very susceptible to the cold, north, winter winds blowing down the Red River Valley prairie lands from Canada. The house is still there today and appears to have had no changes made or upgrading done in the past 87 years. The cottonwood trees in the back yard have become old and gnarled with many dead branches, and are unsightly and serve little purpose as shade trees. The house lies adjacent to and north of the Soo Line Railroad located to the south. Normally the south side of the tracks in most towns was considered to be the undesirable area. It may have been because the prevailing northwest winds carried the soot and cinders from the old steam engines into the main part of town. The pungent coal smoke also permeates the house and penetrates the furniture. A garden was developed on the south end of the lot and actually existed on railroad property.

The house is about ten blocks from where my mother's parents lived on the east side of town. For almost a year my mother's parents didn't speak to her. I was born on April 22, 1923 and my mother almost died in childbirth. That incident sort of broke the ice, and friendly relations were established again. In fact, as time passed, my dad became one of the more favored sons-in-law. Some think this was because he was one of the few with a steady job during the depression and became a good provider for his family. I found out years later that everyone recognized and commented on how clean and well-dressed Rob and Clara's children were when they came to visit. I feel certain we may have arrived looking presentable but it didn't take us long to look just like the kids we came to visit.

On October 11, 1922, the State of North Dakota paid a bonus to the veterans of the Great War. My dad's service time qualified him for 725 dollars. This must have been a very welcome bit of news for a newly married couple. That was considered to be a great sum of money at that time and was probably equivalent to nine months of average salary.

I was baptized in the Emmanuel Evangelical Lutheran Church on May 27, 1923. Sponsors at my baptism were William Kath and Mrs. Charles Kath, Jr.

The Pastor of the church at the time was J.P. Klauster. The church remains today and has seen a number of renovations.

A small scar over my left eye is evidence of my first disagreement with my parents. At the age of two, I said, "I'm going to run far away bye-bye and never come back". My mother gave me a gallon syrup pail with some cookies in it. I got about a block from home, tripped on the curb, fell and cut my forehead just above my left eye and came back home bloody and looking for sympathy.

In 1925, my parents moved to Breckenridge and rented a house south of the tracks and west of Fifth Street. We stayed in this house near the Great Northern Railroad Roundhouse for only a short time before moving to 810 North 10th Street. My mother had hated that south side house since the steam engines usually came by right after she had her Monday wash out on the clothesline. Her white sheets became speckled with soot particles and required a second washing. There were always switch engines working in the area also.

Our move to the north side of town to a house that was the only one on the city block provided Bob and me with plenty of space in which to play. It had a very large yard. In fact, the entire block contained only four lots. My dad rented the one lot to the south and the two lots to the north of our house for use as garden space. He grew potatoes on the south lot and sweet corn and other vegetables on the north lots.

The house on 10th Street had two bedrooms, a large living room and a large kitchen area. The living room had a large Kalamazoo space heater. That was the first word I could spell-KA LA MA Z double O. This stove was located on the north side of the room for the specific purpose of warming any north winds seeping through the wall. The floor was covered with bright colorful linoleum. The walls were not smooth and were covered with colorful, cheap wallpaper. The paper had been put up with a paste mixture made from flour and water. Due to improper mixing small lumps appeared under the paper. If you cut the paper over these lumps, a small amount of flour would trickle out.

A minimum amount of furniture filled the room and the few chairs that did exist were all uncomfortable. I remember a fern stand consisting of a platform mounted on four bamboo legs. One leg of the stand was slightly longer than the other three legs. My mother was going to attempt it make all legs equal in length. She got the handsaw out and cut a piece off the longest leg. However, she cut too much off and then went to work on the other three legs. By the time she quit, the fern stand that had initially been four feet high stood about 18 inches off the floor and was still uneven.

This house also had very little insulation since long icicles formed on the eaves of the house. We were always warned not to stand under them for fear they would fall loose and hit us in the eye.

The kitchen was located on the east end of the house and extended across the entire width from north to south. The ceiling was about 9 feet high on the west side and sloped to about a 6-foot height on the east side. The kitchen was a bright enameled white with yellow woodwork around the windows. A counter extended along the south and east side of the room. There were many windows, and the kitchen was the brightest room in the house. The common ivy vine was hanging from a number of pots located near the windows. The cooking range was also located on the north wall of the room and helped to heat the infiltrating cold air during the winter. The back door of the house was located on the northeast corner of the kitchen.

About 50 feet northeast of this door was a well, and 50 feet beyond that was chicken coop. It was a small building with elevated roosts similar to bleachers at a stadium. I loved to go in that chicken coop to gather eggs. The hens would all start cackling to warn each other that someone had invaded their private domain. The smell of fresh straw and the warm temperature created by the large number of birds made it an interesting place to visit on a cold winter day. Most of the hens just fluffed their feathers when I stole their eggs, but one old hen would peck my hand when I reached under her. She was always interested in raising a brood of chicks.

About 100 feet east of the kitchen door was an outdoor privy - the most comfortable seat in the summer and the most miserable in the winter. A number of years ago, a Reader's Digest magazine contained an article on the outdoor privy and facts relating to it. For the benefit of the young, uninformed and those who have led a sheltered existence, what was the Little Out House really like in its better years? The basic design was the work of some unknown genius to which society will be forever indebted. It had random, angular lines and the undisciplined construction was definitely American Provincial. The most popular color was usually a soft gray, giving it an unpainted look of natural wood. This exterior finish usually blended ideally with the surrounding environment. This natural, rugged look harmonized with the rest of the buildings located on the property. It was so simple, but yet so functional. There were no tile floors, piping, or expensive fixtures to install. Clogged or blocked pipes or overflowing septic tanks were never a problem. No women ever questioned as to who left the seat up. Only two requirements were necessary to make the building operational, a mail-order catalog and the force of gravity. Both were free.

There is a great deal of speculation as to how many catalogs are buried across this land. If the family was predominantly male, the glossy, lingerie pages were the last ones to be used. The catalog usually got a short respite in late summer when crates of fruit, wrapped in luxurious, soft tissue-like paper, arrived in the market. However, this was short-lived, depending on the availability of the fruit and the availability of the resources to purchase it.

Most structures were built by the ultimate owner and were very seldom contracted out to others. A number of engineering problems faced the builder. What was the optimum depth from an economic standpoint? The extra effort necessary to increase the depth a foot or two was measured against the effort necessary to relocate to a new site. The superstructure was fairly simple to construct once the decision as to the number of apertures needed had been determined. This number was not only dependent on the present size of the family, but a rough calculation as to how many more additions to the family might result had to be made. Another consideration that had to be taken into account was the age spread of the children in the family. Some of the older children may be leaving home before the younger ones became of sufficient age to use the Out House on their own.

Shape, size, and bevel of the apertures were important and related directly to family members. Although an artisan should have undertaken this work, it remained as part of the total construction done by the owner. Only he knew the intimate dimensions of the family members.

We had a "two-holer", with one designed for use by adults and the other structured for use by Bob, Mavis and myself. Betty began life using indoor plumbing.

Strangers could at that time, if they were the discerning type, determine the financial and social standing of the property owner by the size of his Out House. The "one-holers" were poor folks; the "two holers" were middle-class people and those with the big four place units partitioned off with a "his" and "hers" section were considered to be the most affluent in the area.

The contribution the Out House made to the family was a passive one. It contributed simply because it was there. Family members then, as now, needed an escape to ponder the problems of the day in solitude. The quiet, secluded place provided an atmosphere that inspired thought and reflection. Many crucial decisions were made as I sat there those warm summers listening to the soft patter of rain falling on the roof and a few flies buzzing around inside. The winter months were a different matter, and the visit that was so pleasant during summer became a test of your courage, fortitude, and strength in the face of adversity. The great moment of truth came on those below zero mornings when the circular openings were surrounded with frost and icy drafts whistled up from the subterranean depths. No pondering or reflection on the previous day's activities took place at that time in this place of seclusion.

Only a few homes existed in that area when we moved there. The edge of the city proper was about six blocks south. Ray and Elroy Cimbura lived across the road from us; George Teherney lived approximately 200 yards to the Southwest, and Plaistads lived 100 yards to the southeast.

As kids, we played our brand of football, and it was usually played in our yard. We had, what seemed at that time, to be a large open space with no trees to interfere with our game. Life was so uncomplicated, and each day was a new adventure.

We began to hear our parents talking about someone they called "Lucky Lindy". Although the conversation didn't mean much to us at the time as the years passed we realized what an amazing feat had taken place. In 1927 Charles Lindbergh took off from Roosevelt Field, Long Island bound for Europe in single engine plane. A prize of $25,000 was offered to the first person that would accomplish such an achievement. After flying 33.5 hours he landed in Paris. He named the plane "The Spirit of St. Louis" and it now hangs in the Smithsonian Air Museum in Washington.   Eighty-three years later one rainy afternoon my wife Mardy and I left for a ride that took us to "Lucky Lindy's" home town of Little Falls, Minnesota.   There is a falls on the Mississippi River, which runs through the city.

About this time, my dad began feeling sick and never had the energy to do all the things that needed to be done. We had a large garden to the north of the house. Today three homes are located on what use to be garden space. After a 10-hour day at the Roundhouse, he would come home to spend the remaining daylight hours in the garden. It became apparent to my mother that he was quitting earlier and earlier in the garden as time went on.

Finally, he went to the doctor for tests, and it was determined that he had a new disease called diabetes. Although this was still a recently discovered disease, a medicine called insulin had been developed a few years prior to this so the disease was no longer fatal. The cost of insulin, like so many other newly discovered medicines, was still extremely high priced. A bottle, which lasted about four to five days, cost $3.85. This meant that more than twenty-five per cent of the 80-dollar monthly salary was going for the insulin. Something had to be done to supplement this loss of income.

It would have been great if some of the procedures were available then that we have today to test for blood sugar. Back then it involve test tubes, Bunson Burners, and litmus paper and its resulting color to relate it to a chart of colors to determine as close as possible what the reading is. Today you prick the finger and a digital reading is displayed on a screen.

My dad began to bring home overalls and other clothing from people he worked with at the Roundhouse. My mother would then wash and iron them and this continued until we moved into town in 1932. In later years, after I had started school, I would deliver the clothes on Saturdays or after school. I remember a Mr. Oxley who would give me a nickel for delivering the weekly package. He lived on Nebraska Avenue on the corner in a large rooming house located southwest from the St. Mary's grade school. He lived in a room on the second floor. A 12-foot wide stairway with a wide oak banister led directly to his room at the top. The strong smell of furniture wax was an indication of the care given to the hard oak stair treads and banister.

About a year after my mother started doing this work, my dad got her an electric "ABC Spinner" washer, manufactured by the Altorfer Bros. Corporation of Peoria, Illinois. It was the 1928 model and sold for 165 dollars, a little over two months wages for my dad. The washing machine not only washed the clothes much cleaner, but it took most of the work out of it. Prior to that time, she did them by hand using the old-fashioned wash board. After washing, the clothes were put in a vertical, cylindrical tank that rotated and spun the clothes fairly dry by centrifugal force.

A much more involved procedure had to be followed in those days to get ready to do a load of clothes. It meant water had to be pumped at the well and carried to the house where it was dumped into copper boilers set on the stove. This was usually done the night before so the water could heat. Chunks of P&G soap (Procter and Gamble) were cut from a larger bar with a paring knife and placed in the boilers so they would dissolve while the water heated. In the summer, the washing was done outside, so the water had to be carried again from the boilers to the washing machine. Washing clothes during the summer was sort of a social event for the kids. Our mother splashed water at us if we became a nuisance and most of the time we probably were in the way more than a help to her. We helped to hang clothes and dump the rinse water when it became too soapy to use. Since the overalls had to be washed in the last batch, I sat with a table knife and scraped as much grease and thick oil as I could from them while my mother did the rest of the clothes. You made each tub of water last as long as you could, and sometimes the colors from one batch would fade into another batch. I was not as color-coordinated then as I am now, so it did not concern me too greatly.

The charge was 15 cents for overalls, 6 cents for socks, 15 cents for a shirt, washed and ironed, and 10 cents for long underwear.

My dad put up swings for the three of us between two large elm trees located in the front yard. One swing was made from a rubber tire and two were wooden seats. I taught Bob and Mavis how to pump the swings to make them go. Robert Louis Stevenson's words, "How I like to go up in the air. Up in the air so high. Until I can look over field and stream. And over the country side" had real meaning for me.

My folks kept chickens for both eggs and Sunday dinners. The roosters were usually selected for the Sunday dinners. I imagine it was because they provided no eggs. They were big, handsome, colorful birds that would strut around the yard all day. Bob never fooled with the roosters since they weren't afraid to turn on him and put up a fight if he chased them. Oh, how they jumped around the yard after they were separated from their heads. It never seemed unnatural at the time and it was almost a game to chase after them and see how close you could get without getting blood on yourself.

In the spring, a number of old clucks would hatch out 16-18 chicks each and that would replenish those eaten the previous year. However, the chicks' lives were in danger if they didn't stay away from Bob. I don't know how many times it happened, but one of his favorite tricks was to catch a chick and put it under a coffee can. The chick did not survive very long on a hot day.

He stayed away from the roosters and a couple of old ganders we had. The geese knocked him down more than once, and then would stand there and hiss at him. That's when he called for help.

In addition to the chickens, my dad started raising rabbits for food. They required very little room or care and multiplied quickly. They were very large and were tame enough that we could play with them in the yard. One of their favorite foods was a carrot top. We soon discovered it was not a good idea to become too attached to any one particular rabbit because suddenly he was no longer there. Although our parents tried to make us believe they had probably escaped, we knew the "chicken" we were eating didn't have funny legs like these did.

We had homemade root beer in bottles and we were each allowed one bottle every day during the summer after our day's duties were completed. We would pump water from the well into a wash tub and put our bottles into the ice-cold water for cooling. All afternoon we would then think of how good that drink would be later in the day. We usually got a sugar cookie to go along with it.

One of our favorite summer holidays was July 4th. My dad was always in charge of firecrackers on the Fourth of July in those early years. The fireworks available for sale were very dangerous. There were 3-inchers, 4-inchers and red cherry bombs. I remember the cherry bombs would blow two-gallon pails many feet into the air, and the firecrackers were more like small sticks of dynamite. It is surprising more people were not seriously hurt. It was not uncommon to hear about those that lost a finger or eye as a result of fire works.

We had a large cottonwood tree sitting in the northwest corner of our yard. One evening one of the kids spotted a little, red squirrel way up near the top. My dad went in for a rifle and with one shot the squirrel came tumbling down through the branches. I really thought that was some shooting. He never did do any hunting such as duck, pheasant, deer or prairie chicken.

Ray Lambert would come by our place on 10th Street on his way to get sand from his pit near the river. He had a team of horses that seemed huge to Bob and me, and these horses were pulling a dump wagon that he used to haul sand. If we were out in the yard when he came by, he would stop to pick us up. What a thrill to drive and be in command of those big animals. When we got to the river and said, "Whoa" they both stopped instantly. It was hard to believe they would take instructions from us. We never cared to be down wind on the wagon when the horses were pulling a heavy loaded wagon up the 10th Street incline leading to our house.

Ray's sandpit was located about three blocks north of our house. It was located adjacent to the river. We were always happy when his pit was about empty. That meant he would have to refill it and that involved pumping water along with the sand from the river. This pumping involved a vacuum type operation, that sucked both water and sand from the river. He had a dished out area in which the sand settled out, and the water returned to the river via a channel outlet from one side of the pit. However, until the sandpit was completely filled with sand, the area also retained water and was just like a large swimming pool. Once the depression was filled with sand, Ray would be able to haul sand from it for about three weeks. After he shoveled on about two cubic yards of sand, we would get to ride back to our house with him. He usually made six trips a day and each time he would stop for us.

One day on the ride to the sandpit, Ray had me stop near a large cottonwood located adjacent to the sandpit. He brought a saw with him and proceeded to cut down the tree. I don't know if he considered it to be in the way or wanted it for firewood. After dark that evening, my dad and I went down there, and he began to cut the tree into pieces that could be hauled on the wagon we had brought with us. To me it was late into the night before we finished. I remember thinking if there wasn't anything wrong with what we were doing; we wouldn't be doing it at night when it was difficult to see. Maybe we did it at night because my dad worked long hours and there wasn't any other time. Ray never said anything to me about it, but I always felt he appeared to be looking for something when he went by our home. My dad had piled the wood on the east side of the chicken coop where it was out of sight of anyone passing on the road.

CHAPTER 5

MY FIRST YEAR OF SCHOOL

In September 1929, I started my first year of school. The school building was located in the north half of the block between 5th and 6th Street in Breckenridge, Minnesota where the present day Post Office building is located. It was a large two-story light brick building with tongue and groove wooden floors. My teacher's name was Miss Fankhandl and I was wondering how she would ever be able to remember all of our names. Each morning, my mother would pack a lunch, and blouse my shirt over my belt. I hated that blousing and as soon as I got a short distance from home, I would shove my shirt all the way down in my trousers again. I had a square, imitation-leather, black lunch box. It usually contained a couple of syrup sandwiches or hard fried egg sandwiches, a carrot or some other vegetable from the late summer season and a couple of cookies. Since there were no plastic bags in those days or no such thing as waxed paper, these sandwiches were usually curled in a U shape by noon. Cold, hard yolk eggs do not necessarily make the best filling for a sandwich. The syrup sandwiches usually contained too much syrup and, by noon, the bread was thoroughly saturated and had that sweet, gummy taste. If the lunch box sat on the windowsill the sun shining on the black lunch box dried out the sandwiches.

School was exciting and a whole New World opened up with new books and new friends. Very few families moved around in those days, and since most of the children were from families who worked for the railroad, many of the friends I made in the first grade continued on through to graduation with me. Phyllis Sagness, daughter of the local variety store owner, was the heart -throb of all the boys in that first year. She was ultimately one of the cheerleaders of our high school basketball team. They lived in an expensive home that was the envy of most families of the city. Phyllis had three other sisters, one older and two were younger. Although they were considered one of the more affluent families of the town, the girls were all liked by everyone in school and had very pleasant personalities. Phyllis, who was in my class, married a Braun from Wahpeton, North Dakota. They settled in southern Minnesota and had a variety store in the town of St. Peter. She has been dead for many years. Her older sister lives in a home on Otter Tail Lake in Minnesota. Her youngest sister lives in Florida and the other sister lives in Montana.

Willard (Snooze) Jenson and Hugh Wing lived next door to each other and one block east of the school. I always walked home with them and Mrs. Wing would give each of us an orange for after school lunch. Those were the first oranges I had ever had and I really liked them. I still think of being a six-year old when I taste orange juice. On Monday afternoon, Hugh would give me Sunday's newspapers, and I couldn't wait to get home so I could read the funnies. Bob, Mavis and I would lie on the floor, and I would read to them. What I couldn't read I would make up.

Hugh lived the way I dreamed I would like to live someday. He lived in a large home on 7th Street in the center of town. That was large warm and cozy and one room was full of toys. He had a wagon that had front and rear wheels that turned simultaneously.   I really thought that was something special, since you could turn around on a dime. His dad owned the Twin City Creamery located on the south side of Main Street just east of the Bois de Sioux River. His parents died while he was still fairly young. I believe Hugh was a junior in school. He had been adopted when his parents were in their 40's.

Just certain things remain in my memory as far as happenings at the Tenth Street home are concerned. I remember one occasion when my parents went out after dark with a large tarp to get straw for the chicken coop. Mavis, Bob and I were told we were being left at home to guard the house. When my parents came home, they rapped on the kitchen window. Mavis and I ran into the bedroom to hide and Bob went to the door to see who was there. I don't know if he wasn't afraid or just assumed it was our parents returning home. I assumed that since we were suppose to guard the house, it had to be someone other than them.

Bob and I had a wagon and one of our usual routes was around the house. An obstacle in our travels was a 2"X12" plank that was a part of the walk leading to the privy from the kitchen door. We would move it out of the way so we didn't have to pull the wagon over it. At the end of the day we always forgot to put the plank back. When our dad came home from work he always wanted to know who moved the plank and didn't put it back. It was sort of a game to see if we could make up a story as to who did it.

At the end of October bad news of a stock market crash on Wall Street was heard. It was assumed it would have no affect on my family since financial losses were related to those that handled the buying and selling of stocks and bonds. As time went on, it was obvious the October 24, 1929 stock market crash would effect everyone indirectly because of its drastic effect on the economy. The middle class in those days was not too involved in the stock market and many didn't know it existed. If they did they didn't understand how it worked or what purpose it served. My dad's sister Adeline and her husband Charley lost 2,700 dollars in a bank failure. That was a huge loss when the average annual salary was 1,000 dollars.

It would trigger a depression that would last ten long years and result in many families being uprooted and on the move in search of work. Many from Oklahoma headed west to California. They were known as Okies. By 1933 15 million were unemployed. Farms were blowing away in dust storms. It would be a period of time that would never be forgotten by those that had lived through it. Many of the older people never trusted banks again, and after the economy improved, they began saving everything they could in order to survive the next depression when it came. The period had such an effect on their way of life that they never changed. They would do without material things unless it was absolutely necessary and put the money away for a "rainy day", meaning for the next tough times or next depression. . Nothing was purchased unless it was paid for with cash. Very few ever opened checking accounts and credit cards and plastic AT & T cards were almost considered sinful.

Fifty-eight years later in October 1987, the Dow-Jones plunged over 500 points, and the day was referred to as Black Monday. Then 79 years after the 1929 crash the stock market plunged over 770 points in 2008. This time world leaders from countries around the world got together to try to resolve the economic problems.

My dad began to take instructions in the teachings of the Lutheran Church about the time I started school. On October 29, 1929, he was accepted as a member of the Emmanuel Evangelical Lutheran Church in Wahpeton, North Dakota. Pastor Robert J. Becker made a special trip to our house on North 10th Street to welcome him into the membership. Shortly after that, we began attending church as a family. Since we had no car, it meant leaving for church over an hour before services were to begin. The distance to the church was approximately 2 miles. We three kids would run ahead, chasing birds, throwing rocks in the river as we crossed over the Red River bridge into North Dakota, hiding behind trees and then jumping out to scare Mavis and doing all the other things kids do to burn up energy. After Bob and I got a little older, we left earlier than the rest and went to a family named Matz, who lived on 5th Street in Breckenridge across from where the Post Office is now located. By leaving early, we could ride to Wahpeton with them and attend Sunday school, which preceded church services by one hour. We memorized the commandments, Psalms, and other church required passages. In due time, we would be required to take instructions leading to confirmation in the Lutheran Church. This usually took place at the age of fourteen. Every Sunday we got a Bible Lesson appropriate for our age, and the following Sunday, questions were asked regarding the lesson and we were requested to recite certain parts that had to be committed to memory. We were very excited about contributing our pennies to help fill up a clear, glass sphere.

One of my Sunday school teachers was named Lydia Witt. She was accused of murdering her husband. She was accused of slowly poisoning him to death using arsenic she purchased at Holicky's Drug in Breckenridge. My wife was a classmate of Pharmacy student Bev Kristjanson at North Dakota State University. Bev was doing her internship at the time at the drug store and was required to testify at the trial.

I don't remember Thanksgiving Day in 1929 being anything special. I do recall my mother had canned much of the garden produce. In early August I would pick all the Golden Bantam corn and cut the corn off the cob and she would put it in pint jars. She even canned a number of chickens so the meat would be available during the winter. There was no such thing as ready-to-fry chicken at that time. If you killed a chicken in the winter, it was very inconvenient to scald it with hot water and pick the feathers off. Therefore, it was better to do this during good weather and can the meat.

Christmas 1929 brought apples plus chocolate covered mounds containing a white sugary interior. The smell of apples filled the house when the curtain partitioning off part of the living room during the winter was pulled aside to get some apples from the room. If the weather was decent we would walk to the German Lutheran Church in Wahpeton for Christmas Eve services. It was over a mile walk. During the services (held in both German and English) the men would sit on one side, the women on the other side. The children sat in the center. We could hardly wait for church to end because then we received a bag containing nuts, an orange or apple, candy and other treats. I had a verse to chant during the Christmas program. I was six at the time and it went like this:

"Ah, dearest Jesus, Holy Child,
Make Thee a bed soft, undefiled,
Within my heart that it may be
A quiet chamber kept for Thee."

I had no idea what some of the words meant. I knew the word at the end of the second line had to rhyme with the word at the end of the first line. I didn't know or care what a 'chamber' was.

As I mentioned earlier, we had a fairly large kitchen, dining room, and living room or front room, as they were known then. During the winter, a fairly heavy curtain was stretched across the opening between the dining room and front room to conserve heat. Since the house was not too well insulated, if at all, the Kalamazoo heater in the dining room would really have to be heated up on cold days to keep that part of the house warm. I think the reasoning was that it would be better to do with less space and have it warm, than to have more space and continually be chilly in the entire area. The kitchen stove had wood placed in it all day long to supplement the heating from the other stove. Since there were no fans to disburse the air, the temperature in the room was directly related to the distance you may be from the stove. The partitioned-off front room maintained a temperature just slightly above freezing and was used as a cold storage area for perishable items.

Ray and El Roy Cimbura lived across the road from our home. Ray was one year older than I was and El Roy was two years older. Since their dad was a boilermaker at the railroad round house Santa seemed to bring them more at Christmas than Bob and I received. We spent quite a bit of time over there during the Christmas Holiday. Not only were more games available to play with but the quality of the candy was better. We ate popcorn balls and sipped hot chocolate as rolled the dice and spun arrows those many years ago.

Shortly after Christmas, a package arrived and everyone was excited. It was a new Airline radio. The main part was a rectangular box about 10" wide, 10" high and 24" long. It had a single large dial in the front with a small knob on each side of it. A set of earphones came with the radio and had to be inserted on one side. We had a selection of two radio stations--WDAY FARGO,

North Dakota or WNAX YANKTON, South Dakota (The House of Gurney). To start with, each of us was allotted five minutes and kept the others advised as to what was taking place. The reception was poor with considerable crackling and static, but it seemed unbelievable that we were listening to music from as far away (50 miles) as Fargo. The radio brought us closer to the events of the day and made us feel we were a part of things that were happening. No longer did we casually hear about things that had happened days before. We now knew about events the same day they happened. Now CNN and other television channels take us to the scene as events are happening.

CHAPTER 6

SECOND THROUGH EIGHTH GRADE

The spring of 1930 holds no special memories. I'm certain my parents had concerns as to what the future may hold for them and their growing family but to Bob, Mavis and I our lives had no weighty problems. Life was carefree, and we only lived for the day. I do remember things such as clothes lines stretched across the rooms on wash day during those cold winter days of 1929 and 1930. Light rope would be strung from one corner of the room to the other corner. The clearance between the bottom of the hanging clothes and the floor was adequate enough so we could run under them. However, our parents had to duck if they moved from one side of the room to the other side. During wash day in the wintertime the need for a humidifier was unnecessary. The room was heavy with moisture. The moisture from the drying clothes would build up thick layers of frost on the windows. We would scratch our names in the frost and create artistic designs by blowing or holding our hands on the part of the window we wanted to melt. Each one of us tried to come up with a clever design and then try to con our mother into picking out the best design. She was much too clever to be led into showing favorites.

Bob wanted to change his name from "Robert" to something else because it took too much time to write. I told him that someday he would be called "Rob", which was not too much to write. To many of the relatives, he was known as Junior and would continue to be known as Junior even after reaching the age of 80.

The trip to the outhouse was always a long and unpleasant experience during the winter months and constipation wasn't always considered something that had to be corrected. In the summer time you tried to schedule your trips to the outhouse around lunchtime. That was the period of the day when all the flies were in the house.

The tramping through the snow on my way to school did not create a hardship for me or at least I don't recall having any problems. Ray, my neighbor from across the street, was one year ahead of me in school and we usually walked together. Bob would not be starting school until 1931 and Mavis, two years later. Although most people from my generation had a distance of five miles to school, our distance only involved about 10 blocks. Most families today would not dream of letting their 6 year-old walk that far through stormy weather in the winter. This became three blocks after we moved into town to 229 9th Street in 1931. Spring came and I received my first May basket. Hugh Wing had ridden out on his bike, left the basket, knocked on the door and rode away. I didn't know what it was all about. My mother explained the meaning of May Day to me and how it was customary to exchange baskets with treats or goodies in them.

Soon school was out, and we had another wonderful, long summer to look forward to and enjoy. However, I hated to say goodbye to my first-grade teacher Miss Fankhandl.

Ray and I vowed the previous year we were going to learn to swim in 1930. Their property ran down to the river's edge, and his dad put up a dock that got us far enough out into the Otter Tail River to provide for a safe diving depth. The river bottom was sandy and the current swift enough to make an ideal swimming hole. Here again I think our parents were so busy with their daily duties they really didn't concern themselves with where we were and what we may be doing. Today parents living adjacent to a river would never allow 6 and 7 year olds by the water without supervision.

Bonnie Mae Lee and the Silverthorne girls came to swim there also. At first we resented this since Ray and I always swam in the nude. We always tried to get into the water before they came over. We soon overcame our shyness and everything was fine after that. One day Ray got some paint and a board and we painted a sign that said, "NO SUITS ALLOWED". That was okay with the girls. Rules were rules and if that was a requirement they were willing to accept it.

This free-style living naturally led to the establishment of a nudist camp later in the summer. We selected an open area in the woods adjacent to the swimming hole. When we tired of swimming, we just went up to this area. We had made an enclosure with branches that provided a circular area that was somewhat secluded. Some of the branches used were plum branches that Ray's dad had trimmed. They had sharp spurs protruding from the main branch. One day while we were all sitting in the enclosure talking, Mrs. Silverthorne quietly approached the entrance, stuck her head in, and, in a very firm voice, said, "You girls get your clothes on and come home right this minute". Ray and I went right through that solid wall of branches. We were pretty scratched up, but we didn't quit running until we got to the river. We swam down the river until we got to the dock. We got our towels we had in the little dressing shack that we had near the swimming hole and headed for home. We expected the worst, but no one came to visit our mothers and nothing more was ever said about it. After that, only Bonnie Mae came to swim with us.

Many families went swimming in the area of the river where Ray Lambert pumped his sand. School buses from the Indian School in Wahpeton would bring the Indian school students to this spot on hot summer evenings. It was still a little scary since it had only been 55 years earlier that the battle at the Little Bighorn River had taken place on June 25,1876.

No swimming pools existed, and this became the city pool with a continuous change of water. Some evenings there were as many as 100 people splashing in the refreshing water. In those days, the suits that were worn were known as bathing suits rather than swim suits, since the main objective for coming to the river was to bathe before going home. Everyone brought soap along and one of the final acts before leaving for home was to have someone soap your back and wash it. You, in turn, would then do the same for that person.

It was in this area of the river that Bob, the Klein boys, Ray and I were just sitting and talking one afternoon. Suddenly someone said, "Where's Junior?" (He was called that for many years, and some of the relatives still call him that.) Then we saw the top of his head bob to the surface. He was approximately 15 feet from shore. Earl (Shorty) Klein jumped in and pulled him to shore. Bob was going down for the third time when Klein pulled him out. Bob said it felt just like he was floating on a big, fluffy cloud or pillow and gently bouncing up and down. He also related later that after swallowing the first few mouths of water he began to feel like he was floating on a cloud. When we got him up the bank, we laid him on his stomach and as he lay there he continued to cough up water for about 15 minutes. We said nothing to our parents about the near tragedy when we got home and

I don't know if they ever knew they almost lost another child. The loss of Kenneth was still very much in their minds.

In 1987, I checked into MedCenter One in Bismarck for some minor surgery. The nurse, after seeing my name, asked where I was from. When I told her Breckenridge, she indicated that she thought she recognized the name since that was where she was raised. I asked her what her maiden name had been, and when she told me Klein I asked, "Did your Dad's first name happen to be Earl?" She said it was, and that he had died in 1978. I then related the story to her about Bob's near drowning, and she indicated she had never been told about it.

This was the summer we began to play such games as KICK THE CAN, HIDE AND GO SEEK, RUN SHEEP RUN, and ANTE, ANTE, EYE OVER. Everything east of Eleventh Street was a cornfield and everything west of Tenth Street was woods, so there were all kinds of places to hide. Today that area where we played is residential and also contains the city high school. I remember losing one of my shoes in the cornfield when running for a goal. I didn't dare stop to put it on, or I would be "IT". Afterwards we went back to look for it, but every row looked the same. I never did find it. We had taken the cornfield row by row and looked for over an hour. I don't remember how I explained it to my parents. In those days you had two pairs of shoes; one pair for every day use and one pair for Sunday.

In reflecting back, I suspect this is when you start learning how to get along with others. Good traits were formed at that time, such as no cheating by peeking to see where the others were going to hide. We also helped the younger ones so they had as much fun as the older ones and were not continually "IT". Many times you made it appear you didn't see the younger ones when they were heading for the goal to yell "free".

That summer our family became a customer of the milkman from Cloverleaf Dairy. A one-horse enclosed wagon was used, and the milk was delivered in glass bottles. The horse knew the route and the customers on the route. He would continue to move ahead and stop at the right places while the milkman made his deliveries. The route was 10th Street, a dirt road with no automobiles. Life was so simple in the 1930s. About ten years later, both Bob and I worked for this dairy, and Bob practically became an adopted son of the Hanson family. He spent much of his high school years living right out on the farm. Clark Hanson, former owner of the CloverLeaf Dairy, moved into Breckenridge in 1946 and continued farming until his retirement in 1968. He died August 19, 1988 at the age of 88. His wife died four years earlier in 1984. Whenever possible, I would stop over at his house in Breckenridge and we would talk about the old days. He liked to dream about how things used to be out on the farm, and what a great life it was. I suspect he doesn't remember all the hard work.

Dick Lubenow farmed near the small town of Great Bend, North Dakota located approximately 14 miles southwest of Wahpeton. He was a bachelor who had never been married. My parents had met him through the Misaeges who were our neighbors. Dick raised Shetland ponies for a hobby and brought one of his ponies and a cart to town one weekend. Although I was only 7 years old, I got to drive it by myself and I went down the road about a quarter of a mile. On the way back, something spooked the pony, and he started to take off. I wasn't strong enough to hold him so we came tearing into the yard at full speed. My sister Mavis age 3 was lying on the ground and one wheel of the buggy ran across her neck. The buggy or cart was not very heavy, and it was primarily my weight that would have made it dangerous. At any rate, she wasn't hurt; she cried a little and had trouble swallowing for awhile, but everything turned out fine. However, Dick got on the cart and made that pony run around the block at full speed as a means of punishing him for the fast ride he gave me. I am certain the pony didn't know what it had done.

One day Ray challenged my dad to a bicycle race. My dad always rode a bike to work if the weather was satisfactory, but he had never done any fast riding. Ray had gotten a new bike earlier in the summer and now felt like he was ready to test his skills. The race started four blocks south of our houses. The road was not graveled and had been bladed often enough to insure a fairly smooth surface. They came past the finish line at what seemed like 100 miles an hour to a young kid. I believe Ray won because of less wind resistance and more stamina.

One of the first things to be done in the spring after the sun had warmed the soil sufficiently was to plow the three lots north of our house. This was done with a team of horses and a walking plow. The face of the plow had a polished surface and it looked like stainless steel. The man guiding the plow had the two lines for directing the horses tied together and placed over his head on the back side of his neck. Most of the horses were trained so they knew where to go during the plowing. The freshly turned earth exposed many earthworms and other insects and attracted many birds. I loved to run barefoot through that cool soft soil.

We had a large garden again during the summer of 1930 and my dad planted more sweet corn than ever before. We had a mechanical planter, which I got to operate that year. It was a narrow V type tool with a can attached to one side of the V. This would be filled with seed corn and as you pushed the V down into the soil with your foot, you pressed the top of the V together, thereby allowing two kernels of corn to fall into the soil. As you lifted the tool up to move to the next hill, the topsoil fell in thus covering up the newly planted seed. Bob and I were to find out later that year why so much corn was planted. We were destined to become businessmen.

Within 10 days or so two hills of green sprouts poked up through the soil. Then after a rain and some warm sunshine the corn grew rapidly. By mid July cobs were forming on the stalks and early in August the corn began to ripen. Each morning, after breakfast we picked 30 dozen ears of corn. These were neatly stacked in a box that was made for our wagon. Bob and I then started out for the influential residential section of town to sell. I took one side of the street and Bob took the other side. He had the wagon, and I would run back and forth with a basket. The corn sold for 15 cents a dozen, and if they bought two dozen, we threw in two extra cobs. I came back from one sale to see some woman loading up a wash tub on Bob's side of the street. I went over to see what the problem was. I couldn't believe he had made such a large sale that it required a wash tub to carry it. What Bob had actually told her was that the price was 15 cents a BUSHEL, and she wanted that quantity. When I told her the true cost, she decided to settle for a dozen ears. He must have learned something from his first sales job because he turned out to be one of the top auto salesmen in the Upper Midwest.

My second year of school began that fall of 1930. I was selected to hold up the "flash cards" for multiplication, division, subtraction and addition. When I sat with the class, I was first with the answer, so the teacher, Miss Ellison, thought the rest of the class wasn't getting much training. So she had me take over her job and I felt very important to do so.

There was no pencil sharpener in the second grade room so we had to go to the first grade room to sharpen our pencils. I was in there when the bell rang to start the first class. I ran for my room and one of the boys in the front row stuck his foot out and tripped me. I went down with my head hitting the steel edge on the front part of the desk. Blood immediately shot out all over the place, and pandemonium developed. Miss Ellison, my second grade teacher, ran to the bathroom to get some wet paper towels. She held these on my head as we started downtown at a fast pace to get to the doctor's office. We were only two blocks from Dr. Mc Mahon's. She was crying so much I couldn't talk to her. I couldn't understand why she was crying. Nothing was hurting me. The doctor bandaged my entire head with a white-gauze bandage and when I came back to the school, I got the same reaction and satisfaction as my son Mark did when he faked a head injury for the Highland Acres class thirty years later in 1960. Before coming home, I had to go over to the St. Mary's School for my violin lessons. I had gotten a violin earlier in the year and I was expected to be the first musician in the family. I came home late in the afternoon and I could see my mother hoeing potatoes in the lot next to the south side of our yard. She stopped and looked in my direction when I yelled to her but she was uncertain it was me. The voice was familiar but why would my head be all white? Finally she determined it was me and she came running. Her first question was "Are you all right?" I had to tell her the cut was deep and about two inches long and exactly how it all happened. She told me that the scar would always remain, but that it probably would never be seen unless my hair becomes thin some day. Now that I am bald, I don't care if the scar shows; there are many other distracting blemishes.

As I mentioned above, I was being introduced to music in my second year of school. I was enrolled in a violin class being taught by one of the Sisters at the St. Mary's Catholic School. The lessons lasted one-half hour and cost 50 cents. Each person was tutored individually, and within a short time, I was able to play "THE OLD OAKEN BUCKET", "LIGHTLY ROW", and make the sound of a cat (MEOW) with the F string. The Sister was a beautiful lady with lovely, smooth skin but her black and white habit scared me every time I showed up for lessons. She moved around quietly and spoke in very soft tones. I always felt that once I showed up, I might never get out of there again. Everything was so spooky. Had there been more than one of us at a time for lessons, I may have felt a little more comfortable. The lessons were given twice a week, and I was starting to get things down pretty well. Then Miss Ellison had me play before the class the morning before my lesson later in the day. That did it. I wasn't going to play before the class twice a week for my entire school life. I asked the first man I met on the street if he wanted to buy a violin. He wanted to know the price, and I told him "ten dollars." That included the case, extra strings, rosin, and an extra bow. I took the money home to give to my dad, thinking it would more than cover the initial cost. It was then that I discovered that the original cost of the instrument was closer to eighty dollars. He had spent a month salary to purchase that instrument. It wasn't until years later that I could appreciate how he must have felt when he knew someone else had that instrument that had cost him 240 hours of labor.

My dad asked me to describe what the person looked like that had purchased my violin. He walked around the school area hoping to find the person and get the instrument back, but to no avail. None of the other children in the family were afforded the opportunity to get a musical instrument, and my lack of ability to understand music today probably dates back to those early lost opportunities.

My first knowledge of General George A. Custer came in the second grade. I was in the bathroom that was located in the basement of the school. A fourth grader, standing at the urinal next to me, asked if I was going to the lyceum that afternoon. I didn't know what "lyceum" meant, but I asked him where it was going to be held. "In the auditorium," he said. "Where did you think it would be held."

I asked him what it would be about and he replied it was a play about General Custer being killed at the Little Bighorn. At that time, it was still fairly recent history, having happened only 54 years earlier. What a stupid name I remember thinking. Little bighorn - couldn't they decide whether it was little or big? I didn't go because the teacher said she would be collecting dimes right after lunch from those who were going to the lyceum at 2 P.M. I gave the impression I would rather stay in the room and get started on the next day's lesson. I was too embarrassed to admit I didn't have a dime.

I never did go to very many school functions that cost money. I just didn't have the nerve or didn't want to ask my parents for the money. I do remember my mother and I walking to school one night to attend a Junior Class Play. I think it was probably a free school function. If I had only realized at the time how important a little thing like that was to her. I'm sure my mother enjoyed our little evening together but at the time it meant nothing special to me. I do recall a large, orange moon rising just above the horizon and my mother remarking what a beautiful evening it was. I continued to run ahead of her on the way home. We fail to appreciate the little things in life until they're no longer available to us.

On another occasion, the program for the month was a demonstration of sled dogs by Eskimos. I was the only one in the class not going. The teacher, Miss Thomas, said that she had found a ticket in the hallway and I could have it if I liked. It never occurred to me that she probably bought it for me. It also permitted her to go. Otherwise, the teachers had to stay with the class. I always felt she did it for me and not for herself.

One time just as recess was being concluded and the whistle to return to class had already blown, I gave the football one final kick. It went up and up and I knew before it had reached its maximum height that it was going to hit the second story window. I held my breath as I saw it go through the window, and I heard the glass start to fall. I hoped and prayed that it was going to be considered an accident, but I also knew the whistle had blown. My only hope was that no one else could remember whether it happened before or after the whistle. Before the whistle would mean it was just an accepted incident resulting from recess activities. After the whistle, it meant I hadn't stopped when I should have.

Before leaving for home that afternoon, the teacher handed me a note and told me to give it to my parents. All the way home I wondered what was in the note; I knew it had something to do with the broken window. I debated whether I should open it and read the contents. I really didn't have the nerve to do that. I also thought I should throw the envelope away; that would make the problem disappear. In the end, I took it home and gave it to my mother. She read it and then said we would have to discuss it with my dad when he came home from work. Basically, the letter said I had kicked a ball through a window after recess was over, and my parents would have to be responsible for paying the three dollars for having it repaired. They paid it but I also realized they were not too happy about it; the three dollars was about equivalent to one day's wages for my dad. That meant a day of shoveling coal for nothing.

I always took the same route home from school each day. About half way home, I passed the home of a little old lady who was named Mrs. Andel. She always brought out two samples of the cookies she had baked that afternoon. One day I came by and she didn't come out. I walked around the block and came by again, thinking that maybe she hadn't seen me the first time. She didn't come out even though I went by there as slowly as I could. The next day the same thing happened. On the third day, I asked someone, who was standing out in the yard, what had happened to Mrs. Andel.

With sadness in her voice she said, "Mrs. Andel had taken sick suddenly about three days ago and was taken to the hospital and died that same day". She didn't indicate the cause of her death and I didn't think to ask.

I was very sad because all I knew about her was her last name, that she made very good cookies and that she liked little children. I went by her home many days with sadness in my heart. I did miss the cookies but I also had become very fond of the little old lady with the sweet, quiet voice.

A large circular saw sat in a vacant lot near where we lived. It was the type of saw that was driven by a tractor with a flywheel and a large belt attached between the tractor and the saw. Two of us were turning it as fast as we could by hand as my brother Bob was feeding wood into it. He got his hand in too far, and the big teeth came right across his knuckles. We ran for home with the blood squirting out. His first and little finger were cut so deep they were hanging down. The other two fingers had deep tooth marks in them. Our mother stopped the bleeding, put flat sticks under the two fingers hanging down and bandaged the hand. Bob still has large scars today, but his hand appears to have come out of the ordeal unaffected.

It seemed as though our mother was always bandaging us for one thing or another. I was running in the neighbor's yard and I tripped and fell. As I put my hand down to break my fall, my hand went down on the broken end of a bottle. The sharp broken edge was facing up. My mother took the skin or membrane from the inside of an eggshell, placed it over the open cut and wrapped it with a part of a white bed sheet. It healed fine but I still have a large scar today. It probably should have had at least ten stitches to close the wound properly.

I remember I helped to pick parsnips, carrots, potatoes, and onions. We always put the carrots and parsnips in boxes and covered them with sand Bob and I hauled from Ray's pit. Parsnips are not very popular today, but are a garden plant with an edible root similar to carrots. They are white in color instead of orange. They could be either boiled or fried. My dad really liked them. We also grew our own horseradish, which was really strong. I was always happy when all the fall work was done. We probably didn't have that much to do, but it seemed like it was disrupting our play schedule continually.

When our mother went downtown to do grocery shopping, she would always wonder out loud if the Brownies would come while she was gone. The Brownies usually cleaned her house when she wasn't around. Since we had no car, her shopping was limited by the amount she could carry. As soon as she left the yard, the three of us would start dusting, cleaning up any unwashed dishes, sweep the floor and do whatever else needed to be done. When she came home, she would come into the house asking the question, "Were the Brownies here while I was away?" Then she would marvel at what a good job the Brownies had done and how they could get so much done in such a short period of time.

One time we decided we would fool her. As soon as she left for town, we took three large catalogs and tore each page into pieces about the size of a half a dollar. We scattered the pieces on the floor throughout the house. When we finished, the floor was approximately six inches deep with small pieces of paper. We met her before she got to the house, and she asked the same old question. "Were the Brownies here while I was away?"

We answered, "Yes, we think we saw them." When she came into the house, she had a surprised look on her face, and then she just started laughing. We spent a half-day in the clean up, and she never wondered about the Brownies again.

The Congress passed the 18th Amendment to the Constitution on January 16, 1920. This amendment made it illegal to buy, sell, manufacture or possess liquor, beer or wine. It was illegal to make it for your own use. It became very unpopular and was eventually repealed by the 21st Amendment in 1933.

During Prohibition, my dad and John Cimbura made their own beer. Many others, I am sure, did also, but at our age we were only aware of these two cases. One day they got a tip that "government revenue men" would be coming around the next day to check on what would be a known as a violation of the law. John and my dad worked late into the night and hid about 300 quarts of beer down by the river that flowed west of John's garage. No one showed up the next day or the following day. On the third day, they went down to the river to get their beer. They found it gone.

There was an old fellow that lived in a shack by the river about two blocks downstream. It was assumed that he had provided the false tip and then watched what was done with the beer. The other possibility was that he, just by chance, had happened to see them stashing it down there and when they were all done, he relocated it for them. They had found some of their bottles under his shack where they had been thrown after they were emptied. The old fellow was told he could have the beer if he would just return the empty bottles, but he never admitted to the theft.

I remember nothing about Christmas, 1930. We received no presents, and I don't know if Christmas trees were put up at that time or not. At least, we didn't have one. We always had apples about that time. This may have been because of the Christmas season, or it may have been because it was the season for apples. At any rate, the smell of apples traveled throughout the house when the curtain partitioning a part of the house from the rest of the front room was thrown back. Even today the aroma of apples brings to mind many memories of my youth.

I continued to read my books to Bob and Mavis. They knew the "Little Red Hen" and some of the other stories by heart. If I tried to change any part, they would immediately correct me. I also read the comics Hugh Wing gave me on Monday after school. His mother saved the Sunday paper for us. There was Maggie and Jiggs, Katzenjammer Kids, Popeye and many others you no longer see today.

Spring came, and I could always tell when the days were going to get nice. We didn't celebrate birthdays, but when they told me I was now a year older, I knew that the warm and sunny days were in the very near future. Dandelions were usually the first plants to signal the start of another season. The common dandelion is not native to this country, but came from Europe and, like those "huddled masses" who sought a better life in a newer world, the dandelion put down roots and thrived. We didn't struggle to get rid of them like people do now. They were one of the first green plants in the spring and the first to bloom on barren ground. There wasn't time or money to plant the blooming flowers that required pampered living in potting soil. The dandelion's first early leaves provided us with a fresh tasty vegetable we called "greens". The leaves were boiled in water, drained, salted, buttered, and served as a vegetable during a meal. It was also served as a salad. My dad also made a wine from the plant appropriately called Dandelion Wine.

In the summer of 1931, we moved to 229 North 9th Street. Mom was pregnant with Betty and I don't know if the move was undertaken because we needed more room or whether the financial conditions changed sufficiently to permit our moving to more spacious quarters. It also may have been a means of getting closer to school and work, or a combination of all of these things.

The house was a two-story building with a number of bedrooms upstairs. Our parent's bedroom was down stairs. The kitchen had a large walk-in pantry. The most interesting and exciting room was the inside bathroom. This was real living and would take some pain out of the winter season. There would be no more going out in the rainy or cold weather to carry in water. In addition to the house, we now had a garage at the end of the lot. Although we didn't have a car, it was a great place to store things. Sidewalks on the north and east of the house permitted us to play outside immediately after a rainstorm without getting muddy. Hard surfaced streets were also quite a change and must have made it considerably easier for my mother to keep the house clean. There were also less muddy clothing to wash.

Somewhere we got the idea that the house was haunted. We thought we heard noises at night. The neighborhood kids told that an old lady lived and died in the house. We were also told that there was money hidden in the walls, but we never discovered any.

We lived on the corner, and the lot to the South of us was vacant. Whether my dad rented the lot or agreed to keep the weeds down for the use of it is unknown, but they put in another garden that summer. We spent time working in it, and also making new friends around the neighborhood. I learned to play baseball from the Cahill kids. We would take an old work glove, stick a handkerchief inside for padding, and play catch all day long. I practiced pitching by the hour and dreamed of playing American Legion ball some day. Jim Cahill and I went to see all the Legion games and on Sundays, a semi-pro team from Breckenridge would play one of the traveling teams such as the House of David or other organized teams. The House of David players all had long beards and they were better than the average players that came to town.

The games were played at the Island Park, and the only entrances to the ballpark were a couple of bridges crossing the Otter Tail River. In order to save ten cents we had a spot on the river where we could swim across, holding our clothes above our heads with one hand and swimming with the other hand. As soon as we got to shore we took off our wet shorts and dressed.

Also located in the Park were the Wilkin County Fair Buildings, where an old fashioned county fair was held every year during the latter part of August. It was at this time that my competition in penmanship with Phyllis Sagness took place. Phyllis always took first prize and was awarded one dollar. Her samples of perfect penmanship were beautiful. I always took second place and received 75 cents. At that time the award money was greatly appreciated and seemed like a fortune to a young boy. Local women entered their cakes and pies in hopes of picking up a blue ribbon. Garden produce of unusual size, shape and color was displayed. Flower enthusiasts competed against each other to gain local recognition as the one that could produce the most beautiful and interesting flower arrangement. Crocheting and knitting skills were presented in the form of completed work. Grains of various types were tied in neat little bundles and used for judging as to length and strength of stock, quality and quantity of grain. Judging was done to select the best animal in each category that was raised and cared for by a 4-H member. Horse races were held on a track that circled the outer perimeter of the island. A carnival usually came in to take advantage of the crowds. It was one of the major events of the summer, and it brought everyone together to share their activities and achievements with each other for the concluding season. It was an exciting time because it was a change from the ordinary things that happened every day. There was no travel for the average person in those days, and only circuses, carnivals, fairs, and rodeos brought in people from the outside world.

In the fall, at least one rodeo was held in the Park. Automobiles would be parked in a circular arrangement to provide the outer boundary or substitute as a fence for the activity area. There were no seating facilities; you simply sat on the ground in front of the cars. If any animals came in your direction, you quickly rolled under a car.

I started fishing by myself during the summer of 1931. Bob sometimes came with me, but he really didn't care that much about fishing. I also think he was too impatient. One could get a box of assorted size fishhooks from Kalash Hardware for five cents. By picking up fifty feet of carpenter's yellow-colored line and finding an old nut somewhere for use as a sinker, you were in business. What carefree and pleasant days those were sitting in a warm summer sun by the river. Birds were singing, and occasionally a muskrat would come swimming by.

The primary bait I used was earthworms and they were easily found by digging in a manure pile. They were always red in color. Bullheads were the main catch and occasionally I would get a walleye pike or sucker. I learned to respect the bullhead almost immediately. They had a sharp prong on each side of their heads and one on top of their backs. When you got stuck by one of the prongs, the fish secreted some type of poison that not only caused the puncture to be quite painful, but there was considerable swelling for a day or so. The smaller and younger the bullhead the more painful the wound.

Bullheads were very difficult to clean for someone my age. I had a board where, as a first step, I would pound a nail through their heads as a means of holding them. Then I would make a cut through the top just back from the head. This permitted me to get a hold of the skin with a pair of pliers. It didn't take too long before I became adept at removing the entire skin by a uniform, straight pull toward the tail. It wasn't too long before I was skipping the step of placing a nail through their heads and merely holding them while stripping the skin. The meat was white and contained no bones other than the main backbone. My catch usually provided the main or basic item around which a summer evening meal was planned. The bullheads were so small that it usually took anywhere from 35 to 50 to provide enough meat for everyone at the table. I continued to provide fish every summer up through 1937. After that, I began to work during the summer and the carefree days between school closure in May and start-up in September were over.

I started the third grade in the fall of 1931. Miss Meitke was the teacher and after a somewhat relaxed environment in the first and second grade, this teacher seemed extremely tough. I remember on one occasion where I had to go to the bathroom. I raised my hand, but she completely ignored me. She either thought we had taken advantage of the previous teachers by requesting permission to leave the room when it really wasn't necessary, or we were testing her. I continued to raise my hand and she continued to ignore me. Finally, I could wait no longer and that warm, saturating feeling enveloped me and the terrible pain was gone. Panic struck me when the excess formed on my seat and continued to run off the edge in a small stream to the highly polished tongue and groove oak floor. It formed in a pool about one foot in diameter at a spot where the sun coming in through the window reflected off the wet floor.

I prayed no one would see it and that it would dry before anyone would have to walk by that location. We were doing penmanship at the time and this teacher had a habit of walking up and down the aisle observing our style. If you were using "finger movement" instead of Palmer Method No. 9, she would rap you across the knuckles with a steel-edged 12-inch ruler. I watched her out of the corner of my eye as she came up and down each aisle, drawing ever closer to where my secret existed. She was ready to head down my aisle, and I knew that in just a few more moments my life would be ruined forever. Just then another teacher came in to ask her something and they went into the hall to discuss it. When she came back, the recess bell rang and we all headed outside for 15 minutes of play. Another case of being saved by the bell.

I was the first one back into the room. I intended to sit on the floor and move around enough to absorb whatever remained. However, when I got there, I found nothing but a light colored spot on the highly polished floor. The varnish had been eaten off the wooden floor. I had been saved from an embarrassing situation by a visiting teacher, a recess bell and a warm, summer sun. It was such a contrast between the light colored spot and the dark varnished area surrounding it that I was certain someone would surely ask me what happened. I wasn't prepared to answer them but the question was never asked.

I remember October 1931 as a time of discussion about a twenty-six year old medical secretary and daughter of a minister who allegedly shot and killed her two best friends in their home in Phoenix, Arizona. She dismembered one body, stuffed both bodies into trunks and checked them as baggage on a train to Los Angeles. Her name was Winnie Ruth Judd. She was sentenced to death by hanging but pleaded insanity and was committed to an institution. Finally in 1971 she was paroled by the state of Arizona.

Betty was born on November 14, 1931, in my parent's bedroom located in the northwest corner of the house on 9th Street in Breckenridge. Bob and I were sleeping up stairs with one of our uncles. I imagine one of my aunts was there to assist with the birth. The uncle was sleeping in the middle, and one of us wet the bed. That pretty well ruined the night for all three of us. I do remember the activity going on downstairs, but none of us were permitted to go down.

The summer of 1932 was hot and dry and was similar to the previous few summers. Unemployment figures were growing larger, and the economy worsened. Although we children were too young to realize life was not normal, I do remember, in looking back, that my parents were concerned primarily with job security and keeping the family clothed and fed. They always planned for a garden to supplement summer meals and canned the excess for winter use. Nothing was wasted. If we had cooked mush for breakfast, the amount left over was fried for supper and used along with whatever else was being served for the evening meal.

Nothing unusual happened in the fourth grade and our teacher, Miss Meitke, continued to be a dictator.

All through the dry years of the thirties, I remember my dad singing:

"It ain't gonna rain no more, no more.
It ain't gonna rain no more.
So how in the heck can I wash my neck.
If it ain't gonna rain no more.

Another popular Government program that was established in April 1933 during the depression recovery period was the Civilian Conservation Corps (CCC). It put the young unemployed to work and took them off the street. Young men were trained in conservation involving flood and soil erosion control, wildlife, recreational areas and improvement in forests and parks. The employees, much like in Army life, lived in barracks and their lives were restricted by many regulations. Their pay was $30.00 per month and $25.00 of that amount was sent home to the individual's family. The Corps completed many wonderful projects, many of which still exist today.

My brother Darrell was born on August 28, 1933, just before I started my fifth year of school. My teacher was Miss Thomas and I remember her as being very beautiful and very nice. I only recall two things from that year of school. A situation similar to what happened to me in the third grade also happened to Wilfred Schwankl. Each day we had a reading period and each pupil was required to read before the class for ten minutes. Wilfred was in front of the class and it was obvious that he was very uncomfortable about something. All at once he let out a scream and headed out of the room. It was obvious from the trail he left behind him which room he was heading toward.

The other incident I remember involved an upper classman named Ernest Skorheim. He was sliding down a wide, oak banister leading from the second floor. About half way down, he caught a loose piece of wood and ran a large splinter about one foot long into his upper thigh.

During the summer of 1934, we moved to 329 North Eleventh Street. This house was located in the northeast edge of town and, by going across the street, you were considered to be in the country. In fact, Miller's, who lived across the street, had horses and farmed for a living. My mother could always tell when Bob had been over helping Mr. Miller clean the manure out of the barn. Bob could never understand how she knew where he had been.

It was a seven-room house with a bathroom off to the south of the kitchen and a bedroom off to the south of the dining room. Two unheated bedrooms were located upstairs. I spent many enjoyable nights reading Tom Swift books and others by flashlight under the covers. In the winter, if I took a glass of water up and didn't drink it all, the remainder had a thickness of ice on it the next morning.

The floors in the house were uneven. If you set a marble in the middle, it always rolled to one of the corners. The floor covering was linoleum and provided a lot of fun in stocking feet. We would run as fast as we could from the kitchen, hit maximum speed about the middle of the dining room, and then slide into the living room, or the front room, as it was called then.

We would also line all the chairs in a row in front of the dining room windows and make believe we were on a train trip. As people went by the house in cars, we would wave as though we were looking out the train window and make believe the people we saw were passing by on the highway. When the train stopped at the station, we would all get off and then go in the kitchen to tell my mother we had gotten off the train to eat. She usually came up with a cookie or some other lunch that made the train stop well worthwhile.

Certain areas of the Great Plains had dust storms all through the '30's. They were the worst in Minnesota and the Dakotas during 1934. Great clouds of dust arose that blotted out the sun - the topsoil of a nation blowing away. The dust drifted like snow with high banks of it piling up against fence lines, buildings and houses. Even today one can find fences, if you dig through the rise in topography near a property line. After a storm, the dust would be lying on windowsills up to one inch deep. Businesses stopped, and cities turned on their streetlights. Cars drove with their lights on in the middle of the afternoon and the lighting had to be on in the homes in order to see what you were doing. We would hang wet blankets over the doors in order to prevent the dust from coming in through the openings. The blowing dirt and sand was damaging to car paint and other painted surfaces exposed to the elements.

Hundreds of thousands of farmers could no longer grow crops on land that had literally blown away. Streams and wells were choked by the dust and drove cattle and sheep mad with thirst before they died and then were buried beneath the dust. The farms and homesteads their grandfathers had carved out of the wilderness had returned to wilderness. Farm-mortgage foreclosures began increasing. Many farmers who owned their land filed for bankruptcy. Drought and grasshoppers added to the farmer's woes. Some of those that did have some money bought up the abandoned farm for the unpaid taxes.

Government programs paid farmers to destroy piglets and other animals in an attempt to increase prices.

These people had no choice but to pack their families and what little possessions they could carry and head west as desperate migrant workers. They were willing to work for any wages at all doing the only thing they knew how to do - planting and harvesting. This they did for others. Most ended up in the states of Washington, Oregon and California working in the fruit orchards. A few years later many became defense workers who prospered and never did return to the lands from which they had migrated.

We were too young to realize there were good times and there were bad times. We just accepted that this is the way things would always be. I guess we never actually gave it any thought. Now that I look back we must have been aware that our financial situation was not as good as some of our friends. My dad would bring brown high-top shoes home from the railroad roundhouse that others had discarded. If they fit me I was expected to wear them. All the classmates in school had black low-cut shoes. I would pull my pant legs down as far as possible in an attempt cover the fact that mine were brown and were not oxfords. I still feel the embarrassment and it affects my decision making when I shop for shoes today.

I did become aware of various government programs becoming a part of our lives under President Roosevelt's Program. In November 1933 a number of programs were established under the National Industrial Recovery Act. Two years later the Federal Emergency Relief Act (FERA) was replaced by the Works Progress Administration. The WPA expanded on the type of work accomplished by FERA. Most cities benefited from the construction of ballparks, golf courses, swimming pools and other recreational facilities usually found in a city park.

All businesses started displaying the National Recovery Administration's (NRA) symbol of a blue eagle with "We Do Our Part" stickers in their windows. The Public Works Administration (PWA) under Secretary of the Interior, Harold Ickes, started building dams, highways, post offices, and other public works. Hoover and Grand Coulee Dams were built under provisions of the PWA. Ted Mann, who later became Project Manager at the Bureau of Reclamation's Bismarck Office, where I would later work, started on Hoover Dam as a young engineer just out of college.

The NRA undertook to mobilize public opinion to force businessmen to cooperate in standards of production, prices and marketing. Eventually, more than two million employers signed the NRA pledge.

The most widely known Roosevelt program was the one set up under the Works Progress Administration (WPA). The gigantic new program gave three and a half million jobs to the unemployed, paying just slightly less than the prevailing wage rates. This was done so the unemployed would not be discouraged from seeking private employment. The WPA could not compete with private industry, and therefore, many of the projects took on the "make work" aspect.

Every city and town across the nation had WPA projects. They ranged from construction to art. Sewer systems dug by hand (trenches seven feet deep), courthouse buildings, airports, schools, playgrounds and hospitals were constructed by the thousands throughout the nation. Theater, writer, and painter groups were formed.

When watching trenches being dug today by mechanical trenchers, it is unbelievable and difficult for today's worker to realize the amount of time spent to open a 100 yards of trench during the '30s. The worker then was so proud of his tool of the trade (shovel). At the end of the day his last duty was to clean and oil his shovel. The steel had a shiny silver sheen. They took a great deal of pride in their work. Those trenches were perfectly straight and uniform in width and depth.

Even though the projects were financed by the government as a means of employing the unemployed and at the same time, helping them maintain their dignity, many beneficial facilities that still exist today were provided for the Country under these programs.

The employee received forty dollars a month, and the supervisor of each group received ninety dollars. Mr. Miller, our neighbor who seemed very old to a young kid, was one of the workers on WPA. He hauled sand and began stock piling it for use in building a new school. The pit was located five miles north of Breckenridge adjacent to State Highway No. 75. The round trip distance was ten miles, and he would make two trips a day. The wagon would hold approximately two cubic yards. He was paid an extra dollar a day for the use of his horses.

Bids for the new school were let on January 11, 1934 and the first shovel of dirt was moved on February 10th. The corner stone was laid on May 14th and the work completed on October 29th. The school was dedicated on November 12, 1934. The school construction had progressed sufficiently to permit classes to begin that year on September 10th. I started the 6th grade. The cost of the school was $210,911.23 and today (2010) it is being used as a Middle School. You can't build a house today for that amount of money. Very few houses where construction is started in the spring can be moved into by fall.

The National Youth Administration (NYA), a division under WPA, provided part-time work for 600,000 college students and one and one-half million high school students between the ages of 16 and 24. NYA also found work for more than two and one-half million youngsters who were not in school. Six years after the NYA was organized, I became involved with the program for a short time. On February 13, 1942 I left for Glenwood, Minnesota to enroll in a course by the NYA that provided sheet metal training. It was especially appropriate at the time I enrolled since all training was directed toward and geared to skills that would assist in and benefit the war effort. It was hinted during our training that we would probably end up in one of the war production plants in the nation.

The NYA program was organized similar to a military operation. We lived in a large building next to a lake west of Glenwood, Minnesota. The Government had leased or purchased the building on a lakeshore west of the city. The building provided living accommodations for 150 of us with our training being conducted in town. We attended classes during the day and studied in the evening. We were restricted to quarters during the week with lights out at 10 P.M. We could request weekend passes and my high school friend Mel Ruud and I usually hitchhiked home to Breckenridge. We had to report back to camp by 6 PM. Sunday evening. Duties assigned were much like those we would come to experience in Army life approximately 15 months later. Washing pots and pans for the chef and other kitchen duties were assignments everyone dreaded.

Our food was provided and we were paid $3.50 a month for such things as toothpaste, soap and other miscellaneous items. I don't know where we got our cigarette money.

My high school girl friend Kay had 2 more years of schooling before graduating. She was the main reason that weekend pass was so important. I was so in love and I thought if I didn't remain in close contact it would be so easy for someone else to take my place. With no money, it meant we had to hitchhike the 90-mile distance. Darkness came early in those winter months and many times it was beginning to storm when Mel and I left for home. Years later I wondered if we caused our parents many hours of concern and worry. Now days everyone remains in contact with cell phones. Back then they didn't know if we were coming home in a blizzard or if we elected to stay in Glenwood for the weekend.

Many WPA projects had more employees than would be economically feasible under today's work standards. Even today, if someone leans on a shovel, a remark by someone old enough to remember the Depression is made that, " he looks like a WPA worker". One of the jokes at the time the WPA existed (1935-1940) went like this: A lady needing her grass cut called the local WPA office and asked if they would send a man over. A short time later a truck pulled up and nine men got off. They unloaded an outhouse, and set that up in one corner of the yard. The lady came out and said, "Why all the men; all I want you to do is cut my grass?"

One of the men said, "Lady, it's like this:
There will be two coming, two going, two
shittin', two mowing and I am the Boss"

As mentioned above construction of the school began the spring of '34, and wood scrap piles began to develop. We lived less than four blocks from where the school was being built. I kept hauling the scraps home with my little wagon and piling them in a bin we had in the garage. My mother used them in the kitchen cook stove for cooking meals.

One day that summer, Bob was shooting sparrows with a slingshot. One of his shots went wild and broke a window in Pelvit's home, who were the neighbors living across the street. As soon as he heard the glass start falling, he ran around to the south side of our house and hid behind a rain barrel. Ben Pelvit came around the house from the other direction and just as Bob was hunching down as much as possible, Ben grabbed him. Bob wet his pants on the spot.

About mid year, my dad developed a pain in one leg. As time passed it continued to worsen, and it soon became apparent it was something that would not go away in time and he knew he had to take some kind of action. Because of costs and lack of medical insurance, no one went to the doctor or checked into a hospital until they were almost near death.

One afternoon, a flatbed truck from Larson Transfer pulled up and two men carried my dad out to the truck on an Army-type stretcher. They were moving him to the depot where he would be put on a train for transfer to the Veterans Hospital in Fargo. I remember him turning on his side on the stretcher so he could wave as they passed around the corner and out of sight. I then went in the garage and cried for an hour. Fargo was so far away and I would never be able to ride my bike that far to see him. I had a feeling he was never going to come home and I would never see him again.

The doctors operated and found a large black spot on the bone of his leg just above the ankle. They chipped this black area off and when they thought they had removed it all, they closed it up. However, he didn't come home like we thought he would. Following the operation, he was placed in the "death room" on two different occasions. I imagine that was the terminology used for the Intensive Care Unit by the patients at that time.

During that year he was confined to the hospital, Mrs. Spreckles (his sister) came by to pick us up during her visits to the hospital. She had a large 12 cylinder Willys-Knight with yellow spoke wheels and black body. There were two large spare tires that were mounted on each side of the car just ahead of the running board and extended into the front fenders. It was a huge car; especially to an 11-year old kid.

The hospital was located north of Fargo, adjacent to the Red River and, except for the landscaped grounds, was surrounded by farmland. A road through the wheat fields led from what today is Broadway in Fargo to the hospital. The grounds had a small man-made stream running through it that formed a small lake in the center. Bob and I had our picture taken in our new white pants and shirts by the lake. We only wore white for special occasions since it was so difficult to keep from getting soil marks that were easily visible.

My dad tried to get some type of pension payments for the family while he was in the hospital. I have a number of pieces of correspondence between he and the Veterans Administration wherein he is trying to justify his claim. The final position taken was that since his confinement was not due to or a result of military action, he did not have a legitimate claim. That decision had to be a blow for him. There was no savings account and no such thing as unemployment compensation existed at the time.

Although very few people were in good financial condition at that time in the thirties, we would find baskets of food on the steps in the morning. There was never any note with it that might make us feel obligated. His fellow workers at the roundhouse had had special drives from time to time to show they were thinking of him. On Thanksgiving, we received a goose. The fellow delivering it said my dad's name had been drawn in a lottery. I guess we didn't believe him and realized they didn't want us to feel it was a handout. The American Legion raised money through a dance held at their pavilion and this was used to buy groceries. There were no places to turn for help like there are today.

His leg would not completely heal and remained an open sore. All the hospital was doing was introducing live maggots to eat away the dead flesh and putting peroxide on twice a day to stop infection. My dad decided he could just as well do that himself at home and requested discharge.

After returning home, he began going back to work. He still had a terrible pain in his leg because we would wake up in the middle of the night and hear him moaning. It was terrible to hear him in pain and unable to sleep. I can't imagine how he could remain awake all night in pain and then go to work the next day.

After he had been home for about six months, my mother noticed a strange clicking sound coming from the mouth of the bottle as she poured peroxide on the sore. In examining it more closely it was obvious the mouth of the bottle was hitting some hard material. It was a small chip of bone about the size of a dime that had worked its way to the surface. She removed the bone with a tweezers and from that evening on, the sore began to heal. In two months, it was completely healed, and his pain was gone. It was wonderful. He was sleeping again and so was the rest of the family.

Years later my sister Judith worked at this Veteran's Hospital as a nurse and tried to look up some old records of her father that might have given some information as to his treatment at the time. However she was unsuccessful and assumed all the records had been destroyed or put in dead storage somewhere.

I started classes in the sixth grade at the new school that fall of 1934. We had a beautiful teacher named Miss Kravik. You notice, I no longer say a "pretty" teacher. I, along with all the other boys, began to experience some strange, new, bewildering, physical changes taking place. We looked at our new teacher in a manner differently from the previous five teachers we had had.

We also did more teasing and showing off. I once brought a live mouse to school. When she was out of the room, we opened the top drawer of her desk and put a thumbtack through the mouse's tail into the bottom of the desk drawer. The mouse could run in a circle with the end of its tail as a focal point. When classes started for the day, we just couldn't wait for her to open her desk drawer. We thought she would think it was really funny.

About forty-five minutes had passed and she still had no reason to open her desk drawer. We were becoming impatient and also fearful the mouse may escape and spoil all the fun. Finally, she assigned us some work and sat down to do some of her own. She opened the desk drawer and let out a blood-curdling scream and headed out the door. She came back with the janitor who promptly removed the mouse. She never did try to find out who the culprits were and we surmised later that she might have assumed the mouse was loose and had somehow gotten into her desk.

Pornography was passed around that year. Comic strip characters such as Popeye and Olive Oil, Maggie and Jiggs and others were used in small ten page books. This material then blew the "stork theory". Life would never be the same again.

Bob and I put up a round oatmeal box with the bottom cut for a hoop up above the doorway between the kitchen and dining room. The dining room floor was covered with linoleum, so we played basketball in our stocking feet, using a rolled up stocking for a basketball. I don't know how my mother put up with the noise but she didn't seem to mind. We had some wonderful one-on-one games. The game we played seems so simple now but we could spend all afternoon on a rainy day playing indoor basketball.

A man named Anzilo Siciliano emigrated from Italy and changed his name to Charles Atlas. He built up his physique using a system of body building procedures which he later dubbed "Dynamic Tension". He set up a business and began selling body building courses by mail. He advertised in comic books and one ad showed a well-built bully kicking sand in the face of a 97-pound weakling. The weakling takes the course and is able to confront the bully. I sent my brother Bob's name in for the course and approximately every six weeks he would receive mail from Charles wondering when he was going to start his bodybuilding. Charles was born in 1893 and died of a heart attack in 1972.

We use to steal watermelons from Dinger's field lying adjacent to the river on North side of 12th Street. We would throw them in the Otter Tail River and then run down west of the Eleventh Street bridge, strip down, form a human chain across the river, and retrieve the melons when they came bobbing by. We quit stealing after Dinger came out one night and fired a shotgun. We thought it was into the air but we really weren't certain. We did hear the buckshot falling around us in the field.

We decided watermelon wasn't good enough to risk our lives for.

In the cool, crisp evenings of October, Bob, Darrell, and I played football on the boulevard. It was mostly just big pile-ups, but Darrell really loved it. We would let him score touchdowns and then he would tell his mother how many points he scored when we went in for the evening. In the winter we flooded the boulevard and made a skating rink. We piled a ridge of snow to make a border and then flooded the inside to a depth of two inches. Then we hoped for cold weather so the water would freeze. I can close my eyes and almost recreate the feelings of excitement and enjoyment we had playing hockey under a bright full moon. We had poor quality clamp on skates. A key was required to tighten the skate to the bottom of the shoe. If the shoe sole wasn't too thick the tightening of the clamp would pinch the foot.

On cold winter mornings Bob and I would wait until we heard someone stoking the space heater in the dining room downstairs and when we were certain it was fired up, we would race down in our long johns. Before dressing, we would hold our clothes up in front of the heater to warm them. It did not seem too strange then but not too many people today would accept a heating system, which at that time was acceptable.

We also played hockey on the Otter Tail River. Our hockey stick consisted of a tree branch having an L shape at the lower end and our puck was a Carnation Condensed Milk can. We would scrape the snow off the ice and use it to build a perimeter around the sides of the rink. We would then go to the upstream edge of the rink, and cut a hole in the ice. The pressure would force the water to the surface. The water would run downstream on the surface of the river ice. If the temperature was low enough we soon had a nice smooth hockey rink.

We also cut a hole in the ice at another location where there was a high hill above the river. We would then haul pails of water to ice down the riverbank slope by Teherney's house. When the slope was frozen, we would go down the hill on skates or by sled. I recently stopped to see this slope the last time I was in Breckenridge and it is not nearly as long, high or as steep as I recall it being back in 1934. I stood there, closed my eyes and for a few moments I was eleven years old again.

We had a number of alternate freezing and thawing periods early in the winter and again late spring. During these periods all the snow in Mr. Miller's pasture melted on warm days and during cold days large patches of ice formed in his field. Bob and I clamped on our skates and had a great time on a natural rink much larger than the area we had flooded at home. There were weeds and grass protruding through the ice but we soon had that shaved off with our skates. We played tag and hockey on these patches of ice and never seemed to tire.

I never seem to have any memories of Christmas that would make it memorable. I do remember one Christmas about 1935 when my dad got a new bicycle. He would no longer have to walk to work. After the Christmas Eve festivities were over, he set the bicycle out on the front porch. The next morning when he went out there the bike was gone. It had been a major purchase and everyone was sick about it. Whoever took that bike on Christmas Eve must have guilt feelings today. As young as I was I felt so sorry for my Dad.

Local entertainment during this time period was attending the Walkathon held at the American Legion Pavilion. Of all the crazy competitions ever invented, the walkathon won by a considerable margin of lunacy. This became a national craze in 1923. All across the nation men and women staggered in near exhaustion to the music of seedy little bands or to the fox trots played by Victrolas. Couples had to remain on their feet and walk in a circular route around the pavilion floor. If their knees touched the floor for any reason they were eliminated from the contest. They were given a 15-minute break every hour. Days passed and one partner would sleep while being held up by the other. Ice packs and smelling salts were used as a means of staying awake. As one of the partners dropped to the floor from sheer exhaustion, the couple was eliminated from the competition.

Similar events were held all over the country. Prizes that ranged from $1,000 to $3,000.were awarded. The prize amount went to the last two contestants that were standing. Contestants were required to perform a skit, song or dance at certain times during the day. A number of contestants died from heart failures. Before the contest was over, couples came to hate each other.

Another form of entertainment was reading roadside Burma-Shave signs as you rode along the highway. It was a form of "friendly sell" rather than "hard or soft sell". However, they have gone the way of the ice-wagon, the steam locomotive whistle and other vanishing sights and sounds whose memory sets America's heart strings vibrating with more than ordinary nostalgia. They were a humorous message in rime

Such as:

Every shaver
Can now snore
Six minutes more
Than before by using
Burma-Shave

Another one was:

Does your husband misbehave?
Grunt and grumble

Rant and rave
Shoot the brute
Some Burma-Shave

And another

The Wolf is shaved
So neat and trim
Red Riding Hood
Is chasing him
Burma-Shave

And another

The chick
He wed
Let out a whoop
Felt his chin and
Flew the coop
Burma-Shave

These signs would continue for miles and no two were ever the same. There were over 7,000 signs in 43 states.

Right after Christmas I went to my Grandmother's home in Hankinson for a week before school was scheduled to start again. I took the GALLOPING GOOSE out of Breckenridge. It went southeast to Nashua and then switched from the Great Northern tracks to the Soo Line tracks and headed west to Hankinson. The 27- mile distance between Breckenridge and Hankinson required approximately five hours by railroad. The train stopped to pick up every cream can along the track. The GOOSE was a one-car unit that hauled freight, people, miscellaneous items and mail.

I spent the week with my Uncles Reuben and Bobby and my Aunt Gladys ice skating, going to movies and other fun things like sitting around the pot-bellied stove cracking black walnuts and telling stories. We were all approximately the same age and liked doing the same things. My Uncle Art, who lived in southern Minnesota, would bring five-gallon pails of black walnuts up to Hankinson every year. The walnuts were difficult to crack and difficult to get at the meat inside. However, we didn't care; that was part of the fun as we sat talking around that old stove.

My Grandfather made and bottled his own beer. He set a batch in a 30-gallon Red Wing crock and continually checked it periodically to determine if it was ready for bottling. When it was ready to bottle the crock was almost empty as a result of his frequent checking and a new batch had to be set.

Whenever he wanted a quart from the crawl space underneath the house, the four of us also got to split a bottle. We had Reuben asking the question all the time, "Do you want a another bottle of beer, Pa?"

It was during this period that Gladys got some cigarettes from my Aunt Orley. We tried smoking them while we were skating one evening. What an awful taste they left in one's mouth. We couldn't understand why anyone would want to smoke. A few years later we were all steady smokers. The two uncles Bobby and Reuben and Aunt Gladys have been dead for a number of years. Gladys never did give up smoking and it contributed to her death.

In the spring I discovered fish migrated up the small streams of water resulting from snowmelt that was running into the Ottertail River. As they migrated up these streams, the width and depth of the stream decreased. I caught Northern Pike by hand in the area along the river west of the 11th street bridge. The water temperature was just slightly above freezing, and the fish were sluggish and slow in their movements. I would catch them by hand or by using a tree branch that had a "Y" shape at the end.

The school year was soon over, and another summer was available for fishing, swimming, and shooting my slingshot. I also got my first single shot 22 rifle, which I purchased from some kid for two dollars. It didn't have an ejector, so after each shot, I had to take a jack knife and dig out the empty cartridge. I spent a great deal of time by myself that summer. The mournful cooing of the mourning doves and the singing of the other birds would wake me early in the morning. I would fix my own breakfast and then would go hunting in what I considered my own private hunting preserve--the wooded area along the river between the 11th street and the 5th street bridges. I would run through the woods imagining that Indians were behind me and I was using my cunning knowledge to elude them. Somewhere in that expanse is a large tree containing my initials. I spent a wonderful, beautiful afternoon doing the carving and I told myself I would come back some day when I am old and see if they are still there. I still want to do that. I just have to take the time.

I also spent a great deal of time at my grandparent's home in Hankinson that summer. One of the first duties Reuben, Gladys, Bobby and I had before being free to go off and play was coal picking. We would each have a pail and we would start down the Soo Line Railroad tracks heading east out of Hankinson. We would pick up the coal that had fallen out of the tender of the railroad steam engines. The engineers soon knew us and if they happened to be coming by on a run while we were picking, they would throw coal off for us. We would then have our pails full in no time at all. We were each required to pick one pail of coal per day. Without their assistance, it usually required that at least a mile of track had to be covered. It wasn't long before we knew the train schedules and timed our trips to coincide with their schedule.

The bakery in Hankinson shipped their baked goods to all the little towns along the Soo Line Railroad between Hankinson and Bismarck, North Dakota. The goods were shipped in cardboard boxes, and the following day the boxes were returned and left at the depot. Reuben and I would deliver the boxes to the bakery and receive a dozen day-old bismarks for our effort. It was only a distance of four blocks between the depot and the bakery. We each finished a half-dozen bismarks in no time at all. My Aunt Dorothy (Reuben's sister) worked in the depot restaurant. If we had the nickel for an ice cream cone, the serving was extra large.

Reuben and I collected copper wire, burned off the insulation, and sold the copper to a junk dealer. We collected tinfoil from cigarette packages and candy bars and rolled it into large balls. Bacon grease was saved, and suddenly scrap iron became valuable. Unknown to us, Japan was buying everything they possibly could from us to support the war effort they had underway.

Many of our summer days were spent down next to the railroad tracks in what was called the "Hobo Jungle". It was a large willow patch near the coal chute where the steam engines stopped to take on water and coal. The unemployed men traveling west would stop off for a day or two to rest up. They came from all parts of the country and had many interesting stories to tell about their lives. We would quiz them about some of the places they had come from and places they had come through before arriving at "Hobo Jungle". Many were married and had families they left behind while they set out in search of work. I have often wondered how many found employment, sent for their families and never returned home again. These men were not like the tramps my parents knew before the Depression. These were high school and college graduates willing to take any work regardless of the pay.

One of the daytime activities was fishing at Lake Elsie. The main catch was bullheads but occasionally one of us got a Northern Pike. The low water elevations and the hot temperatures of the 1930's resulted in much rotted vegetation and a smell that was very unpleasant. The lake today is at a much higher elevation and is a beautiful body of water with many wonderful homes bordering its shoreline. There is a large sand and gravel operation around the perimeter of the lake.

The primary activity at night was going to the Avon Theater. It didn't matter what was playing. We went to whatever was being shown. If we hadn't been able to cut someone's grass or do some other job to earn money that day, Reuben and I would wait for the first show to end. Then when everyone was exiting from the theater, we would face the same direction as the crowd leaving and back into the theater. We didn't think we were doing anything wrong. They were going to show that movie for the second time anyway and there were all kinds of seats that were not being used for the second showing.

My aunts Dorothy and Esther were a few years older than we were. I don't remember where Esther slept since there was only one bedroom downstairs and one bedroom upstairs. The other five us slept in that upstairs bedroom. Aunt Dorothy would tell us scary stories as long as we tickled her feet. Sometimes when the stories got very exciting and we got engrossed in what may happen next, we would forget to continue tickling. Then the story would stop until we started tickling again.

Dorothy and Esther always went to dances in some of the smaller towns in the adjacent area. It was the flapper age and my aunts knew all the latest dances. There was the Black Bottom, the Shimmy and the Charleston. They also indulged in the slow fox trots of the day and let loose during the faster, jazzier numbers. At that time Jazz songs seemed somehow uncivilized and therefore desirable to the young. Many songs during this period were either suggestive or just plain silly. The aunts knew them all and we thought the songs were just plain stupid and made no sense. Now I can see why others at the time thought they were suggestive. Below are two examples:

I'm the Sheik of Araby
Your love belongs to me
At night when you're asleep
Into your tent I'll creep

or

If you knew Suzie like I know Suzie,
Oh! Oh! Oh! What a girl!
We went riding, she didn't balk
Back from Yonkers,
I'm the one that had to walk

It was also an age when women started smoking and drinking. College campuses abolished compulsory chapel attendance, legalized smoking for women and did away with a dress code. They also winked or looked the other way at drinking parties held on campus.

Reuben and I spent many wonderful days together during the summer. We went to baseball games on Sundays, made our own ice cream, snared gophers, and played with a Billy goat he had trained to pull a cart.

All the small towns within a 25-mile radius had their own local baseball teams. Some very good baseball was played on Sunday afternoons during those depression years. It was the major entertainment enjoyed on weekends.

We would go to the pasture of John R. Jones and catch a cow to milk. We then would go to Bolens' chicken coop and steal some eggs from the chickens. The next items required to be picked up were sugar and vanilla at home and then take all these ingredients up to the icehouse located east of town adjacent to the railroad. Here we would get ice and rock salt. These ice cream ingredients were then mixed together in an old one-gallon syrup pail. We would then begin turning the pail back and forth using the handle while it sat in a mixture of ice and salt. In a short time, we had ourselves a gallon of ice cream.

The State of North Dakota paid a penny for gopher tails that summer. We couldn't imagine what the State wanted the tails for and what they could possibly do with them. We took our traps to a field that was filled with scurrying rodents and spent the afternoon trapping them. However, if the State had a use for them we would try to get all we could for them. However, we didn't want to reduce the number of producing rodents, so we began to snare them. We then cut off their tails and released them. That would help the State obtain the tails they needed for some intended purpose. Our revised method for obtaining the tails would also insure there would be plenty of production for next year's harvest. The following summer, true to our assumptions, many of the gophers running around were bobbed tailed, but their young were normal in every way. We would be able to continue supplying and meeting the needs of the State of North Dakota indefinitely.

I remember bringing some clothes home to Breckenridge for my mother to wash. I had forgotten to take out some of the gopher tails and they were getting pretty ripe. She always checked the pockets to make certain there were no stones (I always had a slingshot and the required ammunition with me) or other odd things in the pockets. When her hand grasped the rotten hairy mess, she let out a blood-curdling scream.

One thing that I often think about is some of the unsafe activities that we were involved in. In the thirties the refrigerated cars of the railroad still had to be iced for cooling. Reuben and I would go to the icehouse to help. It required the cutting of ice blocks to the proper size and dropping these into a chute in each corner of the railroad car. The dangerous part was jumping from the ice house platform to the railroad car. Both the platform and car were wet and had chipped pieces of ice lying around. The opening between the icehouse platform and the top of the railroad car that had to be crossed in the jump was about three feet. For the adults this was not much distance but to young kids this seemed pretty great. Had we slipped and not made it, there was about a thirty-foot fall to the rail bed below. Even now it scares me to think how easily we could have ended our lives at an early age.

Each time I returned home from my grandparents' home after a summer visit, my grandfather would take me to the train. On the way we would stop at the local bar. While he was enjoying a beer, he had me looking at the candy case to see what I wanted to take with me. He gave me 10 cents and the decision was difficult because there were so many kinds of penny candy to select from. I changed my decision many times during that period of time it took my grandfather to drink his beer. I can still sense that feeling of uncertainty I had as I looked at that candy case.

The Great Depression continued, but it never really seemed to directly affect us too much. I guess it was because we had almost grown up with it and we had never really known other times.

The dust storms continued and in an effort to end the wind erosion menace, a Shelterbelt Project was begun. Millions of trees were to be planted from

Bismarck, North Dakota to Amarillo, Texas. They were to be planted on quarter lines 132 feet wide in a continuous North-South axis one mile apart. The results of the study the Great Plains Field Station at Mandan, North Dakota had done on 2,700 demonstration shelter belts were to be used in the selection of tree types and methods for planting.

I began to deliver the Minneapolis Tribune that summer. The papers came wired together so I needed to carry a pair of pliers with me to cut the wire. There were usually 50 papers to a bundle.

I wouldn't get out of bed until I heard the train whistling as it came around the curve about two miles east of Breckenridge. I had to pick the papers up at the depot at 5:30 A.M. and it would take me until about 8 o'clock to finish with the delivery. I received ten cents per morning during the week and twenty-five cents for Sundays. The Sunday paper with all the ads was very thick and heavy. I always hoped someone would miscount my Sunday papers. Every extra paper I got, I could sell on the street for ten cents. I don't remember what was done when there was a shortage but that wasn't my responsibility. The man overseeing all the routes had to take one from the newsstand supply and make up the shortage.

The summer deliveries weren't too bad. The sun was up and the weather was warm. I didn't have to rush because there was no school schedule for me. However, in the winter it was terrible to get out of a nice, warm bed, get into cold clothing and head out into what may be stormy weather. We had no heat upstairs where we slept. It would have been so easy to climb back into bed and say I don't need that 10 cents. I still dislike the mournful whistle of a train engine on an early winter morning.

That summer, I also got a short-term job mixing grasshopper poison. There was an old circular butter churn near the County Fairground Buildings in the Island Park. About ten truck loads of sawdust were dumped near the churn. My job was to shovel the sawdust into the churn, put in about five gallons of liquid poison, (arsenic) mix it thoroughly and then dump it and start a new batch. This material was hauled out and spread on the fields. The grasshoppers ate anything and everything. When they ate this sawdust, the poison killed them. I was glad when that job was over; I didn't like the fumes that came out of the churn once it started mixing. I don't know if it was harmful or not. I often wondered if my lungs were damaged in any way from the strong fumes.

During the time I was mixing the grasshopper poison, I discovered an opening leading to the second story of one of the Fair Grounds buildings. A number of us would go up there to play. It was similar to a large haymow and we would fasten ropes to various rafters and swing through the air like Tarzan. We devised a game of tag, but the rope had to be used in catching someone. Evidently with our laughter and yelling we made enough noise to attract attention. The County Sheriff came one day and yelled, "You kids come down out of there." I looked down through the opening into one of the largest gun barrels I had ever seen in my life. I wet my pants on the spot.

Nothing more than a warning was issued but we got out of there immediately. We then went under the bridge between Breckenridge and Wahpeton to talk things over. My fright that day was greater than any fear I would experience years later during World War II. I don't think anyone of us ever forgot how frighten we were that day.

When Franklin Delano Roosevelt was inaugurated as the 32nd U.S. president March 4, 1933 he resolved to put the nation to work. He brought his New Deal to the American people in the form of a number of "alphabet soup" agencies designed to provide jobs, among them:

WPA (Works Progress Administration)
NRA (National Recovery Administration)
CCC (Civilian Conservation Corps)
PWA (Public Works Administration)
AAA (Agricultural Adjustment Administration)

President Roosevelt established the Rural Electrification Administration (REA) in 1935. The REA Act was passed in 1936, with preference loans available to public power districts, public utility districts, municipal and electric cooperatives. Farmers banded together to organize electric cooperatives, with a few dedicated individuals going from farm to farm to get signatures of new members, along with a $5 "sign up" fee.

Poles and lines then began springing up, often with the help from members who assisted the line crews. By the end of the 1930s 90 percent of the rural homes across the country had electric power.

Another program born in the turbulent times of the depression was the Social Security Act signed by President Roosevelt on August 14, 1935. The federal government began one of the most gigantic tasks of its kind on November 16, 1936. It began setting up social security accounts for 26,000,000 workers. From 45,000 post offices throughout the country, postmen set out with forms to be delivered to 5,000,000 business establishments. When the social security program went into effect on January 1, 1937, one cent of each dollar a worker earned, up to $3,000 a year, was put in to the pension. Still existing today, it turned out to be one of Roosevelt's most important domestic achievements and most lasting legacy. Its purpose was to assure the elderly citizens a guaranteed income against the day they could no longer work and to avoid attaching the stigma of welfare to those in need by making the program universal in scope.

The local radio station took requests each day for about an hour. One afternoon my mother called me in for Kool-Aid and cookies. As I sat there eating the radio announcer said, "This next number is for Merle McMorrow, who will be twelve years old on the 22nd." They then began to play "That Little Boy of Mine". I remember the verses and the smile on my Mother's face as the words were sung:

A tiny turned up nose
Two checks just like a rose
So sweet from head to toes
That little boy of mine

Two eyes that shine so bright
Two arms that hold me tight
Two lips that kiss goodnight
That little boy of mine

No one will ever know
Just what his coming has meant
Because I love him so
He's someone Heaven has sent

He's all the world to me
He climbs upon my knee
To me he'll always be
That little boy of mine

Nothing could seem dumber at the age of twelve than to have your mother dedicate a song to you on your birthday. I was hoping none of my friends had heard it. Each day for a week I kept waiting for someone to say some thing to me and I had thought up all kinds of responses I would make. However, no one said anything.

Either they hadn't heard it or forgot about it if they did hear it. If it were possible now to relive those few brief moments, I would try to sit upon her knee and thank her for all the things she had done for me in the first twelve years of my life. Those first twelve years had seemed like a lifetime to me but now I can imagine it was a brief fleeting moment in my mother's life.

My mother worked at Swift & Co. to supplement my Dad's income during the '30s. She received 10 cents a chicken. It was a dirty, smelly job and the high humidity resulting from the scalded chickens made for an undesirable-working environment.

Americans started traveling and not only were better roads needed but a place to stay at night was also a necessity. Rows and semicircles of little cabins started popping up. They were little more than glorified chicken coops when they started. People demanded more and the accommodations became more acceptable. By 1925 the State of Florida had developed 178 tourist courts.

This was the year (1935) my Uncle George and Aunt Mabel and their three children moved upstairs at our place. I remember they also had a small Pekinese dog. I can't imagine what the arrangements were since we had no bathroom upstairs or cooking facilities. George was working on the paving job on Highway 210 between Breckenridge and Fergus Falls. The 27-mile stretch of highway was gravel. I suppose my dad needed the rent and George needed a place where the rent was reasonable. Today large farm homes lie adjacent to the beautiful highway.

George had a '29 Chevy which was parked in our garage. I would sit in it every day and go through the shifting sequence, making the necessary noises with my mouth to simulate the engine rpm's.

I again spent part of the summer of 1936 at my grandparents' home in Hankinson. My Uncle Reuben and Aunt Gladys were near my age and seemed like brother and sister to me. We played tag at the stockyard pens. The top railing of the pens were finished off with a 2" x 12" plank. The various pens had swinging gates and the rules required that you could not go to the ground to chase anyone. You had to run along the top plank and use the swinging gates to catch someone. Gladys fell one time and broke her arm.

Reuben and I became very proficient with slingshots. Our most common target was the grasshopper. They were everywhere and we loved to lift them off the dusty road with a well-placed shot. We were continually on the lookout for the perfect crotch and the elm trees seemed to provide the best location to look. Garages had plenty of old inner tubes since there was no such things as tubeless tires in those days. The tubes were made from real rubber. We also needed strips of rubber for the arrows we shot. All homes had shingle roofs and it was easy to make arrows out of the shingle. We would notch the arrow at the balance point. By fastening a half-inch wide strip of rubber to a piece of wood for a handle and tying a heavy piece of string on the other end with a knot in it, we could send the arrows up out of sight. The knot was placed in the notch of the arrow and then shot like a slingshot.

Another thing we made during my summer visits was a pair of stilts. We'd each get two 8-foot 2x4s, nail a block of wood about half way up on each 2x4, put a leather strap on each block, mount and start chasing each other. It is amazing what simple little things we did to amuse ourselves.

We fished Lake Elsie during the day and attended Laurel and Hardy movies during the evening. If we went to a Frankenstein movie, we would come home and tell ghost stories until we fell asleep. My grandfather would pound on the wall to quiet us down. Cowboy movies were very popular in the 30s. Stars such as Tom Mix, Hoot

Gibson, Smiley Burnette, Gabby Hayes and Hopalong Cassity provided plenty of action. Gene Autry, Roy Rogers and Dale Evans were some of the first to begin singing in the western films. The men in the white hats were chasing those in the dark hats through the hills outside of Hollywood. The movies were not too costly to produce.

Sundays were spent at the ballpark watching teams from the surrounding towns take on the Hankinson All-Stars. Cars would circle the outfield and if a well executed play was made or a home run hit all horns would blast indicating approval.

The sixth year of the drought continued. Horses and cattle were being fed Russian thistle, which had been cut green and put up like hay. The Government paid the farmer to kill and bury his pigs because of a lack of food for the animals. If sold for meat they brought 3 cents per pound. My relatives (Hoefs) living west of Hankinson gave me one small pig from a litter that they were about to kill. I took it home to Breckenridge and built a small pen on the south side of the garage. I picked up food scraps thrown out by one of the local restaurant and also used table scraps to feed him. He became quite tame and was very intelligent. It is surprising someone didn't complain about a farm animal being raised in town. I guess people had too many personal problems other than that confronting them to be too concerned about something so minor.

The pig would follow me around the yard like a dog, and we became very attached to each other. Toward fall my dad said it was about time we killed the pig. I guess all along I knew it was going to happen someday but I just put it out of mind and didn't think about it. I kept hoping he might forget about the pig if I kept him out of sight as much as possible. Then the day came and I ran in the garage to hide. It wasn't long and I could hear my friend squealing for help.

When my dad stuck him in the throat, he evidently didn't get the knife deep enough to reach his heart. When I looked out the garage door I saw the pig running around the yard squealing and leaving a trail of blood behind him. I felt so sorry for him because we had become pretty good friends in those few months I had him. Finally, after the loss of a considerable amount of blood, he dropped to his knees. My dad went over and re-stuck him. It was all over in a minute. I never could eat any of the bacon or pork chops we had that winter. In fact I wanted to leave the table when the discussion got around to how good the meat was. I am certain we would have many more vegetarians if people would see how animals have to die so we can have meat on the table.

I now have a better appreciation for what the Future Farmers of America members feel after feeding, raising, and grooming an animal all year long for a fair, knowing full well the animal will go to the slaughter house after the judging is over and the sale is completed.

I also had squirrels and a white rat for pets. I convinced my dad that white rats kept wild rats away. I don't know where I had gotten this information. I kept the rat in the garage at night. It had a dirt floor and the rat lived under the wood I had brought home from the school construction and stacked in the south end of the garage. One morning, when I came to the garage to get my pet, there was a wild scurry of many rodents heading for the scrap pile. The pet had mated with a wild rat and that blew another theory. There must have been a least 10 in the litter. The mother would come when I called her, but I never saw the others unless I quietly moved up to the garage and quickly opened the door. Even then it was merely a streak of gray that was seen.

We trapped most of the wild ones, but two got into the house by some means. We could hear them dragging things around at night after we were in bed.

My dad bought some poison, and the rats ate it and went outside to die. I no longer told anyone white rats would keep wild rats away.

In the fall of 1936, I started the 8th grade. I recall I had mixed feelings; I begin to feel my youth was rapidly approaching an end. I hated to let go of a carefree existence, but I was also interested in starting to work so I could buy some of the things my friends had and I didn't. I also became more interested in girls and no longer just teased them. It was really a confusing time with mixed feelings and emotions and not knowing how or with whom to discuss them. It would be extremely more difficult today to go through the teen-age years than it was when I was growing up and I can understand some of the pressures the kids have now.

That fall I also began taking instructions that would lead to confirmation the next spring. Classes were held in the Immanual Lutheran Church in Wahpeton on Wednesdays after school. The period lasted approximately until 6:30 P.M. I rode my bike over to Wahpeton and during the winter, I wrapped wire around the tires to give them more traction on the snow and ice. Supper, as we called it then, was over by the time I got home but my mother kept a hot plate of food in the oven for me. The food had a slight crust on it from sitting in the heat for a period of time. The plate was hot enough to require a hot pad under it. I can still recall the excitement as I neared home, wondering what that hot meal would consist of. I guess it would not have mattered what it was. Anything would taste great after a long bike ride on a cold winter's eve.

The next year on May 23rd, Pastor R.J. Becker confirmed four girls and nine boys. I had my first suit - double-breasted with vest. I am sure it was the first suit for many of those in the class. The girls wore white dresses and shoes, and the legs had to be properly crossed for the class picture. Each member of the class wore a pink carnation. No smiles were permitted during the photography session, since this was a very serious matter. A picture of the 1937 confirmation class still hangs in the church. I have one in my first book "Remembrance of Things Past."

I still see Marcus Radig in Bismarck. Wilfred Schwankl died a few years ago and Melvin Fenske lives in Wahpeton. I don't know what has happened to the rest of class.

I had now completed 8 years of schooling.

CHAPTER 7

HAPPINESS AND SADNESS

The summer of 1937 brought the first good news my dad had received in a long time. Notice was given that all World War I veterans would be receiving a bonus and the check could be picked up at the local Post Office. He sent me down to get it, and I brought this piece of paper home that had a figure greater than 1,200 dollars written on it. That was more money than my Dad made during an entire year of work. The Post Office was located just east of the Ridge Theater on Minnesota Avenue between Fifth and Sixth Streets.

A few days later, he bought the lot just south of where we were living at 329 North 11th Street. The total cost was 112 dollars. He then contacted Manley Storey, who was a carpenter and lived across the street. He asked him to build a house on the lot he had just purchased.

The house plan called for a two-bedroom, living room, kitchen but no basement. The original investment was $1,310.40, and the repayment contract called for monthly payments of $15.60 beginning September 4,

1937 (Darrell's funeral date) and continuing on the 4th of each month until paid in full. Total cost was slightly more than $2,700.

The house by today's standards was very small. The kitchen work- space was so small that it is amazing a full meal could be prepared in it. The room was probably about 10 X 10, and when the area for the stove and refrigerator is removed from the total area, that leaves very little space for table and work area. Insulation was put between the studding but the interior of the house had no sheetrock on the walls and remained that way until sometime after I was gone in 1941. A material called Celotex, about 1" thick, held the insulation in place. After the war Sheetrock was placed on the wall by Ray Cimbura, a fellow that had played on our 1940 basketball team.

The deed was recorded in the Wilkin County Courthouse on September 14, 1937, in Book 153 on Page 582.

My Dad was 46 years old and this was the first major possession he had ever owned. He had never owned a car. We shared our parents' feelings about owning their own home. Every other place we had lived, the landlord was the one to benefit if we did make improvements to the place. Now we could see the pleasure it brought to the family when Bob and I went to the river to obtain trees for the front yard. We planted grass and pulled out the weeds that came up thicker than the grass. It was just nice to know that everything we were doing was for the family and not some unknown landlord.

We had an oil burning stove for heat set up in the living room. This heat was supplemented with a wood burning stove in the kitchen that was used for cooking. The living room stove was connected by a quarter inch copper tube to a 55-gallon barrel sitting on a saw horse on the west side of the house. When the deliveryman came, my dad would have Bob or me count the number of trips he made to the house with five-gallon cans he carried to the barrel. Then he felt confident when checking our total number of gallons against what the billing contained that he got what he was paying for. Fuel oil at that time was 16 cents a gallon.

Our kitchen stove had some 3/4-inch cast iron pipes running through the firebox. They continued through the floor and into the crawl space under the house over to the bathroom and up into the hot water tank. The stove, when used for cooking, would also heat water for bathing. However, you could only count on hot water for a short time after the cooking had been completed. The water in the tank cooled very quickly. Usually Bob and I took our showers at school where the water was always hot and available in unlimited quantities.

This was the summer I fell in love. A little movie star two years older than me took the country by storm. She was the highest paid star in the world. Her name was Deanna Durbin (born Edna Mae Durbin on December 4, 1921 in Winnepeg, Manitoba) and I never failed to attend the movies she was in. She was in Three Smart Girls, That Certain Age and Mad About Music. I saw these movies over and over. If they were showing in neighboring towns I would hitchhike to attend. She tired of Hollywood, retired at an early age and moved to France. She was married three times, the first ending in death early in the marriage. The second marriage ended in divorce. Her last marriage ended after 49 years with death of her husband in 1999. She had one son and one daughter and she still lives in France just outside of Paris.

In 1939 I met another little dark-haired 14 year old and my love for Deanna cooled and was soon forgotten.

The fall of 1937 was spent digging and hauling soil from under the house. The initial space was only about 3 feet so I had to lie down while digging. My dad wanted enough space so things could be stored under there and canned goods could be placed below the trap door we had in the kitchen. The material I dug out was taken out by pails and was placed on the garden space in the back of the lot.

I also went out for Junior High basketball that November and it seemed like it would be a fun game. The fellows that would be playing on the future championship team were all ahead of me in school, not because I was slow, but because they were a year or two older than I was.

Nothing memorable happened that winter of 1937-1938. Frank Peterson or the Misaege boys would come over, and we would play poker with my dad. We used Diamond blue tipped matches for chips or money. We each started with 100 matches, and when they were gone, we were supposed to be out of the game. Some time during the latter part of the evening, some red tipped matches would always find their way into the game. The Misaege boys' father and uncle were in prison as a result of a bank robbery. Five years later George Misaege would end up in the same Army unit as I did.

We would usually have a large bowl of popcorn on the table and everyone ate from the community bowl. Lard was used in a cast-iron skillet to heat the popcorn and I never remember using butter as a topping. In fact, we never bought butter; we had the white margarine that required a capsule of coloring to be broken and added to the bowl of white margarine and then mixed with a large wooden paddle to give the margarine the appearance of butter.

There was a huge amount of snow that winter with strong winds piling it into large drifts. We would tunnel into these drifts and carve out a number of rooms. It could be cold and windy outside but we always felt warm and comfortable in our cave home.

We also listened to such radio programs as Jack Benny, Amos & Andy, One Man's Family, Fibber Mc Gee and Molly, and George Burns and Gracie Allen. Radio strengthened the imagination, and each listener pictured each situation a little differently.

We spent much of our outdoor time in the winter down on the river playing our special brand of hockey. Shoveling the snow off a piece of the river formed a rink. We would cut a hole in the ice and the water pressure would force the water up through the hole and flood the rink. After an hour or two, a nice, smooth surface would result if the temperature was low enough. It took a great amount of patience to wait for that water to freeze.

We used a Carnation Milk can for a puck. Our hockey sticks were found in the woods. Any piece of wood that looked like an "L" or a "7" became a hockey stick. Each of us wanted a stick that looked better than those sticks used by those we were playing with. Winter created no unpleasant memories for me, but I still preferred the pleasant days of summer.

The spring of '38 I got my first barber shop haircut. What a pleasure it was to walk with the wind and catch the aroma of the sweet smelling tonic they put on my head at the shop. My dad had never used anything like that. When we were very young my dad used a hand clipper which resulted in much hair pulling rather than hair cutting. Later he purchased an electric clipper, which took much of the pain out of haircuts.

All haircuts after age 15 were the professional type except on one occasion. Years later after marriage I was going to Denver to meet with some of the top people in our Bureau. I wanted to look my best. I asked my wife to clip the hair on the back of my neck. Before I knew it she was practically on the top of my head with the clippers. When I asked her what she was doing way up there, she said, "I'm just trying to get some of the nicks out."

That spring, Government surplus food was distributed from the Wilkin County Court House. Since I was the oldest, my parents selected me to go pick it up. I took the little red wagon and tried to mentally select a routing which would insure that I would not run into any of my school friends. Going to the courthouse was not too important, but coming back home had to be handled just right. I had this wagon full of flour, grapefruit, cornmeal, butter, oatmeal, nuts, sugar, etc. Everything was boldly marked "Government Surplus-Not To Be Sold". I took every back alley and side street not normally traveled by my friends. I was really relieved when I got home and I hadn't run into anyone I knew. I'm sure about half the town was eligible for the surplus and probably a greater number of my friends than I realized were also sneaking down back alleys hoping not to be seen by me. It was always a relief to get home without running into any of my friends.

Weekends and evenings that spring of '38 were spent at the dam by the 5th Street power plant. By rearranging the rocks and riprap below the dam, we were able to funnel fish migrating upstream to spawn into a trap. As the fish came along the face of the dam searching for a route upstream, they would end up in our rock trap. We would then catch them with our hands. Many times, we would catch fish by feeling in the cavities created in the rocks.

One time my brother Bob thought he had a fish and when he pulled it to the surface, he had a big snapping turtle by the head. He sure dropped him in a hurry and from then on, anything I reached for had to flash scales before I would go after it. The biggest fish I caught by this method was a 13-pound Northern Pike.

That summer of 1938 Rueben and I were working on Dick Lubenow's farm. We took one of the Shetland ponies and a cart into Hankinson for the weekend. We staked the pony out in a vacant lot for the night. Some time during the night he got loose and wondered off toward home crossing the railroad tracks on the way. He got his hind foot wedged in a railroad frog. A train evidently approached and in his frightened state he pulled his leg out of his hoof. We found him the next morning grazing along the railroad right-of-way. His bloody stump was sealed over and no longer bleeding. In time a thick scab formed but he could never be ridden again. I don't know what Dick ever did with the pony. The farm was located six miles west and six miles south of Wahpeton. Dick had never married and had two brothers named Johnnie and Tony, living on the farm with him. You could say they were indentured slaves. They never left the farm and Dick's only expense relating to them was a one pound can of Prince Albert smoking tobacco periodically. In addition to farming, he also raised Silver Fox, which were prized as fur capes at that time by fashionable women and Hollywood starlets. The pelt from one fox would bring from 125 to 150 dollars. This was a great sum when compared to the 35 dollars we got paid for working the entire summer. I found out recently that Reuben received only 30 dollars because he was younger. Dick had a way of saving every dollar he could.

The farm was a lonesome place. This was especially true at night. There was no electricity, no radio, or anything else in the way of conveniences. Trying to read by a flickering kerosene lamp was difficult. The days were long and monotonous. Each morning started about 5 A.M. with feeding foxes, milking cows, gathering eggs and feeding the chickens, and then coming in to make breakfast.

Dick would get Reuben and me up and then say, "Okay boys you feed the foxes, and I will make breakfast". As soon as we left to start the chores, he would jump back into bed. When we got back he jumps out of bed and says, "Shucks, I must have fallen off to sleep again.

You boys milk the cows and I will make breakfast." We'd end up making our own breakfast.

We usually got into the field by 8 A.M. and returned home by 7 P.M. Then the chores had to be repeated before we made supper. We normally took a dip in the Wild Rice River before going to bed in order to get some of the day's dirt off. The river had a muddy shoreline so we had mud halfway up to our knees. It might have been better if we had forgotten about the swim and left the dirt on. The bed bugs would have had a harder time getting through the dirt to get at our blood.

Rueben and I each kept a can of kerosene by the bed. During the night we would pick the bed bugs off and drop them into the can. It was one less bug the next night, but we really never decreased their numbers. They hatched the new young faster than we could kill the parents. In the morning we were covered with red raised spots where we had been bitten during the night. We had contests to see who had the most bugs in the cans each morning. The cans' contents would be half kerosene half bedbugs.

I preferred to cook my own meals. If Dick fried eggs, he would break approximately fifty into a frying pan. Occasionally we would see a green one go in and when we mentioned it to Dick, he would say, "Shucks boys, you won't even be able to taste that when I get it mixed up with all the other ones."

The bottom eggs were usually burnt and the top was still slimy and uncooked. He would then cut a pie wedge chunk out and put it on our plates with a comment, "Eat everything, boys. There's plenty of everything." With that we ate day-old bread which he told the bakery he wanted for his chickens. Day-old bread was never sold in the stores.

One Sunday afternoon Rueben and I were testing each other to see who could jump the highest. Anything we could do to help break the monotonous life we were living we did. Things were going along smoothly until I tried to clear a four-foot high barbed-wire fence. I made a misstep on my approach and got hung-up on the top wire by my left arm. Three large barbs held me off the ground. As I hung there I could slowly feel my flesh ripping. With no first-aid material at the farm, we put axle grease on it to keep the flies off and then wrapped a strip of a flour sack around the wound. During the day the perspiration would saturate the bandage and the salt in the rag would cause the open wound to smart. The wounds slowly healed and it is amazing no infection developed. I should have had stitches in one of the wounds.

Later in the summer when the threshing season started, the cooking got better but the days got longer, the temperature got hotter, and the work got harder. Reuben and I tried to prove we could outwork the older men. Our bundle loads were higher and loaded in less time than those of the others. Since each loaded rack took its turn pulling up the threshing machine, it meant we also got to rest.

In addition to the regular chores, we now had horses to feed and harness each morning and care for in the evening after returning from the fields.

The cooks that were hired turned out meals and field lunches that more than offset the disadvantages of threshing. One, whom we called Aunt Bertha, seemed to know what we liked best. Fried chicken and freshly baked pies or cakes were the norm. Lunch twice a day included sandwiches and freshly made donuts with the coffee. It must have taken an awfully large amount of work to keep the crew fed. There were approximately 12 to 14 people on an average threshing crew. The chickens had to be killed, scalded in hot water and the feathers picked and the pies had to be baked from scratch. In those days one could not buy chickens cut and packaged. The pies were usually made from apples and the apples had to be peeled before using for pie baking. While preparation was underway for the three meals, someone had to also be responsible for the two lunches. These lunches would consist of sandwiches, homemade donuts, pie and coffee. There was no such thing as a prepackaged snack. Some of the lunches were equivalent to what we eat for a meal today.

Grasshoppers were still unbelievably great in numbers. I made the mistake of laying a shirt on the ground one day instead of placing it in a vehicle. In a short time, it was completely eaten except for the double seamed areas. The grasshoppers would eat anything they could chew. I imagine they liked the salt in the sweat-stained piece of clothing. As you walked across the field, you would have anywhere from 50 to 100 grasshoppers flying up in front of you as you walked.

We had Sundays off so we usually went to Hankinson on Saturday nights. Dick would head for the bar and we would go to the movie. If we didn't have money for the movie we would wait for the second showing. We would then face the same direction as the audience leaving the theater and then we would back into the theater. After the movie we would sit around with friends and talk until the bars closed. All the farmers came into town on Saturday nights. It was a night to bring in the week's production of eggs and a can of cream. Reuben and I would sometimes help candle the eggs at Kjelstrup's grocery store to make certain the merchant was buying fresh eggs. We also returned the ice cream containers to the creamery from the Vick's drugstore. The person dispensing ice-cream cones could not reach the bottom and approximately a pint of ice cream remained in the container. We made sure that it wasn't wasted.

When Dick came out from the bar we made certain one of us drove home to insure we got there safely. He never came out sober and he usually slept all the way home. We let him sleep in the car overnight since we were not going to attempt to get him out and up on his feet.

For the next six days, we would discuss everything that happened in the movie. We could almost repeat the dialog word for word. The movies in those days pictured a dream world for most of us; a style of life we could only dream about but never expected to experience.

Dick took Reuben and I to the movie Gone with the Wind in Wahpeton one Sunday afternoon in 1939. It was based on Margaret Mitchel's romantic novel of the Old South. It was unbelievably long and unbelievably expensive to produce. The cost per person was $1.50. During the intermission that lasted 15 minutes we had a candy bar and a Coke. Today when I see reruns of the movie on television I feel 16 years old again.

When it rained during the night, it was usually too wet to thresh the following day. We looked forward to rain a great deal more than Dick ever realized. It was like a day off. We would hunt pheasants or ducks along the Wild Rice River east of the farmstead. The birds were plentiful, and what we shot became fox feed. Dick expected that we get something with every shot since we were using his shells. The cost was five cents per shell. At the time I thought pheasants would always be plentiful. I didn't realize one bad winter could wipe them out.

Occasionally prairie fires would start from lightning strikes or from other sources such as carelessly discarded cigarettes. When this happened all those within sight of the fire showed up with water and gunnysacks. If the fire wasn't too large and enough fire fighters responded it could be beaten into submission. This was usually possible at intersecting roads where no stubble or grass was available for fuel. The smoke and heat from the fire caused one's lungs to hurt for days.

There were some enjoyable days on the farm. It is human nature not to appreciate the good things at the moment they are taking place. I can reflect back now about how peaceful and beautiful the sunrises were. The roosters crowing early in the morning encouraging everything in the barnyard to begin another day. The pheasants cackling to each other in the stubble field from the previous day's harvest seemed to be claiming the area as their domain. The mist that was rising off the Wild Rice River and the birds that were singing in the wooded area bordering the stream bank gave a peaceful setting for the start of another day. It was as though all God's creatures were saying, "Get up, it's going to be another wonderful day".

By the middle of August, most of the threshing was completed, and we looked forward to getting back to school. When I got home, my mother would make me take all my clothes off about 50 feet from the house. The clothes were then put in the trash barrel and burned. She was deathly afraid I would bring bed bugs into the house. Once a mattress becomes infested with them, it is almost an impossible task to get rid of the vermin.

It is true all the jobs created under Roosevelt's New Deal helped not only restore self-esteem but helped provide some of the basic necessities of life.

The invasion of Poland began on Reuben's fourteenth birthday. This September 1, 1939 invasion by Germany changed everything. The dismal decade during the period 1929 to 1939 was suddenly replaced by a war economy instead of a make-work economy. Prosperity returned suddenly to a country that had been in a prolonged period of poverty. The millions that had been on the streets and riding freight trains to other parts of the country now were finding their way into factories and other related industries. As the years passed we would find there was a price to pay for the "good times". Families would lose their sons, daughters, husbands, uncles and brothers to the conflict and they felt the price was higher than they had imagined it would be.

The war brought more than good wages; it also brought suffering and heartache.

During the war-years prices for grain were unusually high. Farmers had come to believe these prices would continue on into the future. Technological changes in farming methods and the over production encouraged by the war need soon resulted in surpluses. This resulted in the prices for grain, milk and hogs tumbling drastically. Pork sold for 3 cents a pound and milk was as low as 2 cents a quart.

On August 23, 1988, Reuben and I returned to the Lubenow farm. As I stood there that sunny Tuesday afternoon, I could visualize the location of all the buildings that were on the farm 50 years earlier. I knew there had to be some changes since fifty years had to effect the area in some manner. I was not prepared for the drastic change. Reuben had hunted the area for a number of years and had seen the changes taking place; changes not only on the Lubenow farm but also in the rural area surrounding the town of Great Bend.

The 12-mile trip to the farm from Wahpeton by automobile seemed to take as long as it did when we walked it. The excitement grew as we turned west off the section line road onto the one-half mile approach road leading into the farm. It was obvious from the grass growing in the wheel tracks that very little traffic used the road. This was the road Reuben and I raced on horses at breakneck speed to see who could get to the mailbox first. We didn't receive that much mail but when one of us did receive a letter from home we shared the news and read and reread the letter until each of us could recite the contents by memory. Fifty years had passed and many memories of my youth began flooding back as we neared the Wild Rice River crossing.

As we approached what used to be the bridge across the river that provided access to the yard area in 1938, we found broken timbers and trapped debris. The river was low and the stream flow almost non-existent. We picked our way on foot across the river to what 50 years earlier had been the farmyard. I stood there agreeing with Reuben as to the type and location of each building. The only visible evidence that a farm had ever existed in what was now a soybean field was the filled-in house foundation. Had it not been for that, we would have had a hard time convincing others we were standing in the middle of what had been home to us during those summer months in the depression years.

We walked out to the fox pen area and found that some of the pens still existed among the trees. Trees had sprouted and grown up in the middle of some pens. The woven wire was in a state of disrepair. Some of the wire had been removed and used by others for various uses. As I stood there, the many years and all that had happened since we had fed those foxes in the late thirties vanished and it seemed as though it was yesterday. I realize now those foxes were abused. Many times in the heat of summer they were without water. Their food was inadequate and spasmodic. Dick had purchased crippled horses that could no longer be used for farm work. These were killed, skinned and chunks, including the bones, were thrown into the fox pens. The foxes would pace back and forth looking for a means of escape.

Dick also bought old horses that should have been able to enjoy their last few years grazing in a pasture somewhere. However Dick would work them as long as he could on a bundle team during the summer and then kill them for fox feed. Most of the horses he got were already worked beyond their years and these he killed, as he needed them. When I look back now it had to be and probably was a welcome way to be relieved of their suffering. He paid three dollars for each live animal and received six dollars for the hide.

Each pen contained two foxes. They were fed horsemeat but never enough to satisfy their hunger. They continued to be wild animals even though they were fed and watered occasionally. Today, I would feel differently from the way I felt back then when I saw the animals caged. They paced along the edge of their cage hoping to find an opening and a way to freedom. Although a layer of fencing existed six inches below the bottom of each pen, the fox would dig down hoping to escape by burrowing out of the enclosure.

Reuben worked for Dick a number of years after I left there for the last time. Since I was two years older than he was, I left for work on the West Coast and after a year out there, I returned to enter military service.

As we stood there talking, Reuben indicated that he estimates that he killed approximately 500 horses during his stay on the farm. Dick eventually got a large grinder and a horse could be ground into hamburger in a very short period of time. The bones were ground along with the meat.

The bottom suddenly fell out of the fur business around 1946 and Dick lost a fortune. Male foxes for use in breeding, which he had paid 800 dollars to obtain a short time earlier, were suddenly worthless.

Dick died in December 1953 at the age of 64, and my mother and I went to his funeral in Great Bend. One of his brothers continued to live on the farm for a short time and then was moved to a nursing home. The house was filled with antiques Dick's parents had used in the 1880s and they all disappeared with time. Some people made a practice of going to old abandoned farmhouses and taking anything of value.

That afternoon we drove down the Main Street of Great Bend. It was only a short distance from the farm. We laughed about the Wednesday night movie we looked forward to each week. A screen set up in a vacant lot and planks placed on nail kegs to provide for seats were all that was needed in the way of facilities. All the surrounding farmers would come in for the evening to socialize. As soon as it became dark enough, the movie was shown as the climaxing highlight of the evening. When a train would pass through the town, the projector was turned off and started again after the caboose passed by.

A fellow named Melvin Fenske was confirmed with me in the Wahpeton Lutheran Church in 1937. I hadn't seen him in 73 years and he dropped in to see me this week (3/1/10). I found out he was a neighbor of Dick's and he was filled with stories about Dick and some of the happenings on that farm. He told me that in the winter Dick would open a window, shove a long log through it into the stove. As the log burned away he would shove it a little farther into the stove. He didn't bother sawing it into short pieces.

My feelings for Reuben are rooted in the experiences we shared on that farm during the summers of our youth. It was depressing to see my memories shattered by the reality of the present.

As we left for home that sunny afternoon, my thoughts returned to those long, hot days in the field and the work that never seemed to come to an end. I thought of Saturday nights when we would splurge 10 cents on a pack of tailor-mades (packaged cigarettes) and thought we were pretty important in the large town of Hankinson. The Chesterfield brand advertised the slogan 'They Satisfy' and the slogan for Camels was 'I'd Walk a Mile for a Camel'. I actually thought that smoking Camels was healthy for me because the ads indicated 8 out of 10 doctors smoked Camels. Doctors more than anyone else should know what contributed to a healthy lifestyle.

The rest of the week we rolled our own with Bull Durham or Duke's Mixture and rehashed the movie we had seen in town. This tobacco came in small cloth bags that had a drawstring at the top. You filled your cigarette paper in your left hand by tapping tobacco from the bag in your right hand. Then you would close the bag by taking one of the drawstrings in your teeth while pulling the other drawstring with your free hand. Then you ran your tongue along the glued edge of the cigarette paper and sealed your cigarette. When our bags were empty we usually filled them with Prince Albert from a large can Dick had sitting in the middle of the kitchen table for Tony and Johnies' use.

As we traveled toward home I realized why my bond with Reuben was so strong. It was not the fact that he was my Uncle but that he had been a friend that I could relate to about our shared memories created during our early developing years.

I am happy I went back even though it was depressing. It was difficult to believe so many years had gone by so quickly. It is fortunate that only the pleasant things are remembered from one's youth. Not much thought is given at that time to the future and some of the unfortunate things that will occur. In 2003 Reuben's son Lyle a Lutheran minister, developed esophageal squamous cell carcinoma cancer. After chemotherapy and many other obstacles he had to overcome, he is finally cancer free. He has lost his ability to speak clearly but hopefully in time research and medical procedures will correct that condition. He has written a number of books reflecting his strong faith and they can be found in approximately 30,000 religious bookstores nationwide.

School started right after Labor Day, and I now was a sophomore. We were already into about two weeks of football practice when Mikulich from Bessimer, Michigan, took over coaching duties that year. He had been a star with Moorhead State Teachers College and was determined to teach us everything he knew about football. Since he was new on the scene, more than one of the seniors wanted to challenge his authority but always backed down in the end. By mid-season, everyone respected and admired him and his authority.

Halloween became memorable because of an Orson Wells radio broadcast entitled "War of the Worlds." He produced a classic Halloween broadcast about an imaginary Martian invasion of the earth. The "War of the Worlds," began innocently as an evening of scary entertainment and shortly resulted in national terror. A meteorite fell in a field on a farm in the neighborhood of Grover's Mill, New Jersey, 22 miles from Trenton. Martians were supposedly exiting from the meteorite and invading our country. People committed suicide by jumping from windows and shootings. The broadcast resembled a public service announcement. Location and direction of movement of the invading forces were given periodically. Information as to the best escape routes out of town was provided. The program was so realistic that anyone tuning in after the program had started had no reason to believe that everything they were hearing was not authentic. Newspapers the next day reported about a "tidal wave of terror that swept the nation". As a result of the tragic consequences of this program, legislation was passed to prevent this style of programming from ever being used again.

In early November, my brother Bob almost drowned for a second time. He and Donald Hanson were taking a short cut to the farmstead from school. They took the route across the low area on the south side of the Ottertail River. They should have crossed to the north side of the river by crossing on the 11th Street Bridge. It wasn't that much further to go around and cross on the bridge. In taking this shorter route, they had to cross the river where it bends just southwest of the farm. The ice was so thin that they thought it advisable to run as fast as they could. When they were approximately 50 feet from the opposite shore, they both went through the ice. This was the deepest part of the river since the river current was the swiftest on the curve and the bottom was scoured at this location. Bob was able to get on top of the ice. Then by lying down he slid back to help. When he reached Donald he was pulled back into the icy water. When Bob got out the second time, he told Donald to just hang on; he would go get a tree limb to help pull him out. This he did and Donald was able to pull himself up on the ice with Bob's assistance. It could have resulted in a double drowning like the town would experience a year later.

Basketball started in November, and we had what looked like the makings of a pretty good team. What was needed was someone like Mick who would make us work hard and instill in us the desire to win.

CHAPTER 8

HIGH SCHOOL BASKETBALL

Our sixth grade had a basketball team called the Popeyes. Each mother sewed her version of what Popeye the Sailor Man looked like and placed it on the front of a white sleeveless undershirt. She placed a numeral on the back. I don't know why there wasn't duplication in the numbering. The mothers must have gotten together and eliminated that possibility. Each head on each shirt was different but it didn't make any difference to us. We thought we had a great team until we lost a championship game in Moorhead by a score of 6 to 5.

My next experience with basketball was as a member of the Junior High Team. There weren't too many scheduled school games. We continued to play our alley ball games on the weekends and evenings in the neighborhood. Someone would have their father nail a square bank board on a power pole and then we would choose up sides for some pretty aggressive basketball games. These contests prepared us for some very aggressive games that we would be involved in a number of years later.

Once I became interested in sports I became interested in some of the history of former athletes and teams that had played for Breckenridge in prior years.

It wasn't until 1910 that organized sports became available at Breckenridge High School. Prior to that time, the local jocks had an independent football team and played opponents from the surrounding towns, such as Wahpeton, Benson, Morris, and North Dakota Agricultural College at Fargo, North Dakota located 50 miles north of Breckenridge.

One of the more prominent figures in sports at that time was Phil Canfield. He was involved in all sports, not only as a player but also later as a manager and official. He was a referee for many of the athletic events I participated in during my high school career. I was usually able to draw charging violations on our opponents, which was accomplished with a little bit of acting. However, it was not possible to pull it off if Phil was on the floor. Early in my sophomore year, he pulled me aside prior to the start of a game and said, "You may be able to obtain other awards for your acting but you won't be awarded any free-throws for it while I am on the floor."

Phil became Breckenridge High School football coach during the period following his return from World War I. Lack of funding and facilities prevented a good, organized athletic program from being developed. There was no football or a practice field located close to the school. All practices and football games were held at the Wells Memorial Park located a number of blocks away from the school. The Park was also used for baseball, horse racing, rodeos, county fairs and family picnics.

Basketball was played at the City Hall, which contained the Fire Department and city library on the street level and a small gym on the second floor. Seating at the games consisted of one row of benches, placed between the wall and the out-of-bounds line of the court. Total capacity of the gym was approximately 30 people.

It wasn't until the mid-thirties that a track program was introduced at the school. Coach Henry Booher's work in building a track department was instrumental in creating an interest in track, and resulted in many district and regional championships being won in the late forties and early fifties.

Phil Canfield played on the 1915 basketball team that went to the State Tournament. There were no play-off tournaments to earn a berth into the State. You had to win all your games and then be invited. Only one fan, Roy Larson, accompanied the team down to St. Paul. In their first game against St. Paul Mechanical Arts, Breckenridge was trailing 30 to 1 at half time. The game ended with Breckenridge on the short end of a 31 to 30 score. The Breckenridge team was lost on the large floor during the first half. The floor at home was 35 feet long with a ceiling height of 12 feet. With the basket height being 10 feet, this didn't allow for much arch on the ball being shot.

Other team members of the 1915 team were Wallace Millard, Fred Hanson, Fred Ott, F.L. Pierce, and Harry Busko. Heaviest man on the team was Fred Hanson at 128 pounds.

Lack of funding continued to plague the school. We still were in the midst of a depression, and money for athletics appeared to be unnecessary. This lack of funding restricted participation in sports only to those of high school age. As I mentioned earlier, we did, however, have a boys' Junior High team. Our travel was very limited, although I recall going to Moorhead for a tournament game of some type. We lost the game by a score of 6 to 5, a real heartbreaker.

In my freshman year, I became more interested in sports. I began to practice basketball on the boards that were nailed to the power poles in the alleys of the neighborhood. We organized touch football teams with the neighborhood kids and continued to play late into the fall until it became so cold it was uncomfortable.

In the fall of 1938, I reported for football practice. I had spent the summer on the farm pitching hay, shocking, and loading bundles. I believed I was in pretty good shape. However, Coach Mikulich was out to prove to all of us that we were not anywhere close to being in the shape that he expected to put us into. Mick had come to Breckenridge in September 1938, and it was his first year in coaching. His record as a player and captain of the football team at Moorhead State Teacher College proceeded him and we all knew that our practices would not be a piece of cake.

I have nothing that shows what kind of a season we had and I remember very little about it. I'm certain if the season had been anything but average, I surely would have remembered it.

The basketball season began in November following conclusion of the football season. It was obvious from the start we would have a fairly good team and that we may have a winning season. Many of us had been playing together in the back alleys of the city for a number of years. We had height and there was a feeling during practice that we could win games. By today's standard we could not be classed as a tall team. We had two members who were six feet. The rest of the team varied between 5'-8" and 5'-10". Mick also instilled the desire to win. His theory was: You had to work hard if you expected to win games and if you had to work that hard, you might as well win games. It is a lot more fun.

Our schedule included a game with Fargo Central High School, a team from what we considered a large city 50 miles north of Breckenridge. After the game the team would have a snack at the Powers Hotel Coffee Shop. A singer performed on a small stage in the dining room. Her name was Peggy Lee. She was born Norma Egstrom in the small North Dakota town of Wimbleton located west of Fargo. Her mother died of diabetes in 1924 when Norma was only four years old. Her father was station agent for the small Midland Continental Railroad that traveled between Oakes and Jamestown, North Dakota. He remarried again and in the '30s got on a train and was never heard of again.

Norma and her stepmother didn't get along so she went off on her own to Jamestown. She earned a little money singing at kids' birthday parties and other small functions. Eventually she ended up in Valley City and sang at a radio station. Later she came to Fargo and performed at the Powers Coffee Shop in the Powers Hotel and at the radio station WDAY. She supplemented her income by working as a bread slicer at a local bakery.

Ken Kennedy, the station manager, gave her the name Peggy Lee. She went on to sing with the Benny Goodman Orchestra and wrote a number of songs. In 1955 she was nominated for an Oscar for her role in "Pete Kelley's Blues". She won her first Grammy Award for the recording "Is That All There Is". She led a very unhappy life and had four awful marriages.

The basketball season progressed, and we won the majority of our games. Eight of the team members were sons of railroad workers. Since Breckenridge was a railroad town, the main topic of conversation by tournament time was basketball. We got through the District Tournament without too much difficulty. The Regional Tournament was held at Glenwood. The first night we played Saulk Center. We were behind for most of the game, but we usually came on strong in the last quarter. We won the game 32 to 30 in the last moments of the game. The next night we played Brainerd and the same pattern developed. We fell behind 12 to 6 in the opening quarter and trailed most of the game. In the last period, the score difference began to decrease. Ray Cimbura fouled out in the last minute of the game and his brother El Roy came in to take his place at center. With seconds remaining, he hooked a shot over the heads of the opponents and as the ball swished through the net the buzzer went off. We were in the State Tournament, which was scheduled for March 23, 24, and 25, 1939 at the Municipal Auditorium in St. Paul, Minnesota.

On March 21 at 5 o'clock in the afternoon, about 300 people bid us goodbye at the train depot as we boarded. The windows of all the businesses in town were decorated with signs showing their support and wishing us luck in the tournament. During the train ride to St. Paul the Great Northern Railroad served us 12 of the largest and juiciest steaks I had ever seen. We were about to arrive in St. Paul by the time we finished those steaks.

When we arrived in St. Paul, we were met by a number of police squad cars and escorted, with their lights flashing and sirens blowing, to the Lowry Hotel. We really felt like we were something special. The last time a Breckenridge basketball team had been to a state tournament was 1915. I'm certain they never got the reception we did. Those 24 years between 1915 and 1939 seemed like such a long time. I wondered how anyone could remember what had happened 24 years earlier. Now it has been 70 years since our winning the tournament in 1940 and many events are as clear as if they had happened last week.

On Wednesday, we had an opportunity to work out on the floor. I could imagine how that 1915 team felt. Their games had always been played on a small floor above the fire hall. The ceiling height was slightly more than 10 feet so the shots at the basket could have very little arch. At home, you could usually judge your shots by the wall located behind the basket. On this floor, there was nothing but open space behind the basket.

On Thursday, all the teams were invited to a noon luncheon as guests of the St. Paul businessmen. At 3 o'clock that afternoon, we met Hutchinson and won 34 to 21.

Friday evening at 8 o'clock we played Minneapolis Marshall. We were not favored to win and when the game ended 38 to 22, we knew the dream of winning State was over. Mick's only comment was, "Enjoy yourself for the rest of the Tournament and we'll come down next year and take it." South St. Paul beat us on Saturday night by a score of 36 to 25. The season was over, but it had been an exciting and enjoyable year. I only hoped I had two more years just like it coming up.

We lost five members of the 1939 team to graduation but four of the starting five returned to play on the 1940 team. The Coach told us this was our year to take it all if we really wanted it and was willing to work for it.

I don't understand why the young kids look up to those in sports. Why not adore someone who excels in math, the sciences or drama? The reason I bring this up is because there was a small 7th grader who would seek me out each day. He had a deformed arm and leg as a result of polio and it was difficult for him to walk. Others in his class teased and made fun of him and I don't think anyone understood how deeply he was hurt. He was so withdrawn from others his age and I believe he was embarrassed for being different.

In those days everyone in a small town went home for lunch. There was no such thing as a school lunch program. Each day this boy and I would meet when classes ended at noon. He lived within a block of where I lived. We would start down the street with my arm around his neck. He felt so important to be a friend of this basketball "star". Soon the others quit teasing him and a number asked if they could walk with us also. It wasn't long before 5 or 6 of us would meet every noon. He was now just one of the gang. It made me feel good and they became my strongest supporters at future ball games.

By 1939, the economy was improving and money was becoming more readily available for more and better athletic equipment. This resulted in being able to field a greater number of participants for the football team in the fall of 1939. However, this did not guarantee a winning team. We opened on September 15th at home and lost to Pelican Rapids by a score of 32 to 0. A week later, we out scored Moorhead 7 to 0. The following week we played Wheaton at home and won 25 to 6. I returned a kick off for 85 yards, and the effects of my smoking left me breathless. Our traditional clash with Wahpeton ended in a 6-6 tie. We had two touchdowns called back. Detroit Lakes ruined our homecoming on October 13th, when they out scored us 26 to 7. We played our final game in a blizzard at Barnsville. The field was new and the use of sod was unheard of in those days. The temperature was warm enough that the snow melted as it hit the ground. The field turned into a sea of mud. We were happy when the game ended. I don't know if they ever got our uniforms clean again. The final score was a tie, 6 to 6.

Basketball followed almost immediately after the conclusion of football. We had five returning lettermen and were looking forward to the coming season. Mick had told us this was the year we were going to take it all and we believed him. We compiled nine straight wins before losing to Fargo 26 to 25 in the Red River Valley Tournament held during the Christmas Holidays. Following that defeat, six more victories were achieved before falling to Crosby-Ironton 27 to 18. Wahpeton gave us our only other loss during the season by soundly trouncing us 39 to 27. We had defeated them twice earlier during the season. Although it really bothered us to lose, Mick told us it was good for us. If we went into tournament time realizing we could be defeated, we might play better ball. It wasn't until years later that we realized how much that 28-year old coach really knew. We went on to win five more regular season games. At tournament time we won our three District games, two Regional games and three State Tournament games to win the coveted Minnesota State High School Basketball Championship. Our record for the season was 30 wins and 3 losses.

To me, the most exciting games of the 1939-1940 season were the wins over Crosby-Ironton (26-24) in the Regional Tournament and Minneapolis Marshall (32-30) in the semi-final game of the State Tournament.

The Regional Tournament was played in the Moorhead High School. The final game in the tournament got off to a bad start and we were behind 8-4 at the end of the first quarter and 16-8 as the half ended. By the end of the third quarter, we had cut Crosby's lead to two, 20-18. The game ended in a tie (24-24) and went into overtime. In those days sudden death (the first team to score) was used to determine the winner. Ruud took the tip off from Cimbura at the start of the overtime, turned and sent the ball sailing through the hoop. We won 26 to 24 and we were on our way to State in St. Paul.

The Marshall game was a battle all the way. Cimbura, who, along with Ruud, usually provided the most points for the team, was held scoreless during the entire game. In the final 10 seconds he hooked in what was to become the winning basket of the game.

Marvin Quinn of the Minneapolis Times Tribune described the game this way; "A capacity crowd of 9,600 were on hand to witness a re-match and the defeat of the Mill City team that had beaten Breckenridge a year before. At the end of the first quarter it was Marshal by 10 to 8 and at the half it was Breckenridge 18-14. Marshall had gotten off to a10-4 lead early in the first quarter, but by the time the first 8 minutes had ended Breckenridge was back in the game as Ulness and Mc Morrow furnished the explosive by propelling a field goal each into the twine. The second period was a nightmare for Marshal as Ruud swung into action. He dropped two gift shots to knot the count as Bill Ekberg, 6'-4" center, was guilty of his third personal foul and taken from the game. Mathson got his first field goal to send Marshal ahead again. Then Ruud connected twice from the floor and then later got another pair while Mattson's lone field goal was all the Mill City could muster. At intermission, Ruud had scored 10 points; his last two coming simultaneously as the gun sounded ending the first half.

From the beginning of the third period until the sensational and thrilling conclusion, the battle raged on even terms. Breckenridge with a well-balanced team and capable of substituting at will any of its 10 team members was down 27-25 at the end of the third period. Mattson made it 29-25 shortly after the final stanza got underway. Breckenridge followers slipped back into their seats. Ruud came to life and connected from the floor to narrow the margin. Mattson got a free throw and that was the end of Marshal's scoring with fewer than three minutes to play. Ruud was the man of the hour as he tossed in another field goal and Mc Morrow dropped in a gift through the hoop to knot the score. Mc Morrow toed the line cool and confident and his shot never even touched the rim. That gift shot set the stage for Cimbura's piece of work. Mattson's defense against Cimbura's hook shot was as good we've seen in these parts. However, Cimbura's only two points of the game, coming when it did, was enough to put Breckenridge ahead 32-30 when the gun went off.

My parents went to St. Paul on the special train that was made up in Breckenridge. My dad had a brother (Joe) living just south of the St. Paul downtown area on

Congress Street. After much celebrating on the train, my folks took a cab over to Joe's home. My Dad was going to take a short nap before the evening's game. They never did wake him so he missed the first night's action. I think there had been a little drinking on the train before arriving.

We returned from the Tournament on Sunday and were met at the railroad station by 10,000 people--more than had shown up for President Roosevelt's whistle stop a few years earlier. The following Sunday Bernie Bierman spoke at a celebration held in the High School Gymnasium. We were presented with cowhide suitcases and gold medals. The luggage, after it no longer was in style, was kept on a shelf in storage shed as a constant reminder of my youth and of a coach that taught us all much more than the fundamentals of basketball. Before our move from Bismarck to Fargo it was disposed of along with some other garbage.

The Gazette-Telegram issue, dated April 4, 1940, carried the headline NICE RIDING COWBOYS in two-inch high letters. Individual pictures of the team members were under the headline. In the center of the paper was a large picture of a young coach named Walter (Poker Face) Mikulich. The caption above the picture read, "FOLKS, MEET A SWELL FELLOW!" The editorial for that issue spoke of Mick in glowing terms. In part, it said, "Coach Walter Mikulich is a man who says very little, yet gets results. Game after game, with the score very close, we watched Walter sitting on the bench with his poker face. When a bad play by the Cowboys was made, Walter didn't jump around like a wild man. He would just sit there and think what was wrong with the attack, or defense of the team."

I guess what put Mick head and shoulders above any other coach was also covered in the same editorial. It went on to say, "The true character of Walter Mikulich was shown near the close of the championship game.

Breckenridge was leading Red Wing by seven points with over a minute of play left. On the bench were four players who had seen no action during the entire game. Turning to these lads, he told them to go into the game and take over the duties of the first squad. The second team barely got into the game before Red Wing sank two field goals to close the gap to a three-point margin for Breckenridge. The expression on the face of Walter, who was sitting on the bench, showed no trace of excitement. He seemed to know his boys and had explicit faith in them. When the game ended, with Breckenridge the winner by three points, every man on the squad in years to come could tell about winning the championship of Minnesota as a member of one of the best basketball team that ever played in the State Tournament. What could one expect but to have a champion basketball team when a man like that is the coach."

The entire issue was primarily devoted to the results of the Tournament, the celebration that followed, and the coach that made it all happen.

The 1940-1941 season would seem anticlimactic for me. I missed the fellows that had graduated. Some I had played with all my life. It also was now obvious that the fun years were not going to go on forever. This was to be my last year of school, and the uncertainties of the future began to concern me. I didn't want to stay in Breckenridge but how could a person get out? I finally decided I would have as much fun as possible this last year and worry about the future when I had to.

Our football season was a disaster. We won our first game against Pelican Rapids and then lost the next five and tied the final game.

In basketball, we had the height and experience and I guess I would consider the season a successful one. We continued to improve during the season and finished up winning eight of our last ten games. We went into the District Tournament with some of our players on the injured list and others on the sick list. The game against the Morris Tigers was fairly even all the way through. In the final minutes, we fell behind and lost 33-27. Schwankl and I were named to the All-District Team, quite a surprise when you consider that we were members of a loosing team. That ended my high school career in athletics, but the one thing that made my three years in sports most memorable was Coach Walter Mikulich. Winning was important but he taught us so many more things that prepared us for the years that were ahead. I would meet Mick 3 years later in August 1944 at the Mussolini Forum in Rome, Italy. The area consisted of a number of buildings and other facilities that Mussolini had had constructed in anticipation of holding the 1944 Olympics in Rome. The Army took it over after the capture of Rome and used it as a Rest and Recreation Center for the military. We had both come out of hospitals in the region and ended up at this Rest Center. His comment to me, when he came up behind me in a chow line, was, "Small world, isn't it"? I turned around and couldn't believe it.

Members of the two basketball teams that went to State Tournaments have kept in touch with each other. A number of reunions have been held; one in Breckenridge in August 1980; one at Bigfork, Montana on Flat Head Lake in September 1985; one at the home of Dick and Margaret Smith on Otter Tail Lake in August 1990; and one in Bismarck, North Dakota, in August 1992. Coach Mikulich celebrated his 80th birthday during this reunion in Bismarck and we had a little party at the Radisson Inn during a breakfast. The last reunion was held on August 4, 1995, at the Smith home on Otter Tail Lake.

The Breckenridge High School Basketball coaching staff also held an open house in honor of the 50th anniversary of the 1940 team. The event was held August 10, 1990 at the Senior High School in the Commons from 1:00 to 3:00 P.M. A short program was held at 2:00 P.M., followed by lunch. The local newspaper took a photo and ran a "yesterday and today" picture the next day. It was fairly easy to determine which picture was taken in 1940 and which one was taken in 1990. It was great to be together. Only one member of the team (Mel Ruud) had died. Although we were all in our late 60s, we acted like a bunch of kids in their teens. The intervening years just disappeared. We knew it was the last gathering where we would be together but no one wanted to mention the fact. The bonding couldn't have been stronger.

A Diamond Jubilee Champions Reception was held on March 28, 1987, during the annual boys' Minnesota State High School Basketball Tournament. The reception was held from 5:00 - 7:00 P.M. for past state championship teams, honored players, coaches, hall of fame coaches, etc. Rush McAllister, Sid Cichy, Ray Cimbura, Orlo Johnson, and I attended.

Individual members also meet for various reasons at other times. Four of us (Cimbura, Mc Allister, Johnson and I) attended the State Tournament in March 1990. We were the featured team of 50 years prior in the Tournament Program Book.

When the 1940 class graduated, half the members of the championship team moved on to other things. The war was intensifying, and it was obvious we would eventually become involved. Ultimately, it would drastically affect all our lives.

All members of the 1940 team entered military service during World War II and, although some were wounded, all returned home at the conclusion of hostilities. Following is a brief personal history of what happened to the coaches and members of the team members after high school graduation.

Coach Walter Mikulich entered military service in June 1942 and received his basic training at Camp Walters, Texas. He then went to Ft. Benning, Georgia in January 1943 and attended Officers Candidate School. He married Vivian Murphy in Aberdeen, South Dakota in

July 1943. Vivian had been a teacher in Breckenridge during Mick's coaching period there. He then shipped overseas to Italy with the 88th Infantry Division. He was wounded and spent time at a Rest Camp and Replacement Depot in Rome. It was here where we met in August 1944 and spent a week together. Mick returned home and was discharged from service at Camp, Mc Coy, Wisconsin in March 1946. He returned to a coaching and teaching position in Breckenridge in September 1946 and remained in that position until June 1948. He then attended Graduate School in Iowa. After coaching two years in West Allis, Wisconsin, he and his family moved to the Panama Canal Zone. He was involved in the athletic programs of the Zone schools. He remained in this position from 1951 until his retirement in 1974. He and Vivian had a son born in November 1946. His wife and son live in Everett, Washington. Mick died on December 28, 2005 at the age of 93. Mick's wife Vivian died June 2, 2010 in Everett, Washington at the age of 94.

Assistant Coach Vernon Zehren grew up in Breckenridge and played on the high school team. He and Mikulich were teammates on the Moorhead State Teacher's College football team. After graduation he returned to Breckenridge to a coaching and teaching position. After returning from four years in the Navy, Vern joined the faculty in Little Falls, Minnesota as football and basketball coach and later becoming athletic director. He was an avid sportsman and spent his entire life working with young people. He was instrumental in beginning a gun-training program for young people in the Little Falls area. He died of a brain tumor on December 2, 1986. He had two sons.

Sid Cichy grew up in Kent, Minnesota and after grade school, came to Breckenridge to finish his education. He enlisted in the Naval Air Corps and flew missions in the Pacific during World War II. After college he was involved in education and became a renowned football coach in the area. Sid married in 1944 and had eight children. He died on January 7, 2007 of Alzheimer's disease at the age of 85. Among numerous awards presented to him over the years was one he richly deserved. He was named 1975 National High School Coach of the Year. He was also named High School Coach of the three-quarter Century. Sid died the day of Coach Walt Mikulich's funeral.

Ray Cimbura joined the Army Air Corps in 1942 and served in the Signal Corps. He married a high school classmate in 1943 and had three children. He had an electrical firm from 1946 until 1952 after returning from Service and then became an engineer for the Great Northern Railroad. Ray retired from railroading in February 1986. He died March 2, 1991 at the age of 68. His wife Ferne died May 10, 2009 in Fargo at the age of 87.

Orlo Johnson grew up in Doran, Minnesota and took his high school training in Breckenridge. He joined the Army Air Corps and took his basic training in Lincoln, Nebraska. He finished gunnery school in Los Vegas and prepared others at various bases around the country. Orlo was discharged from service at Leavenworth, Kansas and then received a degree in Accounting at the University of North Dakota. After working with various firms for a number of years, he began his own business in 1963. Orlo married in 1951 and added three Norwegians to the population of Minnesota.

Rush McAllister entered military service in December 1942 and served with 14th Armored Division until his discharge in February 1946. He then continued his education with a degree from Michigan State in Hotel Administration and Business Administration in March 1949. He married in August 1949 and had five children. He retired in November 1986. Rush died December 29, 2004.

Merle W. Mc Morrow worked in the Puget Sound Naval Shipyard in Bremerton, Washington for a year in 1942 following graduation from high school. He returned home in December 1942 to enlist in the Army Air Corps. However, enlistment of personnel was terminated before he could obtain a release from his Draft Board in Bremerton. He then volunteered for the US Army Paratroops. He was scheduled for shipment to Anzio, Italy in May1944. As mentioned earlier it was in Rome where he met Coach Mikulich. Mikulich illegally commissioned him a second lieutenant for one week with some gold bars he had remaining after his being promoted to captain. The two of them spent the week at the Officers' Clubs in Rome. From Italy he parachuted into southern France with the 1st Airborne Task Force. He was involved in the Battle of the Bulge in Belgium with the 101st Airborne Division. He was sent into Berlin on Occupation Duty for five months at the end of hostilities. He was discharged in December 1945 and married his high school sweetheart in June 1946. He graduated with a degree in Engineering from North Dakota State University in August 1949. He worked for the Department of the Interior for 35 years and retired in December 1980. After that he was involved in the establishing a family medical supply business for three years.

Richard Miksche served in the Navy Seabees and after attending St. John's University he was involved in the family hotel and liquor business in his hometown of Breckenridge. Dick had six children and still lives in Breckenridge today (2010).

Mel Ruud attend the University of Minnesota for a short time after graduating from high school. In January 1942 he and Mc Morrow attended NYA School for sheet metal training and then went to Seattle for work in the shipyards. Mel returned at the end of 1942 and enlisted in the Marine Corps. He was discharged in October 1945. He married Alice shortly after returning home and had two sons and two daughters. The two boys were born in Minnesota and the two girls were born after he moved to California. Either as a result of death or divorce Mel married Arlene and they lived in Hesperia, California. Mel (known as John by Arlene) spent many years as California Deputy Inspector licensed by the State to insure that hospital construction met established codes. Mel died February 8, 1985 of cancer.

Eugene Stanbra returned after Service and began a career with the Burlington Railroad. Very little was known about Gene as to his life after graduation. He did return for a basketball reunion on August 4, 1995. He was a very private person but likeable. He died a number of years ago.

James Thomas attended St. Mary's Grade School and Breckenridge High School. He spent two years in college before entering the service in early 1943. He was sent to Europe in December 1943. He returned to the States in December 1945 and began working for the Post Office in Breckenridge. He married in November 1946. He left the Post Office in 1957 and moved to Billings, Montana. He owned and operated a Big Boy drive-in for 19 years. He retired in 1977 and purchased a cherry orchard on Flat Head Lake near Bigfork, Montana. He was treated for cancer in 1993 and died on September 29, 2006.

Vern Ulness returned to Breckenridge after serving in the US Army. He obtained employment with the Great Northern Railroad and continued with the company until he was placed on disability retirement. He married on July 25, 1948 and had one daughter. He moved to Los Angeles in 1966 and remained there until his death on December 21, 2004. His wife preceded him in death. He had one granddaughter.

Only three members of the 1940 team are still alive today: (2010) Johnson, Miksche and Mc Morrow.

Robert Colbert was team manager in 1939. He was a corporate attorney for a major bank in Minneapolis for many years. He is retired and lives in Tucson, Arizona.

The trainers were Frank Matejka, my brother Bob, and Cliff Thomas, a brother of James. The cheerleaders were Gerry Matheson, Phyllis Sagness, Pat Connolly and Marvin Peterson. Frank Matejka, my brother Bob and Gerry Matheson are still living. Frank lives a few blocks from me in Fargo, North Dakota.

On Thursday March 11, 2010 my wife Mardy and I drove to Breckenridge to attend the last home game of the season that the basketball team would play. Their team is tall, fast and should go a long way in the upcoming tournament. They handily defeated Osakis, a team that played in the 1940 Region 6 tournament on March 19th and was defeated by Detroit Lakes.

I was surprised to be introduced at half-time as a member of the 1940 team. Mardy had mentioned this fact to the lady sitting next to her and then this lady went down and conveyed this information to the person announcing the game. My Aunt Maxine mentioned it to her son that she had heard it on the radio.

CHAPTER 9

MY FINAL THREE YEARS OF HIGH SCHOOL

I covered my high school sports activities in the previous chapter above. Except for the two trips to the State Tournaments in 1939 and 1940 our sports program was pretty average and uneventful. However, it was during this time that I noticed a cute, dark-haired, little eighth grader watching us practice the afternoon of January 27, 1939. There was sufficient interest on my part to cause me to investigate who she was. My investigative work not only helped me find out who she was, but also provided me with the information that a certain fellow was giving her the rush. I also found out her name was Kathryn (Kay for short) Jonietz. I realized that faint heart would not win fair maiden and by the end of February, I had mustered sufficient courage to sit at the same table with her in the library study hall. I had gotten a copy of her school schedule to know what periods of the day she would be in there. Some of my teachers, mistakenly, thought I had turned over a new leaf, and was now beginning to spend my free time more productively. However my free time was spent thinking about her.

It must have been obvious to Mikulich that I was smitten with the little eighth grader because after a particularly bad ballgame, he mentioned that if I got my mind off the "skirts" I might be able to play a better brand of ball.

On March 7th, she stayed around until practice was over and I walked home with her. The following day the District Tournament started at Benson, Minnesota. We won that night and the following night. On March 10th, Kay came to Benson on the school bus for the championship game. We won and advanced to the Regional Tournament.

On March 16th the Regional at Glenwood pitted us against Sauk Center and Brainerd. We won both games and left for St. Paul on March 21st. Kay rode her new bike to the railroad depot to see us off. On March 23rd, she came to St. Paul on the "Special Train" that was run for the purpose of bringing fans from the Breckenridge area to the Twin Cities. She saw the kids at the Ryan Hotel, visited with me and then took the evening train home. I was on Cloud 9 thinking she had come all that way to see me. We won the first game at the Tournament and lost the next two. We returned on March 26th and it was shortly after that I found out Kay preferred me to the competition I had. It must have been my charm because I didn't have any money.

On April 13, 1939 I helped her rake the yard and met her mother. I was sixteen, she was fourteen and her mother seemed old at thirty-six. After finishing the yard, we went for a bike ride. From then on, we were sitting together constantly in study hall. I had completely forgotten the Deanna Durbln of Hollywood who I was in love with at the age of 14.

On April 28th I went with her to the bus when she left for the Band Festival at Moorhead. The following month a friend of mine, who was able to get the family car, picked me up and we attended the Band Banquet on May 17th when she was awarded a letter in music. On the way home, I held her hand. By May 22nd, Miss Johnson was lecturing us for too much talking in study hall.

School was rapidly coming to a close, and for the first time I wasn't looking forward to summer. I knew we wouldn't be seeing each other as frequently. She would be involved with her summer activities, and I would be working. The final days involved final tests for the year. Because of her marks, Kay didn't have to take any final tests in any of Mikulich's classes. Instead, he had her checking History, English, and Math papers for him. Mick's mother didn't raise any dummies.

We spent time together at Well's Memorial Park after the last day of school. Shortly after that, she left for Williston on June 3rd to visit the Zaparas and other relatives in the area. She met her cousin Wilbur's future wife Irene. She returned on June 9th, and we spent the evenings together for the next week attending the Carnival that was playing at the Island Park.

Kay spent most of the summer with the band, going on Good Will Tours to surrounding small towns. The band played in the bandstand at the local park. Many of the towns and cities of America had a bandstand in the parks back in the '30's and early '40's. A Sunday afternoon of entertainment consisted of going to the park for a noon picnic and then listening to a band concert the rest of the afternoon.

I began working at Clark Hanson's dairy farm that summer of 1939. Work began at 4:30 A.M. since there were 55 cows to be milked and bottles to be filled and loaded before being on our way into town by 7 A.M. for delivery to Breckenridge and Wahpeton customers. There were two rows of cows with about 52 in each row. We had two milking machines and they were used beginning at the end of each row. Two of us would start milking by hand and by the time we met those handling the machines we had milked about 13 cows each. I use to feel sorry for those cows that had stood in water out in the pasture in an attempt to get away from flies. They loved to come in for milking because we sprayed each cow with a fluid that repelled the flies. Their teats were cracked and bleeding. I knew they were in pain during the milking period. Before turning them back into the pasture after milking we would rub a salve on their teats similar to Vaseline that contained healing properties.

Milk was 8 cents a quart and we not only made home deliveries in the two towns but also delivered to grocery stores and other conveyance stores. In those days cookies were stored in little bins with covers that were hinged. Every morning we would lift the covers and take a few cookies back to the delivery truck. A morning lunch of cookies and milk was then taken. The merchant was aware we were taking the cookies and it seemed acceptable to him. Today it wouldn't'' be acceptable to anyone because of sanitary reasons.

If the customers paid their bill each month they received a free pint of whipping cream. After completing the delivery the returned bottles had to be washed. The bottles were placed in a soapy tub. We had a machine similar to a drill press. Two vertical steel shafts with brushes on the end spun continuously. We took the bottles from the tub and inserted the open end of the milk bottles up on these shafts. From there they went into clear water rinse tub and then into a second rinsing.

We also had machines for filling the bottles and capping them. The caps were imprinted with the Cloverleaf Dairy logo. The milk was not pasteurized as it is today. Milk run through a machine called a separator removed the cream from the whole milk. The 15 to 20 gallons of skim milk remaining after the cream was removed were given to the hogs and chickens. Today skim milk is a pretty precious commodity and many prefer it to whole milk.

The cows had to be milked again at 4 P.M. This was a 7-day a week job. We did have Sunday off from 1:00-4:00 o'clock. Some of the older workers, who had more sense than teenagers, spent the time catching up on their sleep. However, my brother Bob, the Hanson boys and I always headed for town to make the most of the three hours of free time that we could call our own. We also spent every evening in town and usually got home shortly after midnight. We were averaging about 4 hours of sleep each night and each day around 3 o'clock we would swear we were going to stay home that evening and go to bed. As soon as 7:30 arrived it always happened. Someone in the group would wonder out loud what was going on in town. Before we knew it we were headed in to check things out. We could always sleep tomorrow night.

It was during one of these evenings that I met Phyllis Bladow. She was from Hankinson and was visiting a friend in town. I was flattered by all the attention she showered on me. After a short time she even came out to the farm on certain afternoons during milking time. It doesn't seem very romantic but on occasions she would hold the cow's tail while I was milking. The flies were terrible and there aren't too many things worse than getting a dirty tail swished across your mouth.

Before I knew it, the summer romance was over, and she went back to Hankinson. Years later in the early 1970s she worked as a nurse in the Cooperstown Hospital where my son Tom started as Hospital Administrator.

Kay spent the last week of August in Williston visiting the Zaparas and others at the farm. All the boys were still home, and they teased her unmercifully, especially Wilbur. He still loved to tease her whenever we visited them in California.

School started again and I was now a junior. Kay was beginning her freshman year and we thought we were in love. She was continually on my mind during every waking moment. Neither had the courage to even mention the word "love" but we spent every possible moment together. We enjoyed our nights at the movies and lunch afterwards at Hart's Cafe. A steak sandwich with beverage, hash browns, toast, a large piece of steak and dessert cost 35 cents. It doesn't seem like much now, but it was equivalent to the earnings I received for one and one-half hours of work. Our conversations would tie up that cafe booth for as much as two hours. We didn't have a car so it was either remain there in the café and talk or walk the streets and carry on our conversations. Walking was fine in early fall but as the air temperature dropped toward the end of October the café booth was the preferred location. I don't remember what we talked about but what was important was that we were together.

By October 6th, I found the courage to kiss her for the first time. It might have happened sooner if it weren't for that streetlight near her back door. I kept hoping that bulb would burn out. We were much too young to be spending so much time together. We should have been meeting and spending time with others but neither of us wanted that. We should have been more involved in school events and activities. However sharing every possible moment with each other was the only important thing to each of us.

Saturday nights were usually spent at the movies. Before going Kay had to hear the Lucky Strike program "Your Hit Parade " and she could usually predict which song would be No. 1. Songs during that period were I'll Walk Alone, On Slow Boat to China, Marsy Doats, Elmer's Tune, One Dozen Roses, Juke Box Saturday Night and A Nightingale Sang in Barkley Square among others.

On November 5th, Wilkie lost to Roosevelt in the Presidential election and eleven days later, tragedy struck the city when two small cousins, Roy Douglas and Jim Fischer, went through the ice by the powerhouse on 5th Street and were drowned.

Later in the month a lover's quarrel developed. I can't remember what it was about. Kay began seeing Eddie Hemness from Wahpeton. His only claim to fame, as far as I was concerned, was that he could roller skate and I couldn't. The two of them were at the American Legion Pavilion every free moment they had. I'd go down there and look in the window. I know the skating techniques displayed were put on for my benefit. My heart ached.

This love affair with Eddie lasted until December 22nd and then erupted in a quarrel. They continued to see each other by chance, but the meetings remained cool. These meetings continued through January, February, and March 1940. On March 21st I sent Kay a note and a picture by mail.

Our basketball team left for the Minnesota State High School Basketball Tournament in St Paul on Tuesday, March 26th. Kay came down to see us off, but she was just one of many and no conversation was held. However, two days later Kay and her mother came down to St. Paul and stayed at the Ryan Hotel. I did talk to her at the Tournament and again on April 21st during an Appreciation Program held at the school on a Sunday afternoon. At that age it is difficult to put into words all the feelings you would like to convey. I wanted to tell her I was in love but I didn't know how to express my feelings in words that didn't sound silly.

The following day I gave her the gold medal we were awarded for winning the State Tournament. From then on, things seemed to run fairly smooth.

On June 16th, I again left town to work for Dick Lubenow. I came into town for the Carnival on June

29th and met Kay there. Today it is so simple to stay in contact with someone by cell phone. Back then you tried to frequent the places you thought someone might be in hopes of running into them. I also saw her the next day for a short period before returning to the farm.

On July 11th, Kay left for Williston and, after a short visit with the relatives, she, Lorraine, Ken, and their mother continued on to Everett and Tacoma, Washington for a brief visit with relatives in that area. They then continued on to the Golden Gate International Exposition at San Francisco.

Each day, I would ride a little buckskin mare the one-half mile to the mailbox to see if any mail came from Kay. In fact, as I mentioned earlier, Reuben and I would race down there and back. It is amazing one of us wasn't killed as we came at breakneck speed across the wooden bridge spanning the Wild Rice River and into the farmyard.

Her letters telling about the ride on the Bay Ferry, Chinatown, parks, and beaches were a welcome relief from the uninteresting and unpleasant life we were living. I envied those that could travel and see the sights of the world. About all that I had seen up until that time was Fargo and Minneapolis. I also felt fortunate that Kay would take the time to write and tell me about all the exciting things she was doing. I missed her terribly and couldn't wait for school to start. I knew that then we would be back together. We would have a whole year to spend every possible moment together. I didn't want to think about graduating and leaving her behind in school for two additional years. There were so many others that would want to make certain she didn't pine for me too long.

Our work that summer was similar to that which we had performed during the summer of 1938. Our only recreation was hunting pheasants and going into Hankinson on Saturday night. The pheasant cover along the Wild Rice River was ideal protection against fox and other predators. The river passed the farm on the south, meander a mile to the east turned and flowed past the farm on the north. The pheasants were numerous and I believed at the time that it would always remain that way.

On the way to the field in the morning to thresh the grain bundles that had been shocked a couple of weeks earlier, we would toss our pitchforks in an attempt to spear pheasants. They were running around everywhere in the ditches on both sides of the road. It had been a dry spring and there was a very successful hatch. The birds weren't afraid since they were use to horses and farm equipment.

One Sunday I took the big, Belgian stallion and went to pick berries. I used an empty one-gallon Karo syrup pail. I had the pail about half full when I started for home. As the stallion got up to a gallop, the berries in the pail began bouncing up and down. The noise scared the horse and the faster he went, the more the berries bounced. I couldn't hold him back, and he was going too fast for me to jump off. If I had had enough sense to throw the pail away, everything would have been all right. I thought as soon as we come into the farmyard he will slow up and then I will jump off. However, he headed straight for the barn at full speed. I thought he might slow down when we got to the barn but he didn't. The clearance between the top of the barn door opening and the top of the horse's back was about 18 inches. He continued into the barn, and I got swept off as he entered. I'm certain I left some impressions in the wood above the entrance opening. I walked around in a dazed condition for approximately a half day. I would imagine I got a concussion. One wonders sometimes how we survived the teenage years considering some of the stupid things that were done. Another stupid thing a person never wants to do is standup barefoot on the back of a horse and urinate on an adjacent electric fence. The horse leaves you doing an aerial flip.

Kay got back from California on August 10th. I didn't get through at Dick's until August 17th. That has probably been the longest week in my life. The days just dragged by. I wanted to hear all about her trip out west but more importantly I just wanted to be with her.

The week finally passed and it was nice to be together again. It had seemed like an awfully long summer, that summer of 1940. She filled me in on everything she did and saw in San Francisco. I was happy for her and probably a little bit envious thinking that I would probably never get to see some of those wondrous sights.

Kay and her family went to Tracy, Minnesota on Labor Day, as they had done for many years. A celebration called BoxCar Days was held each year with parades, carnival, shows in the park, and other activities, which brought people into town. Her Aunt Ida lived there at the time. I hated to see her leave town. My imagination always ran wild. What If she was killed in a car accident or what if some other terrible thing happened to her and I wasn't there.

School started that fall on September 3rd. We had been practicing football for about two weeks, and our first game with Pelican Rapids was only 12 days away. Kay was active in the marching band and the opportunities to see each other during classroom hours were not as great as I had hoped. We did share our evenings together by walking, talking and going to movies.

Her cousins Wilbur and Adins Zapara from Williston were attending Science School that fall. They had a car and Adins, Phyllis Larson, Kay and I double-dated quite often those last months of 1940. After that quarter of school was over, they went home and I didn't see them again until about 1960.

On December 3, 1940, Harry Miksche died of cancer. His funeral was on December 6th, and I was one of the pallbearers. Harry and I had spent many hours together during the years of 1939 and 1940. He was at our house quite often and every time he came over, my Dad would say, "Are you here again? Don't you ever stay home?" I was always a little embarrassed because I knew my dad was kidding but I didn't know if Harry knew that. Harry was the only one I knew who was not afraid of my Dad. He would talk back to him and then my Dad had to laugh. Today I find myself saying some of the things my dad use to say and I think it embarrasses my wife Mardy.

Harry had the use of a 1939 Buick and we put many miles on it. His funds seemed enormous at that period in my life and when I didn't have show money, he would buy the tickets and treats. He was interested in photography and had his own dark room in a shed behind his house. We took many pictures and then did our own developing. He was also the only person I knew that was involved in 8-mm movie photography. In fact, he took some coverage of the 1940 Minnesota State High School Basketball Tournament that I was unaware existed until my son Mark surprised me on my birthday in 1987 with a video tape of film Harry had taken.

Harry's Dad and Mother may have known that he had cancer and tried to make his remaining time happy by giving him everything he wanted. Cancer was not discussed in those days and many of us at the funeral didn't know why he had died. I do not recall any long period of illness. It seemed strange to be a pallbearer for someone who, a few months earlier, had been so full of life and energy. When you're young, you have the feeling of immortality.

Kay and I exchanged Christmas gifts; I gave her a Schafer Pen and Pencil set and red furry mittens and she gave me a nice leather billfold. It was so difficult to come up the money for a type of gift you would like to buy.

On New Year's Day, 1941, a group of us went ice -skating. I really wasn't supposed to be ice skating because a different set of muscles is used in skating than is used for basketball. Mick was not too happy that Kay and I were spending so much time together. But what did he expect from teen-agers in love.

On January 12th, Johnnie Lipps, one of our classmates killed Alex Holabak over some problem relating to Holabak's sister, Rose. Alex was buried on January 15th. The Gazette-Telegram's headline on May 5, 1941 was "John Lipps Case Goes To Jury". Shortly after being found guilty, he entered prison.

On January 18th, a group of us arranged for a sleigh ride. Mr. Miller, who lived across from me on 11th Street, had the horses and a bobsled. It was a beautiful Saturday evening, and the twenty of us were looking forward to two hours of fun and laughter. The sled was lined with hay and straw and the temperature was such that a light jacket was sufficient. We were just getting started when an accident happened that could have been a real tragedy. We were crossing 5th Street (Highway 75) on the avenue that leads to the bridge that crosses into the Shirley Addition. Had we been a little further into the intersection, the car would have hit the sled loaded with teen-agers. Surely, some of them would have been killed. The horses had the hide torn loose from their legs. I remember feeling especially sorry for one of the horses, since he had been blind since birth. I wondered at the time what he was thinking as to what had happened to him. Mr. Miller was so shaken up by the ordeal that I'm certain it was an incident that contributed to his death a short time later. Mr. Miller took his sled and horses home, and we went over to Shirley Sagness' home for hot chocolate.

Kay and I were constantly together that spring of '41. There wasn't much to do other than go to every new movie that came to town but just being together was enough. We listened to the North Dakota State Basketball Tournament on radio. Wahpeton beat Bismarck on March 13th, Minot on March 14th and became State Champs on March 15th by outscoring Grand Forks 45-27. The next day, on Sunday, we were in Wahpeton for the homecoming of the North Dakota State High School Champions. Kay played in the Pep Band. Most members of that team are dead today. I guess that isn't so surprising. Most of the members of our team are dead also.

We saw Coach Mikulich and Miss Murphy at the movies on March 17th and we both decided things were getting pretty serious with them. I wanted to tell him we might start winning a few ball games if he would get his mind off the "skirts" but I didn't dare do it.

Mick took the team down to St. Paul on March 28th to see the Minnesota State Basketball Tournament. We came back on the afternoon of March 30th. Being under 30 years of age, Mick took on quite a responsibility. Watching over a bunch of high school kids in a large city was no easy task. A few did get quite rowdy and the school was assessed a hundred dollars for damage at the hotel where we stayed,

On April 3rd, Mick took Richard Miksche and me up to the Agricultural College in Fargo to see Stan Kostka about school scholarships. Stan was Athletic Director. I still remember my feelings at the time. It was difficult to accept the fact that my high school days were soon to be behind me. All the security of home and friends would no longer be a part of my life. Being a teen-ager has probably been difficult for every generation. I had mixed emotions. I wanted to get out of high school and go somewhere but at the same time I was concerned graduation was coming up too quickly. After that I would have to face the uncertainty of the future. Prior to graduation, everything had been predetermined and scheduled for me. After graduation I would have to make all my own decisions and be responsible for them.

I also realized I would no longer be a part of Kay's daily activities. During the previous two years we spent every possible moment together. So many pleasant memories were created during that period. It was as though it would never end and we gave very little thought to the future and how it might change for the two of us. Now she was a sophomore and all the school activities of band, school plays, sports, and other daily happenings could no longer be shared and discussed with her. I wanted so much to be with her in her final two years of school. I was also afraid that the exciting things that were important in her life would be of little concern to me since they would relate to school, and the important things happening in my life would be insignificant to her. I guess I was concerned that we would probably grow apart once our interests were no longer mutual. I also knew there were many other boys standing in the "wings" that were interested in her and I visualized this as a perfect opportunity for them to share the void in Kay's life that my leaving would create. As I write, I can totally experience those feelings I had almost seven decades ago. I would not enjoy living through that period of my life again.

On April 10th, Kay's parents bought 1941 green Mercury. Three days later on Easter Sunday, Kay and a number of her girl friends were permitted to take the car and go riding. They ended up in Fergus Falls, which I'm sure her mother never knew about. The kids just never got to use the family car as frequently in those days as they do today. In fact, if kids today don't have their own car by the time they are 16, they feel as though they're being deprived.

On April 15th, I gave Kay my graduation picture. I wanted to leave as many things as possible with her to remind her of me when I was gone.

On my 18th birthday, my mother invited Kay for supper. She had never been over to our house and I didn't want her coming now. I was embarrassed that the interior of the house was not finished and that I might be further embarrassed by some member of the family like my younger sister Betty asking, "When are you two going to get married?" I argued with Kay all day hoping she would refuse to come over but she was there at the designated time. The meal came off without any hitches and I was presented with a wristwatch for graduation. It wasn't until years later that I realized what a sacrifice on the part of my parents that watch must have been. The cost of $29.95 was equivalent to two weeks work later that summer when I was employed with the Wilkin County Highway Department. Toward the end of the evening, I began to relax and later in the evening, Kay and I went walking.

Kay participated in the Band Festival in Moorhead on April 25th and 26th. The afternoon of the second day Rich M. and I went up to Moorhead in his parents' car and Kay and Beverly M. came home with us.

The Senior Class Play was titled "The Bride's Stand In" starring Eleanor Leathart, Phyllis Sagness, Jeanne Auman, David Strand, Vivian Dretch, Leonard Stensing and Bill McCullough.

Kay served at our Junior-Senior Prom on May 10th. Cliff Thomas was Master of Ceremonies, and Walt Mikulich was the principal speaker. He injected humor in his usual informal manner. I got Rush McAllister's car, and Kay and I went out to the New Lake east of town after the Prom to discuss our futures. I was wishing we were both the same age, and I could spend the next two years in school with her.

Graduation was held on May 29, 1941 and though I am sure my parents attended I don't remember their presence that evening. There were 57 in the graduating class - the largest class in history of the school. Our class flower was the red rose and our class colors were blue and silver. Hugh Wing, my first grade buddy, was class president. That evening after graduation was over, almost everyone went to the local nightclub located on Highway 75 north of the fifth street bridge. Drinking became the primary activity during the evening. Kay got me home at a reasonable hour but I'm certain my parents knew I had been drinking. Most of the remaining part of the night was spent in the bathroom. The next morning I thought my mother might say, "How do you feel"? I saw no reason to bring up the subject. They were probably happy that graduation night was over and nothing more serious than a hangover resulted.

On May 31st, Kay left for Williston. She was to be the Maid of Honor at Wilbur's wedding to be held on the evening of June 1st. The cousin who continually teased her was on his best behavior that evening.

CHAPTER 10

From Graduation
to Military Service

Kay spent the summer of 1941 with the Drum and Bugle Corps sponsored by the local American Legion Club. They participated in such summer events as the Firemen's Convention at Alexandria and the Water Carnival at Detroit Lakes. During this period I worked at Hanson's Cloverleaf Dairy Farm. The hours weren't any shorter and the work wasn't any less strenuous than they had been two years earlier. However the farm operation required the need for about six employees and the days were no longer lonely like they had been at Dick's farm. We also were only a mile from town so our evenings could be spent shooting pool, attending movies or just dragging Main Street.

With the need for that many employees, a full-time cook was needed to assist the owner's wife with meal preparation. The owner hired a cook about my age named Thelma Holden. Some new scenery around the place made conditions more bearable, especially at mealtime. Kay was in St. Paul for a week so Thelma and

I went to the movies a few times. After she got back, I told her about Thelma and about our being out a few times. Things got a little cool but I thought I should at least be able to see other people and I was truthful and open about it. I was certain someone would mention our attendance at the movies. About three days later she called and indicated there was a good movie on at the local theater. I told her I couldn't come into town that night. I did have a plausible and legitimate excuse for not being able to come into town. I don't remember what it was now. Later the reason for not being able to make it was no longer valid and I was now free to go. However I had no way to contact Kay so I asked Thelma if she wanted to go to the movie. Unknown to me, Kay also went to the movie with some of her girl friends. Thelma and I came into the darken theater and unknowingly and unfortunately sat down in front of Kay. After a short period of time, she leaned ahead and whispered in my ear, "Hello, it's getting pretty serious, isn't it?"

My response was a startled, "No it isn't." I didn't remember any part of the movie after that moment.

Later, in that month of July, Thelma got fired. I don't know the reason but I suspect the late hours affected her efficiency during the day.

In no time at all, Kay and I were again sharing our free time with each other. On Wednesday, July 30th, she and four other girls went to Hart's cabin on Detroit Lake. They swam, napped, went boat riding, read and went into the town of Detroit Lakes. Two of my classmates and I went out to the cabin on Saturday, August 2nd and came back on Sunday afternoon. The lake was like a mirror and the full moon on Saturday night made for perfect swimming. Life is made up of such memories.

The summer drifted into August and the field corn was just starting to ripen and we would have corn-on-the-cob cookouts. One group would go out into the country to look for the corn while another group would get the pots of water boiling. It was the type of good clean fun experienced in those days except for the method obtaining the corn. Kay always loved corn well enough to steal for it.

On August 7th, Kay got a letter from a committee requesting she become a contestant in the Red River Valley Queen Pageant. Jean Hoverson won the Pageant contest and later in 1947, became Homecoming Queen at North Dakota State University (formerly NDAC). Kay took second in the contest, but she was first as far as I was concerned.

I went to Mansfield, Ohio on September 1st. My cousin, Frank Bresnahan and I went to my Uncle Phil's home and intended to get defense work there. I'm sure we could have found employment in some defense-related work such as machine shops but neither one of us was ready to break the ties with home. I think I was homesick before we ever got to Mansfield. I got back home on September 10th, having been in a train derailment at Fort Wayne, Indiana. Two people were killed and a number shaken up. The car I was in remained upright and bounced along over the railroad ties. The luggage stored in the overhead racks began tumbling down and dirt and cinders came through the upper portion of the railroad car. It was a scary experience but would also give me something to tell about when I returned home.

After returning home, I went over to the athletic field. It was difficult to accept that my school days were over. I also wanted to see the fellows that I had played football with the previous year and talk to Coach Mikulich one more time. I knew I had to get on with my life but with Kay still in school I just found it difficult to make the break. I had wished I could have been born two years later so we could have shared her last two years in school.

I immediately went to work for the Wilkin County Highway Department. Since I moved in again at home,

I felt I should start contributing something toward the maintenance of the household. I bought a refrigerator, the first we had ever had. Prior to this time the milk, butter, and other perishables were placed in a pail and lowered into an old, metal, hot water tank that had been placed in the ground. The temperature at the bottom of the tank was the same as the ground temperature and registered about 55 degrees F. The tank was next to the steps by the back door. Although things were kept cool, the humidity was high in the tank, and you had to be selective as to what was placed in it.

Another purchase I made that fall was a 9x12 living room rug. The refrigerator cost 60 dollars, a month's salary for me. I don't know or remember what the rug cost but the purchases helped offset some of the guilt feelings I was experiencing by living at home. My brother Bob was working and living full time at the dairy farm and I felt I should be living somewhere other than at home.

My work with Nemo Thompson that summer and the County Highway Department had a great deal to do with the position I would end up in two years later when I entered the military. We spent the summer doing surveys for new road construction. When this type of activity was reflected as past experience on my military record, I was placed in a surveying position that involved laying or aiming artillery pieces. Many times little events in life have a bearing on the direction that life will take. Had it not been for that little bit of surveying I surely would have ended up in the infantry and that could have resulted in a much shorter life expectancy?

Construction of County bridges using creosoted timbers resulted in rising fumes during the hot days of summer. These fumes would actually blister our faces. I often wondered what it did to our lungs.

I worked on into the fall hauling gravel from open gravel pits and then spreading it on county roads by the use of a shovel. Today no one would think of loading gravel on a truck by shovel and then taking the gravel to where it is needed and unloading it by shovel. That would only be feasible if wages were still 25 cents an hour.

As the weather turned colder in November and early December, I moved into the courthouse to plot some of the survey notes obtained earlier in the summer.

Ten days before that the Japanese envoys Kurusee and Monura met with Secretary Cordell Hull to discuss peace between the two countries. However, the Japanese struck at Pearl Harbor on December 7, 1941 and my world and my life would change dramatically for ever.

Toward the end of December I rode a snowplow opening up county roads. As the start of a next year dawned, I began to notice that less and less of my friends were around town. Draft age was 18 to 36 and the County began filling their draft quota from this age group. I continued my employment with the Wilkin County Highway Department. When all roads were opened I went back to working in the courthouse, plotting field notes.

The numbers in the courthouse also began to decrease as more people were being lured to the higher paying jobs in the war industries. I was beginning to feel that if I didn't make some decisions soon, I may become mired down and I never would get out of town. I again had mixed feelings as to whether I should go into Service or find a job on the West Coast. The war clouds boiling over Europe in 1939 and 1940 were just as real now in this country. Patriotic slogans and recruitment posters were everywhere. More and more countries were being drawn into the conflict each year. Japanese successes in China and the havoc they caused at Pearl Harbor created greater lusts for their military. They overran one outpost after another in the Pacific. All this was going on as I worked a snowplow wing opening up county roads. It seemed I should be doing something more important, something more patriotic and something more glamorous and exciting.

I turned in my resignation notice to the County on January 10, 1942. I could have sat out the war in that county court house basement plotting plan and profiles for county road construction. However, if I did that I would have guilt feeling the rest of my life. The County Highway Department needed men desperately since most had gone to the West Coast or other war-related jobs in other areas. I turned down the pay offer they made to me in an attempt to encourage me to stay.

I was beginning to do those things that would ultimately lead to my leaving town for one reason or another. I was nineteen years old, restless and beginning to feel life would pass me by if I remained in the small town of my youth. So many conflicting thoughts and uncertainties passed through my mind. I had no one I could formulate a life plan with. I did realize that I had to set a course for the future. I am certain my parents would have been very happy if I had sought their advice. What teenager ever goes to their parents for advice?

On January 16th, Kay's 17th birthday, we went to the Wilkin Cafe for dinner. As I looked into her eyes across the table from me I wished I could visualize what the future would bring for the two of us. We were both so young and for the first time we knew the decisions to be made were ours alone. I also realized the time we shared together became more precious each week. We were so much in love and so fearful of what the future might or might not bring. Our carefree high school days with all their memories were now behind us. It was the spring she would graduate from high school and go on to college. I had no idea as to what I would do or should do. It was one of the most difficult periods in my life.

On February 6th, a warm and moonlit evening, a group of us got together on the river just north of the present site of the Breckenridge High School. We skated, built a bon-fire on the river's edge and gathered around the fire to roast wieners, marshmallows, and drink hot chocolate. There was laughter and other teenage noise. No alcohol or drugs, which is so prevalent today at so many of the gatherings, were considered necessary to have a good time. For the next three years, I would relive the pleasant memories of that warm, beautiful, winter evening. I believe that was the date that I finally accepted that a break with home, friends and the town would have to be made; a break that had been so difficult to make.

A week later, I took a box of candy over to Kay's home and informed her I was leaving for Glenwood.

On February 13, 1942, Mel Ruud and I left for Glenwood, Minnesota to enroll in a sheetmetal-training course. Mel and I were good friends and had played basketball on the 1940 Minnesota State High School Championship team. The training school was sponsored by the National Youth Administration, an agency formed earlier in the Roosevelt Administration specifically for training youths in vocational skills. It was part of a Recovery Program similar to the Stimulus Package proposed by the Obama Presidency during 2009. It was especially appropriate at the time we were attending, since all training was directed toward and geared to skills that would assist in the war effort.

The building in which we were housed held about 150 students and was formerly a resort on the lake lying west and adjacent to the city of Glenwood. Food and lodging was provided to us and, in addition to that, we were furnished $3.60 per month for other such necessities as toothpaste, hand soap, etc. The operation was not too much different from a military operation. We attended classes during the day, studied in the evening, and had a lights-out curfew at 10 o'clock. Friday and Saturday nights were free to go into town and passes were required to leave for the weekend. You had to return by 10:00 P.M. Sunday evening. Each student drew a turn on K.P., which involved washing dishes and pots and pans. Another requirement, as part of the duties, was to assist the chef when help was needed. Beds had to be made each morning before leaving for class.

Mel and I usually hitched-hike home for the weekend, leaving about 4:30 P.M. on Friday afternoon and hoping to arrive home in time for the high school activities such as basketball. We had only been out of high school a short time and many of our friends were still students. Those older than us had gone into military service.

Being able to catch a ride always was subject to the weather. If it was nice people were always going somewhere. It may only be to the next town. There wasn't the stigma associated with hitchhikers then that there is today. Practically everyone would stop. There was always a concern on our part that if we accepted a ride to the next town that may only be 6 miles away, we may miss the chance at a 75-mile ride. We also preterred cars that sprouted aerials, since we may then be able to listen to the radio as we traveled along. Radios in automobiles were not too common in those days.

Weather predictions were not as reliable and scientific as they are today. We'd leave in what appeared to be ideal weather, get half way home and see a snowstorm or blizzard develop. Of course, as soon as the weather worsened, the opportunities for a ride were also greatly reduced. Most small towns on State Highway No. 9 were fairly close together and we would walk the distance between them on the chance that we would find someone there that might be going to Breckenridge. One time we got between towns when a sudden wind, snow and a drop in temperature developed. We were walking almost directly into the northwest wind. Mel was not as warmly dressed as I was and at one point he suggested we lie down in the ditch and sleep for awhile. I realized he must have been very close to that feeling experienced when one begins to freeze. I convinced him the town of Herman was just a short distance ahead of us and we could sleep there. About this time a farmer turned onto the highway from a side road. He was on his way into town for a beer. We flagged him down, and he wondered out loud what in the world we were doing out on foot on a night like this. I guess we could have asked him also what in the world he was doing out on a night like this. We rode into Herman and went into the bar with him. It was warm and fairly quiet since the weather had discouraged customers.

The bartender closed his business at 1:00 A.M. and as the evening had progressed, so had the intensity of the storm. No one would be venturing a drive to Breckenridge until the weather cleared up. The bartender agreed we could sleep in one of the booths until he opened his business the next morning at 8 o'clock.

The next morning was clear and bright and as we left for Breckenridge, the sun sparkled on the newly fallen snow. Life began anew with another day and no thought was given as to what might have happened had the thirsty farmer not come along the night before. We made the decision to retrace our steps and return to Glenwood.

I don't know if our parents were worried or not. We never told them if we were coming home for the weekend. There was no telephone in our home and besides, the phone was never used for long distance calls unless there was an accident or death in the family to report. It was just assumed a long distance call meant an extreme emergency. The call had to go through many operators, with each one relaying the call to the next switchboard. The person answering the phone had to be confirmed by the operator as the one that the caller was trying to reach. So it was very obvious to the one receiving the call that it was a long-distance call and their first response was usually, "What happened"? My son Mark's philosophy of "What is there to worry about; if you're dead, you're dead" had not been developed as yet at that time.

We did stay at the school a few weekends. Mel and I organized some touch football teams and we played each other. We had a few beautiful days in February where we played in short-sleeved shirts. The temperature was up in the high 50's and the little snow we did have was melted. We had some good times during that two months we spent at the school. I've often wondered what happened to the good friends we made there and did they survive military service. So many people briefly pass through certain period of one's life and then just disappear forever.

In the early part of April our training was considered complete. Rumors began to fly as to where we would be going and what we would be doing. Early on the morning of April 14th, we boarded buses and were shipped to Shakopee, Minnesota. The next morning, we were assembled with groups that had come from other training centers and then were loaded on a special train for Seattle. Never had life been so exciting and never had I been so far from home. Would I ever want to come home to the little railroad town in the Red River Valley after seeing the wonders of the world?

As we begin our westward journey, I realized we would be going through Breckenridge. We had stopped at Willmar for water and coal but it was obvious by our speed, as we approached the east edge of my hometown that we wouldn't be stopping there. I had wished I could have notified my parents some way that I would be going through town at a certain time. Not that I wanted them to be down at the station, but just having the opportunity of sharing with them some of the exciting things that were happening to me. As we whistled through town tears came to my eyes. Even though I was anxious to get out of town, all the familiar streets and buildings brought back memories of my earlier years. I guess, subconsciously, I knew things would never again be like they were in the past. Never would the same group of kids all play together. It would be impossible to recreate the same feelings experienced in our youth since the world and each of us in it were changing too rapidly. As we passed the Wells Memorial Park, I reflected back to the period when the school year was ending and we went down there for the class picnic. The boys would play baseball and show-off for the girls sitting on the sidelines. Finally, the time would come for the picnic itself and the highlight, at least for me, was the bottle of strawberry pop we got as a drink to go along with the peanut butter sandwiches. You needed something in those days to get the sticky peanut butter off the roof of your mouth. It wasn't homogenized in those days. The ball games Jimmy Cahill and I had sneaked into by swimming the river were still fresh in my mind. The rodeos I had attended with the family in the park brought back memories of more pleasant times. Kay and I had spent many pleasant hours at the County Fairs and summer carnivals during the past three summers. We had attended band concerts on beautiful summer evenings and at the time we never thought they would end. All these thoughts flashed through my mind in the few brief moments it took to pass through the city of my youth. I had only spent 17 years there but years contained and were filled with so many memories. As the train began crossing the bridge over the Bois de Sioux River into North Dakota, I turned for one final look at the area I called home and wondered what the future held for Mel and me. Would that ever be my permanent residence again?

I am sure the trip west was just as thrilling to the majority of the kids on the train as it was for me. Many of us had never traveled within the State of Minnesota and now were traveling across the country. No one wanted to convey the impression, though, that what they were experiencing was something unusual. However, when we got to the Rocky Mountains, it became very obvious that very few had ever seen mountains before. Noses were pressed to the windows to view the tops of the peaks as we followed along and adjacent to the mountain streams.

As we drew closer to Seattle, someone spotted snow-capped Mount Rainier rising up against a dark blue sky. We were fortunate, since we found out later that the mountain is very seldom visible from Seattle because of weather conditions. However, on this day, it was welcoming us as the Statue of Liberty must have welcomed the early immigrants coming from Europe. Seagulls also began to appear. I could feel an exciting new period in my life was beginning to open up. I wanted to remember everything so I could share what I was seeing in my first letter home.

We didn't want to give the impression when we disembarked at the station but I'm sure we all looked like the country boy making his first visit to New York City. Barrage balloons were flying everywhere in the blue sky. They were lazily floating around at 700 to 1000 feet and were anchored by heavy cable to a wench and motor mounted on a concrete slab. The balloons had short pieces of cable hanging down from their side and were intended to discourage Japanese fighters and bombers from trying any low level strafing and bombing runs along the West Coast. The Japanese had attacked and landed on the outer islands of Alaska. Suddenly the war became real to me and it was no longer something I read about in the newspapers like I had been doing back in Minnesota.

We arrived at King Street Station (also known as Union Depot) in Seattle on a beautiful, warm sunny morning. At home the temperatures were still in the high thirties and snow covered the ground. We were billeted in Government buildings until we could be assigned to war-related jobs in the area. In the meantime, I was put to work painting buildings within the compound. This work lasted approximately two weeks and during this period I lost track of Mel. In fact, I hadn't seen him since we debarked at the railroad station. I would not see him again for another 38 years. At the end of the two-week period, I got a notice to report to the Personnel Office at the Puget Sound Navy Yard in Bremerton, Washington.

Threatening gestures by Japan in the late 1800s about taking possession of the Philippine Islands prompted the United States to consider a Pacific Ocean naval fleet. In 1891 190 acres on Puget Sound were purchased and construction of a dry dock was begun. By 1901 the site had had been elevated to what was Navy Yard status. By 1913 a second dry dock, capable of repairing any battleship existing at that time, was constructed. In 1916 a third dry dock was complete and used for building submarines. With threats from Hitler widespread in 1940 another dry-dock was built. Employment rose from 6,000 to 17,000 prior to the war. After the Japanese struck at Pearl Harbor the Navy Yard went into full production with 3 shifts of 50,000 employees.

After World War II the name was changed to Puget Sound Naval Shipyard. Employment fell off and then picked up slightly during the Korean Police Action. In 1960 a large dry dock capable of handling the large aircraft carriers was constructed. An additional 327 acres of hard land and 338 acres of submerged land were purchased to increase the size of the base.

I had heard Mel was assigned to the Kaiser Shipyard in Seattle. It was difficult to know and accept they had separated the two of us because together we could give each other moral support and could share things we had in common back home.

Life was still exciting but now also a little bit frightening. Up until this time, we had always done things in small groups. There had always been a group leader or an older responsible adult one could turn to for answers. Now I was to leave on a ferry all by myself. What if I couldn't find the shipyard? What if they really didn't have a job for me when I got there? Having never been this far from home before and being without money, all kinds of things kept popping into my head. Everything would have to work out just the way they said it would for me to survive.

I was furnished a ferry ticket and would board the Kalakala Ferry docked on Pike Street at Pier 52. It was the largest boat I had ever seen and it carried many cars. We passed through submarine nets that were placed to prevent Japanese submarines from enter the area that would give them access to the shipyard. The trip took approximately an hour and a half.

The ferry dock landing in Bremerton was located right near one of the entrances to the shipyard. One major concern was eliminated before I had too much of an opportunity to think about it. I showed my papers to the Marine guard stationed at the gate and asked where the Personnel Office was located. Again, another item of concern disappeared. It was the first building inside the gate. The Personnel Office had information showing I would be reporting for work. Everything was starting to fall nicely into place. Maybe the world wasn't such a tough place to venture out into on your own after all.

I was assigned to the X-17 Shop (Sheetmetal), given Badge No. 35293, and designated a sheetmetal helper for Ronald Rockwell. My first job was to help install sheetmetal lockers in the officers' quarters on a mini-aircraft carrier. In June and July, ships that were capable of steaming under their own power were beginning to come in from Pearl Harbor. Repair of these ships was given priority, since the crews were available, trained and ready to go back out to sea. The country was woefully unprepared for the conflict we were about to be engaged in. Trained personnel were woefully lacking.

One of the first requirements when the battleships came in was the removal of shells. Each shell weighed in excess of a thousand pounds. This removal would continue around the clock for up to three days on battleships before all shells were off the ship. At the conclusion of this work, the ship would be riding two feet higher in the water. Many of the ships had been temporarily patched to make the trip back from Pearl Harbor. The sailors on those returning ships had some terrible stories to tell regarding the activities encountered that Sunday morning of December 7, 1941.

We worked seven days and had the eighth day off. Pay was $1.08 per hour for regular time; $1.13 for swing shift and $1.20 for graveyard shift (12:00 P.M.-8:30 A.M.). I worked the day shift for the first two months and then went to swing shift. It required an adjustment in one's sleeping and eating habits when a transfer from one shift to another was made. I never did work the graveyard shift and I don't think I would have like it. Some asked for that particular work period and I could never understand why. Both men and women worked in the shipyards and later, after hearing what was going on down in the double bottoms of the ships, I could better understand why they preferred that particular shift. Their activities were not conducive to increased war production, but it may have improved the morale on the home front for the shipyard workers at the Puget Sound Navy Yard.

The usual tricks played on the new employees were also tried out on me; tricks such as being sent over to another shop for items like left-handed monkey wrenches. Even when you were suspicious that everything wasn't on the up and up, you, being a new employee, were afraid to question a request from the supervisor. It is amazing we won the war with all the time spent on nonproductive fooling around. Another favorite trick involved welders. Almost everyone working in the shipyards wore a horseshoe shaped strips of metal around the outer edge of the heel of their work boots. As one welder would be working overhead, another welder would tack his boots to the steel deck of the ship. This was usually done just before the noon whistle would sound. The welder would then have to get out of his boots, find a chipper to chip the boots off the steel deck, and then get the rough edges of his boot ground off.

The toilets, or heads as they are called in Navy lingo, consisted of toilet seats fastened to semi-circular steel troughs similar to a hot water tank cut in half. A continuous flow of water was pumped through this sloped channel. A favorite trick was to find someone in a dozing position. A crumpled wad of toilet paper was then lit with a match and placed in the upper end of the trough. The torched paper would start down the channel, and when the fire passed under the sleepy goldbrick, he usually bounded to life.

Shortly after starting at the shipyard I got together with five other single fellows, and we rented a house in Charleston a suburb of Bremerton. We paid the outrageous sum of 90 dollars per month. I say outrageous because my Dad was making a mortgage payment of $15.60 and I thought that would be a more realistic payment for our house of comparable size. However, as high as it may have seemed for a house, it was still only 15 dollars each, or about two days pay per month.

Each person fixed his own lunch for work, and it usually consisted of a thermos of milk, some meat sandwiches, a tomato, and some cookies.

A typical day on swing shift meant getting up around 9:30 A.M., having breakfast downtown, going back home to fix lunch about 2:30, and then reporting for work at 4:00. When we got off work at 12:30 A.M., we went out for our only large meal of the day, and then home to bed. On our day off we occasionally went to Seattle and I spent the July 4th holiday at the cabin owned by Tiltons. My supervisor, Rocky, was a son-in-law of Tiltons. The cabin was located on the Hood Canal just a short distance from Bremerton. While there, I met a girl named Amy who was a neighbor of the Rockwells. About a year later, I sent her a pair of Paratrooper's Wings after completion of jump school. This proved to be a very unwise action on my part, as you will discover a little later in your reading.

Lack of home cooking or the uninteresting lunches we were packing led us to start looking for other accommodations. In July, we discovered a widow (Mrs. Fellows) at 627 Washington Avenue who was renting rooms in her home. It was much closer to work and the lady next door packed lunches and served meals. Rooms were 18 dollars a month and the meals and lunches cost us 8 dollars a week. The meals were terrific - family style with all you could eat. The sit-down arrangement with about ten at a table gave the setting a homey atmosphere. I think that was the beginning of my weight problem that has continued to grow over the years.

In August, I received a letter from my mother informing me she was considering a divorce. I responded with a pleading letter asking her to reconsider. My argument was that since the economy was improving, she could expect to be receiving a better quality of life. I assumed that she was unhappy because we were financially unable to have all the things she may have wanted or would have liked. She followed with a letter indicating she had given it considerable thought and was going to proceed with the action. I was heartbroken and angry.

I gave no thought to the fact that this was probably more difficult for her than anyone else. I should have been thinking of her happiness and if this is what she wanted, I shouldn't have made it more difficult for her. All I could think of was what such an action would do to the continuity of the family.

That was the last communication we had for over three years. I was feeling sorry for the rest of the family and myself. My feelings were that she was robbing us of the opportunity of doing the things together as a family. Never would gatherings for Christmas, weddings, graduations and summer reunions be a possibility again. If she went ahead with her plans, all these things I visualized as happening someday would only be dreams.

Bob told me much later that he could see it all coming. One day my Dad sent him to Ray's, a small grocery store about three blocks from home, for a loaf of bread. On the way home, he saw Larson's Transfer coming down the street. This time they weren't coming to take my Dad to the train depot and the Veterans Hospital, but rather to move my mother to south 3rd Street. So little time had elapsed between visits to our house by Larson's Transfer. The first visit in 1934 temporarily broke up the family by taking my Dad away to the Veteran's Hospital for almost a year. The second visit in 1942 permanently broke up the family by taking my mother and sisters away. The drastic effect on the children would be much greater than realized at the time and only each can convey his/her own feelings regarding the changes in their life that the divorce action brought about. It was shortly after this that the move to the Clark Hanson farm became a permanent arrangement for Bob. A year later, after Bob was in the Service, my Dad would inquire of Mrs. Hanson when he saw her, "What do you hear from our Bob?"

Judy was just one year old, but Mavis and Betty were 15 and 10, respectively. They remained with their mother and, as small as the town was, all their friends knew what had taken place.

I place the bulk of the blame for the divorce on Emma Jean Richter, who was living with a bachelor two doors south of us. She continually seemed to be creating dissatisfaction and implying that mom's life left a lot to be desired. Emma had very little to do at home since the bachelor was a railroad engineer and would be gone four or five days out of each week. This would leave Emma with time on her hands and she usually spent her evenings downtown at the bars. She could play an accordion and she would accept drinks or money for her performances. Mom was easily influenced by others, so when Emma kept telling her each day how much fun she was missing, it probably began to seem that way. At age 38 she probably couldn't remember doing much of anything other than raising four children and burying two. Emma's constant coaxing to get out and have some fun didn't make it any easier.

As early as 1929, my parents began going to local barn dances with the Mathesons. The Mathesons were neighbors who lived within two blocks of our home when we lived out on north 10th Street. Alfred (Red) Matheson, after a few drinks, would usually become involved in a fight at these dances. It was also apparent to the neighbors that Red and his wife were having family problems. I suspect a spark between Red and my mom may have been kindled as early as that. By 1938, he was paying her a great deal of attention and this may have been flattering to her. I was working for Red as a helper in his well drilling operations. I hauled five-gallon buckets of water continuously all day from another well about 100 yards away to supply the drilling operation with a water slurry mixture that would bring the drilled material to the surface. I made 50 cents a day or five cents an hour.

I was supposed to be ready for work at 7:00 A.M., but mom would never call me until Red pulled up to the house. He would then come in, have a cup of coffee and wait until I was ready. I could never understand why she couldn't remember to get me up. As the years passed, I soon forgot about her failure to insure I was up and ready for work.

Then suddenly years later when I received that letter in August, my memory flashed back to those mornings when I was never awaken in time to be ready for work. It was now obvious to me that it was a deliberate action on her part so Red could come in each morning for a few minutes.

My work in the shipyard continued into the fall. I was making good money and half of what I was making I sent home to the First National Bank in Breckenridge. Late in November a new song, "White Christmas", sung by Bing Crosby, along with a movie by the same name was showing at Admiral Theater in Bremerton. During that week I attended that movie three times. I loved the falling snow and suddenly I wanted to be home. Nothing will cure homesickness like going home. I resigned my job, giving the excuse I was going home to enlist. There was a certain amount of truth in that. All the movies had a patriotic theme and with so many servicemen in the area, I did feel a little out of place. I was at the age of most of those in uniform and to be walking around in civilian dress made me feel very uncomfortable. You were assumed to be 4-F (unfit for military duty) if you were a certain age and still walking around in civvies.

I arrived home on December 2, 1942 and within five days Wilfred Schwankl and I went to Minneapolis to enlist in the United States Army Air Corps. The Federal Building where we made application was on 3rd Avenue just off Washington Street in Minneapolis. We both registered and were informed we needed draft releases from our draft boards. Since Wilfred's draft board was in Minneapolis, he got his draft release immediately. I had registered in Bremerton and my board at home had to write to them for the release. Not knowing how long this would take, Wilfred didn't dare wait for me. There were already rumors that the Air Corps was about to close all enlistments. He signed up on December 11, 1942. I received my release from the Bremerton Draft Board December 24th and returned to Minneapolis after Christmas. I was informed the Air Corps took no additional enlistments after midnight on December 15th. I was a little upset and decided that if they wanted me they would have to draft me.

Wilfred and I had started school together in the first grade and also were in the same confirmation class at the German Lutheran Church in Wahpeton. We had also played high school basketball together and it would have been nice if we could have gone into service together.

Wilfred left for service on February 23, 1943. Kay and I, along with Betty Johnson (whom he later married), double dated the previous evening and had a great time together. We watched the sun come up over the buildings of the Wahpeton Science School. I don't know what Kay's mother thought about her late arrival home. Wilfred went on to become a B-24 bomber copilot. From Minneapolis, he was sent to Merced, California for training. After completing his training, he began ferrying B-24's from the East Coast through Greenland, Iceland and into England. His ferrying operation began in April 1944 and continued until October when he began making bombing runs. He completed 57 missions with the 8th Air Force, flying his last mission in April 1945. He was then transferred to the States where he began training with a B-29 group. He had completed 90 hours of flying time and was probably scheduled for Japan when the war ended in August 1945 with the dropping of the two atomic bombs. He was discharged two months later in

October. He and his wife Betty spent their retirement years on Pickerel Lake a short distance outside of Fergus Falls, Minnesota. Wilfred hosted a reunion for his bomber crew one year and they all were able to attend. He died a few years ago and his wife continued to live at the lake for a period of time.

I often wondered what my fate might have been had I gotten my draft release at the same time he did. Would we have stayed together through training and been assigned to the same bomber group? I may be alive today because I didn't get in. The losses in the 8th Air Force were very great during 1944. As many as 60 B-17s were shot down in a single raid. That meant 600 men lost in one bombing run. It leaves much to wonder about as to what my fate may have been.

Mel Ruud, who had gone out to the shipyards with me, also came home in December 1942. This I didn't find out until we had a basketball reunion 38 years later in 1980 at Breckenridge. He joined the Marines, fought in many of the major battles in the Pacific and came through the war in great shape and although he had a few close calls he was uninjured. He settled in Minneapolis after the war, raised a family and eventually relocated to California as a contractor and inspector for the State supervising hospital construction. He died of cancer on February 8, 1985, the first to be lost from our 1940 basketball team.

The year 1942 had been an exciting one but it also had its sad moments. It was just tough to be a teen-ager and have to handle all the little uncertainties that come up in a young life.

One year after I left for my first exciting period away from home, I was right back where I had been, working with the Wilkin County Highway Department. The hourly wage was still 25 cents, exactly the same as it was during the summer and fall prior to the time when Mel Ruud and I went to NYA School at Glenwood.

However, my job provided spending money and I knew it would not be a career for me like it was for some of the older fellows who had been with the County all through the Depression Years of the '30's. I also knew it would not be too permanent, since I was expecting my "greetings" letter from the local draft board any day. I was actually looking forward to leaving town again.

I had saved 600 hundred dollars during the six months I was working at the shipyard. One of the first things I did when I got home was car shop. No new cars had been produced for over a year, so used cars were at a premium. People knew that the car they had would have to last through the war. Because of gas rationing very little driving took place during the war years.

I did find a 1937 green 4-door Chevrolet and spent half of what I had saved to make the purchase. Kay and I were no longer restricted to distances that could be covered by bicycle. We were now free and capable of going to places like Fergus Falls and Hankinson. It was a wonderful feeling as a teenager to have a set of wheels. Kay and I parked west of Wahpeton one evening after a movie and played the radio so long the battery was run down and the car failed to start when we were ready to leave for home. I don't know why I didn't start the car occasionally to recharge the battery. It might have been because of how precious a gallon of gasoline became in those days. I can't remember what we did. No one carried jumper cables in those days. I often wondered how I got Kay home. It would have been wonderful to have a Cell Phone at that time.

Prior to leaving for service, I passed the car on to my brother Bob for safekeeping. He sold the car after graduation and headed for the West Coast. For 64 years, we have had discussions as to what has happened to the money he received from the sale. Did he invest the money for me in stocks and bonds or is it sitting in a savings account or certificate of deposit account somewhere? I can just imagine how the compound interest has increased during the past sixty-seven years.

I spent the three months of January, February, and March as "wing man" on the snowplow. It was an unusually severe winter that year and considering the type of design and construction used for roads in those days most county roads needed plowing. Since most trees and shrubs were planted adjacent to the road, they created the effect of a snow fence when the wind blew. This meant a week's work could be undone in a matter of an hour after the wind and ground drifting began. Then we would start over on the same old roads. After each cut through, the depth became greater the next time it had to be plowed. More than once we opened roads where the snow was so deep it was possible step over telephone lines when we were on top of the snow drift we were cutting through.

Many times after a blizzard we would find pheasants almost frozen to death. The hens had enough sense to burrow into a snow bank or get into some protective cover. However the roosters would stand out in the open facing the wind. Their beaks would fill with snow and they would come close to suffocating or would freeze to death. We would take the birds into the cab of the truck and when they thawed out sufficiently we would open the window and give them little push. With the beating of wings they were airborne and into the closest cover, running as they hit the ground.

During the period January 27-28, 1943, hearing proceedings in the divorce between my mother and dad were held in the 16th Judicial District Court in Breckenridge. On one side of the courtroom sat my mother, my sister Mavis and some of my mother's friends and on the other side sat my dad and me. We were no longer the family that had shared the hardships of the Depression. We had now chosen up sides to oppose each other. I don't recall the actual testimony but I remember each attorney questioned the children in a manner that attempted to discredit each parent. I recall thinking, why do we have to go through this? Why do all these nasty things have to be said about each of them? If they no longer want to live together why can't they just tell the Judge that and have the marriage dissolved. Why do the children have to sit here and glare at each other across the aisle showing dislike for each other as means of showing loyalty and support for the parent? I assume the reason for the hearing was because my dad contested the divorce. He didn't want it to take place.

The trial began at 10:00 A.M. and ran to 3:00 P.M. each day. At noon, my dad and I went to Hart's Cafe for lunch. I had a hot beef sandwich and milk the first day and the cost was 35 cents. The second day we each had the special pork chops and mashed potatoes. The cost for each dinner, which also included apple pie for dessert, was 65 cents. It is the only time I can recall eating out with my dad. At the time, it didn't seem too important or anything special but the following year during times when I was on lonely outpost duty I often reflected on those three hours we had spent together. I thought of so many things I should have asked and some of my feelings I should have expressed. There was so little I knew about his early years as he was growing up. The sharing and expressing of personal feelings was never encouraged so it was difficult to make it happen. His letters to me in service always began with the salutation "Dearest Son".

At the conclusion of the trial on the second day, the Judge indicated he wanted to review some additional evidence before making his decision. He promised his ruling in the very near future.

Although I was gone into service by the time the Judge made his ruling, it was obvious to me before I left what the outcome would be. The Judge had requested some additional information and testimony on June

18th and then declared the divorce final on June 22nd, twenty-one years and one month after their wedding vows promising "until death do us part". Two days later the decision was filed with the Clerk of Court and the family that had worked together, laughed together, read stories together and cried together at two funerals were now no longer considered a family. By law, it no longer existed, dissolved by a piece of paper on June 22, 1943. Ruling of the Court included the following provisions: (1) My mother would have custody of Betty and Judy. (2) My dad would pay my mother's attorney, Louie Jones, the remaining balance of 55 dollars due him at the rate of 10 dollars per month beginning July 1, 1943. And (3) my dad would pay my mother 50 dollars per month for herself and the minor children until advised otherwise by the Court.

I was already in Service and Bob had left for the West Coast. We could no longer be directly affected by the aftermath of the divorce but my thoughts kept going back to Mavis and Betty. How would they be able to handle this with their friends? Judy I didn't know and I realized this would all be history by the time she grew up. I knew there would be whispers and nasty remarks by other children and it would continue all through school even though Mavis and Betty were totally blameless for the things that had happened. This may have contributed to Mavis' decision to quit school in her sophomore year. Kids can be very unkind without realizing how deeply they are hurting someone.

Betty's comments on that particular period in her life were "It was a lonely and confusing time. We moved to a small, upstairs apartment on the other side of town. Mom got a job as a waitress at the Hamburger Inn. Judy was a baby and I remember many nights of rocking her to sleep, crying and praying for things to be like they used to be when we were a complete and functional family. For a long time, I had hopes my parents would resolve their differences and get back together again. I didn't like Red because I felt he was taking our mother away from us. I remember coming in one night, and the living room was quite dark. Mom was on the couch with someone that I thought was Red. I felt myself become tense and then I realized it was my dad. They were talking and again I was hoping they would get back together".

Betty was in her sixth year of school. Divorce at that time was not a very common thing; it carried quite a stigma with it. One day after school, on her way to see her mom, some kids were teasing her about the divorce. A classmate, Harold Sussenguth, stood up for her and told them to leave her alone because it wasn't her fault. She indicated, "Even now when I think of that event, I ask God to bless Harold. He was my lifesaver that day and he doesn't even know it."

Betty goes on to say that since Mavis isn't here to speak for herself, she would provide a few thoughts of her own. She said, "Mavis was fifteen; it was wartime, and a great number of sailors were stationed at the North Dakota State School of Science. Everyone was trying to cram in a lot of living and loving before going away to fight for our country. Mavis started dating too much, too soon. Then she quit school and went out to the State of Washington with four older cousins to work in an aircraft defense plant. Again, too much growing up, too fast. She should have been home with her mom and dad thinking about her first Prom. Anyway, I felt sorry for Mae. She was so much fun and had a gift for making people laugh, but she longed for love and security and always seemed to look for it in all the wrong places. Her gift for making others laugh covered a lot of her deeper feelings."

Early in March, I received a letter from the Government and I knew what it contained without opening it. It did not come as a complete surprise. I had been in for a haircut about ten days earlier. The owner of the barbershop was a man named Stephens, who also happened to be the chairman of the local draft board. Each Board was responsible for furnishing a certain number of names that were eligible for military service. They had quotas to meet each month. I had mentioned I was looking forward to receiving my draft notice. I was still depressed about the proceedings that had taken place during the latter part of January. News, such as a divorce spread like a prairie fire in a small town. It was not a common action taken in those days and when it did happen, it drastically affected those that were directly involved. Stephens could understand that I would like to remove myself from an environment that left me self-conscious. Although it may not have been true, I always felt there was some whispering taking place when I was in a group of people. Since we had won the State High School Basketball Championship three years earlier, everyone in the town of less than 4,000 persons knew me. It was not as easy to leave a town then as it is today. Reporting for military service provided a perfect and justifiable reason for leaving. It also meant it could be an all-expense paid trip with someone else being responsible for all the decisions that had to be made.

CHAPTER 11

Military Service-World War II

Details regarding my military time are contained in a separate book titled "From Rome to Berlin via Bastogne". It was published in 2009 and is available from Amazon.com and other sources including BookSurge.com. It is an expanded version of material that was contained in an earlier version of the book From Breckenridge to Bastogne. I sold approximately 2,000 copies of that book at book signing sessions at B Dalton's before Father's Day, Memorial Day, July 4th and other holidays each year. I still have a few copies of that book in both paperback and hardcover.

After receiving my notice, I realize my youth was over and life for me would be drastically changed for the unforeseeable future. I would now be able to leave town with an all-expense paid trip. I also realized my life would no longer be my own. I would now be told what time to get up and when to go to bed. I would be told what to wear and what I would be doing each day. That was acceptable to a nineteen-year-old kid.

On April 8, 1943 a group of local inductees were to leave by bus for the Ft. Snelling Induction Center at St. Paul, Minnesota. The bus was scheduled to leave from the Wilkin County Courthouse at 9:00 A.M. I showed up at 8:15, not because I thought I might be late, but because I wanted to get there before anyone else. That would permit me to board immediately if the bus came early. I knew no one would be there to see me off since my dad had said good-bye to me that morning before he left for work at 5:30 a.m. He didn't feel he should or could come over to the courthouse from work. I didn't want to be a part of the group when the farewells were being conveyed. I was still sensitive about my parents' divorce and I was concerned someone might ask me where my mom and dad were. I didn't know where my mom was living and I am certain she wasn't aware I was leaving for Service that morning.

It worked out the way I had hoped and I was sitting in the back of the bus when the first parents showed up that morning at 8:45 AM with their sons. Although we had been told we would be back home for a week after the initial orientation and swearing-in processes had been completed, there were still a large number of tearful partings. I was beginning to think that maybe it wasn't such a bad idea after all that no one had shown up to see me off.

We spent most of the day getting down to St. Paul. A couple of stops along the way were made to pick up some additional inductees from towns on the route who were also scheduled to report for military induction.

The food at the Ft. Snelling Induction Center was great. We ate at long tables set in rows under a tent. The food was served family style with 16 men at a table. Large steel pilchers of ice-cold milk sat at each end of the table. They were continually filled as the young teen-agers devoured not only huge quantities of milk but also all the other varieties of food. For many that had come from the larger cities, such quantities of food at one meal had never been available to them. Everyone thought the Army was going to be great. However, each would have a rude awakening and reality would set in as soon as each reached his training camp.

We completed all the prerequisites for induction by April 12th. I was given a week off after the induction ceremonies to return to Breckenridge and complete any unfinished business. It was also a time when I spent every possible moment with that lovely, dark-haired high school senior. It was going to be a difficult adjustment when the week was over. We would be setting out on different paths and I wondered whether all the wonderful memories of our high school days together would be sufficient to insure our feelings would remain strong during our lengthy separation. I knew there were boys in her class that were interested in her. Although it bothered me there was nothing I could do about it. I could only hope she felt as strongly about me as I did about her.

I should have shared a part of that week we were given with my dad. Even after all these years I have a feeling of guilt. It could have been the last visit for a very long time. It also could have been the last opportunity for a last visit. No thought or words were ever expressed that I might not return and I gave no thought to what his feelings might have been. I wished many times during those lonely hours on outpost duty in Italy and France that I had spent a greater part of that week with my dad. We could have gone fishing together or just sat around in the evening and talked. I realized in later years how little I knew about his early life before I was born. I should have had him share with me what his Army life was like and some of the things he had experienced in World War I.

After the week was up we returned to the induction center. Our days were filled from morning to evening with the prerequisites necessary to becoming a soldier. As I returned to Ft. Snelling, I had a strange feeling life was going to be drastically changed for me. I now knew my childhood was definitely over. It had been entirely too short.

During the period I was at the Reception Center at Ft. Snelling, I would be celebrating my twentieth birthday. I knew the Army had my records and was well aware my birthday was April 22nd. I couldn't imagine how they might make the day special for me. I fell asleep the night of the 21st thinking of what the possibilities might be. I thought I might even be excused from any duties that day. The next morning at 0430 hours a sergeant rudely shook me and said in a gruff voice, "Soldier, you are on KP today"? With the flashlight shining in my face, I sat up and said to him, "There must be some mistake in your records. It is my birthday today". He replied without any sign of exhilaration or emotion in his voice, " I don't give a damn if it is President Roosevelt's birthday. You are on KP". And then he was gone. I wanted to but I knew I better not lie back or I would fall asleep again. I was very disillusioned with the Army. I couldn't believe they wouldn't have more compassion for a person on his birthday. I was to find that this was inconsequential compared to what could happen to me later in my Army life.

One fellow that I went down to Fort Snelling with showed me a brochure he had gotten somewhere explaining a new branch of service that was being developed. It would not only provide excitement, thrills and a new, novel way to travel, but would result in an extra 50 dollars a month in jump pay. It was called the United States Army Paratroops. Imagine getting 50 dollars a month for being in service and an additional 50 dollars for flying around in airplanes. The total of 100 dollars was 40 dollars more than I was making at the Wilkin County Highway Department working 240 hours a month.

I had never been any further off the ground than halfway up the Hankinson water tower or up in the coal chute on the Soo Line Railroad in Hankinson. In the mid-30s my Uncle Reuben and I had jumped off a number of buildings using umbrellas and talked about what it would be like to jump out of planes and gently float to earth. Neither one of us had ever been up in a plane. We probably would have refused at that age if someone had asked us if we did want a plane ride.

The fellow inductee and I decided the United States Paratroops was the branch of Service we wanted to enter. I was sitting in the front row when the Orientation Officer asked if there were any volunteers for a new branch of service called the United States Army Paratroops. I raised my hand and he pulled my sheet out of a stack and placed it in a separate envelope. He then asked a couple of additional times and got no further responses. I was getting concerned and as I looked around the room and I saw my friend sitting in the back of the room. I gave him a puzzled look and he just smiled. At the conclusion of the meeting I asked him what happened. He indicated that after giving it further consideration he concluded that jumping out of planes could be dangerous.

I had to sign a sheet that stated "I do hereby volunteer to jump from a plane while in flight and land on the ground via parachute".

We were issued uniforms and a kit containing personal items such as toothbrush and toothpaste, shaving cream and razor, comb, etc. We were given shots for about every imaginable disease. This was followed by a physical examination. Nothing seemed slower than standing in a long line with nude men waiting for your turn to see the medical officer.

When the physical was completed there was another line with an officer that asked such questions as "Do you like girls?" I thought what business is that of his.

In those days "gay" meant "excited with merriment and a synonym was "lively". Most of us had never heard the word "homosexual" and wouldn't have known what it meant if we had heard it.

When we fell-out in what would become our daily mode of dress, we were a sad looking group. None of the uniforms fit properly. We had all pictured ourselves to look like those men we had seen in the movies. I guess we hadn't realized the uniforms came without ribbons and decorations. That was something one had to earn.

I was issued an Army Serial Number (37558391); a number that would become a part of me just as much as my name. Dan Chapman who had lived down the street from me for 47 years after the war evidently was in camp at the same time. His serial number is very close to mine. Whenever we talked about the military I reminded him he still owned the taxpayers a considerable amount of money. He was in the Timberwolf Division (104th) and his first day in combat was spent in Belgium. The Sergeant told Dan and his foxhole partner named Crawford from Texas to be especially alert since German patrols had been sighted in the area. Crawford kept falling asleep on his watch so Dan said he would take over. About 0200 hours an 88-mm shell came in. Crawford was dead and Dan was badly wounded. When personnel from his outfit came around the next morning one of the men remarked, "It looks like one of them is still alive." Dan recalls his thinking at the time, "I hope they are talking about me."

I often reminded him of the incident and of all the expense the taxpayer incurred for over a year in training, food, transportation, clothing and medical expense for his one day of combat. Our last discussion on the subject was just before his death on July 9, 1999. He indicated to me that money would be set aside in his will to reimburse the Government.

Since I was the only one in our class who had volunteered for the paratroops, I was put on a regular passenger train at the depot adjacent to Washington Street in Minneapolis with travel orders that read Toccoa, Georgia. I had never heard of the place. The rest of the class was going as a group to some other destination and traveled by troop train. I was beginning to have second thoughts. Why hadn't I just stayed with the rest of the fellows? There is safety in numbers. I was scared, lonely, and homesick. Suddenly the prospect of going into service no longer seemed interesting and exciting.

The rest of my activities relating to basic training, jump school, overseas duty in Italy, the jump into southern France on August 15, 1944, Battle of the Bulge beginning on December 16, 1944 and occupation of Berlin are contained in the books mentioned at the beginning of the chapter. There were so many pleasant memories resulting from military service. The 3-day passes into Nice, France during the fall of 1944 with lodging at Belgian King Leopold's winter home gave us a feeling of how the rich and famous lived. A 3-day pass to Paris in February 1945 provided memories that last a lifetime. The period from May 7 through July 1, 1945 was spent in Bavaria in southern Germany. We were in a beautiful mountainous setting and living in chalets. We hunted deer in the forests and fished trout in the cold, mountain streams. If the fish were not biting a hand grenade would bring eight or nine to the surface. Then we would flip a coin to see who had to wade out into the icy water to retrieve them. Life was wonderful. The war was over and we had survived.

Our "band of brothers" still meet at annual reunions and have traveled to Europe a number of times to visit battle sites. We have many French and Belgian friends in the areas where we fought. They welcome us with open arms during our visits and are eternally grateful for returning their freedom to them. Those sites are peaceful and calm today but are remembered for their moments of fear and concern.

I along with 698 other troopers loaded on to the SS Walter Forward at Le Harve, France on December 3, 1945. Excitement ran high because it was a day we had dreamed about for an awfully long time but never thought it would ever arrive.

Two days out of port we ran into a terrible December storm and many of us felt the old Liberty Ship would not survive. We had heard that other similar ships had problems with their steel welds not being able to withstand the pounding waves of the stormy Atlantic. No one was allowed on deck when the storm first hit; not even ship's crew. The bow would rise up high and then fall back hitting the water with a blow that caused the entire ship to vibrate. Everyone prayed that the welded seams would hold together. As the bow slipped under each wave you could hear the water splashing across the deck. The screw at the stern would spin freely in the air and also cause a terrible vibration. Those that tried to eat left most of it on the deck. They couldn't keep it down because of the pitching and rolling of the ship. The smell of regurgitated food mixed with oil fumes from the engine room made everyone sick. The steel deck was slippery and going from the mess area to the bunk created a real challenge. It was best to just stay in the bunk and wait out the storm.

After four days we reached the edge of the storm and were allowed up topside. What a relief to breathe fresh air again.

We arrived in New York Harbor on December 16th. Class A uniforms with neckties (which we hadn't worn since March 15th when we were presented with the Presidential Unit Citation by General Eisenhower in Mourmelon, France) and overcoats were the dress for the day

What a wonderful sight to sail by the Statue of Liberty. Fireboats gave us a "Welcome Home" salute. They also gave us a salute with their water sprays, whistles and horns. Tears were in the eyes of more than one as they lay over the ship's rail. Each was thinking his own private thoughts and I am certain many were thinking of those who went overseas with us but never had the opportunity to return.

Even today I think of that half hour period that it took to pull into the harbor, it is impossible to convey the joy and happiness that was felt. It was the conclusion of an episode in each of our lives and each of us has his own story to tell.

Four tugs pushed our Victory Ship into the Hudson River, and then sideways against the army pier in New Jersey. What a wonderful feeling we felt coming down that gangplank and being back in the good old U.S.A.

We were trucked to Camp Patrick Henry for processing and then sent to Camp Mc Coy December 20th for discharge. I arrived in Minneapolis a couple days later. I hopped on a streetcar to go see my mother. For three years everywhere we went transportation was free. The conductor in a very loud voice so all could hear asked, "Are you a special character, or what? The fare is 10cents." I sheepishly returned to the front of the car and dropped my dime in the container. I didn't know if I was going to like civilian life after all.

I arrived home Christmas morning. Fluffy snowflakes were gently falling. My footprints were the only evidence of life in the city. Homecoming was so different from how I had visualized it would be.

Many of the officers and some of the enlisted men remained in service after the war was over. Some of them were caught up in the Korean War in 1950 and a few died in that war.

An attempt was made to remain in contact with the men of the Unit and this led to the forming of the 517th

PRCT Association. With the coming of the computer age it became a little easier with e-mail to remain in contact and eventually a web site was created where a wealth of information about the members and their activities is posted today.

There have been many returns by members of the Unit to where time was spent during the period 1943-1945 in Italy, France, Belgium and Germany. We are always warmly welcomed and have many friends in the first three countries mentioned. They have adopted graves of our fallen comrades and placed and care for monuments at known locations where men have been killed.

I was President of the Association in 1999-2001 and 2009-2011. We are now in the process of reorganizing to turn the Association over to the second generation. The veterans are now too few in number and are either unable or unwilling to remain actively involved. For quite a period of time we held National Reunions every two years in cities around country. During my presidency in 2001 the National Reunion was held in Bismarck, North Dakota where I lived at the time. Some were a little reluctant to come to North Dakota but loved it by the time the reunion was concluded. Those attending from France and Belgium were thrilled. To them that was where the West began and anything about the wild, wild West thrilled and excited them. They had the opportunity to see real Native Americans and observe bison grazing along the highway on one of the bus trips. They told me that that opportunity alone was well worth the long trip over to America.

Our last reunion is scheduled for July 2011 and will be held in Atlanta, Georgia. Many of the members of the Unit will have been friends for 68 years.

CHAPTER 12

Life Immediately After WW II

During World War II price for grain was unusually high. Flax sold for more than eight dollars a bushel. There was a great demand for linseed oil for use in paints. Corn and wheat prices were also very high and farmers had come to believe these prices would continue long into the future. However, technological changes in farming methods and the over production encouraged by the war needs soon resulted in surpluses. This sent the prices for milk, grain and hogs tumbling drastically. Pork sold for 3 cents a pound and milk dropped to as low as 2 cents a quart.

I, like many of the returning service men, found adjusting to civilian life difficult. The daily routine seemed to require no challenges and contained no excitement. The contacts that continued to be made with the wartime buddies established that each handled their return to civilian life a little differently. Those from the California or coastal area had taken what was called their 52-40. The Government had a program where returning servicemen could sign up for unemployment if they couldn't find work. If they were unsuccessful in this endeavor they could collect 40 dollars per week for a period of 52 weeks. I had one buddy from Long Beach who spent the entire year lying on the beach. After that he began selling fitness equipment to the Hollywood stars.

As mention later in the book, I returned to my pre-service job in the Puget Sound Navy Yard in Bremerton, Washington. It was a difficult period. Many had stayed in military service and there were times when I wished I had. There was an indescribable closeness with those that I had served with. There were moments in the evening after retiring when I wondered what they were doing. I wondered if they also had had second thoughts about continuing their military service. A number of officers continued in the Service and most ended up with Korean service during the early 1950s.

After spending almost 6 months in Washington State Kay and I left for Los Angeles to be married. We had car trouble on the way down and had no other option other than to sell the car to an automobile agency at a six hundred-dollar loss.

After the wedding we spent two weeks in Long Beach attending plays and museums in the downtown area. Our apartment was 50 feet from a nice sandy beach and we spent way too much time in the bright California sunshine. A major burn can be received in just a few hours. Activities enjoyed during that two-week period are contained later in the book.

Kay and I returned to our hometown in Minnesota. I spent the summer of 1946 shocking grain for Leo Yaggie, a local farmer living approximately 3 miles east of Breckenridge along and adjacent to US Highway 210. The shocking of the thousands of bundles lying on a 160-acre field seems to be an impossible task to accomplish. However, at the end of the day it was a satisfying feeling to see many of those bundles standing in hundreds of shocks. I also spent a short time working for Al Holzbauer. Al's wife was a sister to Yaggie and had come from South Dakota in 1939 with all his worldly possessions in a hayrack pulled by a team of horses. Yaggie had given them a half section of land. I stopped to see Holzbauer August 29, 2010. Al and his wife had some ten years but the son told me they had talked about me enough that he felt as though he knew me.

My new wife and I spent the summer living with her folks. Weekends were spent at some lake in the State. My wife's father loved to fish and so did I. However, he didn't have an outboard motor and that meant I was assigned the oars each time we moved to a different spot. I was young and was still in terrific shape so I was happy to do it. As a result of that summer of fishing, we formed a close bond that lasted up to the time of his death at the age of 103.

Kay's family background can be traced back to the mid-1850s without too much difficulty. Her descendants originated from Eastern Germany and the Ukraine.

Her paternal grandfather, Franz Jonietz, was born October 8, 1855, near the Oder River in Upper Silicia in the village of Szczedrzyk. He died at the age of 85 and is buried in the small cemetery in the village of his birth.

Franz married Katherine Bednorz, who I assumed was born and raised in the same area, in 1883. She was a year younger than Franz was.

They had six sons born between 1883 and 1901. Kay's father, Thomas, was second in order of birth and was born on December 21, 1887. Thomas' youngest brother Ludwig died in 1978 at the age of 76. Two brothers died at an earlier age, Anton at age 50 and Franz at age 31. The other two brothers, Leonard and Paul, were 76 and 91 respectively, when they died.

Our son Tom visited with his grandfather's brother Paul in Berlin during his trip to Europe in 1970.

Kay's grandmother, Katherine, died in 1914 at the age of 58. Her grandfather remarried seventeen months later on March 5, 1916 to Pauline Kokat. He was 61 years old at the time, and the new bride was 29.

Seven children were born of this second marriage - two sons and five daughters. The two sons, Josef and Max, were killed in 1942 during the Battle for Stalingrad. One daughter, Agnes, died in 1985. Agathe, Maria, Hedwig, and Gertrude continue to live in the birthplace of Kay's father. Agathe's husband, Feliks, died on November 24, 1989.

Josef, Kay's uncle who was killed at Stalingrad in 1942, was married in 1940 and had two daughters. His wife, Anni, never remarried. I corresponded with Anni and Monika, a granddaughter of Josef and Anni for a number of years.

Kay's other Uncle Max, who was also killed in the same battle, had never married.

I also correspond with Kay's cousin Margarete, a daughter of Paul. Margarete's daughter, Claudia, and her granddaughter, Alice, came to Bismarck for a one-month visit in September 1989.

We have written to Kay's Aunt Gertrud and have received a photo of Franz's grave in Szsczdrzyk.

Prior to December 1989, it was difficult to move west from East Germany. After the prewar countries of Eastern Europe became independent and free of Soviet influence, the ability to relocate was no longer impossible, and many did move west. However, three of Franz's daughters mentioned above that remained at their place of birth do visit some of the relatives in the West occasionally. Agathe has a daughter living in Aachen, who she visits occasionally.

Kay's maternal grandfather, David Vaselenko, was born in 1875 in Sheepeke, a small village about 65 miles from Kiev in the Soviet Ukraine. He had three children at the time he migrated to the United States, Pauline, Fred, and Kay's mother, Sally.

They filed on a homestead in Bull Butte Township, North Dakota, where Kay's grandmother's brother, Mike Baybarz, helped them build a sod house.

David married Katherine Baybarz when he was 23 years old. She was 21 years old at the time. Six years later in July 1903, they arrived in America. Kay's grandmother, Katherine, had an uncle who had homesteaded in the Williston, North Dakota area and it was for this reason that they also came to northwest North Dakota.

Kay's grandfather, David, was killed at the age of 38. Shari Zapara, who wrote about the incident in her family history, states the following: "In 1914 David Vaselenko was hauling grain for a close friend. An argument somehow started. The friend was a man of quick temper and in his drunken state, he killed David. He hit him with a stove lid and hit him so hard that a piece of his skull was knocked loose and brains were scattered about. He put David out by the horses so it would look like the horses had kicked him and killed him. Grandma (Kay's Aunt Pauline) said that the man would get drunk and want to fight. When he was in this condition at home, instead of hitting his wife (because he knew he would kill her), he would go out and break the hayrack. Grandma and her family finally found what in truth happened, but no one had any money, no one cared so the man was never sent to prison. After the incident, he went to Canada, but because he felt so bad about killing his best friend, he didn't live long himself."

Kay's grandmother continued to operate the farm with the help of her two oldest children, Pauline and Fred. During the early 1930's, she lost the farm during the height of the Depression. Her son, Fred, took over the farm, survived the rough times, and had a successful operation at the time of his death on July 18, 1948. Fred's wife, son and daughter continue to receive benefits today from the 1903 homestead. She lived on the farm for a short time before moving into Williston. In 1939, she moved to California where she lived with her son Andrew and his wife Mary, who operated a grocery store in San Pedro. She died on April 18, 1951, of stomach cancer and is buried at Forest Lawn Cemetery in Glendale, California.

Soon the summer was over and Kay and I moved to Fargo, North Dakota. I registered for college at what now is the North Dakota State University. Because polio was so prevalent and it was assumed crowds contributed to the disease, school didn't start until October 1, 1946. I decided I would continue straight through the summer courses and finish in three years. Many of the other veterans going to school under the GI Bill also elected to follow this plan of action. Most were married and since they had already lost three years of their lives due to military service all wanted to get through school as quickly as possible and get out into the job market. It worked for me. I was gainfully employed with the Department of the Interior in September 1949.

CHAPTER 13

MY FIRST YEAR HOME FROM SERVICE

It had been almost three years since my parents had divorced. It also had been almost three years since I left for service. During this period my dad had always worked the holidays so others could be home with their families. So this Christmas morning 1945, as I walked in the door at 5:30 AM, my dad was just leaving for work. His eyesight was diminishing as a result of his diabetic condition and he wasn't certain who I was until I spoke. I detected a slight shudder in his shoulders and I could see the relief in his face that I had returned safely. We had a brief conversation and then he dutifully left for work. It was so different from what I had imagined as a homecoming for so many months. It was always visualized as a happy moment. Now suddenly it was over and I had a void feeling. I thought is this what I had spent so much time thinking about. The few moments spent greeting each other and then the silence after he left gave me an empty feeling in my stomach.

After my dad was gone I sprawled across the bed hoping to catch a little sleep. Because of the excitement of returning home, a day I had dreamed of for so long, I didn't sleep at all on the train. The sound from the car wheels hitting the joints in the rails sounded like I'm going home, I'm going home, I'm going home.

Now there was no excitement. I wondered what my buddies were doing. As I mentioned above my return was so much different than I had expected. Suddenly I was sad. It was strange world I had returned to and I wasn't certain I was going to like it.

Later that day I went to Kay's home for Christmas dinner. Another family had been invited and the conversation during the meal seemed so trivial and unimportant. The topics being discussed were of no interest to me and my mind kept wandering back to the separation center where I was bidding farewell to my buddies. It was a joyous group all excited about leaving for home and promising to remain in contact with each other. Over the past three years we had talked about what this day might be like and now it had arrived. As with me I am certain the others also felt a degree of sadness set in. We had as they say today been a band of brothers. Now that band had been broken into many separate pieces and the brotherhood disappeared as each went separate ways.

On New Year's Day, 1946, Kay and I spent the day together walking around the town that had held so many memories before I left for Service. We were trying to fill each other in on the many little things that happened to each of us since that evening we parted two years earlier in Willmar, Minnesota. The events I experience in those two years were not totally understood by Kay and I could not convey to her how important they had been. Her two years of events seemed so unexciting to me. It was as though the two of us had lived in different worlds.

In the evening we went to the movie "Week-end at the Waldorf" at the Ridge Theater. Try as we might neither of us were able to capture those feelings we experienced prior to my leaving for Service. We were so in love and so afraid that separation would result in something happening to that love. It would take time since we were strangers in a world I felt uncomfortable in. I'm sure Kay could sense I was not the same person I was when I last saw her in February 1944. Thus ended the first day of the 1946 and my first day home in this strange new world.

Three days later Kay packed her luggage and returned by train to her job with the Restaurant Association in the Puget Sound Navy Yard in Bremerton, Washington. We had spent such a short time together after my return home from service. I continued to search for that special feeling I thought I would experience when I got home. Each day became worse. I had visualized coming home and all the high school classmates being there. We would sit around Casey's Bar and compare war stories. Suddenly it dawned on me the war had been over for nearly five months. The local servicemen had drifted home during that period, a few at a time and found the same situation existed as I did. They changed into their civilian clothes and got on with their lives. I also decided then that if military uniforms were out, I better start shopping for clothes.

It was a strange experience. We hadn't worried about our wardrobe during the previous three years. Once a year we would change from summer uniform to winter uniform. Now each morning we had to make a decision as to what we would wear for the day. You can imagine my difficulty in going out to select a wardrobe that would convey what the well-dressed returning serviceman was wearing. However, I am certain my knowledge of fabrics and the ability to color coordinate made my selection the talk of the town.

My dad and I went up town each evening, drank beer, talked and then went home. He was happy to be with me but to me, the routine seemed so unexciting and boring. I am certain he would have been happy if I had spent more time at home. This would have been a great opportunity for me to catch up on all the things that might have happened to him during my absence. However, as with most others the age I was, we thought only of ourselves. We wanted to get on with our lives. I could have just as well spent a month at home painting his house, repairing broken items, fishing with him and create a closer bond between the two of us.

None of my friends were around, and the town had nothing in the way of activities. I sometimes suspect young people in the smaller towns take up drinking out of boredom.

On January 10th, I sent Kay a telegram telling her I would be arriving in Bremerton on January 13th. The train was still extremely crowded with returning servicemen and I had to stand about two days of the three-day train trip. I ate more often because it provided a chance to sit for a period of time at the lunch counter.

Kay met me at the Seattle depot and we took the ferry over to Bremerton. It is a nice ride and very scenic. It also was nice to be back where the first exciting things in my life began four years earlier. However, the original thrill I had experienced in traveling to that area of the country was not there this time. I guess I had seen too many things in the last three years to be overly excited but the memories of that first trip still lingered. The first sighting of Mt. Rainer was remembered as vividly as if it had happened a week earlier.

I had arranged for a room at the Fred Tilton home on Warren Avenue. Fred was a father-in-law to the Ronald Rockwell to whom I was an apprentice in the Sheetmetal Shop prior to my release for military service in December 1942.

This was only a couple of blocks from where Kay was renting. We would meet in the morning and walk to work together and usually have breakfast on the way.

Shortly after arriving in Bremerton, I began looking for a car. I ultimately purchased a 1942 Dodge for $1650, which had 60,000 plus miles on it. In those days the reading on the odometer wasn't too meaningful. It could have been rolled over once, or turned back by an unscrupulous owner. It may have also been a taxicab in Seattle where I purchased it. Compounding the problem was my lack of knowledge relating to the service and maintenance of a vehicle. It never occurred to me that one of the first things I should have done was change the oil and filter, lubricate, and check the transmission fluid. This all contributed to the future problems we would have on our way to California in June.

Kay and I continued to enjoy each other's company for the next five months. We went on picnics, skiing at Mt. Rainier, drives along the Hood Canal, trips to Seattle, over to Puyallup for the Daffodil Festival and visiting other sights in the area.

Kay was aware my personality had changed, but I couldn't tell her the reason for the change or the cause. I really didn't know, but I suspect it was resentment against what we called the "civilians". They didn't seem to understand or care what we had gone through, and their main concern seemed to be how soon they might be able to get butter and stockings again. Most servicemen thought, "Oh, how they must have suffered".

I picked up where I had left off at the shipyard three years earlier. As a returning serviceman, my job was available as a guaranteed right. I was back at X-17 Sheetmetal Shop working with Eugene Rockwell. However, everything seemed anticlimactic. The old wartime excitement associated with the activities of our work was no longer there. I no longer pressed out mess trays from square pieces of stainless steel or bench pressed steel cabinets, desks and lockers for officers' quarters for ships no longer being built. The purpose and goals existing during wartime were lacking. Even Rocky, who had no idea how it sounded to me, made the remark, "If only the war would have lasted six more months, I could have paid off the mortgage on my house." No more overtime. How sad I thought that was.

We went out to dinner on Kay's 21st birthday and I gave her a music box. It was a miniature piano and when the top cover was lifted the music began to play I Love You Truly. We were both so young and felt we had a future ahead of us that would never end. On January 23rd I slipped a diamond on Kay's finger and we began to plan that future in a little more detail. The next day at work she was the center of attraction and everyone wished her the best.

Kay's sister, Lorraine and her school friend, Sally Halvorson, were also working and living in Bremerton. We all spent many evenings together, roller-skating, bowling, movies, and riding. Since Kay did most of her own clothes, she also spent quite a bit of time at the USO where cutting tables and sewing machines were available for her use. She was sewing her wedding gown.

On Valentine's Day, Kay was at the USO and Lorraine and I were home. Suddenly the pictures on the wall began to move back and forth. Lorraine and I looked at each other to assure ourselves that we weren't just imagining something. As soon as I realized it was an earthquake, I knew we had to get out of the building. We ran to the vacant lot across the street. It was the first quake either of us had ever experienced.

On March 15th and 19th nylons became available at Penny's. Lines formed that were two blocks long. Kay had no money with her, so she had me run home to get some. The run home caused me to perspire. I then stood for two hours in a cold, gentle rain to get one pair of stockings. This resulted in the worst cold I ever remember having and did not endear me to these strange civilians with a warped sense of values.

On April 12th, Kay got a large monthly increase in pay amounting to $7.52. I don't know if the people where she worked thought this might make her reconsider her decision to marry and move away. Maybe she was just eligible for the pay raise.

On April 21st, Easter Sunday, we put on our Sunday's best and went to Seattle. After attending church at the Immaculate Conception Catholic Church, Sally, Lorraine, Kay and I had a picnic in Woodland Park near the University of Washington.

The next evening after work, Kay I went out for a drive along the Hood Canal and on our return to Bremerton, we celebrated my 23rd birthday by having dinner at the Missouri Cafe. Afterwards we drove along Washington Avenue to a point that leads to the oceanfront. We parked and watched a full moon rise and reflect off the water. It never occurred to us that evening that a lifetime is a fairly short journey.

Lorraine was quite interested in a Navy man named Ralph. Everywhere we went in a group, Lorraine and Ralph were included. On April 25th Ralph left for New York and as far as I know, that was the end of the romance.

One evening after we dropped Kay off at the USO to sew on her gown, Lorraine asked to drive the car I had purchased. We told Kay we would be back in an hour to pick her up. As we continued down the street all signal lights changed perfectly as though they were synchronized to our speed. Each light turned green just as we got to it. As we left the downtown area, the streets became somewhat narrower. As an approaching car drew nearer, Lorraine looked over at me and asked, "Is there enough room to get by?"

"Certainly", I said. "How long have you been driving?"

"I've never driven before; Mother always got too nervous when I wanted her to teach me," she said.

I told her to pull over to the curb and stop. I often wondered what might have happened had those green lights not been so perfectly timed.

Early in May, we went to a carnival at Port Orchard and spent a weekend at Paradise Inn on Mt. Rainier. Kay, Sally, Lorraine and I received skiing instructions and then started up the mountain by towrope. Kay had a little trouble hanging on to the rope, especially after the man behind her told her that she had a hole in her slacks. We got bad sunburn and a few bruises.

On May 20th, Kay started sewing on her wedding gown. Almost nightly, she was at the USO making certain she would finish the gown before we left for California on June 5th.

The morning of June 5th, we left Bremerton at 6:30 A.M. heading for Tacoma and south to Portland. How stupid I must have been. The car I had purchased two months earlier had never had an oil change while I had it and no telling how much longer it had been before I got it since the oil had been changed. In fact I don't even recall ever having looked at the dipstick. So we start blissfully for Los Angeles, a city more than a thousand miles away and not knowing if there was oil in the car.

We stopped a short time in Portland and then continued on our way. About 8:00 P.M. near Wolf Creek, Oregon, the car engine developed a knock. The town was small and would not have the garage facilities necessary to fix the engine. Since we were on the downhill slope leading to Grants Pass, I shut off the engine and coasted mile after mile. I don't know if Lorraine was serious or not, but her comment was, "The car runs better with the engine off. Why don't we go all the way to LA this way?"

Even if she had been joking, I was in no mood for funny remarks. We had a deadline to meet and just didn't care about including trouble delays in our schedule. The church was available to us for June 12th and may not become available again for weeks or even months.

We got a hotel room but I worried more than I slept. What if they didn't have the necessary parts or what if it took a week to fix? The next morning, I took the car to Carner's Automotive Service Company, the authorized Dodge dealer in town. It was suspected that we had bearing problems but an attempt was made at one other option in hopes it would correct the problem and get us on our way. We got about five miles out of town and the same noise started. We turned around and came back while it was still possible

A decision had to be made. The car needed new bearings and possibly a new crankshaft. This could take a week to repair, and we could not afford that much time. I decided to sell the car. I had paid $1,650 for the car, but under Office of Price Administration guide lines; I could only receive $1,050 for it. The car had cost me about a dollar a mile plus gasoline. I was going to say plus gas and oil, but evidently I didn't spend too much on oil.

Kay and Lorraine had just thrown their things from their apartments in the back seat and now all the little items would have to be packed. We started looking for boxes so that all the unnecessary things could be shipped home. We put Lorraine on the corner with all the items we wanted to pack and ship. Old women would come by and ask her if she was holding a rummage sale. One of the items Kay insisted on keeping were old magazines so that she could see in the future how much the styles had changed. The box of magazines cost 20 dollars to ship home. This was equivalent to two days wages at that time. Later, we moved the magazines from Breckenridge to Fargo. Three years later we moved the magazines from

Fargo to Bismarck. After storing them about 20 years, they were moved to the local landfill. When I asked Kay about the style changes, she said, "I can always go to the library and look at their old magazines if I ever want to see how they have changed".

Had I been able to see into the future while standing on that corner getting those magazines ready for shipment home, there may never have been a wedding to worry about.

We got everything ready, shipped off on a bus to Breckenridge and then we boarded the 8:30 P.M. Greyhound to Los Angeles. We arrived the next morning at 9:30 and took a cab over to Elvina's home.

On June 8th, we went to City Hall for blood tests and then were taken to San Pedro, where Kay's mother and dad were staying with Andy and Mary Vaselenko. The next day we spent at the beach, the most relaxing day we had in quite some time. On June 10th, we got our marriage license and then went to Alveria Street and to Chinatown with Elvina and Dennis.

Finally, the evening of June 12th arrived. It was a beautiful evening, but I was beginning to wish it was over. The wedding was held at the Wee Kirk O' the Heather Church at Forest Lawn Memorial Park in Glendale. The church is an exact reconstruction of the little church in Dumfriesshire, Scotland, where Annie Laurie worshipped during her lifetime. It was a small wedding with only 24 close friends and relatives in attendance. The minister was Joseph Calderone, Elvina's first husband. Tom Zapara was best man and Lorraine Jonietz was Maid of Honor. The usher was Kay's cousin Leonard Zapara.

Rose petals fell from the ceiling as Kay came down the aisle. A soloist sang "I Love You Truly", "Because", and the "Lord's Prayer".

Her gown had a very full net skirt and brocaded satin top with sweetheart neckline and cap sleeves. She wore long white gloves and a fingertip veil. Her shoes were white sandals, and she carried a bouquet of white carnations and white orchids.

After the wedding, coins were dropped in a wishing well out in front of the church. I put her rings on and recited a wish that we would both always be as happy as we were this beautiful evening. We then went over to Kay's cousin Elvina for a reception and had pictures taken. We found our clothing in our suitcases had been sewn full of rice. Later in the evening, we were taken downtown by a car that must have had every tin can in Los Angeles tied on behind it. We spent two days at the Clark Hotel and then left for Long Beach, where we rented an apartment at 1530 Ocean Boulevard right on the beach. We remained at the apartment for nine days and spent our time at the "Pike" during the day and went downtown in the evening. The Pike was an amusement park located across the bay from where the Queen Mary is presently anchored. The "Pike" was demolished many years ago. We saw the opera "Naughty Marietta" and went to a number of movies. Some of the days we just walked the beach looking for shells and spent our time swimming.

On June 22nd, Tom and Leonard Zapara and Lorraine picked us up, and we went up into the mountains exploring for gold and fishing for trout. For the next week after that, we spent our time visiting Warner Bros. Studios, Hollywood stars' homes, CBS Studios and Forest Lawn.

On June 30th, we spent the day at the beach and then left for home by train at 8:30 P.M. We arrived in Breckenridge on July 3rd at 3:00 P.M. The next day Kay's parents, Kay and I went fishing.

On July 8th, an Alfred Slorby and I met at the intersection of 7th Street and Mendenhall Avenue. I was driving my new in-laws' car at the time, and I now had another 112 dollars to pay out for repair of a left front fender and grill. It took eleven days to complete the repair work, and I am sure Tom and Sally were not too happy about being without a car during that time.

I spent the summer working at the farm of Leo Yaggie, located on the north side of Hwy. 210, about three miles east of Breckenridge. Most of the work related to grain harvesting, but I did spend one week in which I cleaned the hog barn. After working in the middle of the mess for about an hour, you can no longer detect any smell. However, that was not true when I got home. Kay would insist I strip down in the back yard and then she would wash me down with the garden hose. After a few nights, I had a feeling the neighbors were gathering at their windows when I came home from work.

We spent the rest of the summer at Kay's folks. We usually all went fishing on weekends and attended the Wilkin County Fair for a week in August. My brother Bob was separated from his wife, and we saw him occasionally, since he lived in Breckenridge. Early in September, I bought a trailer house from Clark Hanson that needed considerable repair and maintenance. I began fixing it up so it would be ready to move into by the time school started. Kay sewed drapes and made a bedspread to match. I repainted the inside and repaired a corner which had a hole knocked through it. On September 26th, Clark pulled it to Fargo for us, and we placed it on the campus lot across from the old Pharmacy building. We moved in and it was nice to be by ourselves for a change.

I registered for school on Tuesday, October 1st. School had been delayed that fall because of the polio problem. They suspected that the disease was more prevalent where crowds gathered. Kay started working in the Business Office at Old Main shortly after I started classes.

I went out for football that fall, but after coming home bruised each evening, I decided after one week I could find better things to do with my late afternoons.

I also reported for basketball when the season started and did make the Baby Bison squad. We had a fairly successful season, losing only two games and winning 13 straight after the Christmas Holidays. The highlight of the season was the two wins over the University of North Dakota Sioux.

We spent the Thanksgiving and Christmas Holidays at Kay's folks. Christmas shopping didn't take long; there wasn't that much money to spend. Tommy was old enough to enjoy the Christmas lights and the attention he continually got from his grandparents. It is hard to believe Tom is today (2010) almost as old as his grandfather was that first Christmas we spent at his grandparents.

So ended my first year as a civilian and I think I had adjusted very well in that time. I was just about like the rest of the civilians.

CHAPTER 14

College Years 1946 through 1949

When I came home from California on July 3, 1946, following our wedding, my intentions were to apply for admission at the University of Minnesota. This I did near the end of July, thinking I was plenty early since school wouldn't be starting until September. In a few weeks, I got a response indicating they had 38,000 students returning from the Spring Quarter, which was about the maximum they could handle at that time. They suggested I apply the following Spring. I knew if I took a job somewhere until that time, there still wasn't any assurance that I would be accepted in the spring. There was also a great chance I may get in a rut and never start school. I was also afraid that if I settled down in Breckenridge, even for a short period, I might get so entrenched that I wouldn't get out.

After receiving the U of M's letter, I began thinking of some other options. I didn't want to get too far from familiar surroundings. I still needed the security that came with being near those I knew. I had taken on the responsibility of a new wife, which was a little scary after having no real responsibility for the three years prior to that. Life suddenly was no longer carefree and simple.

About the third week in August, I sent my application to the North Dakota Agricultural College in Fargo. A few days later, I received a notice that I had been accepted in the School of Engineering. However, classes would not be starting until October 1. There was a concern that Polio was much more prevalent where crowds gathered during warm weather. This delay was fine with me. I needed to find some type of housing for the new bride. I had made a hurried check of what was available near the college and found out very quickly that nothing suitable was available within our price range.

I then purchased an old trailer from Clark Hanson for 600 dollars. He had been using it as a headquarters in the field during harvest time. It was obvious, from a cursory check, that a lot of cleaning and some repair work would be needed before it would be habitable. I repaired the roof leaks and did some painting, and Kay sewed curtains for the windows and a bedspread for the bed. The trailer was so small that in order for one person to move from one end to the other, the second person had to sit down on the bed. Our cook stove was a combination toaster and dual hot plate we had received from my brother Bob as a wedding present. It remained under the stairway for many years at 917 Midway Drive as a reminder of what can be done with so little. Kay turned out gourmet meals with that two-burner hot plate.

I registered for school on Tuesday, October 1st. Tuition was approximately 30 dollars a quarter, and our books were around 15 dollars. We were also allotted a certain amount of money for paper, pencils, and other supplies under the GI Bill. I remember the question arose as to whether the slide rule should be qualified as a necessary tool in our education. It was a major item since the cost was in the neighborhood of 15 dollars. It was argued that not only would we need it all through school, but would probably use it the rest of our lives in our work. It wasn't too long before it became a museum piece, and today many people don't know what a slide rule is. In addition to the tuition, we received a check for living expenses. Initially it was 65 dollars a month. This was later increased to 75 dollars, then to 90 dollars and to 105 dollars when Tom was born. So you could say Tom was worth 15 dollars a month to us during our college time, not counting expenses such as diapers, buggy, Pablum, ABDEC, etc.

After receiving our check shortly after the first of the month, we usually went up town for dinner and then to a movie. Toward the end of the month, we were on a steady diet of goulash. Macaroni was very cheap, and hamburger was around 19 cents a pound. I still like it, but Kay has to force it down.

Our school activity ticket, which came as part of our registration fee, included on-campus entertainment. On February 3, 1947, we saw Paul Robeson. Other plays and lyceums were presented throughout the year.

We spent many of our weekends in Breckenridge, usually going by train Friday after school and coming back Sunday evenings by bus. The time schedules for the two modes of transportation were ideal for us since the train came through at 5:00 P.M. and the bus left at 7:30 P.M. We were home for longer periods of time during major holidays.

During the summer, Tom and I went fishing every weekend. He loved to fish more than anything else he did. Kay and Sally occasionally went along, but most of the time they preferred to sleep in. Sally would fix us a big breakfast about 5:00 A.M. and pack a big lunch. We would then start out for Norway, Stalker, Blanche, or Star Lake. I would be eating all day long, and there was still food remaining on the way home. Tom would say, "Eat all you can, and what you can't eat, throw out the window, or she may cut us short the next time." Sometimes we didn't arrive home until 10:00 P.M., and then there were usually fish to clean after that. Tom liked beer, and he got mighty thirsty sitting on a hot lake all day. Otter Tail County was "dry" at that time, and it was always a fast ride to Foxholm, which was in Wilkin County, to the little passenger train coach along Highway 210 that had been converted to a tavern.

It seemed as though Fargo experienced many more snowstorms at that time than they do now. We looked forward to storms since it brought a day of relief from school, a day that could be used for catching up on some studying or a day to sleep late and party with the neighbors. We usually played whist or monopoly.

On February 12, 1947, Kay got a new oven, and my weight was never the same again. She loved to bake, and it was never the same thing twice; she loved to try new recipes. She made Baked Alaskan for a group of women one evening. It is an ice cream dessert with a topping of meringue. The directions indicated the dessert should be placed in the oven at 450 degrees for 40 seconds to brown the meringue. Kay left it in the oven for 40 minutes, and you can imagine what happened. The dessert was served with spoons.

On April 13, 1947, Kay attempted to make donuts for the first time. It became an all day's project, and, eventually, I became involved in it. The dough was so sticky that once you got it in your hands you couldn't get it off. We finally got a few donuts made, but they were too tough to eat. We put them out in the built-on shed, and even the mice refused to touch them. I suggested she sell the formula to some glue factory.

Kay's mother brought her an icebox on April 18, 1947. We were gradually accumulating all the requirements needed to establish Kay as a full-fledged homemaker. There were a few things she had to master though, before receiving a certificate. One was making toast. We had the old-fashioned type toaster, which required the sides be dropped down and the toast turned over. She was making toast one noon for egg salad sandwiches. All at once the smoke came pouring out of all the windows of the trailer. Kay came running out of the trailer into the middle of the complex, yelling, "The trailer is on fire, the trailer is on fire." Everyone came over to help, and then found out it was the toast burning. She thanked them, and then, went in to proceed to burn two more slices.

Most of the students living in the trailer courts went to school year around. Our main objective was to get the education, get steady employment, and try to make up the three years of life most of us had lost by being in service. The depression years were less than ten years behind us. Nothing was more important and desired at that time than security and a decent income.

On weekends during the summer months, we either went home or, if we didn't, we would rent a cabin with the Ericksons, Hofstrands, or Pratschners and go to Star, Lida or Pelican Lake. It was right after one of these weekends that Craig Hofstrand was born on May 19, 1947. We were a little concerned he might be born in the boat.

The July 4th weekend in '47 was spent at Stalker Lake with Ken and Lil and Howard and Lorraine. Neither couple was married as yet. Howard had never fished, and we were going to teach him how to cast. One thing we failed to tell him when he brought the rod and reel around in the circular motion of casting that he was suppose to hang on to the rod. All the equipment went sailing out from the boat. We attempted to snag it with the other lines, but gave up after a half-hour. We spent most of our time swimming and sunning. Before the weekend was over, everyone had painful sunburn.

After returning to Fargo following the July 4th weekend, Kay was shopping at de Lendrecies. She bumped a rack full of dishes, and they came tumbling down. Kay moved back quickly from the scene of her destruction, and then as the crowd started gathering from all over the store, she also started moving toward the scene of her crime asking, "What happened? What happened?"

We had unexpected company occasionally. Two days after Kay's de Lendrecies' episode, Van Norden stopped to see us. We went to the Gardner Hotel for dinner. It would have been nice to have such things as credit cards in those days. I don't know where we came up with extra cash out of the clear blue when we needed it. A few days after Van left, Leonard Zapara from Los Angeles stopped in on his way to Williston. He was driving a beautiful, red convertible, which made us both envious.

On July 19th, Van Norden came again on his way to Alaska to go hunting and fishing. We again went out to dinner. He may have been paying for the dinners; I don't recall, but I am sure we never had enough cash lying around that would make two dinners out possible in the same month.

Early in August, we began preparing for the wedding Lorraine and Howard had scheduled for August 4th. Howard and his brother Merlin arrived in Breckenridge on August 2nd. The next day Howard's folks from Nebraska arrived. The wedding was held in the First Lutheran Church on Sixth Street. Kay and Merlin were attendants. The bride and groom spent the first night in the Wahpeton Hotel, and then honeymooned in the mountains of Colorado. The temperature remained around 100 degrees the day of the wedding. Air-conditioning was a luxury of the future at that time.

Shortly after the wedding, Kay's hay fever settled in her lungs. Toward the end of August, her condition became so severe that her boss, Edith Toring from the Business Office, took her to the doctor. The doctor sent her to the clinic, and she was diagnosed as having bronchial asthma. She spent the next three days in bed.

On October 3rd, Kay had a major purchase delivered to Trailer 47 S. Her Singer Sewing Machine had arrived. Oh, Happy Day! No more running to Ceres Hall or Roosevelt School. She spent her entire savings, $162.50, which had been accumulated over the years. It represented everything she had saved from baby sitting jobs, working at the little store on south 5th Street, and working at the commissary in the shipyard. The rest of the money she had earned was spent on shoes.

We spent the Thanksgiving and Christmas Holidays of 1947 in Breckenridge. We were home a week at Thanksgiving and went home on December 19th for Christmas. We attended the Red River Valley Holiday Basketball Tournament. In no time at all, the holidays were over, and we took the afternoon train back to Fargo on January 4th. It was a little tough to have to think of school again.

We saw Bob frequently all through January, February, and March. We always enjoyed his company, and if we didn't just sit around and talk, we would go to a movie or the college basketball game. It was nice to see so much of him.

Kay got her new Sunbeam Mixmaster on February 13, 1948, and the next day I got a Valentine cake. I also got many more high calorie things after that.

On my 25th birthday, Kay had all the neighbors in for coffee and cake. I had completed my first quarter century.

Our civil engineering class left for Bismarck early Friday morning May 21, 1948, on its way to view work progress on Garrison Dam. I had never been to Bismarck before, and I couldn't believe what terrible shape Main Street was in. The large potholes were so numerous that it was impossible to miss them when driving. We stopped long enough to eat at the GP Hotel lunch counter and then drove up to the dam site. It was difficult to believe they had to build a town before they could start building the dam. Every construction project I had ever been associated with in the past never was involved in the welfare of the workers. It was interesting to see the size of the equipment and the enormity of the project undertaken. Never had I heard of a job that would take eight years to finish. We left the construction site shortly after lunch on Saturday and arrived back in Fargo at 6:00 P.M. We had 18 members in the class, and the trip required 3 cars. It was an enjoyable field trip, but much too short. I never dreamed at the time that I would end up working and living in Bismarck the rest of my life.

The following weekend Kay and I went to Breckenridge for Memorial Day. I found a good buy on an outboard motor. Vertin Furniture had a new 5HP Champion for 139 dollars. We spent the weekend with her folks at Blanche Lake and what a treat it was to go fishing and not have to row to our favorite spot. The motor was noisy, but for the times it was considered large and powerful. We were now able to move with ease and try many locations on the lake. I use to sort of discourage moving before we got the motor, since I always had to do the rowing. After the acquisition, I wanted to troll all the time, but Tom preferred still fishing. Rather than race from one spot to another, I would troll between locations.

Early in June I got a small crow that had fallen out of a nest. I fed him worms and hamburger, and he ate constantly. I guess that is why they grow to full size in such a short period of time. I named him "Blackie", and he started following me everywhere. When I went to class he would sit on the building until I came out. I don't know how he recognized me from all the other students, but as soon as I came out, he would start his screeching and fly from tree to tree until we got to the trailer. Then he would fly down to the steps. You didn't dare leave anything lying around like keys or he would pick them up and fly on top of a building or power pole. He would come to eat when I called him, and he loved to sit on my head when I walked around.

One weekend Louie, Ericksons, Kay and I went to Star Lake to fish. We took Blackie with us, and he sat in the front of the boat with Louie. Louie thought it was great sport to feed the crow worms. However, he would hang onto the worm. After the crow would swallow most of it, Louie would pull the worm up again. Before leaving the lake we gave the crow to Roeds, the people who rented the boat to us. We found out later that the crow had been in the back of their pickup, and they were unaware of it when they went to town. Somewhere along the way they lost him.

We spent our second wedding anniversary at a cabin on Star Lake. We spent the weekend fishing with Pratschners and Ericksons. I gave Kay two sterling silver soupspoons.

The July 4th weekend was spent again with Howard, Lorraine, Ken, Lil, Tom and Sally. As usual, the time was spent fishing, swimming, eating and reading. Everyone got the annual sunburn. This was usually the first anyone got any sun and no one had sense enough to take it easy. We spent this holiday at Star Lake.

Kay's Uncle Fred died at Williston on July 20th, 1948. Kay took the train the next evening and arrived in Williston at 7:20 A.M. Sally, Tom, Agnes, Alex, Andy and Kay's grandmother were already there. The funeral was held on July 23rd, and Kay came back to Fargo on July 25th.

On August 16th, Kay told her mother she thought she was pregnant. Everyone was happy, but I was a little concerned too. I would have felt better if I was out of school and had a job lined up. Hopefully, everything would work out all right.

We left on a Northern Minnesota and Canadian vacation with Joe and Audrey Pratschner in their '38 Ford on August 21st. We spent a short time in Bemidji, taking a speedboat ride, seeing Paul Bunyon and other tourist sights. From there we went on to the Skyline Drive in Duluth and then to a cabin on Rainy Lake. The mosquitoes were the largest I had ever seen anywhere.

We fished a little in that area and then went on to Ft. Frances and Kenora in a few days. We ended up shopping in Winnipeg, which seemed to put more energy in the women. They ended up buying yarn, silverware, and china. We were all happy to get home.

On August 30th, Steven Robinson and I started working for S.J. Groves Construction Company on a new paving job being put in for Highway 81 north of Fargo. Our job was to remove the steel forms placed for use in placing the concrete and then move them ahead to be reused on the uncompleted portion of the highway. Being out of shape made the work that much more difficult the first few days. The forms weighed about 150 pounds, and we were loading them all day long on the flatbed of a truck. It also seemed that the wind was blowing against us each day so that when we lifted the forms all the sand and gravel on the forms would blow back in our faces. At the completion of the first day of work, Steve and I just came home and lay on the grass. We didn't eat or go into the trailer. We just slept there until the next morning. Steve said recently if it hadn't been for me, he would not have reported for work the next morning. Steve doesn't know it, but if it hadn't been for him I wouldn't have reported for work that next morning either. As the days continued, the work seemed to become easier. By the time the next quarter started, we were in pretty good shape, and we were also a little more certain we wanted to finish school so that we could do something other than move steel forms for a living.

On September 12th, Tom, Sally, Lorraine, Kay, and I left for Jamestown at noon to attend Ken and Lil's wedding. After the reception was over about 11:30 P.M., we went to the car to leave for home. Tom had to go to work the next morning. We got in the car, and the key broke off in the ignition lock. We fooled around for awhile trying to find someone who might be able to fix it, but finally gave up. Tom and I found someone at 3:30 A.M. who was going to Fargo. We bummed a ride and got to Fargo in a couple of hours. Kay slept in the car at Jamestown and Sally and Lorraine spent the night in the show window of the local car dealer. The car was fixed by 9:30 A.M., and they arrived in Fargo about noon.

When Tom and I got to Fargo earlier that morning, we bought a few rolls and then walked over to Moorhead where he was going to hitchhike to Breckenridge on Highway 75. I got him to the edge of town and then walked back to the college. Later in the day, he came back to the trailer, and I found out he didn't have the nerve to put his thumb out indicating he wanted a ride. He then rode home with Sally.

We were riding around town with the Pratschners the evening of November 6th. We saw a car hit a little girl on Broadway. She was taken to the hospital and died the next day. That sight flashed back to me a few years later when I saw Mark lying in the middle of Rosser Avenue.

Kay's dad came to Fargo for a checkup on November 20th. They diagnosed his condition as pernicious anemia, and he would need shots for the rest of his life.

The next day we were notified that our new 6 cylinder, 90 hp, maroon, 1948 Plymouth was here. What an exciting day that was. We had been waiting two years for this notice. We cashed in the bonds we had and made the other necessary financial arrangements required and picked up the car on November 24th. The basic cost of the car was $1,671.80 and then another 432.05 dollars for extras making a total cost of $2,103.85. One didn't dare say take some of the extras off or you may end up waiting another year. We picked up my dad and Edith and drove to Fergus to get plates and insurance. From there, we drove to Fargo to show them our trailer at the college. We then returned to Breckenridge that same evening. What a pleasure to drive.

Since the car was maroon in color, it oxidized easily in the sun. However, I polished that car weekly with Simonize polish. I was just sick when I found gravel chips or where someone had slammed a door into the side of it. I dreaded parking lots and tried to stay out of them if I could.

We drove the car until 1966 when I sold it to Fred Robinson for 40 dollars. He blew the engine by exceeding a hundred miles an hour on a trip to Montana. That was the end of what had been our pride and joy in 1948. It was the car used to bring Tommy home from the hospital. I guess we have never felt as sentimental about any other car as we did that first one that we had waited for so long.

Kay and I drove to Breckenridge November 25th. The next morning at 5:00 A.M., we left with Tom and Sally for Lincoln. We arrived at 4:30 in the afternoon, and Lorraine had a large turkey dinner ready. The next day we spent time visiting points of interest in Lincoln, and then left for Breckenridge at 5:15 the morning of November 28th. We dropped Tom and Sally off and continued on to Fargo, arriving home at 6:00 o'clock.

We again all spent the Christmas holidays in Breckenridge. Kay and I, along with Bob's daughter Sandy, spent a day in Hankinson. After the gifts were opened Christmas eve, we all played monopoly. Ken went in for surgery on his wrist on December 27 and came home from the hospital three days later. He had hurt it during the summer harvest season.

On New Year's, Eve, 1948 Kay, Edith, my dad, and I went to Hankinson. He saw some friends from there, but it just wasn't like it used to be. I guess everyone finds his or her hometown that way. You expect it to be like you remembered it being and then are disappointed.

The New Year started out with Van Norden walking in on January 15th. He stayed long enough to have breakfast and then flew on to New York. He spent three years after discharge from service playing and trying to get over his love affair that didn't work out in Bad Reichenhall, Bavaria.

The next day was Kay's 24th birthday and we drove to Breckenridge. Her mother baked a birthday cake, and we all told her how old she was getting. We came back to Fargo that evening.

On February 2, all the women Kay worked with in the Business Office at the college held a shower for her. The shower was held at Edith Torning's home. Edith was Office Manager.

I had been working at Armour's Packing Plant at West Fargo all day Friday and when I got in that evening I was told to get right down to the Gardner Hotel. Pictures were been taken to determine winners in the Beard Contest. I had been unloading a boxcar of coal all day, and since I didn't have a chance to shower before having my picture taken, I am sure the beard was exceptionally black because of the coal dust it contained. On February 25th at half time in the basketball game between the AC and UND, I was selected as the winner in the untrimmed division. I received a Schick electric razor.

Kay had her first flat tire in her life on March 9th, but as she tells it she was very lucky. She happened to be within six blocks of a service station so she just drove over and had them fix it. What they did to fix it was put a new tire on and threw the shredded one in the trunk for my review.

We finished exams on March 17th, and Merle Erickson and I started working full time at Armour's during the break between quarters. Our job was to clean the ramp leading up to the slaughterhouse. We were given a horse for use in pulling a stone boat on which we loaded this wet, sloppy, smelly, manure. It was necessary to wear rubber boots since the depth extended half way up to our knees. I led the horse up the ramp and when we got to the top Merle would pull the stone boat around by the use of a rope attached to the back side. It took a fairly good tug to pull it around and on the morning of the second day the rope broke as he pulled on it. He went down on his back in this 18 inches of slop. Although we were surrounded and saturated with smell, I kept telling Merle all day not to come near me because he smelled.

Our pay was about 80 cents an hour, which was not too bad, but we got all the jobs the steady workers didn't want. We unloaded carloads of salt used in curing the hides. It was accomplished using two-handled scoops with small wheels on the bottom and we would run at this pile of salt and try to embed the scoop to get a load. If the salt was damp, it tended to bind together like sandstone, and then a pick had to be used to break it up. We also unloaded boxcar loads of coal. That was a dirty job, and we came home looking like minstrel singers.

Kay and I were setting money aside for Tommy's baby buggy. Kay had picked out the $29.95 blue model, which had a few extras on it such as sunshield, heavy-duty springs, and the removable main body that could be used as a crib.

Kay went in for her checkup on March 2, and Doctor Darner told her he was going to let her go into labor, but her pelvis was very narrow and her progress during labor would have to be monitored very closely. She went in again on March 30th, and the Doctor said the baby would be later than he initially thought. Then on April 1st, Kay woke up with labor pains at 7:00 A.M. I took her to the hospital at 10 o'clock. Our neighbor, Merle Erickson, thought it would be great if Kay had an April Fool's baby. He had been telling her for about two weeks that was the day the baby would be born. She was in labor all through that day and that night. At 5:00 A.M. on April 2nd, they gave her a spinal, followed by a second one at 9:30 A.M. At 10 o'clock, I was called out of a Double E lab I was taking and asked to report to the hospital. They needed my approval to proceed with a C-Section immediately, or there was a chance the baby's skull would be crushed. Doctor Darner was out of town the early part of April so Doctors Hunter and Nelson performed the surgery.

Baby Tom was born at 11:00 A.M. He weighed 8 pounds 2 1/2 ounces, was 18 1/2 inches long and had lots of black hair, which is something you can't say for him now. Kay kept imagining all kinds of freakish things. She was certain he looked like a monkey, and his feet and hands were not normal. She insisted the doctor bring him in so she could examine him. For two days after he was born, the doctors and nurses would ask her if she was satisfied with what she got.

On April 9th, I took Tom and Kay home. Kay's mother came to help and stayed until April 14th. That was actually longer than she would have had to stay. Tom was such a good baby, all he did was eat and sleep. Many times Kay had to wake him so he could eat. She was afraid that if she didn't he might starve. Kay got that blue Welsh buggy on April 21st, and four days later, took Tom for a three-hour ride. On the 28th, he got a rash from head to toe, and everyone became very alarmed. Doctor Poindexter was called, and he indicated it was probably heat rash. Use of calamine lotion for a couple of days cleared everything up, and the first catastrophic event in the life of a new baby was over.

We took Tom to the lake for the first time on May 15th. We went to Pelican Lake with the Ericksons. Four days later we went to Hankinson for my sister Betty's graduation exercises. Kay stayed in Breckenridge with her mother until the following weekend. Sally then drove her back to Fargo on the 25th.

We spent Memorial Day weekend at East Battle Lake with Tom and Sally. It had become a major operation to go anywhere now. It meant the buggy, diaper pail, stroller, and all kinds of small miscellaneous things that we had never had to worry about before now, had to go along with us.

We spent our third wedding anniversary out at Star Lake. Kay's Uncle Andy and Aunt Christine were out there also for the weekend. They lived in Williston, but had some good friends who lived at Star Lake.

I started ushering at the Star Lite Drive-In Theater located just north of the campus at a spot where the entrance to the airport is now situated. After getting everyone settled in for the evening, I was to continue with such duties as questioning those settled down in the back seat as to whether they could see all right. That type of work could be hazardous to one's health, since one big fellow raised his head up and told me, "Mind your own damn business and get the hell out of here." We tried to help people remember why they had come out to the theater.

The July 4th weekend was spent at the Star Lake again with the time spent swimming and fishing. Tommy got lots of attention, so much that he probably didn't get the amount of sleep he should have.

In August, I started working at a Mobile service station two blocks north of the Great Northern Railroad crossing on Broadway. The hours were long, but the work was interesting and the time went fast. When

I wasn't pumping gas, I was fixing flat tires or doing oil changes. That was back in the days when a service station provided service. Everything under the hood was checked and all the windows in the car were washed. Gas was 31 cents per gallon.

I graduated on August 19th, and all those from Trailer City brought their children along to the ceremonies. Tom and Sally came up from Breckenridge. The exercises were held at 10 o'clock in the morning, and Tommy was on time for this one. We even got him a decent pair of shoes. He was late for the one held twenty-three years later, and the shoes he had on appeared to be twenty-three years old. In the afternoon, I went back to work at the station.

I sent out twelve applications for work and heard from only two - the Bureau of Reclamation and the North Carolina State Highway Department. I decided to accept the Bureau's offer and got my physical on August 24th. Kay had been packing for two weeks and was just about through. Kay's father Tom came to Fargo on the 28th with a trailer, and we loaded my school desk and a few other things we said they could have. We went to Breckenridge with them that day. It was a little sad to leave the campus trailer and all the friends; there were a lot of memories associated with it and we knew that once we left the campus, we would never be able to duplicate anywhere else the type of activities we experienced there.

Many happenings were experienced at college that still brings smiles to our faces when they are discussed. Merle Erickson, who lived in the trailer next to us, was always giving Kay ideas on how to improve our life in the trailer by completing what he called minor construction projects. He would suggest certain shelving or other types of work, and then indicate he had scrap material that I could use in doing the work. Kay would become so enthused that I had no choice but to complete the suggested project while my neighbor Merle sat at home and chuckled. Forty years later he still called her to let her know he had some scrap lumber available if there was something she needed constructed.

On another occasion, Steve Robinson was told a new phone was installed at Merle's and he was given a number to call to check out the phone's operation. Of course, no phone had been installed and the number given to him had been picked at random. Steve laughed right up to the time of his death many years ago as to how naive he must have been to keep trying to call the number he had been given.

Ruby Erickson gave Kay a permanent one Saturday morning. They ran out of wave set and sent Merle and me uptown to get another bottle. We ran into a few friends, had a few beers, and in no time at all it was six o'clock. Some time during the afternoon Merle ducked out to buy a present, since the next day was Mother's Day. By the time we left for home, all stores were closed for the day. I had to go home without the wave set and a gift. To make matters worse, Ruby came over the next day to show Kay her Mother's Day gift. Dan Chapman tells the story around Bismarck whenever two or more people gather in one place. He adds a little each time he tells it, and I hardly recognize the true facts any longer.

College was now behind us and life would become more serious in the years ahead. However we would never forget those college years. We also would never forget some of the people we met during those college years. Unfortunately most of them are dead now. It is unbelievable how quickly the years have passed.

CHAPTER 15

Campus Life in Trailer City

During the second half of the 1940's, one of the fastest growing communities in the State of North Dakota was Trailer City. It was located on the campus of what was then known as North Dakota Agricultural College. The trailers were interspersed among the Vet, Science, and Pharmacy Buildings, the Men's Dorm, Ceres Hall, the Student Health Center, and the football stadium. Additional units with corrugated metal siding were located north of the campus and the area was known as North Court. Some of the trailers were privately owned and some were owned by the college and rented to the students. The west end of the football stadium was where the entrance to the Student Union is presently located. Student housing was located between the east side of the stadium and 13th Avenue and all along the south side of the football stadium. Kay and I were initially located in the West Court Area by the Vet Building. All ten trailers were privately owned and varied greatly in size, shape, and quality. Our trailer was small and had been used originally by the Singer Sewing Machine Company for use in on-the-road demonstrations. We had purchased it from Clark Hanson, a farmer, who used it as a field shack. I had worked on his dairy farm before the war. The roof needed repair and the inside needed painting. After Kay finished with her decorating the place seemed quite homey.

The nicest trailer was comparable to the Air Stream. It may have been an Air Stream; at least it looked like one with the shiny stainless steel outside. Everything inside was built-in and very neat.

There was no class distinction made, however, because of living accommodations. In some cases parents had helped some with their housing, where in other cases the individuals came up with the best they could afford. We found the quarters quite livable and comfortable considering what else was available at that particular time. No housing had been constructed during the war and the available facilities in the way of apartments were priced beyond the means of the average student.

Our ten trailers were located on the west side of the street directly across from what is now known as the old Pharmacy Building. The units were placed in a U shape with a combination bathroom-washroom building located at the end of the open part of the U. The college had provided this building. We rented the space for seven dollars a month, which included electricity and water. With a flat rate like that in affect, many electric heaters were used in preference to other types of heating.

The total number of trailers on the campus was 172. Married students occupied all and substantially all were World War II veterans attending on the GI Bill. Population of Trailer City was approximately 500 people. After all the available space on campus proper had been filled with trailers, the North Court area was developed north of the campus in what later became the football stadium. Today football is played inside in what is called the FargoDome. North Court units were constructed on site and the siding consisted of sheets of corrugated metal.

A mayor and Trailer City Council was elected each quarter to represent the residents and govern the community. The city was divided into six wards and town meetings were held periodically. Other officers elected were Secretary, Treasurer, Social Chairman and Publicity Chairman. Kay was elected Secretary in 1948 and Council member in 1949. Many social clubs, such as the Women's Club, were formed.

During 1947 and 1948 we began to settle into a routine college schedule. It may be considered boring by today's standards, but we had a great time. All activities revolved around a close knit group of friends. All were in their mid-twenties, were married and were anxious to complete college and get out into the workforce. Some of the close couples have remained friends through the years, but each year a few more die.

All through college we shared with these people the excitement and joys of their first-born, the purchasing of their first car, and the moving to more spacious and modern facilities, as they became available on the campus. We had coffee together late at night when the studying was completed. A few times when my brother Bob stayed with us, he couldn't believe people would call at 11:00 P.M. and invite us for coffee and cake.

Life styles completely changed during those college years. Evening meals were frequently shared with one or two other couples. Social calendars were filled on a day-to-day basis in the wash room where the women gather to do their laundry. Group knitting or sewing sessions were held with various women getting together in a specific trailer. Serious sewing had to be done at Ceres Hall on campus or the Roosevelt School, since no one had the luxury of a sewing machine at home.

Whenever a major storm resulted in the cancellation of school, it meant whist parties and other social gatherings were scheduled. We were such a compact unit that we all lived closer to each other than we did to the bathrooms. Our location was also ideal for attending school. We were never more than two or three minutes away from our farthest class and we never had a parking problem. For most of us that wouldn't have presented a problem anyway; we just didn't have cars as yet.

On August 27, 1947, we sold our trailer to Fred Turner from Dickinson for 310 dollars and moved to the college rental unit #47S. It was located on the east side of the Pharmacy Building and sat next to the board wall surrounding the football stadium. This was a standard unit with no plumbing, and required the outside use of washroom and bathroom. The college also had expandable, which were similar to Wingfoots in style and design. One side contained a bedroom and the other side contained a living room. We immediately placed our name on the list for one of these units since the available space was so much greater.

The trailers had no telephones and the heating was done with a fuel oil stove. During the winter when we went to Breckenridge or any other place for that matter, we shut the heat off while we were gone. This meant nothing in the way of canned goods or houseplants could be kept in the trailer. The units were poorly insulated and the blankets on the bed were usually frozen to the wall if an air space wasn't maintained between the bed and the wall. The trailers were warm and cozy as long as the furnace was fired up. The volume that required heating was small so it didn't take long to heat it up after returning from a trip and it didn't take much to maintain a temperature once it was warm.

That Fall I built a lean-to enclosing the entrance, not only to reduce wind but also to buffer the cold air when the door was opened. It also provided some additional storage space. I was to find out later that the more storage space I provided, the more Kay needed.

On June 26, 1948, we move to the expandable. These trailers were referred to as "the Moderns" since they had all the facilities such as indoor plumbing and running water. Were we happy. It was heaven with all that room and there was no longer a need to go outside to wash your hair or go to the bathroom. It is surprising we didn't have more colds than we did when we lived in our other trailer. We would go to wash our hair and by the time we got back to the trailer the hair would be frozen stiff. With the additional space, large groups could be accommodated and whist parties were the preferred social activity.

Sally and Tom came up to Fargo frequently to see us. It was usually on Sunday and they left right after dinner in the evening. My brother Bob was switching for the railroad and much of his work was scheduled in Fargo during 1947 and 1948. He would have dinner with us and then the three of us would go to the college basketball game or to a movie.

On February 21, 1948, Kay, Bob and I left for Breckenridge in Bob's Ford. We broke down in Wolverton and, after considerable delay, we found someone that knew a little about auto mechanics. We would go to Breckenridge on Friday evenings and then take the 7:30 P.M. bus back to Fargo on Sunday evening. When we returned two days later, it was really storming and shortly after we arrived in Fargo everything was closed down as far as travel was concerned.

Four days later Bob was back in Fargo and we went to the Jack Frost Parade. We saw quite a bit of him during the rest of February and all of March. On March 28th Kay, Bob and I went to Hankinson for Easter

Sunday dinner at Mom's. Kay got to meet many of the relatives while she was down there. One of the few she hasn't met as yet is Boyce. Boyce was my cousin and he was always planning to run for office. He wanted to be mayor of Minneapolis or Governor of Minnesota. However, after John Kennedy was shot he had no interest in running for President.

Trailer City always found an excuse for special parties, Halloween being one of them. It was always great to get together with those other than your own special circle of friends to find out what was happening in the rest of the campus community.

Trailer City had a great group of people with common interests, similar goals, and a desire for a great future. We still see many of the friends made during that period in our life and eventually the conversation always gets around to the happy days of our youth in Trailer City. The sad part about it is that you don't realize at the time that you are experiencing some of the best years of your life and you're really not taking the time to fully enjoy them.

Members from Trailer City held a reunion in October 1990, during Bison Homecoming. We stayed at the Holiday Inn, attended the football game and had Sunday morning breakfast together as a group. It was fun, but not possible to experience the feelings and excitement that existed in earlier years.

I walked the campus area that had contained our "living space" in 1949. Buildings have sprung up in the open areas. The football stadium has been moved north and the Student Union commons area is located on what use to be the playing field. All college games are now played indoors in the Fargodome and the field that had been moved north is now a practice field. The stadium seating has been sold to another college.

The area on which our last trailer was located is now a large, open, grassed area with walkways and benches. The traffic speeding past on 13th Avenue reflected an accelerated life style that we didn't dream would be present 50 years later. Large trees now provide shade in what use to be our housing area.

As I sat on one of those benches, the present day students streamed by unaware that the area they were passing through once housed a young group of students similar to them; a group that had hopes and dreams for a future comparable to their dreams. Probably not everyone achieved the goals they might have liked but I am certain they were better off for having spent those years at college.

Merle and Ruby Erickson were our closest neighbors during the major portion of our campus life. Some of our fondest memories of college life are related to them in one way or another.

We still see them when we visit Minneapolis and I feel it is because of those early-shared experiences that a strong bond of friendship still exists today (2010).

PHOTOS

My dad entered the US Army on May 17, 1917 and was sent to Jefferson Barracks, Missouri and then to Ft. Bliss, Texas. He was discharged at Dodge, Iowa on September 27, 1919.

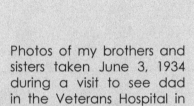

Photos of my brothers and sisters taken June 3, 1934 during a visit to see dad in the Veterans Hospital in Fargo, North Dakota

Betty and Darrell taking care of 1936 snow at 329 N 11th Street in Breckenbridge

My sister Judith with our mother and parents

Family Photo taken in 1937
Father-Mother-Merle
Mavis and Robert
Betty

Kenneth and Darrell had died earlier and
Judith wasn't born until 1941

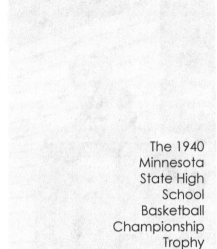

The 1940
Minnesota
State High
School
Basketball
Championship
Trophy

Picture of my father and me. He was 26 years old and I was 20 years old. His picture was taken in May 1917 and my picture was taken in September 1943. He was discharged in September 1919 and I as discharged in December 1945.

I was discharged on December 21, 1945 at Camp Mc Coy, Wisconsin. I spent 3 days in Minneapolis, Minnesota visiting my mother and sisters. I left for Breckenridge, Minnesota Christmas Eve at 10 PM. One other passenger was on the train. I arrived home at 6 AM, picked up my duffel bag that had been thrown on the depot platform and headed for home. It was a much different homecoming than that I had thought about for almost three years. I met my father as he was leaving for work.

Later that Christmas morning I went to Kay's home. When we had parted in March 1944, she indicated she would be waiting with camera in hand for my return.

The above picture was taken as a remembrance of our first day together after my return.

My sisters Mavis, Betty,
Judy and JoAnn

Merle and Mardy

Don and Betty Petron with Rosalynn and Jimmy Carter.
Betty is the author's sister.

CHAPTER 16

A Decade of Fear and Changes

The decade began with the Cold War continuing to escalate. People began breaking ground in backyards to construct atomic bomb shelters. Prices ranged in the neighborhood of $2,000. No one really understood or could comprehend what may result in the event of an atomic attack. Water and other supplies were stored in public buildings and many were trained in radiation detection using Geiger counters. I was on a team that was trained and would go out after an atomic attack to measure the extent of radiation existing in an area. The raising of the Iron Curtain resulted in cessation of communication between the Americans and the Soviets. The arms race began in earnest and the two nations began producing ICBMs (inter-continental ballistic missiles) as rapidly as they could. North Dakota, as well as a number of other States, had Minutemen silos with missiles that could be fired within a minute's notice.

The closest the world came to nuclear war was during the 1962 Cuban Missile Crisis. Russia was attempting to place missiles in Cuba just 90 miles off our shore. Russia agreed to remove the missiles from Cuba if the United States would remove its missiles from Turkey. It was a face-saving agreement by both sides.

As the Cold War slowly melted into our history books after the Berlin Wall came down, the younger generation has no concept as to amount of fear experience from Communism.

It is an unstable world today as threats from other nations continually surface

The scientific and mass production advances made during WWII changed the way people lived. New housing units were mass-produced and helped relieve the shortages that had developed during the war years when all construction material was diverted to the war effort.

Five years after hostilities ended WW II the Korean Conflict began and would continue for 3 years before a cease-fire was agreed to. Almost 60 years later the Peninsula is still divided with armies facing each other at the 38 Parallel.

Credit cards and color television came into being in 1950 and the first organ transplant takes place. Salk polio vaccine was introduced in 1952. McCarthy witch-hunts took place in Congress in 1953 and a year later the French were defeated at Dien Bien Phu by the Viennese. Elvis Presley became an international star with Love Me Tender film. Sputnik 1 was the first satellite to orbit the earth launched by the Russia in 1957. A year later De Gaulle became President of France. Castro took power in Cuba in 1959. Alaska and Hawaii become states that same year. By the end of the fifties most American households owned a car, a washing machine, and a television set.

Many silly things that emerged disappeared just as quickly. All young children wore Coonskin hats as a result of a television show called Davy Crockett. Hula-Hoops were the rage for a short time. Phone booth cramming where up to 22 students would crowd into an outdoor booth. Students were able to cram 40 of their friends into a VW Bug.

CHAPTER 17

My Employment Career

My employment career actually covered more than three decades beginning in the late 40s and ending in 1980. I had graduated with a Bachelor of Science Degree in Civil Engineering from the North Dakota State University in Fargo on August 19, 1949. Up until 1960 the school was known as the North Dakota Agricultural College.

The government anticipated a depressed economy would result after the booming wartime industry came to a conclusion. That was another reason for the passage of the G.I. Bill providing for educational benefits for returning servicemen and women. It was believed most would end up on unemployment.

I had sent out 12 applications to various firms earlier in August and received favorable responses from two. The North Carolina State Highway Department and the Bureau of Reclamation, an agency under the Department of the Interior indicated an interest and made me an offer. I decided to accept the Bureau's offer, which would keep me in the area where I grew up. I was told to get a physical at the Government's expense, which I did on August 24th.

My first tour of duty was to be in Riverton, Wyoming and I would be working on drain design for an irrigation project scheduled for rehabilitation. A new drainage system for an existing irrigation project was to be constructed. I had been selected to design the system.

The day before I was scheduled to leave for Wyoming I received a call from the Bureau Office in Bismarck. They indicated I should stop in for a discussion on my way through town. I couldn't imagine what they might want to discuss other than maybe provide me with some insight as to the Bureau's mission and goals. I reported to Peg Homan in Personnel who explained to me what the District Office was involved in and inquired as to whether I might prefer employment in Bismarck.

The District Office of the Bureau in Bismarck was to be responsible for the distribution and sale of power generated by the dams constructed as part of the Pick-Sloan Project authorized by Senate Document No. 191. This Document provided for the conservation, control and use of water resources of the Missouri River Basin. The work was authorized in April 1944, but no funding was to be furnished until after the conclusion of World War II. The dam at Fort Peck had been started in 1934 as a WPA Project to provide employment during the Depression years. The dam was completed in 1938.

Construction of Garrison Dam, located approximately 70 miles north of Bismarck on the Missouri River, was begun in 1946. The Bureau would be responsible for the distribution of power generated at the dam.

I came to Bismarck on September 7th and following the discussion I had in the Bismarck Office I returned to Breckenridge to talk to Kay. She also preferred a location closer to home. I then indicated to the Personnel Office that we were interested in the offer made to us in Bismarck. I was really excited because a number of my classmates were having problems being accepted for work they had applied for. The country had not converted as yet from a wartime economy to civilian economy. I was also happy to find a position fairly close to home and family.

My official starting day was September 12, 1949. I was put on a one year promotional period and started my career on a Monday morning. My grade was GS-5 and my starting annual salary was $2,984.00.

The Bureau had established an office in Bismarck in 1942. There were about 5 people working above the bank located north across the street from the old Sears Roebuck store on Main Street and 4th.Avenue. The work of this group consisted primarily of investigation and preliminary planning. A recession was anticipated following the completion of the war and about 50 irrigation projects along the Missouri River were being planned for development. However, the reservoir area needed for the proposed Garrison Dam precluded the development of these projects since the reservoir water would inundate the proposed irrigated areas.

Garrison Dam would be generating power by 1952. In order to distribute this power when it became available, plans were underway to construct facilities for the distribution of power generated by the power plant. The Bureau had survey crews out obtaining centerline locations and profiles for transmission lines. The power was to be made available to cities such as Valley City and Breckenridge. It was also sold to co-operatives that in turn would make it available to small towns and individual farm families. The cities of Bismarck and Mandan declined to purchase power for a municipal system because the local investor-owned utility convinced the two cities that there would be frequent outages with Government furnished power.

My first assignment was working for George Seaworth. After 60 years, he and I are still closely associated with each other and remain good friends. After we were both retired we were members of the Bismarck Lions Club and a Wednesday Morning Breakfast Club. He is now 95 years old and I have an opportunity to see him when I return to Bismarck from Fargo for various reasons; mostly funerals.

My initial work consisted of taking the field notes coming in from the surveyors and plotting the information on plan and profile sheets. These sheets would then become a part of the specifications used by contractors in preparing bids for the construction of transmission lines. I continued with this work through the end of the year. I was notified on December 12th that I, along with Don Raatz, would be going to Montana on a two-month detail on January 3, 1950.

Don Raatz and I left for Wolf Point, Montana at 9:30 A.M. on January 3, 1950 in my 1948 Plymouth. The weather was stormy and cold and we were to discover it was going to get much worse that winter before it got better. We arrived in Wolf Point that evening at 6:00 o'clock and checked into the only hotel in town. The town is located in the center of the Fort Peck Indian Reservation. Early residents of the area were members of the Assiniboine and Sioux Tribes. The Reservation capitol was located in Poplar, Montana.

The lands that were originally scheduled for irrigation development were situated in the northeast Montana and northwest North Dakota. The water for development of these lands would come from Ft. Peck Reservoir, which formed after the construction of Ft. Peck Dam. The Construction Office established at Wolf Point was to be responsible for the construction of the Missouri Diversion Dam, the main feature for the diversion and regulation of the supply water used in development of the North Dakota lands. Construction of the diversion dam was underway.

The lands suitable for irrigation in northeast Montana had never been surveyed or delineated. Our instructions were to conduct surveys on the Culbertson and Brockton Bench areas. We had a surplus World War II Army Ambulance vehicle for a survey truck. The vehicle had high clearance and was a 4-wheel drive. This was the only thing that could have gotten us around in that country. All travel was off-road work and the snow was two feet deep on the level.

Raatz and I shared the same facilities at the hotel. It was a basement room with a small kitchen off to side. Each morning before leaving for work, we each packed a lunch for ourselves. It normally consisted of a couple summer sausage sandwiches, an apple, roll, and a couple of candy bars and lots of hot coffee in a thermos. The temperature consistently stayed at 20 degrees below zero during the day and dropped to 30 degrees below at night. This continued until about the middle of February and then it got colder. The day it dropped to 58 degrees below zero we didn't go out into the field. After 10 days of 40 below, it actually seems warm when the temperature got up to 15 below. After it became apparent that due to the deep snow and cold temperatures, our work was not very cost effective, the Bismarck Office decided we should return to our headquarters. We did not object in the least.

During that two-month detail I spent most of my evening hours downtown for a number of reasons. The hotel environment was not too great and a movie occasionally seemed to break the monotony of the life style we were living. The Montana bars were open 24 hours a day, seven days a week at that time. Slot machines were in every place of business and the most popular machine was the one that took silver dollars. Montana did not fool with paper money at that time. Everyone converted the paper into silver at the first opportunity and that was when the dollars were real silver. The bars also had kitchens and served full course meals. I would eat my evening meal there and then watch the ranchers play poker. The stakes were high in some games and it was not unusual to have a rancher lose his favorite horse, saddle or, in some cases, lose his entire ranch in a game. The rancher covering a bet did not have to produce his horse or title to his ranch. His word and a handshake were all that was needed.

We left Wolf Point at 8:15 A.M. on February 28th and arrived back at the Bismarck Office at 4:55 P.M. My only concern now was that we might be directed to return later in the spring when the weather permitted a more productive operation. However, laboratory testing of soils taken from that area concluded that the soils were not suitable for irrigation. The work on the Missouri Diversion Dam was wrapped up and instructions were given to find a diversion point further downstream. Since the lands most suitable for development were located in Central North Dakota, a diversion point on Garrison Reservoir was selected.

My expenses for the two months of detail were reimbursed at the rate of 6.00 dollars per day and $0.07 cents per mile for travel expense, for a grand total of $381.28. The mileage I had claimed, as read from my speedometer, was 616. However, the official mileage from Bismarck to Wolf Point, Montana according to the Household Goods Carriers' Bureau Mileage Guide No. 5, Supplement No. 1, was 604 miles. Seaworth pointed this out to me and deducted 84 cents from the voucher. I have since recovered from that financial setback.

The following morning, Wednesday March 1st, I left for Breckenridge and popped in to surprise Kay and Tommy. On Sunday we left for Bismarck at 1:00 o'clock, stopping at Trailer City in Fargo for a couple of hours to visit friends who were still there and then on to Bismarck, arriving at 9:00 P.M. The Montana detail was over and life would get back to normal.

After returning from leave I was assigned irrigation design and layout work on the Baldhill Area, a part of the Garrison Diversion Unit project. I found this work very boring and frustrating. You would complete a design and then changes would require a redesign.

In April 1950, I transferred to the Land Acquisition Division. I wrote and checked legal descriptions of right-of-way easements. These parcels were being acquired from the landowners for use in the transmission line construction. Maps were drawn to accompany the legal descriptions that were filed in courthouse. I worked for a year in this Division. Bob Dorothy was also in the Division during this period. The District Land Officer was A.J. Palmer.

In April 1951, I was promoted to GS-7 and transferred to the Office Engineering Branch. I worked for Wendell Dennis who was Office Engineer of the Transmission Lines Field Office. After plotting plan and profile and writing easement descriptions for transmission lines, I was now computing quantities and preparing payment vouchers for contractors' completed work. This work not only involved transmission lines but included the construction of approximately 17 substations throughout North Dakota and a radio communications system requiring 140 and 200 foot towers placed throughout the State to provide communication in vehicles working on the power distribution facilities. I continued this work for two years. Both jobs during the period from April 1950 until April 1953 were located in the old International Harvester Building, later known as the L. P. Anderson Building at Main Avenue and Mandan Street.

This work also required some field trips occasionally to view or determine percentage of completion of contract work. My first official travel, other than the Wolf Point detail, was a trip to Rolla, North Dakota to check out the Rolla Substation. It was a two and one-half day trip and the per diem rate was six dollars per day. I was paid 15 dollars for the trip and my total expenses were only 9 dollars. I was certain I would become wealthy just from travel reimbursements.

In April 1953, I moved back to Office Engineering Division in the building on the southeast corner of Third Street and Main Avenue. I was working for George Seaworth again and had been promoted to GS-9. My work now involved cost estimating for all project works and specification writing for transmission lines and dam facilities. Heart Butte and Dickinson Dams had essentially been completed and Jamestown Dam was in the final stages of construction late in the year 1954.

Condemnation action was required to obtain reservoir acreage from one landowner for Heart Butte Dam. He continually refused to cash the $50,000 check sent to him for the reservoir acreage. That amount of money was comparable to 17 years of salary that I was making at that time. He would come into the office periodically and request that we get those damn fish off his property. He refused to accept the court's decision. This went on for several years. Each year the check we had issued the previous year had to be cancelled and a new check issued. He never cashed them and continued to tell us to get our fish off his land. Then one day we were furnished information that he had died. We reissued the check in his wife's name. She remarried shortly after that and used the money for a very lengthy honeymoon.

In the fall of 1954 I was detailed to the Contract Administration Branch of Transmission Division to help with work association with the construction of 230-kv Transmission lines between Bismarck and Fargo. About this time, we started construction of our home in Highland Acres. I had a working agreement with the Administrative Assistant, Alice Hanson, that permitted me to work on the house in the afternoon and then I come to the office for four hours in the evening to compute quantities and prepare payment vouchers. It worked out great and we were able to get into our new home before Christmas.

In 1955, the Transmission Division moved their office to Fargo to be closer to the work associated with the Fargo-Morris 230 kv Transmission Line. I then went back to design work in Office Engineering Division. I continued working there until March 1956, at which time I transferred to Project Development Division, and was given a promotion to GS-11. I was now in a supervisory capacity with a number of engineers under my direction. Our work was primarily on Garrison Diversion Unit; a planning report was scheduled for submission to the Congress by 1959. The report provided for one million acres of irrigation development along with recreation, fish and wildlife, municipal and industrial water development. The report was furnished to Congress and after a review by the Congress, it was recommended that the scope of the Project be scaled down to one-quarter million acres of irrigation as a first stage. For the next two years we worked on a revised report. This report was submitted for congressional review in 1962. While awaiting favorable consideration and authorization of the new plan a Reduction in Force became necessary in order to keep the office open with a nucleus of personnel. Some transferred to other offices within the Agency and some took other offers of employment.

In April, 1961 I accepted a position as Location Engineer-GS-12 and began work relating to finding a centerline location for a Yellowtail Dam-Glendive 230-kv Transmission Line. A dam on the Bighorn River southeast of Billings, Montana had been in the planning stages for a number of years and was scheduled for construction during the summer of 1962. The dam was to be named for a Native American named Yellowtail. He strongly opposed the use of his name but to no avail. Paul Willmore and I selected a switchyard location on the east side of the dam site. The transmission line would originate at this facility and terminate in the switchyard at Glendive, Montana approximately 220 miles northeast of the dam.

Paul had his own plane, which he preferred to use on Bureau business. This reduced his overhead for hanger fees and insurance. After completing our work relating to switchyard selection we stopped at Hardin for gas. We got caught in a blizzard and spent my 38th birthday and the weekend in the small reservation town.

This transmission job was the beginning of a 2-year detail. I would leave for Miles City, Montana on Monday mornings at 3:15 A.M. on the Northern Pacific Railroad. I would eat breakfast in the club car as we passed through the Badlands. The sunrise against the scoria hills reflected a red glow across the landscape and the deer grazing near the tracks created a beautiful morning scene. I would arrive in Miles City about 8:30 A.M. and meet Sam Moss, who was my Chief of Surveys. After a week of work selecting a segment of the alignment I would return to Bismarck leaving Miles City on Friday at 4:30 P.M. and arriving home at 10:20 P.M.

The initial requirement was to fly the proposed alignment using maps to try to select a paper location. After this was done, aerial photos were taken and then the proposed location was plotted on the aerials. The standard joke during the aerial reconnaissance, when passing over a relatively rough area known as the Hysham Hills, was, "Fly a little higher so it won't look so rough."

After completion of surveys, a plan and profile of the centerline was plotted. Spotting of tower sites to obtain the desired span lengths between tower sites and insure adequate ground clearances was the next required step. This paper location for the tower sites then had to be field checked to insure the proper foundation and drainage conditions existed. Since much of the topography was too rough to permit use of a vehicle for field checking, we started out using tote-goats; a small two-wheeled vehicle similar to a small motorcycle. However, it was more tiring fighting the vehicle than the advantages gained by its use. We then tried horses, but the time spent caring for the horses each morning and evening, plus the fact that they had to be hauled out and then returned to the initial starting point each day resulted in considerable lost time. We ended up deciding to just walk the alignment. We did this twice during the summer of '61, a total of 440 miles.

The wildlife in the backcountry of Montana was beautiful. The early morning hours always produced antelope, deer, and coyote. The antelope continued to graze throughout the day and were very curious animals. If we placed a lath with a flag on it to mark some particular point in the field, they would be drawn to it and eventually pull it down. They would also come close to check us out; I gathered their eyesight is not too good and they came to investigate anything that is unusual.

The alignment from Yellowtail Dam to Hardin, Montana crossed the Crow Indian Reservation and the Campbell Farms, a large cattle and grain operation owned by a Texas corporation. The operation involved over 55 square miles of area. The Custer Battlefield is a few miles southeast of Hardin. The alignment between Miles City and Glendive crossed an area that is rich in agate. Sam Moss and I picked up what we felt were the largest and best agates. Immediately after a rainstorm, it was possible to find arrowheads in the cultivated fields exposed on the plowed earth.

On hot summer days we were careful in opening gates. It was not unusual to find a rattlesnake lying in the shade of the gatepost. I brought a few rattles home for my sons Tom and Mark. The easy way to kill the snake was with the use of a shovel. You would arch your body to keep your legs back beyond striking distance, and then bring the shovel down with one hand to cut off the snake's head.

By May of 1962 the line location was firm and specification were issued for construction. I was then detailed to Miles City as Office Engineer. This work continued through August and consisted of preparing payment vouchers for completed contract work, preparation of extra work orders and change orders.

Miles City was a typical Montana cowboy town. They had a bucking horse show early each year to provide horses for the rodeo circuit. This was followed by a local rodeo. Gambling of all types was wide open and prostitution was permitted, but everyone acted as though it didn't exist. If some stranger in town or an employee from one of our other offices questioned what the building on the edge of town was, they were informed, with a straight face, it was the Riding Academy. All the locals were dressed in western attire and the older and more beat-up a cowboy hat was, the more it was cherished.

I returned to duty in the Project Office in September 1962 and was designated the Field Engineer. John Johnson from the Bismarck Office assumed my Office Engineer position in Miles City, Montana.

My work now involved all survey and other fieldwork associated with Garrison Diversion Unit and other smaller units along the Missouri River scheduled for irrigation development. This work lasted until I became Division Chief in February 1963. I was now responsible for all the work involving design, geology, surveys, preparation of specifications, construction, and contract administration. Much more travel was required for consultation with other agencies and firms. Denver, Minneapolis, Chicago, and Canadian cities in the Provinces north of North Dakota were the most frequent locations visited in completing the work. Whenever possible I took the family along and the evenings were family time.

Visiting Denver on business was always interesting. Engineers from all over the world would come to the Bureau's Design and Research Center. A van from the Center would come around to the various hotels each morning and pick up the visitors for the day and then take them back after work in the afternoon. On one occasion I was sitting next to two Russians who were over here under the President Nixon's Cultural Exchange Program that was in existence at that time. As we drove to the Center, which was on the west edge of Denver, I could tell they were impressed with the number of vehicles traveling along the six-lane highway. Finally one turned to me and asked, "How can parts be kept on hand for so many different types of vehicles?" He assumed every different color and shape was a different vehicle and required different engines and different parts. I just smiled and said, "They do it by computer." I could tell he was perplexed and wasn't certain I was giving him the total story. I wasn't; the Cold War was still very much in evidence. I often wondered what conclusions were reached when the discussion with the other Russian engineers was held in the evening.

Much of the work during the years 1963 and 1964 was involved with the Canadians on the Pembina Unit in northeast North Dakota. The Pembina River Basin was located in both countries and, therefore, fell under the jurisdiction of the International Joint Commission, a body organized in 1909 to handle transboundary water disputes and matters.

As mentioned above I tried to combine business and vacation on some of the more exciting out of town trips. Each January specification reviews for construction work were held in the Denver Office. Kay would accompany me for the three days and spend her time in the department stores. Denver weather was usually pleasant and it was a break from the type of weather we were having in Bismarck at that time. Instead of flying we would take the 9-hour trip by car so we would have a vehicle while we were there. Many times we would take an extra day or two and drive home on Sunday.

International Joint Commission meetings held with the Canadians were, at the Canadians request, usually held in Fargo during the summer and in Minneapolis during the winter. When our sons' schedule could be coordinated with these meetings, they would go along. They would spend most of their time in the motel pool. Training sessions also provided an opportunity for a number of mini-vacation trips. One that comes to mind was a Middle Management Course held in the St. Paul Hilton on February 7-9, 1968. Room rate was 9 dollars per day. One of the most interesting training sessions I was involved in took place in Sacramento. The course lasted a week and I think I gained 10 pounds that week. The food was terrific and the quantities were enormous. Ice sculptors decorated the tables and the décor of the dining room was something out of a magazine. The dining room was located in the clubhouse on a golf course that bore Arnold Palmer's name. Adjacent to the clubhouse was an airstrip for fly-in golfers who came from as far as Los Angeles for the weekend.

On August 5, 1965 Garrison Diversion Unit was authorized and the Table of Organization for a construction office was changed and expanded. In January 1967, I applied for a position advertised as Chief, Design Branch and was promoted to GS-13. In March 1973 I took the Office Engineer, GS-14 position until December 1973 and then became Construction Engineer, GS-14 until August 1974. When Makoff came from Grand Coulee Dam that August and became Construction Engineer, I became Chief, Engineering Services Branch and continued in that position until my retirement on December 29, 1980.

Many humorous things happened over the years and I will share three incidents with you.

John Bauley was a Party Chief on a survey crew. One of the survey members was a German who had come to this country as a refugee shortly after the World War II and was not totally familiar with everything. Bauley stopped in at a hardware one morning to get some nails. Since Hans had to go to the bathroom, he went in with John. Bauley told him the bathroom was probably in the back. In about 10 minutes Hans is back, but he tells Bauley he couldn't find a handle on the toilet to flush it. Bauley realizes that Hans has just sat down on the first floor model he could find out in back, not realizing these had been taken out of their boxes for use as display models in the front of the store.

Bauley's only comment to Hans was, "Lets get the hell out of here".

We could only guess the store manager's surprise and comments when he came to pick up the stool for movement (pardon the pun) to the front of the store.

On another occasion we had a fellow from California who applied for a vacancy on one of the survey crews. He had never been to North Dakota. He gave up his job with the Forest Service, towed his house trailer up here, and reported for work one Monday morning in October. After a week of work, it was obvious to the Survey Party Chief that he was not going to carry his share of the work. The second week the members of the crew were giving him tips of what to do when the impending winter hit the State. He was told to never get more than 50 feet from other crewmembers. If for some reason, he was sent more than 100 feet from the survey vehicle, he should tie a nylon rope to the van's door handle so that if a sudden blizzard came up, he would be able to find his way back to the crew. The crew indicated one of the members from last year's crew didn't heed their advice and they weren't able to find him until the following June when the snow melted. That Friday at the end of work he went into Personnel, resigned, and towed his trailer back to California at his own expense.

A new survey crew member reported for work and was told he could go through Personnel later after things began to slack up a little. The other crewmembers told him the Personnel Officer was a woman and one of the toughest things to get through was the complete physical she would give him in her office. For two weeks he thought about this and finally the day arrived when he had to report to Personnel. Peg Homan, Personnel Officer, told him to take his jacket off. This was the start of the moment he had thought about and dreaded for so many days. Peg took his fingerprints and found his hands trembling and ice cold. She asked him a number of questions required for his Personnel Folder and then told him that was it.

He said, "What about the physical?"

She knew nothing about the torture the crew had put him through for the past two weeks and merely told him there was no requirement for a physical.

During my time with the Bureau, our Regional Office had a private plane for our use. Initially it was an old twin tailed Beechcraft and then continued to be updated as the years went by. After authorization of the Garrison Diversion Unit Project we got a Cessna 172 and then a pusher-puller Cessna 210. According to the flight logs, I logged about 30 thousand miles in our Bureau planes. My first commercial flights were in the early 60's by turbo-prop and they were quite exciting. On September 3, 1970 I accompanied Congressman Mark Andrews on a flight over the Garrison Diversion Unit Project.

We had various visiting dignitaries and cultural exchange groups over the years that were taken out to view project works. I've had people out from Iraq, Iran, Afghanistan, Denmark, India and Thailand. A few I brought to the house for lunch or an evening visit and it was interesting to observe some the things they were curious about. One spent a great deal of time studying how the drapes were drawn by the use of a cord. The grass cloth on the walls fascinated another.

After thirty years of retirement, I occasionally stop in at the office on 3rd and Broadway. However, the span of time between visits has increased greatly because there are fewer and fewer employees I still know. The Bureau's mission has changed and, in addition to maintenance of existing facilities, authorization was recently passed that directs the Bureau to plan and construct the Red River Water Supply Project. The development will provide a source of municipal, rural and industrial water for the Red River Valley, serving the cities of Fargo and Grand Forks in North Dakota and Breckenridge and East Grand Forks in Minnesota.

We met many wonderful people during the years we were associated with the Bureau. Many remained in the Bismarck Office and retired here. Many transferred to other offices throughout the 17 western states and many worked in the Regional and Denver Offices that we came to know and appreciate for their talents. We had our own Bowling League and our own softball team. We played against a traveling team called The King & His Court. It consisted of 4 players; catcher, first baseman fielder and the King did the pitching. His name was Eddie Feitner. Very few got a hit off of him. He a ball speed 114 miles per hour. His specialty was control and he could pitch from second base. I got hit by one of his pitches and my shoulder was blue for two weeks. As the years passed, Eddie's son replaced him on the team.

My first Project Manager, Bruce Johnson, died in 1990 in Phoenix, Arizona. Project Manager G.A. Freeman, who lived in Bismarck after retirement, died in January 1993. Project Manager Ted Mann lives in Lacey Washington, and is now 103 years old, if alive. Project Manager Ed Lundberg died a number of years ago and his wife Ann may still be living in Las Vegas. Project Manager Warren Jamison worked with Western Area Power Association in Denver until his retirement and was Manager of the Garrison Diversion Conservancy District in Carrington until his death in 2004. Darrell Krull was Project Manager when I retired in 1980. He has since left Government Service and works in the Las Vegas area.

I might have gained more financially had I been willing to accept offers made which required relocation. We had many opportunities to accept foreign assignments under the AID Program (Agency for International Development). However, I guess Kay and I weighed the advantages of staying put against the additional materialistic things that could be gained and decided we would give our sons a permanent location during their early adolescent years. They can always call Bismarck, North Dakota their hometown. I know a number of people who have never remained in one place long enough to establish roots. This is especially true of military people who have made the military their career.

It is difficult to condense over 30 years of activities into less than sixteen pages. That is about two years of activities per page. However, many of the details would only be of interest to other fellow employees who were working at the time. It would be nice to meet with former employees and reminisce but most are gone. All in all, it was a great time in my life and I enjoyed every minute of it. It would be terrible to work at a job you disliked, but I guess it is being done by some every day of the week. I run into many that can't wait to retire.

CHAPTER 18

Memories of Otter Tail Lake

Good memories are the most precious items of our treasurers. As they are nurtured through the years, they take on new importance and have more value than material possessions. The summer periods at Otter Tail Lake in Minnesota provided such memories in abundance. We watched our children develop through childhood, pass through their teen-age years and mature into adulthood. Initially we thought summer activities at the lake would go on forever.

Kay's parents purchased a cabin on Otter Tail Lake in the spring of 1955 for a sum of three thousand dollars. The cabin located on the West Side of the lake on the West Half of Lot 14 of Pleasant Grove, was purchased from R.K. and Corinne Pettit. The land on which the cabin is located is a part of a larger parcel (Lot 2-Section 32, T. 134 N. R. 40 W.) issued to a veteran who had been in the military service of the United States. The initial grant had been made to Private William Alford, who fought with the New York Militia in the War of 1812. Joseph A. Dean issued the first recorded deed to the property on March 1, 1870.

Otter Tail Lake is a beautiful body of water approximately ten miles long and three miles wide. On warm, sunny days the watercolor is a bright, robin egg blue, but on cold, cloudy days it becomes an ugly and uninviting greenish gray. The location of the cabin is such that the prevailing northwest winds have little effect on the water surface or beach area. However, a southeast wind will result in white-capped waves and a beach littered with washed up weeds and dead fish. The beach is composed of sugar-like sand that extends throughout the lake bottom. The lake is ideal for swimming, since it has a gradual slope to its bottom. The water depth is approximately six feet at a distance of two hundred feet from shore. Walleye fishing is good during the early months of spring. Water related activities are the most popular use made of the lake during the summer months. The variety and size of the water toys have changed over the years. Initially truck innertubes were used for floating on the waves. Now with powerboats available commercially produced tubes for towing by the boats are available. Water skiing is popular as well as parasailing.

On May 29, 1979, Tom and Sally Jonietz sold their interest in the cabin to their children for a sum of six thousand dollars. In August 1980, the interior of the cabin was completely gutted, enlarged, and insulated to provide for better use of the facility.

During the first thirty years of cabin use, very little change resulted in neighborhood owners. Scotts lived to the south and Vyes and Hirons to the east. Approximately 20 plus years ago Mrs. Scott converted her cabin to a year-around home after the death of her husband. She died of cancer approximately fifteen years ago. Her children and grandchildren took over the use of the cabin for a few years and then sold it to

Sam Toft from southern Minnesota. The Vyes both died and their children took over the management of the cabin. After a few years, they relocated to different areas of the country and eventually sold their interest in the cabin to Pughes. The Pughes purchased a lot on the east side of the lake, built a new home and then sold their interest to a Dr. David Hunter from California. The Hirons divorced and final disposal of property included the sale of their lake home. It would be interesting to be able to foresee what will happen to the Jonietz family cabin in the future. It is surprising how quickly generations come and go. Since the death of Tom and Sally, who were the catalyst for gathering at the lake cabin, the desire to schedule dates at the summer retreat is not very strong. We bought the cabin and Kay and I continued to spend time there during the summer months. As her health continued to fail it was more of an effort for Kay to spend time out there. It was a long drive from Bismarck. Hauling bedding and other washing back and forth also was an effort. A lengthy stay became necessary to justify-the effort, time and expense involved in making the trip. By the mid-1990s Kay indicated she no longer was interested in spending time at the cabin. In October 1995 we spent time with Tom, Patty Mark and Diane at the cabin. McKenzie and Tom had been pheasant hunting and came back to the cabin for the night. I believe that was the last time Mark and Diane saw Kay because she died approximately 38 days later.

After Kay's death on January 8, 1996 I lost interest in spending time at the lake. There were too many memories that surfaced as the sun settled each evening. The singing of the birds added to the sadness. Sitting alone at the lake in the quiet of the evening my mind would slip back to the earlier years. In the latter part of the 1950's it was fairly simple to get the entire family together at the lake for summer holidays. Memorial Day, July 4th and Labor Day were the three holidays that were set up as the best time to schedule family gatherings. The children were small, fewer in number and not too involved in personal summer activities. It was a phase in their lives that only lasts for a few brief years and then their activities and needs change as do those of the parents.

Grandpa started every morning by loudly calling out "Daylight in the Swamps." Another favorite expression of his when we were fishing with the children was "It's a keeper" regardless of the size of the fish. This made each child believe his/her fish was just as important as other fish that were caught.

One of the initial requirements on Memorial Day was the dock installation. Grandpa Tom had some black, hip boots that became a part of his uniform-of-the-day. He would wade into the lake and began driving steel support units into the sand with a sixteen-pound sledge. Grandpa would have grandsons Tom and Mark check for alignment and others would be bringing the sections of dock down to the water's edge. Everyone had a job. The very young carried a hammer and can of nails. There was always some dock repair done on each section before moving it onto the support points. When completed, the dock was declared useable for sunbathing.

The July 4th celebrations at the lake were most memorable to me. It seemed as though all the families could make that holiday. Groups would arrive at different times preceding the 4th and the cousins would scream and yell as each car arrived at the cabin.

Comments by the adults related to how much each child had grown since last seen. The line-up photo as to size had to be taken each year. The seven grandchildren would line up from the shortest to the tallest. For a few years the line-up sequence usually related to age. As time passed the girls began to stretch out and age was no longer the governing factor.

Usually Grandpa Tom sat on the green, slatted, wooden, chair above the beach and counted his "jewels" as they played in the sand. The grandchildren were his treasurers in life and he always made each of them feel important. He always commented on the numbers of fish each caught on our outings to Lake Anne and the size was always exaggerated.

During their early years, the children built sand castles, dug holes in the sand with their shovels and watched them fill with water. They helped seine minnows, and caught sunfish from the dock. During the July 4th celebration, they used firecrackers to blow up sandcastles and soldiers. One year they set an old, wooden battleship on fire, and pushed it out into the lake and then tried to sink it by tossing firecrackers at it. "Foofie" was the only person disturbed by their activities. In the evening everyone would gather at the lakeshore to watch the fireworks display around the lake. Some years when the insects were thick the viewing was of short duration.

A couple of trips each year were made to Lake Anne; a small body of water located about six miles away from Otter Tail Lake. The group would rent the available boats and a pontoon and then congregate in an area known to be good for catching sunfish. The older members would be kept busy removing fish and baiting hooks for the younger members. How the little ones would scream and jump when they caught a fish. Grandpa had his lawn chair set up on the pontoon and his contribution consisted of shouting encouragement to the young ones and expressing amazement at what they were catching. When we arrived home, everyone had to brag to those that stayed behind about the number and size of fish they had caught. Then followed a meal of fresh fish.

Many evenings after the meal was completed, the children would begin gathering twigs so a fire could be built along the east property line. Marshmallows would then be toasted for the purpose of making S'Mores or they were toasted and eaten plain off the stick.

As the children grew older, we began to play baseball and football in a large open area adjacent to and owned by the nursing home. It was located a few hundred yards north of our cabin. Mark had an Old English Sheep Dog that loved to play football. He weighed about 100 pounds and he slightly injured Tom with one of his tackles. Tom was willing to have fly balls batted to him all afternoon. That open area seemed so large to him when he was young.

That property has now been broken up into 100 -foot lots and sold for a quarter million each. Evergreen trees have been planted on the lots.

A southeast wind always provided large waves that were ideal for bobbing around on with large, tractor tubes. We would tow the tubes out as far as we could walk and then enjoy a leisurely ride in on the white-capped waves. In later years, rubber boats became available on the market and were much safer for use by the younger members of the family.

The evenings were spent eating popcorn and looking at color slides. We would hang a white bed sheet on the wall for a screen and each family would show slides of their activities, which had taken place since the last time the group had been together.

On warm, sunny days, a floating tube trip down the Otter Tail River was a pleasant experience. We would begin at the southwest end of the lake where the river exits and make about a three-mile trip to where the river enters Deer Lake. We brought pop and snacking food along for the trip. The depth in most reaches of the river averaged about five feet. As we slowly drifted down the river, we saw schools of fish race for the weed beds and small turtles dive for cover. Tom and Mark would jump from their tubes in an attempt to catch the turtles before they could hide among the reeds. Mother duck and her train of little ones would head for shore to get out of the way of the tube invasion coming down the river. When we got to Deer Lake, an adult with a pickup would be there to haul tubers and tubes back to the cabin.

As the children got older, their toys got larger. Tom got a catamaran, which provided many exciting and thrilling experiences on windy afternoons. Mark got a canoe, which provided sore muscles anytime you went out with him. We got a 19-foot Larson boat with a 188 I/O Mercruiser engine, which was ideal for water skiing and just plain sightseeing. In the latter part of 1980's Mark and Diane bought a large, beautiful boat capable of carrying thirteen people.

Our two dogs loved the lake and were very disappointed if, for some reason, they could not go along. They would both sit by the car while it was being loaded to see if they could detect any message that might indicate that they were invited along on the trip. If I said the words, "Sure you can go along", it meant each would race around the yard in circles to indicate they understood and to show their pleasure.

Jet was a Black Labrador and just loved the water. She would fetch balls all day long if someone continued to throw them out for her. She did a beautiful swan dive off the end of the dock each time a retrieve was required. We suspect she developed heartworm from mosquitoes at the lake at a time when the disease was not very well known. She died a terrible death. The heartworm burrows holes through the heart and the heart can no longer pump oxygen to the required areas of the body. The dog basically suffocates.

Decca, an Old English Sheep Dog, was not a water dog, but did not mind the water if everyone else was splashing and playing in the lake. He would put his head under water and attempt to catch small fish or frogs along the shore. Sand fleas would become trapped in his heavy, dense coat and if he didn't receive a good bath after returning home, the fleas died and gave off a terrible smell.

The dogs seemed to know when we were going to the lake either by the type of luggage we brought out to load in the car or some sixth sense. They loved the activity and freedom at the lake and always joined in the fun. There was one exception; on the July 4th holiday they preferred to remain in the basement away from the firecrackers and bottle rockets.

Tom and Patty had Labradors and they loved it at the lake.

We bought a 65-foot lot on the east edge of Otter Tail Lake in 1975 and spent one summer developing the beach area. The reeds growing in the water approximately one hundred yards from shore were removed. The wild, willow growth on shore was cut and the root material grubbed out. When we finished, the cleared area provided a nice, sandy, beach for volleyball and other activities. The time spent together doing those things did not mean much at the moment, but in looking back they were hours of shared enjoyment. After a few years, we sold our interest in the lot to Tom. The lot continued to increase in value and the beach has again become overgrown with willows. Removal of the reeds resulted in beach erosion from wave action created by a northwest wind. Code requirements no longer permit construction of a home on any lot less than a 100 feet in width. I don't know what can be done with a 65-foot width other than selling it to the adjoining property owners.

The town of Battle Lake, located about ten miles from the lake cabin, is the site of a flea market held every weekend during the summer months. A visit to this event takes place at least once during every family get-to-together. Dozens of vendors display everything from baseball cards to paperback books. Some are displaying antiques for sale while others promote their crafts and artwork. The area takes on a carnival atmosphere for two days and then on Monday mornings the area is empty and strangely quiet. This space is no longer available for the flea market. The property was purchased and a large Assisted Living facility is now located on the site.

Phelps Mill was another point of interest that was always visited during each period spent at the lake. A William E. Thomas, who operated a flour mill and feed business in Fergus Falls, Minnesota had become interested in constructing and operating his own mill. He purchased some Otter Tail River property from Mathew Sharp and some adjacent railroad land in 1886. He moved his wife Liona to a small cabin constructed on the grassy slope above the site where he proposed to build the mill. He and his construction crew spent two years building a wooden dam and mill, known as the Maine Roller Mills. It began operating in December 1889. Although Liona was never physically strong and was in constant pain, she helped her husband by feeding and caring for the hired help. She endeared herself to her neighbors and in 1891, they gave her maiden name "Phelps" to the village that grew up around the mill. In the late 19th century and the early 20th century, the mill was the only place for many miles around where wheat could be ground into flour. Some early history about Hankinson, my birthplace, contains references of trips made by local residents to Phelps Mill for the purpose of having wheat ground into flour. The material indicates the 150-mile round trip took a period of ten days.

About the second decade of the 20th century, the use of the mill was discontinued. Other mills and the availability of electrical power decreased the importance of Phelps Mill and it soon fell into a state of disrepair. In the 1970's the State of Minnesota recognized the facility as a historical site worth preserving and began some restoration. It has now become a tourist attraction and is visited by many each summer.

When we first visited the Mill during the children's early years, it was merely for the purpose of crawling around the steel substructure beneath the building to find a place to fish in the protected water. We would place boards on the steel framework and drop baited hooks in front of the fish we could see from our darkened position.

Today the area is used yearly as the site of a summer art and crafts show. Artists and craftsmen from a wide area display their work and offer it for sale. Food vendors also blanket the area, so there is no need to leave at mealtime. Grilled chicken, pork chops, steaks, bratwurst and many other choices permits the visitor to spend the entire day, if desired. The State of Minnesota has invested funds in the Mill and has developed it as historical tourist attraction.

Although no one realized it at the time that it would be the last large family gathering, family members began showing up about mid-July. On July 18, 1985, Tom and Sally came out and had a walleye fish dinner with us. The following day, John, Deb and Eli showed up in the afternoon. Lorraine, Howard, Scott, Ardell, and the girls followed them. No sooner had the welcoming committee extended their greetings, Tom and Pat came. During the middle of the night, Vickee, Randy, and the kids came. Saturday Ken and Lil came, followed by Mark and Diane.

Tom fixed a turkey on the grill (or I should say, instructed others as to how it should be done). After dinner, everyone did different things; some went tubing on the river, some water-skied, and some went swimming, read or napped.

In the evening, we had popcorn and played Trivial Pursuit. On Sunday morning, July 21st, I fixed pancakes for breakfast. It was a noisy, joyous meal and I remember thinking at the time that these types of gatherings were numbered.

After the meal that morning, everyone either went swimming or fishing. Late in the afternoon, Grandma Sally invited everyone to a Smorgasbord at the cafe in Amor. We had a separate large room for our use. There was much loud, jovial conversation for approximately one hour. As Tom and Sally watched all the merriment, they probably realized it was the last time that they would experience a gathering of their family. We can only guess what was going on in their minds.

After the meal was finished, the group began to break up. Mark, Diane, Tom, Pat, Scott and family and Randy and family left for home. Little Sally left the next day. By July 30th, everyone was gone and I think only the adults realized we had seen the passing of an era.

As the children grew up, their responsibilities became more demanding and their visits more infrequent. Very seldom does more than one family at a time occupy the cabin today. The noisy and joyous atmosphere is a thing of the past and the age of those early visitors has turned the place into a retreat for relaxation.

The last great family gathering was Grandpa Tom's 100th birthday party. The celebration was held on August 2, 1987. Since his birthday fell on December 21st, it was obvious that not many would be able to attend on that date. As it turned out the only ones not attending the gala celebration were David and Scott's family.

Tom, Pat, Mark, and Diane had arranged for a large tent to be erected in the yard facing the lake. A large red, yellow, and blue, banner containing a 100th birthday message was hanging above the head table. Helium-filled balloons and streamers were everywhere and gave the interior of the tent a festive air. A large, decorated cake denoting a century of life was reluctantly cut and served. A printed program listing descendants and their birth dates, along with pictures of Tom was prepared by Pat and made available to those attending. It not only will serve as a reminder of a memorable day, but also will provide useful information regarding family birthdays and marriage dates.

Grandpa Tom was already a resident of the nursing home when his 100th birthday was being celebrated. It became necessary to bring him out to the lake and Diane arranged for this in a very special way. A long, white chauffeur-driven limousine from Fergus Falls came to the lake to pick up Sally and her three children. Stereo music and champagne were available in the Limousine. Diane had provided Lorraine and Kay will a string of pearls to provide the elegance the occasion demanded.

When the Limousine arrived at the nursing home, all the nurses came to the front door to see Tom off for a day of celebrating. Mark, Tom, and I had gone on ahead to video the arrival at and departure from the Home. We then got back to the lake in advance of the Limousine to video Tom's arrival there. A great number of pictures were taken and it appeared Tom J. was aware of what was happening.

The party began at 2:00 o'clock. German music provided by Howard was playing in the background throughout the afternoon.

During their early years the grandchildren were lined up by age and size each year and a picture was taken. This was done again during the birthday reunion and I feel certain it was the last opportunity to see so many gathered at the lake at the same time.

Debbie, John, and Eli drove straight through in 18 hours from Moses Lake, Washington, to spend a few hours that afternoon and then left on a non-stop trip for home. I'm sure it was a tiring ordeal, but I am certain it is an event that Eli and everyone else that attended will remember the rest of their lives. They were witnesses to an event that their grandfather and great grandfather had predicted would take place. He had predicted for 35 years that it would happen.

Shortly after Deb, John, and Eli left, Sally, Gerald, Mark and Diane also departed. Vickee and Randy took the "star" of the afternoon and returned him to the nursing home by 6:00 P.M.

It had been a hot and humid day. So much time and effort had gone into the planning and execution of an event that would only last a few hours, but it would be a day the younger generations would remember all of their lives.

The next morning Ken and Lil and Tom and Patty left for home and only the memories of an exciting day remained.

The promise Mark had made to his Grandfather many years before had been kept. He had said to him, "You live to be 100 years old and we will throw the 'Party of the Century' for you." He certainly did that. Only after it was over did the rest of us realized how much planning, and effort Tom, Patty, Mark and Diane had put into the event to make it a gala occasion to remember.

No trip to the lake would be complete without at least one trip around the lake. This involves a number of stops at various pottery shops and ice-cream stores. A stop is also made to look at the lot on the east side, a lot that now belongs to Tom.

As the children grew and their activities became more diverse, the gatherings for the July 4th celebrations ceased. It is probably all for the good for it would be impossible to recreate the excitement and fun experienced in those earlier years.

The fall of 1992 and the summer of 1993 were spent remodeling the cabin. Tom and Mark helped as their schedules permitted. New siding and windows were installed and painted. The bathroom was gutted and rebuilt. The interior paneling was painted white. Cable TV was installed. New flooring of 1/2 inch 4 x 8 sheets were installed throughout the cabin and carpeted. New electrical and plumbing systems with a water softener replaced the previous systems. Electrical heat (limited) was also installed. A washer and dryer were brought to the cabin in 1994 to eliminate hauling sheets and towels home and then back again. In 1999 a central heating and air-conditioning system was installed as well as a dishwasher.

Kay and I spent a few weeks each summer at the cabin. We sit in the screen porch during the cool of the evening and listen to the lapping of the waves as they break on the sandy beach. Many sounds we never heard in earlier years because of the children and family now has become so clear and familiar. The Minnesota Loon gives his mournful call to another. The robins singing at the end of the day and the Canada Geese cackling to each other as they return to their haven of safety at Fergus Falls add to the wildlife harmony at sundown. As darkness settles in, it becomes quiet and peaceful. Memories of the fleeting years race through our minds as we remind ourselves we were as much as 30 years younger than our oldest child when we first came to Otter Tail Lake. Another day has past and a part of another year has ended. Do the young really appreciate the time in life they still possess? And just as each year will end, so must our lives end, but we will always be thankful for the memories and joys our children provided to us at Otter Tail. We only hope that many years in the future they will look back on their days at the lake as learning and loving experience.

As mentioned earlier, in October 1995, Tom, Pat, Mark, Diane, Kay and I spent our last day together as a family at the lake. We had raked leaves and made other preparations for closing the cabin for the winter. We sat on the floor in front of the sliding door and just talked for a couple of hours. A certain amount of depression always developed at that time of the year for me. I always felt it could be the last summer that we as a family would spend at the lake. Then the premonition became true a short time later.

Little over two months after we all had been together at the lake Kay died on January 8, 1996. I lost interest in the lake for a couple of summers. Then in the summer of 1999 I had a new roof put on the garage. As mentioned earlier I installed central heating and air-conditioning, a dishwasher and garbage disposal. It is too bad Kay could not have enjoyed some of these items. Just having a washer and dryer would have eliminated drudgery of hauling laundry back and forth between Bismarck and the lake.

About 4 years after Kay's death I married her best friend Mardy Chapman on December 9, 2000. She lived a short distance down the street and we had been neighbors for 40 years.

Mardy and I have enjoyed many summer days at the cabin. We had our morning coffee on the screen porch as we watched the rising sun reflect off the lake. The humming birds come for their first meal of the day from the feeder hanging next to the screen. We watch the mother wren feeding her young in the birdhouse Mardy's father built for her so many years ago. In quiet stillness of the early morning the birds are singing and it is the beginning of another beautiful day.

For a few years Mardy's grandchildren came to the lake and we felt young and needed again. We would watch them play and scream on a floating diving board anchored in the lake. One summer the youngest grandson added water skiing to the list of many other accomplishments he has been able to enjoy. He and I had a couple of days we spent fishing and his main catch was small mouth bass. I felt so sorry for him the evening he lost his favorite fishing rod. What happened I don't know but he was almost ready to go over the side of the boat to retrieve it. We did try to snag his rod using my line but I knew the possibility wasn't very likely. After 30 minutes he agreed our chances of snagging it were not very good and he accepted the fact that he wouldn't see that rod again.

We would walk to the lakeside store for ice-cream cones. Simple little activities but they seemed to enjoy it. They couldn't imagine nor could we express to them how we enjoyed listening to their youthful conversations.

They loved to jump off the bridge where the river exits from the lake, After floating a short distance they passed over the dam into the river and then returned to the bridge to do it again. Suddenly they were grown and had various demanding schedules with college, jobs and marriage. How quickly the years pass and only photos remain to permit one to enjoy their earlier years.

Now our days at the lake are pretty quiet and restful. Mardy and I take our old dog Macy for a walk along the lakeshore in the morning and evening. Gone are the days when she would get us up at 5:00 A.M. for an early morning romp. Now she was willing to wait until 9:00 A.M. to go for that first walk. She, like us, has a much slower pace and is willing to lie down when we stop to sit on a bench adjacent to the lakeshore. We sit for a moment listening to the waves splash against the shore. The old dog that use to retrieve thrown objects from the lake is now satisfied to lie near us as we rest momentarily. The same old route she has been taking since she was a pup still proves exciting for her. She remembers the location where she almost caught a chipmunk and many years later thinks it may show up again. Her actions during late summer of 2009 became slower and she was satisfied to walk by our side rather than checking out each weed patch and wooded area. By mid-November she had difficulty coming up the stairs at our home in Fargo. We don't know if she was in pain or not but we accepted the fact that it was our time to insure she wouldn't suffer. We took her into the Companion Hospital and told them

Macy was ready to be put down and cremated. Macy lay on the floor while the vet looked for a vein. She looked up at us as though she was saying, "Thank you; you have given me a good life and it is now time to say good-by. Don't grieve for me. I hope I was all you wanted me to be." Then her eyes slowly closed as she looked up at us as if she was saying goodbye. Then she was gone. A part of Mardy and I went with her. She had given us so many wonderful memories.

Mardy and I picked up her ashes on March 30, 2010. We went to the lake to spread them along all the old trails the three of us had taken so many times. It was a beautiful sunny day with the temperature in the high 60s. It was almost as though she was with us as we stopped at the same lakeshore bench to rest.

Each time in the past one of her first obvious requests when we arrived at the lake was, as she left the car, "May I go swimming?" As soon as we said, "Macy can go swimming" she would then head for the lake and swim in circles for half-hour. On recent trips she merely went to the water's edge and barely got wet. Swimming had become another difficult task. So we spread a hand full of ashes across the lake surface. She was a great dog and we miss her.

Mardy and I bought a new powerboat and a fishing boat shortly after being married. I guess we thought we were still young and would always be. I tried to water ski the summer I was 85 years old but couldn't get up on the skis. I maintained there were too many passengers in the boat and it didn't have the power to pull me up. There's nothing like an old fool.

This summer (2010) all of Mardy's family came to the lake for one last gathering. This also includes her great granddaughter born last November. All her grandchildren were so young a short time ago and now some are in high school, some are in college and some are married with children. Those few brief years when they were growing up can only be enjoyed as memories or through photographs. I have had the opportunity to see two sets of young people grow up—first that set of my family and then those of Mardy's family.

We have now given thought to turning the cabin over to my two sons this year. There are so many memories associated with the cabin in the past 54 years. There are children and grandchildren who have grown to adulthood and have never seen the cabin. They may have second-hand knowledge related by their parents, as to what some of the activities were that took place during those 54 years. Only memories remain that cannot be relived.

The thought mentioned above actually became a reality early in October 2010. At the end of the summer season the dock and lift were removed from the lake and disposed of. The ownership of the two boats also changed and the contents of the cabin were distributed to various individuals. On a beautiful Sunday afternoon (10-10-10) we build a campfire. The temperature was in the low 80s. Art and Judy Azure, Bob and Evie Mc Morrow and Mardy and I roasted hot dogs and ate potato salad. The end of an era had arrived and we left the lake for the last time.

CHAPTER 19

Construction of our First Home

I recall a summer day in 1954 during a visit to Breckenridge when my sons Tommy, Mark and I drove around town to look at the various houses I had lived in as I was growing up. They were 5 and 2 years old and I was probably doing it more for my benefit than for their benefit.

There were five units located throughout the city that I had lived in. A year is eternal to a child and although it seemed as though I had lived in some of the houses forever and ever, it had really been a very short time in some of the homes. The longest period was five years in the house on North 10th Street. It was located on the north edge of town about three blocks from the city's developed area. Today that entire area is residential with paved streets, schools and playgrounds.

As I stated, Mark was two and Tommy was five at the time of this trip. I was explaining that I lived in this particular house when I was between certain ages and I lived in another house when I was another age. Finally I came to the house at 327-11th Street North.

I told them, "I lived in this house from the time I was 14 until I left home for good at 18. This house was really ours because we owned it."

Tom thought for awhile and then he finally said, "When are we going to really own our house, Dad?"

We sat in the street in front of the house and memories came rushing back. I told him of some of the things Bob and I used to do when we lived there. It was not the house I saw as I talked; it was a series of memories of the late '30's involving Bob and me. I wasn't really talking to Tommy. I was conveying my thoughts in words.

I finally realized Tom was waiting for an answer and I answered him saying, "We'll start seeing what we can do about owning our own house." His question is what really motivated me. There was no reason to wait any longer.

Many of our friends were seriously considering a start on their first house in 1954. Steinbruck and Raatz, two fellows from the office, started that summer. This sort of started a chain reaction and by late summer many from the office were formulating plans to start building.

We looked around the city in an attempt to decide where we might want to locate. We eventually decided to bid on one of the lots located adjacent to the golf course on the north side of Boulevard Avenue between Washington and Griffin Streets. The city was accepting bids and we put in a bid of 1,100 dollars for a lot located about 4 lots west of Washington. The lot went for 1,400 dollars and we started searching again.

We then starting looking at lots in Highland Acres, a development area in the northwest part of the city. A veterans group from Jamestown initially started the development and a few homes were built on South Highland Acres Road in 1946. There were no city sewer or water systems to the area and the development was not moving. The veterans group began having financial problems and sold the area to Hedden Real Estate.

We were initially interested in the lot southwest of the one Bob Dorothy purchased, but another person had an option to buy. Bob and I worked in the same office. Edie and Jim Boucher eventually bought and lived on the property.

We borrowed 800 dollars from my dad and on August 16th we purchased Lot 9, Block 10 for 1,500 dollars. It seemed like a fantastic price to pay for one-third acre. Good farmland was going for 50 dollars an acre at the time.

We obtained a 4.9% interest rate on an 11,000-dollar construction loan from Gate City Savings and Loan in Fargo. Hart Insurance Agency handled their local accounts for them in Bismarck.

Under the terms of the loan agreement, money would be released periodically as construction progressed in order to pay for material and labor. It was a little frightening to be so far in debt. Would we ever be able to repay that amount of money in twenty years?

We obtained a basic set of plans by August 21st and started making the modifications to them that would give us what we wanted. Every evening we would go out to the lot to look and plan. Highland Acres was still pretty primitive and undeveloped. Nothing existed in the area except the few houses that had been built on South Highland Acres Road. All the existing streets in the area were unpaved. Jackrabbits roamed the area and the coulees were full of pheasants. Russian thistles from the hills to the north would blow across the lot on windy days. When standing on that lot I must have been experiencing the same feelings my dad felt back in 1937 when he stood on his lot. It was the beginning of a new way of life. Everything that was done was done for the family.

The basement was completed by September 19th and five days later I had completed waterproofing the concrete walls on the outside. With the exception of the first ten days of October, the weather throughout the construction was perfect. Early October was rainy and cool. We were impatient since we realized it wouldn't be too long before the snow started flying. However it turned out to be a beautiful fall. The daytime temperatures would reach 60 degrees during the afternoon and the sun shone almost every day.

Bob Dorothy and I hired a Howard Steffes from Dickinson to help us frame in the structures. In my case, for 600 dollars, he would frame the house, roof and shingle, put in windows, do the siding, and install the front and back storm doors.

Bob and I worked with him a few days at my place and then a few days at his place. When Steffes' work was done Bob and I moved on to our own work that was necessary to get the places ready to move into before Christmas.

By October 20th all interior studding was completed and I arranged for Keim Electric to do the wiring. The service entrance was rated at 60 amps, which is very low by today's standards. There weren't such things as microwave ovens, television sets and self-cleaning ovens. When we built the addition to the house in 1979, we changed to a 150-amp entrance. The lake home modification provided for a 200 amp. service entrance.

Kay started priming the siding on October 21st and, with a few interruptions for changing Mark's diapers, finished by November 3rd. She then began putting on a blue topcoat on the siding. Before getting all the way around the house, we decided we didn't like the color. I began following behind her with a red finish coat. People were beginning to think we weren't communicating.

During this painting period, we lost track of Mark. We found him in one of the bedrooms with one wall partially painted with the red house paint. It took many coats of the inside wall paint to cover the bright red spot.

We finished with the siding by November 7th and the window trim by November 11th. Later that Armistice Day we went to the parade and then to the American Legion Club for dinner. After waiting in line for two hours, we were nearing the serving windows when they ran out of food. We ended up somewhere else at a restaurant in town.

We begin to put concrete down on one-half of Bob's basement floor. The mix was pretty sloppy and too wet to work. We decided to go pheasant hunting for a few hours to let it start to set up. When we got back, it was ideal for finishing. However, by the time we got to one end of the basement, it was setting up so quickly that it became difficult to work. We tried the best we could to get the floor as smooth and level as possible and finally gave up at 9:00 P.M. Irene reminded us for years that her laundry room floor was not as smooth as she would like it.

We calculated our concrete needs as closely as we could, since any surplus was wasted in the surrounding area and we paid for it. My estimate for the second half of our basement floor came up short and 9 square feet in the southeast corner didn't get patched until the following week.

Both basement floors were completed by November 20th and we started insulating on November 28th. Every little crevice was filled, some no wider than a knife blade. This was then followed with drywall. I had helped Joe Pratschner the year before, so he now helped me. The large, open areas went quickly, but places like the closets took much measuring and cutting. The drywall work was completed on December 13th. I then started taping and sizing in preparation for painting. During this same period that I worked on the drywall, Hindemith was doing the heating and Amick was installing the plumbing. Both jobs were finished by

December 14th and it became more pleasant working in the evenings when the temperatures begin dropping quickly after sundown.

I was still smoking at this time. I used to work every evening until after midnight. I recall this one night I got home and after being in bed for thirty minutes, I begin to wonder whether or not I had put out the cigarette I had been smoking before I left for home. I wasn't certain if I snuffed it out or set it down somewhere. The more I thought about it, the more uncertain I was as to what I had done with it. I knew I wouldn't get any sleep until I checked it out. If the fire whistle had blown about this time, I'm certain it would have given me heart failure.

I got dressed again, traveled across town and looked over the area where I had been working. I got home and fell into a peaceful sleep about 2:00 A.M.

After December 14th, I began bringing packed boxes each time I made a trip to the house. Two days later we hired Ted's Delivery to move our furniture across town. They arrived at 8:00 A.M. and were finished just before noon. Total cost for the move was 25 dollars. Kay and I continued to haul boxes, which she had packed and we were finished by 10:00 P.M. and residing in our new home.

What a wonderful feeling to be able to make as much noise as we wanted. In the apartment we always were concerned about the noise the children would make and what the owner, who was living upstairs, would think. We told the boys they could run and scream all they wanted.

We had no inside doors, which could be locked before we left for Breckenridge at 11 o'clock on December 24th. Anyone coming up to the door had only to turn the doorknob to gain entry. There was less concern in those days about break-ins, but it may have also been our thought that there wasn't that much to take if they did come in.

Before the final portion of the money from Gate City Savings and Loan and the balance of the loan would be made available, an inspection as to completion was necessary. We had none of the interior doors hung, no cabinet doors on in the kitchen, no hardwood floors installed in the bedrooms and all rooms were unpainted. Early in February two men arrived out in front of the house. The temperature was down near a minus 25 degrees. They rolled down the car window, looked at the house, made a few notes on the clipboard, and then drove away. I breathed a sigh of relief.

Kay's health continued to deteriorate and she began to have trouble getting down and up the basement stairs. By the late 1970's, we decided we needed to bring the laundry room up to the first floor. Kay drew up a set of plans as to what she wanted in the addition. We had the excavation done in August 1979 after we returned from the army reunion in Minneapolis. The extension involved approximately 420 additional square feet and provided a half-bath, laundry room and kitchen. We made the former kitchen area into a formal dining room

All major items of work were completed in time to enjoy Christmas. I had torn up the concrete in the basement floor to provide for a new drainage system in the addition. Tom helped me mix concrete on Christmas Day to get the drain trench refilled. It was a beautiful day and we had heard the Soviet Union had just invaded Afghanistan.

Total cost of the addition was approximately 15,000 dollars and we were sorry we hadn't done it many years before. It was too bad it wasn't done while the boys were still home.

We built a garage at this same time; a luxury we hadn't had before then. I installed a natural gas heater. A thermostat regulated the temperature. It was a joy to get into a warm car on cold winter days.

CHAPTER 20

Family Medical Problems

This chapter also covers a long period of time. However to keep all related items together it is necessary to begin about the time the first medical problems occurred and then try to tabulate, in sequence, the problems as they happened. This chapter could be of little interest to all other than those who know the family.

This, like some of the other chapters, will be used mainly for reference purposes. The questions often arise as to what date Mark fell on a stick he was carrying in his mouth or when did Tom have measles. Those kinds of questions can be answered by searching for the answers in this chapter.

Some reference to a trip to Minneapolis for laser beam eye treatment may also be mentioned in more detail under the chapter on trips and vacations. This cannot be helped since in one case it deals with travel and in the other case it deals with the purpose for the travel.

This chapter like a number of other chapters may prove uninteresting to most other than family, relatives and friends. This is mentioned again in order to give you the opportunity to skip to areas of the book that you may find more to your liking.

Regular examinations or checkups were never scheduled during our early years. One saw a doctor or went to the hospital only after a problem developed. As was the case with my brother Darrell, this could prove to be a poor practice. My only time in a hospital during my first 21 years was a brief visit to St. Francis with Coach Mikulich to have an X-ray of a sprained ankle received in basketball.

During February 1944, I was placed in the Camp Forrest Army Hospital in Tennessee for an eye infection. We were on maneuvers at the time.

I was also in the hospital in Naples, Italy in June 1944 and again for a week in Rome in August 1944. Both were Italian hospitals taken over by the Army.

As a young girl, Kay spent time in the St. Francis Hospital for removal of her tonsils.

During the final month of pregnancy with Tom in 1949, Dr. Darner advised Kay on March 3rd that she had a very narrow pelvis and natural delivery would be very difficult. However, he was going to let her go into labor.

On March 23rd Dr. Darner indicated the baby would be at least a week late. Kay's labor pains began at 7:00 A.M. on Friday, April 1st. She was taken to the hospital at 10:00 A.M. She then continued with 30 hours of labor and during that period she was in extreme pain. On Saturday morning, April 2nd, I was called out of the Electrical Engineering Lab at the university to obtain approval to do a C-Section. She spent about a week in the hospital and then came home with a little guy we called Tommy.

Kay began preparing for Mark's birth on February 6th, 1952. She went in for her final clinic visit on that day. She was scheduled to report into the hospital on

February 7th and the C-Section would be performed the following day. I took Kay to the hospital at 3:30 P. M., Thursday, and the hospital personnel spent the rest of the day preparing her for the following morning. Irene Dorothy, a next door neighbor, took care of Tommy.

Kay was prepared and taken up to surgery at 8:00 A.M. on Friday. She was able to watch the first half of the preparation before she went under.

Tommy's brother, weighing 8 pounds 14 1/2 ounces, was born at 8:40 A.M. and Kay was conscious again at 11:20 A. M. She had severe after pains. Kay's mother came later that day.

Dr. Cochran took Kay's stitches out on February 14th and she went home the following morning at 9:30.

Mark came down an alley and out onto Rosser Avenue in Bismarck on September 1, 1954. We were living in the basement apartment on the south side of the street. When we heard the screeching of brakes we rushed up the stairs to see a body lying in the center of the street. You imagine the worst. He had been hit by a car and was covered with blood. We rushed him to the emergency room at St. Alexius Hospital. They took 12 x-rays and put in 6 stitches to close the wound on his forehead. While waiting for a report on the extent of his injuries his mother and I were visited by the police in the hospital. They wanted to know why we had left the scene of an accident without reporting it to them. I will let you imagine what my response to them was.

Tom got the Red Measles on May 2, 1956. Mark was feeling fine until May 15th and then he and Vickee each had the measles. Everyone was fine and out playing again by May 20th.

Mark was running across Ferguson's backyard with a stick in his mouth about 6:00 P.M. on July 2, 1956. He tripped and fell on the stick, which was pushed down into his throat. I took him to the hospital where it required surgery in his throat to close the wound. I was home by

10:00 P.M., but Mark had to stay overnight. Kay went up to the hospital the next morning at 8:00 A.M. She stayed, and since Mark was feeling pretty good, she was able to check him out of the hospital at 1:00 P.M., July 3rd.

Kay's hay fever continued to worsen during the fall of 1956. Dr. Wasemiller gave her 3 new pills while we were in Breckenridge on September 1st.

Tom got his last permanent tooth (a molar) in January 1958. Mark lost his first tooth in July 1958.

Kay fell and hit her head outside of Dan's Super Value on November 5, 1959. She had a slight concussion and a backache after the fall.

Tom damaged five front teeth in a sledding accident at the coulee by East Highland Acres Road. He went to the dentist on December 1, 1959. The dentist indicated that he would need two gold crowns until age 19 or so.

We all got polio shots on July 14, 1960.

Kay had considerable dental work done during 1959, 1960, and 1961, which included gold crowns, root canals, and bridges.

Kay went in for blood tests on November 21, 1960. Dr. Dahl indicated she has diabetes and he recommended pills and a very strict diet.

Mark was taken for a check up on February 9, 1961, to Drs. Nugent and Woodward. He was back at the clinic on February 13. It was determined that he didn't need glasses; he was born with spotted pigment. I sat with Dr. Woodward at breakfast in March 1995 and he told me that he had read in a medical journal recently that anyone with spotted pigment is 30 percent more likely to have colon cancer if anyone else in the family has had colon cancer. He said they should be checked every year. Since I had colon cancer in December 1979, this finding should be of concern to Mark.

A dog bit Mark on June 11, 1961, at the ballpark on South Washington Avenue. We went to the hospital ck against rabies. The dog was kept in isolation for five days.

We had Mark's adenoids and hearing checked on July 17, 1961. Although his hearing is fine, we found years later that he only heard what he wanted to hear.

Kay had an irritated eye and the clinic found a small chip of enamel embedded in the eyeball. After removal, she felt fine.

Mark got a blister from a pair of shoes that rubbed on his heel on September 16, 1962. In a short time, it developed into blood poisoning with a red streak running up the back of his leg. Dr. Dahl checked him the next day in the clinic and told him to take pills and keep hot packs on it.

Kay developed double pneumonia on August 12, 1963, while we were on a camping trip to Lake Superior and Sault Ste. Marie, Ontario. It was brought on by her method of hair drying. Each morning after washing her hair, she would hold it out the window as we were going down the highway at 60 miles per hour. She wasn't sick, so she spent one restful week reading magazines in the hospital.

Kay's hay fever worsened during the fall of 1964. Many nights she had trouble breathing. She was on all of the latest medication available at that time.

Kay broke her front tooth off on March 22, 1965.

Mark's eye was swollen shut each morning. We took him to Dr. Ellingson for x-rays. It was eventually determined that he was allergic to some materials in his pillows. We took Mark to the clinic on September 24, 1969, and we were told he had strep throat. He spent a few days in bed.

Tom came home from Fargo on October 1, 1969, with mono. Dr. Dahl stopped by the house and gave him a shot. The next morning Tom went to the clinic for blood tests. He was given some medication and told to get plenty of rest.

318

Beginning in 1971 Kay had many days where she wasn't feeling well. Her diabetes had become much more severe since she hadn't taken the doctor's advice to lose weight, eat healthy and get more exercise.

Tom had an emergency appendectomy at 5:15 P.M. on May 4, 1971.

Kay had two hours of dental surgery on July 11, 1971 and then found out she didn't need it. She continued to have root canal work and other dental work completed during 1972, 1973, 1974, 1975, and 1976. They eventually wanted to pull all her teeth and do implants. However, her jawbone would not support such a procedure. She ended up with dentures.

Mark went to the clinic on October 14, 1971, and found out he has mono.

Mark had surgery in Fargo on January 24, 1972 to remove 4 wisdom teeth. We left for Fargo at 2:00 P.M. and found his room full of visitors when we got there; Shirleen, Duke, Paula, and Tammy. Mark was still groggy. We went to Breckenridge for the night and returned the next morning at 10:00 A.M. We met Tom coming out when we entered the hospital. We had a quick visit before he left. Mark was beginning to feel pretty good.

Mark went to Fargo on March 21, 1972, to see Dr. Lamb about nose surgery.

Kay had an asthmatic attack on February 9, 1974 and the next month she went to the clinic for blood tests and a physical on March 20, 1974. They determined she needed a hysterectomy soon. She had the 2 ½- hour surgery at 8:00 A.M. on April 3, 1974. She remembered nothing between 8:00 A.M. and midnight. She had her stitches out on April 10th and I brought her home that same day at 2:00 P.M.

Kay's blood sugar reading went down to 68 on May 23, 1974. Kay went to the clinic on June 12, 1974, and Dr. Dahl was puzzled; she either had chicken pox, shingles, or herpes. She was given a cortisone shot and after a number of weeks, she ended up with a deep scar on her forehead from shingles.

We got a call from Mark on October 14, 1974. He went to Dakota Hospital Emergency Room for an appendectomy. We called him twice the next day and everything was fine.

Dr. Ellingson spent three hours checking Kay's eyes on April 3, 1975, and then informed her she would have to go to the University of Minnesota for laser treatment.

Dr. Harris at the U of M performed almost 6 hours of eye tests on May 12, 1975.

Dr. Dahl discovered a lump in Kay's breast on May 20, 1975. Dr. Goughner sent her to the hospital for a mammogram. On May 22nd, 1975, she had a biopsy taken at 4:00 P.M. in the hospital. The next day they did surgery at 8:30 A.M. and she was back in her 4-bed ward by noon. Everything was fine.

She was happy to get out of the 4-bed ward by May 24, 1975, and we went to the lake. She got the stitches out six days later.

We made 8 trips to Minneapolis during 1977 for laser treatment to stop eye hemorrhaging. All work was done at the University of Minnesota.

We started the year 1978 with a trip to Minneapolis on January 28th. Kay had an eye exam scheduled for January 30th at the University of Minnesota. During the exam, it was determined she had a detached retina and would require surgery to reattach it. The procedure was usually no more than 50 % successful. She reported to the hospital on January 31st at 2:30 P.M. Charley Volk was on duty, which delighted Kay. He was a school friend of our son Tom and had spent many days at our home during his youth. The surgery was scheduled for the following day at 2:00 P.M. and would be performed by Dr. Knoblock. Kay spent a long morning writing letters.

She was up at 5:00 A.M. the morning following surgery and was experiencing no pain. She did considerable walking in the halls during her stay and was discharged on February 5, 1978.

We returned to Minneapolis on March 30, 1978, for a 2:30 P.M. examination. Charley Volk did the examination. The eye looked good, but the surgery was not successful. She would be blind in that eye and no known procedures could correct it.

Kay's right eye started hemorrhaging on October 31, 1979. We called the clinic at the University of Minnesota and she was advised to come down immediately.

She flew to Minneapolis the next morning and Tom picked her up at the airport. They had lunch with Patty and then went to the University. Charley Volk was on staff.

Dr. Knoblock put Kay in the hospital on November 2, 1978. She had blood tests and was told the vessels are not clotting enough to have laser treatment. She was discharged that same morning at 10:30 A.M. She and Tom shopped until the plane left for Bismarck at 6:40 P.M.

Kay spent 5 hours at Mid-Dakota Clinic on November 27, 1979. After a series of X-rays, fluid was found in her lungs. She was given medication and had her lungs x-rayed again on December 5th.

We were under construction with our new addition when, during one of her inspection trips, she missed a step on December 19, 1979. She fell and cracked some ribs. She went into the clinic on December 22nd, but all they told her was that she would have to wait for the ribs to heal.

During an eye exam on June 4, 1980, Kay was informed she needed cataract surgery. This she had done in September 1980.

Almost every night I would walk Decca, Mark's dog along the railroad tracks by Fraine Barracks. About November 1980, I noticed a pain in my stomach that just wouldn't go away. I was so weary after each walk, I could hardly make it home. It was a weakness that was more than physical. I assumed I might be developing an ulcer since the time schedule for a number of items at work was so tight. I had been meeting with the Canadians in Denver trying to resolve issues relating to an Environmental Impact Statement. It had a December 15th completion date.

Eventually everything worked out fine at work, but I still had the pain. I retired on December 30, 1980. During a routine physical exam on February 3rd, a lesion was discovered on my colon. I had had a continuous weakness the prior three months and then I discovered blood in the stool just before retirement.

My early retirement was a result of two things. Kay's kidney failure and the need to go on dialysis three times a week and the election of Jimmy Carter as president. Carter and the environmentalists were out to kill the project I was working. They were successful.

Dan Chapman drove me to the hospital on February 8th and I was prepared for surgery on Monday, February 10th. Elvina, Kay's cousin, had come from California on February 9th to stay with Kay.

As they say on the television program "Cheers", I went under the knife at 7:30 A.M. on the 10th and was in the Recovery Room by 9:30. They removed two feet of colon. It was a cold day with wind chill of 68 degrees below zero. It was not an ideal California day for Elvina.

Bob and Terry came on February 14th and Elvina returned home later in the day. Bob and Terry went home the next day.

Donna Makoff picked Kay up at the dialysis unit and then came to get me. She took both of us home on February 18th.

Kay learned to take insulin shots at the hospital on March 10, 1981.

Kay had another of many eye hemorrhages on April 3, 1981.

Kay continued on dialysis every third day during the entire year of 1981. Many times she got extremely sick when her blood pressure would drop way down. This was true on September 10 the day Mark and Diane stopped to see her at the hospital before leaving for Chicago. It happened again on December 3rd and 4th when her pressure dropped to 50.

I was servicing the Dickinson-Belfield-Watford City area for Zee Medical Service. I was staying in a small motel on the east side of Belfield. About 2:30 A.M. June 8, 1982, I got a terrible tightness in my chest. I was certain I had the flu. I tossed around until about 5:30 A.M. and then went over to the Trapper's Kettle for breakfast.

By seven o'clock, I was on my way to Watford City and the surrounding oil fields having Zee first aid cabinets. I felt weak and had a fever and a cold sweat all day. I got back to Bismarck about 10:00 P.M. and went to bed without eating. Mark called three times that day. By the following day I was feeling well enough to be up and around.

I went in for my annual physical on July 21, 1982. During the examination Dr. Dahl asked when I had had my heart attack. I told him I didn't think I had had one, but did mention the flu and the symptoms I had earlier the previous month in Belfield. He said it sounded more like a heart attack than the flu. He did an EKG and found some damage in the heart muscle.

During a routine dialysis session on November 8, 1982, a problem developed. About 4:00 P.M. Kay's blood pressure dropped to zero and her heart stopped beating. The nurses began corrective procedures with no results. They then called Code Blue and personnel from all over the hospital began showing up. Her chest was massaged until the resuscitation team arrived. There was no carotid pulse felt by the nurses. After about two minutes of CPR by the team, Kay's heart began beating again. They rushed her to ICU with tubes dangling everywhere. Since I was working with Zee Medical and on the road, they could not locate me.

She felt fine after arriving in ICU and requested a TV set be brought to her room. The nurses advised her that no one in ICU ever watches TV. She insisted and the nurses got the doctor's permission to grant her request. Her biggest complaint was that her new bra was cut in half when they started giving CPR.

Tom and Mark flew in the morning of November 9th. Dan and Mardy and many others came up to visit. Kay remembered nothing about what had happened. She complained about her chest hurting from the CPR. Considering how fragile her bones were and are, they probably broke a rib or two during the CPR procedure.

Kay was transferred from ICU to a regular room on November 11th. She continued to have pain from the rough treatment administered in trying to revive her.

Tom flew back to Minneapolis at 3:00 P.M. on November 13th. Early that day, Mark left for Fargo and Fergus.

Kay had an angiogram by Dr. Eshoo at 1:00 P.M. on November 13th. He concluded she had blockage in a small and large artery. He also determined she had had a heart attack some time previous to his examination.

A similar episode to the one above happened again on December 13th. She started dialysis at 2:30 P.M. Her blood pressure at 3:10 P.M. was 140/60 and she was doing fine. However, at 3:35 P.M. the blood pressure was found to be 118. Just prior to that she was talking to the nurse and then suddenly grabbed her chest and said, "It hurts". After that she became unresponsive. Again the Code Blue went out over the intercom system. She was given 3 or 4 shots of 5% normal saline and 35 cc intravenous with no results. Again there was no pulse. The resuscitation team worked on Kay for three minutes before she became responsive. She was then given seven shots of the same saline solution and moved to ICU. She was also given nitroglycerin for the pain experienced in her chest. Since she was now feeling good, she again requested a television set. A new nurse crew tried to convince her that it was highly irregular for someone in ICU to have a television set. She once again insisted on seeing a doctor and she ended up with her TV. I had been working in Minot all day and didn't get home until 8:00 P.M.

They put Kay in Room 3333 on December 14th and she came home the following day at 11:00 A.M. after dialysis.

Irene D. and Ella O. brought dinner over on December 19th and Lois D. on the 20th. On December 21st, we went to Chapmans' for dinner and on Christmas Day Linda and Casey C. had 11 people for dinner.

We left Bismarck for Minneapolis right after Kay came off dialysis at 10:30 A.M. on March 10, 1983. I had a Zee Medical meeting in Chicago the next day. We arrived at 8:00 P.M and had dinner with Mark and Diane at the Bonaventure and then went over to Tom's house. Unknown to us at this time, a kidney would become available to Kay the next day.

I flew to Chicago the next morning. Shortly after the meeting began, I got a call from Pat in the office in Bismarck. She indicated the University of Minnesota had called and was trying to locate Kay. They had a kidney available for Kay and it was already 35 hours old (They don't like to transplant after they become 60 hours old). I called the hospital and told them to page the shopping centers. I gave them a list of those she most likely would be shopping in. Unknown to me, Kay, Diane, and Mark had gone to Bank's and then to a new shopping mall in St. Anthony. I got back from Chicago at 7:00 P.M. and when Mark picked me up at the terminal I asked, "Did

the University Hospital get in contact with your mother?"
He didn't know what I was talking about.

We then hurried home to Mark and Diane's
apartment and called the hospital. They then requested
Kay come in immediately for tests to determine if the
kidney was compatible.

She went in for the tests at 10:30 P.M. We sat around
talking and waiting all night for the call the hospital
promised to make as soon as they knew the results of
the tests. At 5:00 A. M. the call came that one of the four
characteristics required was available and considering
the age of the kidney, they were going ahead with the
surgery at 7:00 A.M.

Approximately 4 hours later the surgery was over
and the doctor said everything looked good. Kay was
woozy all day. She had nine tubes in her arm, oxygen in
her nose, and a catheter. The kidney started working that
same day. She remained on round-the-clock-monitoring
and everything continued to look good the next day.

Pat, Tom, Mark, and Diane came up on March
12, 1983, and I left for Bismarck at 3:00 P.M. to return to
work.

Kay still had no food or liquids by March 13th. The
tubes began to come out two days later. Many visitors,
cards, and calls kept her day busy. Jeff Chapman and
Patti paid a surprise visit.

On March 17th, Kay found out her kidney was from
a 32-year old woman in Iowa who had died of head
injuries sustained in an automobile accident. Because of
her age, Kay would not have been eligible to receive a
donor kidney, but an experimental drug was to be tried.
On March 18th, Kay started receiving oral cyclosporin
and the last tube was removed. She also had physical
therapy and ultrasound.

Beth and John Wahlstad were up to see Kay the
evening of March 19th. The next day Ken, Lil, Becky, Jon,
Arlene, and Sandy, as well as the kids and Patty came

up. Sonji (Becky's friend), Mary Dunn, Mark and Diane were up the next day.

On March 22, 1983, I came to Minneapolis at 1:00 P.M. and after the nurse had given Kay instructions on her medications, we were able to leave. The family went to dinner at Le Bistro.

We left for Bismarck the next morning and it was a race between rest stops. Who said the kidney was not working?

The staples used in Kay's March 11th surgery were removed on April 1st at St. Alexius Hospital during one of her regular blood exams.

My feet went out from under me over by the Highland Acres School when I was walking Mark's dog Decca in December 1984. I landed on the back of my head and saw more stars than the heavens have on a clear night. I lay there for about ten minutes waiting for things to clear a little. Decca couldn't understand why we were not heading for the coulee. Except for a small egg-shaped lump on the back of my head, everything was fine the next day. I probably had a concussion but didn't realize it.

We were at Rubellke's for dinner on December 18, 1984. About 9:00 P.M., Kay began having stomach pains. By 10:00 P.M., they were so severe she couldn't stand it. We went to the emergency room. Kay doesn't remember a thing all night. The next morning at 11:00 A.M., Dr. Hamar removed her gall bladder and told me it wouldn't have been too long before gangrene would have set in. They put Kay in ICU on December 21st and she remained there for two days. She didn't remember anything about her stay in ICU.

I called Mark and Tom after the surgery was over. Tom came to the hospital on December 21st and Diane, Mark, Tom and Sally came on December 23rd.

They put Kay on telemetry on December 22nd, and she spent most of the time sleeping. She had her first food in four days on December 23rd, but no water.

Dr. Hamer agreed, after Kay insisted, that he would allow her to go home for Christmas. It was two days earlier than normally considered for discharge time. She came home the afternoon of Christmas Eve and watched while everyone pitched in to get dinner ready.

Sally cooked the Christmas Day dinner. No gifts got wrapped that year.

Mark, Di, Grandparents Sally and Tom left the next morning after breakfast. We took Tom to the airport on December 27, 1984, at 6:00 A.M.

Kay hurt her back on February 1, 1985. It continued to get worse all through February. On March 1st, she couldn't get out of bed or walk. We canceled a March 4th appointment we had in Minneapolis.

Against her better judgment, Kay was even willing to try a chiropractor. This made matters even worse and after five treatments, I said no more.

On March 18th, we went to Dr. Kilzer for back x-rays. He found that the bones in her spine were crumbling and disintegrating from medications she is required to take. He put her on Florical. She stayed in bed for 9 weeks.

On April 6th, she was able to eat her first breakfast in the kitchen since February 1st. Two days later she was able to get out of bed without any help and was also able to walk alone.

On April 22nd, she broke a rib. She went to Dr. Kilzer on May 2nd because of the pain, but he said all she could do was wait for it to heal.

She continued to break ribs from such activities as reaching into he washer or bending over to pick up a piece of paper. Her back has also been a continuing source of pain.

I had four skin cancers removed on May 15, 1986, and three additional on June 4th. Two had continued to seep fluid periodically. I had assumed it was a burn resulting from some overhead soldering I had done. Solder had fallen on my chest on one occasion He removed four additional cancer spots on March 18, 1987. In 2005 I had a lesion removed from my nose that resulted a large chuck of meat being taken out. It is probably a result of never wearing a shirt or cap during the summer when I was young.

Kay had some dizzy spells periodically between January 8, and April 1987. She had an appointment with Dr. Wangerod, Neurologist, on April 29, 1987. He did a series of inner ear tests. Everything checked okay. She followed up with a balance test with Dr. Gene Balzer at MedCenter One on June 9th.

In early June 1988, I began to get terrible leg pains. They continued periodically up until 1995, but continued until I had my left hip replaced in November 1996. I had a knee x-ray on April 13, 1995 and Dr. Bopp indicated they got a good buy on knee replacement components recently and could give me a reduced price on a replacement.

We were at Tom and Pat's for Thanksgiving in 1988. As Kay was going out the door into the garage, she missed a step. She fell, hurting her leg and back. There was a long recuperation period again before she felt what she calls normal.

For years, I had been bothered with an ingrown toenail on my left large toe. I continued to remove it myself when the pain became too great to bear. I finally decided it could be corrected once and for all. I went into the foot clinic on January 3, 1989, and the doctor removed three pieces about the size of a dime. On January 16th, he went to the head of the nail and scraped the sides. This resulted in the nail growing straight instead of angling off to the sides. I have had no problem since.

We spent Christmas with Mark and Diane in Fargo in 1989. Kay had a dizzy spell in the bedroom while dressing on the morning of December 24th. She hit her head as she fell.

We stopped at the truck stop in Tower City on our way home on December 26th. Kay fell again in the rest room and hit her head against the wall. I was sitting in a booth that had a common wall with the rest room. When I heard the noise, I knew it was she. I rushed in there and had to help her off the floor.

Kay's next dizzy spell was on January 26, 1990. She fell and called to me. I came in and got her into bed. The dizzy spells were unpredictable and could not be anticipated. She hurt her arm, head, tailbone and hip.

She went in to see Dr. Wongerard on February 6, 1990. He x-rayed her tailbone and hip to determine if there was any damage from the fall. He also told her to keep her head elevated. The clinic also put her on a 24- hour heart monitor on February 27th. It was uncomfortable, but it came off the next day and proved nothing. She went to Dr. Dunnigan on March 2, 1990, for heart tests, and everything checked out fine. He wanted her to have a MRI.

Kay had returned from the home of Betty Lu Lannoye the afternoon of January 8, 1991. As she was entering the bedroom to change clothes, she felt dizzy and then blacked out. As she was falling, she twisted in an attempt to get to the bed. In doing so, she bent her ankle as she went down. She limped around until January 14th, and when it became obvious that her condition wasn't improving, she went to Dr. Olson for X rays. Her ankle was broken and he put it in a cast. I got a wheel chair for traveling around the house and of course, for covering the Mall. I got a plastic chair that could be set in the tub for showering purposes.

On January 21st, Dr. Olson looked at Kay's ankle and put her in a hot pink walking cast and boot. He told her she would be in that for at least a month. Her bones do not heal because of diabetes and other complications.

I had a root canal done by Dr. Honkola on January 28, 1991. Dental work is nothing now compared to the procedures used 50 years ago. It is almost painless except when the bill comes.

Kay had Dr. Olson cut her cast off on February 8, 1991, to remove some pressure. The new cast was removed February 18th. She was then fitted with a splint, which she was to wear for three weeks. Dr. Olson indicated on March 12th, she would need a half-cast for another three weeks.

About 4:00 A.M., April 10, 1991, I found Kay lying on the bathroom floor. Dr. Dunnigan ran a series of tests on April 10th, 11th, and 12th at Mid-Dakota Clinic. At the conclusion of his tests, he had Kay admitted to St. Alexius Medical Center at 5:00 P.M. on April 12th.

She spent a week in the hospital going through a series of tests. They discharged her on Friday afternoon, April 19th, and then scheduled her into the University of Minnesota for additional tests.

St. Alexius Hospital was going to fly her down in the medical helicopter. However, they indicated that since she wasn't sick, insurance would not pay for the flight. The cost would be 3,000 dollars.

I asked, "If she isn't sick, why the hurry to get her down there. She could ride with me since I intend to go down."

They agreed that riding with me would be all right.

I think it was an another case of utilizing some equipment to justify its cost.

We got to the U of M at 11:55 P.M. on April 19th and checked in. Although it was only 5 minutes away from being April 20th, I could not use that date. It was reflected on the bill as 620 dollars for April 19th. That was an expensive five minutes. We should have sat in the car in front of the hospital for 10 minutes.

There were no doctors on duty over the weekend and the personnel that were there weren't certain as to why she was being admitted. They had her in the Dialysis Unit for the first day until she convinced them that was not where she belonged.

Since the doctors didn't come in until Monday morning, Kay sat in a 660-dollar room for two days while she waited for something to begin. It was imperative to St. Alexius Hospital that we get checked in immediately. Had Kay been flown down, she would have sat around even longer.

The results of the tests conducted the previous week in Bismarck were to be available to the doctors at U of M on Monday morning. Nothing was included in the material I hand-carried with me. I called the doctor in Bismarck and he indicated he had arranged everything with the doctor at U of M. When I informed him nothing was here, he indicated the residents at U of M had gotten into the picture and screwed things up. I then asked him why the CAT scan hadn't been sent and he blamed that on St. Alexius personnel. I told him I would do some investigating on my own to determine as to where the blame lies. He promised to get all material together and ship it by overnight courier.

They began to monitor Kay's heart on April 21st. They still believed she must have had a heart attack.

None of the tests conducted in Bismarck was acceptable to the U of M Hospital, so a repeat of all the work done the previous week was begun.

A neurologist checked her on April 22nd and the following day she had two EKG's and a chest X-ray. Two heart doctors came in to see her.

She had a stress test and a MRI at 9:30 A.M. on April 24th.

An angiogram was done on April 25th. If everything looked fine, they would then do a Cardiac Electrophysiology Study. This study would evaluate abnormal heart rhythms. The procedure involves inserting a long, narrow tube called a catheter into the blood vessels leading to the heart. The catheter winds through the four-heart chambers and records electrical activity to identify the irregularity and its sources. The problem can be controlled, in some cases, with medication. In other cases, cardiac ablation, a procedure involving the sending of a small amount of electrical energy into the irregular heart beat source, may permanently cure the patient.

During the study, the doctor used wires to attempt to recreate and record abnormal heart rhythms. The test lasted several hours during which Kay was awake.

They were unable to create the abnormal rhythms they were trying to achieve. Had they been able to determine blockage in a certain location, they were going to do by-pass surgery.

One final test called a Brain Wave Test was to be conducted before they would clear her for discharge. They completed the study on April 26th and readied her for discharge Friday afternoon. There must be something magical about a one -week stay in the hospital. St. Alexius was also in a hurry to discharge her once Friday afternoon rolled around. It was concluded that she had a defective valve in her heart, which she had since birth.

All week Kay had complained about her back pain because of the hard bed. They kept informing her they were ordering a foam mattress from supply. As she was dressing to leave Friday afternoon, someone walked in with a blue foam, waffle-pad and began stripping the bed to put it on under the sheets. We informed the person we would be leaving in approximately 15 minutes.

She informed us, "You may as well take it with you; it has been charged to your account. The cost was $25.70 and it was included in the billing. We never did find out why it wasn't brought in the first part of the week when she had requested it.

We went to Tom and Pat's for the night and left for Bismarck the morning of April 27th.

Kay continued to have her blood chemistry checked on a regular basis all through 1992.

Dr. Dunnigan ordered X-rays on July 8, 1992, for Kay's back to determine why she was experiencing so much pain. The X-rays showed many hairline cracks in her spine resulting as side effects from all the medication she takes.

After the high school reunion was over, Kay went to Perham for lunch with three classmates on September 8, 1993. Coming back from the restroom at Strom's Steak House, she didn't see a step in a darkened hallway. She fell and hit her head on a brick wall. In an attempt to break her fall, she fell on her hand in a turned-back position. This not only broke her wrist, but also shoved the bone back out of alignment.

She reported to the Perham Hospital where they X-rayed her wrist and put it in a temporary cast. I believe the break was so severe they didn't want to attempt to set it there. They suggested she have it taken care of in Bismarck.

We stayed at the lake until Saturday, September 11th. We went to the Bone and Joint Clinic on September 13th for additional X-rays. Surgery was scheduled for early morning on September 15th at which time a steel plate with four screws was attached to the bone.

An irregular heartbeat was detected during surgery and, instead of treating Kay as an outpatient, she was moved to the hospital. They monitored her for four days and did an ultra sound one afternoon. She was discharged Monday, September 20th.

Follow-up X-rays were taken and they revealed the healing was satisfactory. Final check of the wrist was made on December 12th. The pain continued, but the doctor indicated this would be the case for some time.

The Homemakers' Club went out to lunch at the Radisson Inn on December 9th, 1993. After the luncheon, Irene Dorothy pulled up to pick Kay up. As Kay reached to open the door, she slipped on ice and snow. She hit her head on the curb when she fell and she also broke a rib or two and damaged some bones in her back. When Irene saw her fall, she moved the car ahead to get it out of Kay's way. She almost ran over Kay's head. She was house bound until December 14th when she went to the Bone and Joint Clinic for X-rays. The exam confirmed the broken bones and nothing could be done other than rest and wait for the healing to be completed. She had a follow-up exam on January 25, 1994, which confirmed Kay was mending.

Kay's hand continued to give her problems all during 1994. The pain was continuous and a visit to the Bone and Joint Clinic on November 9 and 22, 1994, established that a nerve may be pinched by one of the screws put in during the surgery of the previous September. It was also decided that carpal tunnel surgery could also help to relieve the pain. The surgery was done on December 5, 1994. Steel pins were also put in Kay's thumb to fuse the joint so she could match her thumb and first finger for holding a fork or pen.

She became totally dependent on someone for all her daily activities. All Christmas parties and a trip to Minneapolis for Christmas had to be canceled. She had clinic calls in January and February 1995 and her last check on the surgery was April 13, 1995. Her hand continued to give her problems and she was beginning to favor the use of her left hand. The doctor told her that the diabetes has probably damaged the nerve in her hand as well as the nerve leading to her foot. She will just have to live with it.

I had x-rays taken of my knees, hip, and back on March 29, 1995, to determine if anything could be done to ease the pain in my leg. My knees are fine. I have a slight arthritic condition in my hips, but a nerve lying between two disks causes the pain. I can take medication when the pain becomes too great or I can have cortisone shot every six months. Surgery is only recommended if all else fails. It is all part of the Golden Years. Since my hip surgery in November 1996, I have had no pain. Evidently it was not a nerve between two disks that caused the pain.

Kay continued to go to the clinic on April 13th, 17th, and 21st, 1995, since her creatine kept going up. It was in the 2.5 range for a number of years. It moved up to 3.2 and the doctor is concerned that the kidney either has a blockage or is dying. Increased medication is being given in an attempt to determine the cause of the problem

The blood tests taken on April 21st showed there was no change in the creatine reading; it remained at 3.2. An ultra-sound also showed there was no blockage in the bladder or kidney.

Saturday was my birthday and Chapmans brought dinner over and ate with us. Late in the evening while I was walking Kay to the bathroom her legs buckled on her. She settled to the floor. I was able to lift her up and get her back in a chair. However, at 4:00 A.M. this happened again in the bathroom. This time I couldn't get her up so I called the police. She is so fragile that any place you try to lift her it hurts. When the patrolman and I could not raise her because of the pain, we called the ambulance. They rolled her on a blanket and then lifted her on a board. They took her to the emergency room at St. Alexius Hospital. I informed them at ER that she was merely weak. However, they insisted on an EKG, chest X-ray, blood tests, etc. Three hours later their report read "Diagnosis-General Weakness".

I went in for a Colonoscopy on April 24, 1995. I followed all the preliminary requirements necessary to prepare for the exam. In fact I went the extra mile. We were permitted to eat such things as Jell-O, juices, and other light foods. However, I wanted to be clean as a whistle when I went in that morning. I reported at 7:00 A.M. and the first thing the nurse said to me was, "You need an enema."

"That's not necessary," I said, "I'm clean as a whistle."

"Doctor's orders", she said.

By the second enema, I realized why the doctor had ordered the procedure to be done.

By the third enema, the nurse and I were on a first-name basis.

She asked, "What kind of whistles have you had in the past"?

At the start of the sixth and final enema I looked down and said, "Jan, you look familiar".

She stopped her procedure long enough, looked up, and said, "Merle, if anyone tells you you're full of it, believe them".

By 11:00 A.M. Dr. Hamar came in and told me that everything had checked out fine.

Adele Gorder had helped Kay get out of bed that morning and got her dressed. I had prepared breakfast before I left for the hospital.

Charles Volk checked my eyes on April 25, 1995. I have a cataract beginning to form on my right eye, but it is minor and he said it would be years before anything will have to be done about it.

Since Kay's creatine was in the 3.2 plus range, the Mid-Dakota Clinic wanted a kidney biopsy done at the University of Minnesota.

We left Bismarck at noon on May 9, 1995. We arrived in Minneapolis at 9:30 P.M. and then to Tom and Pat's. Kay checked into the University of Minnesota Hospital at 4:00 P.M. on May 10th, Pod D, Room 502. She was given a chest X-ray, weight taken (131 lbs.) and vitals taken.

Her kidney was checked for blockage on May 11th by use of ultra sound. She was taken down for a kidney biopsy at noon, but because of a low blood pressure of 80, the procedure was canceled until a doctor could check her heart. Dr. Murray checked the heart at 5:00 P.M. Her heart and blood pressure were okay. Dr. William Warren indicated the biopsy would be done the next day on May 12th.

It was determined the kidney was fine following the biopsy at 11:30 A.M. However, since they found blood in the urine, she had to remain in the hospital until that cleared up. That meant staying in the hospital through Saturday. She was released late in the afternoon on Sunday, May 14th. Patty picked her up since Tom and I had gone to Otter Tail Lake the previous evening to open the cabin.

She had to monitor her blood sugar four times a day in an attempt to stabilize it through diet.

We spent Tuesday afternoon, May 16th, attending two training sessions at the University. We left for the lake the following morning and stayed until Saturday, May 20th.

We stopped for lunch in Fargo on our way home. Kay tripped in the parking lot of the restaurant. Although I was holding her, I could feel her wrist crack as she started down.

She had it X-rayed at the Bone and Joint Clinic on May 22nd and it was put in a splint. A return visit was scheduled for June 12th and it was determined the break was healing properly.

During a scheduled clinic exam in November 1995, Dr. Beach determined that an ulcer on Kay's ankle was inflamed and the bone may be infected. An X-ray was ordered and his suspicions were confirmed. It was the first time I ever heard Kay give any indication that she might be giving up hope. She asked the doctor, "Am I going to die"?

Surgery by Dr. Bopp was performed on November 15, 1995 to scrape the infection from the bone. She was released from the hospital on November 20. A home health care nurse came out for a week to perform daily dressing changes. However, I indicated I could perform the dressing changes and continued to do so through December 1995. Kay didn't like someone coming in. She wanted things done according to her schedule. It involved wrapping a rope-like medicated material in a circular position in the open ulcer.

Kay had a clinic appointment scheduled for the morning of January 8, 1996. The previous day her blood sugar fluctuated drastically between highs and lows. I kept calling the doctor since she didn't want to go into the clinic. I was giving her orange juice in an attempt regulate it. That evening (January 7th) Chapmans called and said they were bringing dinner over. I indicated it was not a good time and they responded they were coming anyway. Mardy came into the bedroom and talked to Kay. All Kay kept saying over and over, "How am I going to get to the clinic in the morning". We said that we would take her in a wheel chair.

Chapmans left and I continued to sit with Kay. I held her hand and when I gave it a gentle squeeze she would respond. I could tell by 2:00 A.M. that her systems were beginning to shut down.

She should have entered a nursing facility many months before. She may have received better care than I could give her. However, she had a terrible fear of being placed in a nursing home and I was going to do everything I could to prevent that. She was totally worn out and tired of clinic visits, hospital stays and being kept alive by medication. I could tell that my well being was also far from good. A number of times she had fallen and I had a terrible time getting her back on her feet. She was dead weight and I just didn't have the strength to raise her without some assistance from her. This she couldn't give. She went down in shower and I spent a half-day getting her up. After that I sat her in a plastic chair in the tub so she didn't stand during her showers. I was doing what was considered three shifts in a nursing facility.

As I sat there a million things went through my mind. I relived our lives from that first moment she opened that gymnasium door and peeked in on our basketball practice. I thought I've never seen a dark-haired angel before. Everything that happened after that flashed through my mind. Then an hour and 21 minutes later I knew she was gone when she gave a big sigh.

I lay there crying and thinking of all the wonderful things we did and shared during the previous 57 years. A couple of hours later I knew I had to call the police to report her death. An ambulance came to pick Kay up and as the emergency medical personnel took the stretcher through the front door I knew Kay was leaving for the last time. I silently said good-bye as I watched her leave. The tears streamed down my cheeks. We had never discussed how we would or should handle a permanent separation from each other. The home we had dreamed about, planned for and constructed 42 years earlier was now just a house. It had seemed such a short time but that period contained so many pleasant and wonderful memories. Now I no longer wanted to live there because the memory of her passing through that front door would always haunt me.

Kay died at 3:21 a.m., Monday, January 8, 1996, at home. Her concern a few hours earlier about how she was going to get to the clinic was no longer relevant.

The funeral was held a few days later at the Seventh Day Adventist Church in Bismarck with burial in the plot I have at the North Dakota Veterans Cemetery in Mandan, North Dakota. Dan Chapman wrote a eulogy for Kay and it beautifully described the type of person she was'

On November 18, 1996 I had my left hip joint replaced with titanium joint. While waiting to go in for surgery, a nurse came into the room with a cloth tape measure and quickly measured my leg. My son Mark was quite concerned. He thought it was a very rough measurement and one leg would surely be longer than the other. The nurse was measuring my leg for an elastic stocking. The pain I had had for so many years disappeared and within two weeks I was walking without a limp.

After a number of tests, it was determined I needed open-heart surgery to by-pass some blocked arteries leading to the heart. On February 8, 2000 I checked into St. Alexius Hospital early in the morning for a number of preliminary tests with surgery scheduled for the afternoon. I had some physical therapy in the hospital for a few days and sent home on February 12th. It was a 4-way by-pass using the vein in my left leg.

I had 4 hernia operations in 2004, a number of hospital stays for blockages as a result of adhesions relating to my colon surgery in 1980.

During a routine eye examination in Bismarck in 2004, Dr. Charles Volk suggested I should consider replacing my corneas. Dr. Elizabeth Davies at the Minnesota Eye Institute transplanted the left eye cornea on December 1, 2005 and the right eye on May 11, 2005. The corneas came from two different individuals, one from a 50-year old and the other from a 57-year old. My sight has gone from 20/400 to 20/40.

I have tried to eat right, get some exercise and hope to live to be a 100 someday.

CHAPTER 21

Our Sons' Scouting Years

In 1959 when Tom was 10 years of age, he became involved in Cub Scouts. No Pack was available in our area so we became involved in organizing what would become known as Pack 119. Kay was appointed Den Leader, Allen Fisk was Cub Master and I was his assistant. Kay had an Assistant Den Leader and Cliff Conrad, an older Boy Scout, was Den Chief. The Den met weekly three times a month and a Pack meeting was held in the evening of the fourth week at the Highland Acres School.

The Den usually met at 4:00 P.M. after school in the home. Kay planned programs or field trips. The boys earned the Bobcat badge first by learning the Cub Scout Promise, Law of the Pack, handshake, salute, sign, motto, and the meaning of "Webelos". After earning the Bobcat badge, a boy works on achievements to earn the Wolf badge. Additional work leads to award of the Bear badge.

Other mothers assisted Kay from time to time with the activities and trips. Some of the field excursions taken that year were:

January 13th	Conrad Publishing Company
February 3rd	Legislature and Museum
February 5th	Blue and Gold Banquet
May 12th	7-Up Bottling Company
May 20th	Cub Picnic
July 2nd	Attended Baseball Game
August 8th	Merle Took Cubs on Nature Hike
October 12th	Eddy's Bakery

The Blue and Gold Banquet was held in November at 6:00 P.M. at the school. This was a dinner attended by parents and was the big social event for the Scout year. This also gave the scouts an opportunity to show off their uniforms and awards. Earlier in the day Mark had run a large sliver in his arm and I had to come home from work to remove it.

The Cub Scout Carnival was held on March 1st. The cubs from many packs around the city displayed their talents in totem pole painting, rope tying, woodcarving, etc. Tom's early experience in ropes has paid big dividends now that he is involved in sailing.

Kay developed a Canadian Mounted Police Theme for one of their monthly programs. All scouts made uniforms and the Bismarck Tribune photographer came over the afternoon of April 1, 1959 and took their picture. The picture of the Scouts appeared in the local paper.

Kay had a Cub Scout picnic for the Pack on May 20, 1959 and she serve homemade ice cream. Another picnic for Pack 119 was held on June 5, 1959, at Ft. Mc Keen south of Mandan.

A large Pack supper was held the evening of October 26th. This was the last major function for the year and everyone's thoughts turned toward Thanksgiving and Christmas.

A Cub Pack dinner was held on February 25, 1960 at Roosevelt School. Plans were made for Scout-O-Rama and meetings throughout March involved the booth that Pack 119 would have ready by the first part of April.

When Tom reached 11 years of age, he graduated from Cub Scouting. A Boy Scout Troop 14 was organized. Many of the boys were two to three years older than Tom, which made quite a difference at that age. The older boys played the usual tricks on the new, younger boys coming from Cub Scouts.

We had an active Scout Committee and the fathers of most of the boys were involved in one way or another. We never lacked for drivers or volunteers to take the Troop somewhere.

Meetings were held weekly at the Lutheran Church of the Cross. Following a general type meeting, the scouts would break up into their respective patrols and do work toward earning merit badges that would result in scout advancement. Periodically a Court of Honor would be held to present merit badges and advancement in rank badges.

On May 20th the scout troop went on an overnight. It was Tom's first outing with the troop and no problems were encountered. It was difficult to get the scouts away from the campfire and into their sleeping bags. They slowly gave up after 1:00 A.M. as the conversation and the number of scouts around the fire continued to decrease.

On Sunday, July 17th we got Tom up early to pack for Scout Camp at Heart Butte. They left at 10:00 A.M. Since I had to register all scouts for the week's camping, Mark and I drove out in our car and then came back at 4:00 P.M.

It was a terribly hot week. We went out for the Parents' Program on Wednesday and the temperature was still 108 degrees at 7:00 P.M. Earlier in the week Tom found a mouse in his sleeping bag which just about sent Kay into orbit when she received a card from Tom telling her about it. I told her that if this is the worst thing that happened to him in life, she shouldn't concern herself with it. I went out on Friday and spent the day with the Scouts. We returned on Sunday afternoon, dirty, tired, and hungry.

Eagle Scout Award required the earning of 21 merit badges. Tom earned 20 merit badges and failed to get the one associated with water--Swimming. Now he is "old seaman", has a sailboat and lives on the water every chance he gets. So I guess you could say he is an honorary Eagle Scout. I felt so sorry for him after he had worked so hard and had come so close to being awarded the honor. In my heart he has always been an Eagle Scout.

Tom continued into the fall in Scouting with camp outs and hikes. The following spring Mark started in Scouts and he and I went to the Blue and Gold Banquet on February 23, 1961. I began working in Montana that spring of '61 and for the rest of that year I had very little opportunity to spend the amount of time I might have liked to spend with the Scouts. The detail to Montana couldn't have come at a worse time. The boys were in their developing years and I was going to miss out on a part of it. It also became very clear that their years at home were numbered especially in the case of Tom. In a few years he would be away at college. That Saturday morning he was born seemed like only yesterday. Parents have so little time to enjoy their children before they are gone to make their own lives.

However, it was either accept the detail to Montana or prepare to transfer to other areas where Bureau work was plentiful. We were awaiting approval and authorization of the Garrison Diversion Unit irrigation project and it's accompanying appropriations. This didn't come until August 5,1965.

The obtaining of field data and then bringing it back to Bismarck to work on resulted in a week's stay periodically. This kept me partially involved with the Scouts.

I spent an overnight with the Troop on January 14th. It was anything but warm. I recall the prediction was for -25 degrees. The more resourceful scouts had located a straw pile earlier in the evening. They placed about a two -foot thickness down before erecting their tents. This insulation blanket below their sleeping bag prevented the cold from the seeping up from the ground surface. Most sat around the campfire until they were so tired that even the cold couldn't keep them awake. You always had someone doing foolish things like placing an unopened coke bottle near the fire to warm the liquid. They were unaware that a bottle lying too close could become a potential bomb.

A week later Jim Dybdal and I took the Scouts ice fishing on a small lake north of Wilton. The day was warm and the air was filled with laughter and yelling of boys keeping each other informed as to what they were catching. It was enjoyable seeing them so carefree. Jim and I knew that in the not too distant future unforeseen problems for some and daily responsibilities for others would cause them to reflect back on their scouting days and recognize the benefits of the Program.

The following month on March 26th I took the Scouts on a hike north of town. We went north on River Road and then west to a point where a steel tower transmission line crosses the Missouri River. We were about five miles from town. We cooked a late afternoon lunch and then started for home. The distance of the hike was probably more than it should have been. I had some seasoned scouts with me, but I also had some that had recently come out of Cub Scouts. In order to stay in a fairly compact group, we couldn't move any faster than the slowest scout. The old Scout Motto "Be Prepared" was not always followed by all the Scouts. The weather was fairly nice when we left town, but now the sky had clouded over and the wind became gusty. When we were about halfway home a wet, heavy snow began falling. Those in canvas shoes and without mittens began to suffer. These adverse weather conditions cut our travel speed an additional fifty percent and we didn't arrive home until 7:30 P.M. By this time there were many anxious mothers and a number of them had called Kay.

Early in April 1961, the scouts began tying hangman's nooses at 10 cents each. We had contracted with Jim Dybdal to do 1,000 hangman's ropes for a promotion he was doing for a new company named Dakota Beer. The nooses were to hang in front of establishments that sold Dakota Beer with a note hanging down that read, "Well, I'll be hanged; they have Dakota Beer". After a poor start, the brewery went broke. The building is at the east end of Main at 26th Street.

Scout-O-Rama was held about mid April that year of 1961. Troop 14 had a booth that provided information on weather forecasting. Ed Schaefer (Later Governor of North Dakota and Agriculture Commissioner) was the weatherman. The boys not only learned a lot about prediction of weather through their visits to the Weather Bureau, but provided the general public with a better perception of what is done before a weather forecast is issued.

A Court-of Honor was held on June 13, 1961, at 7:00 P.M. at the Lutheran Church of the Cross-.

Scout outings continued through that summer and the boys worked on their merit badge requirements. With Mark in Cub Scouts and Tom in Boy Scouts, Kay was kept busy by attending meetings and Courts-of Honor that summer and fall.

I took the Scouts out ice-fishing again on March 10, 1962. They enjoyed building fires, roasting wieners, and involving themselves in horseplay.

I came from Montana long enough in April to help with Scout-O-Rama. The activity was held in the World War Memorial Building on Sixth Street. Each scout troop and pack that elected to be involved was allotted 100 square feet (10X10). The event was held on a Saturday, and after a feverish day of activity, the scouts were ready to shut down at 9 o'clock and clean up the mess.

Dr. Phil Dahl and I took the Scouts on an overnight on May 25th. It was just interesting to sit around the campfire and listen to the Scouts talk. Sooner or later someone would start singing "Ninety Nine Bottles of Beer on the Wall" and this would go on until late into the evening. Slowly individuals would begin sneaking off to their tent and sleeping bag. No one wanted anyone to be aware that they just couldn't take staying up all night if they had to.

On May 26, 1962, Kay and Mardy Chapman served for Tom's Patrol at Burt Zimmer's home.

Tom went to Heart Butte Scout Camp on August 10, 1962. Kay and I drove out to camp to pick up Tom, Dick Ottenbacher, and Mike Ball when camp was completed.

Mark joined Webelos in October of that year.

Tom and Mark continued to move up through the ranks and by December 4, 1962 when the last Court-of-Honor was held for the year Tom was only a few merit badges short of the Life rank award.

The following spring, at a Court-of-Honor held on March 25, 1963, Tom received the Life Award and Mark was awarded the Tenderfoot Badge.

Scout-O-Rama was held on March 31 that year. It was always a lot of work for a one-day show. It was also a lot of fun and it gave the Scouts an opportunity to show off their handicrafts to the public.

Less than a week after Scout-O-Rama, we took the Troop out to Medora for their first camp out of the year. The caravan of station wagons, pickups, and cars left Bismarck early the morning of April 27th. The morning was beautiful and it appeared as though this would be one camp out that would not be adversely affected by the weather. However, the next morning when everyone crawled out of his tent, the ground was white. The sagebrush and buffalo grass had about two inches of fluffy snow. About 11 o'clock that morning a warm sun started melting the snow and turned the area into a wet, messy, ground surface.

Danny Daner gave us all a good scare when he got himself in some quicksand. He purposely got himself into the situation and then, when he found he couldn't get out by himself, he became a little concerned. We were able to get a rope around under his arms and with a number of adults pulling, we gradually eased him up to solid ground. No one fooled around in the soft, wet sandy areas after that.

Church services were held on a high, rocky area overlooking the campsite. Services held in that locale reflected the beauty of the Creation. The sun reflecting off the snow in the scoria capped peaks was an artist's dream.

After Services, a noon meal was prepared over an open fire. A contest was held to see which Patrol could come up with the most interesting and appetizing meal. It was surprising what was accomplished with crudest of utensils.

We left for home Sunday afternoon tired and dirty, and although no one would admit it, I think they were all happy they were going back to the comforts of home.

The Scouts went down to Ft. Yates on May 31, 1963, and except for Scout Camp, that pretty well ended activities for the summer months. Troop 14 had the week of July 14th designated as their period at Heart Butte Scout Camp. Both Tom and Mark went out.

I picked them up six days later on July 20th. Both were tired and happy to be home where the schedule was not so hectic.

I took my Patrol on an overnight on September 27th. The weather was beginning to cool, but it was comfortable sitting around a campfire. The tents and sleeping bags kept the early morning frost off the campers and they objected to climbing out of those bags until the sun was fairly high in the sky.

Another Court-of-Honor was held on November 11th and scouting activities were pretty well concluded for 1963.

We held a Scout Skating Party on January 26, 1964, to begin the new Scouting year. The afternoon was crisp and clear. We had a big bonfire and later in the evening we roasted wieners and had hot chocolate. It was one of the last Scout outings Tom and Mark shared. They didn't sense it, but I realize they would be taking different paths as the years continued to pass.

On Friday April 23, 1964, Tom, Mark, and I left for the Bad Lands with other Scouts. We came home Sunday afternoon about 4:00 P.M. We had spent our weekend in some pretty rough terrain known as Magpie Creek.

On May 1, 1964, a trip to the Turtle Mountains was arranged. We camped on C.P. Dahl's property near the Canadian border. The boys were permitted to cut the poplar trees existing on the property and they were in their glory. Never before were they permitted to cut live trees. They built towers and other structures from the straight, slender trees. C.P. Dahl was hoping they would clear his property.

Before breaking camp for home, rainy weather set in. We had trouble getting the vehicles out to the main road. Judge Ralph Erickstad arranged for a school bus and all the boys were taken to a motel where they could shower and clean up. We got back to Bismarck on Sunday May 3rd.

Mark continued with the scouting program in 1964, but Tom's interests were starting to move more toward cross-country, basketball and Legion baseball during the summer.

I had my Patrol pass their Merit Badge in Cooking by preparing a meal over an open fire built in our garden spot in the back yard. For years afterwards, I continued to turn up charcoal every spring when I spaded the garden plot and it brought back many pleasant memories. A large Indian hammer was discovered in preparing for the fire pit.

The October 12th Court-of-Honor was held and Troop 14's awards were becoming so numerous that the Council began to take notice of their achievements.

I took some of the older Scouts out for some trap shooting on November 8, 1964. We went out on South 12th Street south of what is now known as University Drive. We were down in one of Wachter's old, abandoned gravel pits. It was amazing how well some of the Scouts could shoot. Today that area is well developed with commercial structures.

Mark continued to earn merit badges on into 1965. He attended Scout Camp at Heart Butte July 11-17. Kay and I went to Heart Butte on Wednesday evening. A ceremony, inducting Mark and others into the Order of the Arrow, was held. It was a beautiful evening for an awards ceremony. Tom had also received the award the previous year. After the ceremony, Kay went home with Betty Rockne. I remained and came home the following evening at 8:30. Mark came home Saturday afternoon and then slept the rest of the day.

Tom was playing Legion baseball that summer, so they no longer shared mutual interests at Camp, as they had in the past.

On August 1, 1965, I took Mark and Mark Flickenger to Apple Creek for a two-day camp out. They needed it to qualify for one of their merit badges. Two days later they were ready to come home.

The October 17th Court-of-Honor was held in the National Guard Armory. The number of people had grown too numerous to continue holding the awards ceremony in the Lutheran Church of the Cross. The Troop membership had grown tremendously. Kids that normally would not have joined a scouting unit now felt that they were missing out on something great. As a result of the increased membership, the number attending on awards night also increased. It was on this night that Mark received his Life Award.

On April 11, 1966, Mark, along with four other members of the Troop, met with the Eagle Board of Review. All candidates passed the examination. The presentation of the Eagle Award on May 16, 1966 was very impressive. A news release reported the scout's accomplishments to the public. A reception was held at Dr. and Vivian Dahl's home afterwards.

The Troop left for the Bad Lands on my birthday, 1966. We camped in the Cottonwood Campground and it was so quiet and peaceful. The tourist travelers had not started traveling and we had the whole area to ourselves. It was a beautiful weekend, much different from the April in 1963 when everyone looked out his tent to see about 2 inches of snow. It was the type of weekend one can only relive and enjoy in one's mind.

Later that summer the Troop left for the Bear Tooth Mountains at 5:00 A.M. on July 16, 1966. We spent all day getting to a point above Red Lodge and camped for the night just off U.S. Highway 212 near the Base Camp from which we were leaving. The next morning everyone was up early to help with the packing of the horses. When we got through, they were loaded with tents, sleeping bags, food, and all the other necessary gear needed to spend a week in the mountains 50 miles from the nearest town. The trip to the campsite involved the climbing of 10 miles of rough, rocky, trail. Fording of small streams would be required a number of times. Mark had a beautiful horse to ride, as did a number of others. However, there were not enough horses for everyone. It soon became apparent to the tenderfoot riders that an occasional walk would be a welcome relief. The inner thighs became very tender and sore from the constant rubbing against the horse.

Since the campsite was at the 10,000-foot elevation, the trip took about 5 hours. The elevation and the constant upward incline of the trail required frequent rest breaks for the prairie dwellers. The thinning oxygen became apparent as we continued our climb.

The Campsite was located adjacent to Rock Lake No. 2. We unloaded the gear from the horses and turned them loose as per instructions from the owner. The horses immediately headed back down the trail for the base camp.

A mountain stream formed from snowmelt flowed through Upper and Lower Rock Lakes. Rainbow trout were plentiful in the lake and it soon became the main course of each meal. The Scouts had brought waders, which permitted the fishermen to enter the lake to cast for their trout. Many caught fish for the first time in their life.

One day was spent climbing over the mountain range adjacent to our campsite. We were aware there was a glacier named Grasshopper Glacier on the other side. Grasshoppers were visibly encased in the clear ice. The explanation given was that a swarm of grasshoppers passing over the mountains were suddenly enveloped by a snowstorm and were entombed in a heavy snow depth. Each year the depths and pressures increased. The quick freeze had preserved the insects.

The nights were cool, but the days were warm and beautiful. At the end of each day everyone was satisfied to just sit around the campfire and tell stories or sing songs. The stars were so much brighter up there and the silence was unbelievable. You become so adjusted to the noises of a city that you actually shut them out. The experience and enjoyment of being in a complete silence is difficult to explain.

We returned to Base Camp on July 22, spent the night in sleeping bags, and arose early in the morning to pack the vehicles. As soon as everything was packed, the Scouts each found a place where they could curl up in the vehicle and catch up on their sleep.

The slides taken during the trip were shown at the November 7th Court-of-Honor. We attended two more scout functions; the November 28th Scout Meeting and the Eagle Awards presented at the February 20, 1967 meeting. This was our final involvement in the scouting program. It had covered a period of approximately eight years. It now was time to watch, as our sons became involved in other activities, including girls. There had been many enjoyable moments experienced and many pleasant memories created during that 1959-1967 period, but like always, one stage in life has to end so another can begin. We were left with many pleasant memories and I think they are the men they have become because their mother started them in the scouting program.

Many of the adults that were involved in the program are no longer around but because of their involvement their sons are better citizens because of it.

CHAPTER 22

Vacations and Trips

This chapter and also the events reflected in it are also difficult to separate to include into other chapters. I will include everything I recall in one location. This will began with trips taken early in our marriage and when the boys were young. The initial outings could not be classified as vacations.

Webster's Collegiate Dictionary defines "VACATION" as a period of rest and relaxation, a holiday. Webster and Kay have always differed on their interpretation as to what a vacation is. To her, a vacation has always meant, "Cover as much distance as possible in the shortest amount of time and see the greatest number of attractions and sights without regard for the need for sleep or rest."

To me, a vacation has always meant "Spend as little time as necessary to arrive at a somewhat permanent location; relax and leisurely enjoy the surrounding places of interest and return home rested and refreshed for a resumption of routine activities."

Others have said a vacation is what you take when you can no longer take what you have been taking.

We have also discovered that before leaving on a trip one should place all the clothing and money on the bed that is to be taken on the trip; then put half the clothing back and double the amount of money.

Never have we heard the children say on a trip, "We sure love riding in a car," and then see them promptly fall off to sleep.

Our longest trip was 8,000 miles in 21 days, averaging about 400 miles per day. This distance was cover in spite of the time taken for rest stops, meals and to "smell the flowers".

The standard joke after returning home used to be "let us get the pictures developed so we can see where we have been and what we have seen. I had been driving for three weeks and seeing nothing but taillights and blacktop. Mark and Kay had been sleeping, and Tom had been taking pictures out the side windows,

For a number of years after arriving in Bismarck in 1949, our trips consisted primarily of short journeys into the surrounding area and infrequent trips to Breckenridge. This was primarily due to two reasons: (1) we didn't have the finances to get too far from home, and (2) the capacity of our car was not great enough to carry all the paraphernalia Kay thought was necessary to sustain a small child. A few of the required items included a diaper pail, buggy, stroller, bathenette, diapers, jumping swing, and mattress pad.

My earned vacation time was 13 working days during the first three years of employment, 20 working days between 3 and 15 years of employment, and 26 working days after 15 years of employment. If these days were scheduled in a manner to include a holiday, which fell during the week, it was possible to take off 9 consecutive days and only use up 4 vacation days.

My first book written primarily for the family included 220 8" by 10" pages of the many trips taken and not just those classified as vacations. I had done this primarily to keep the events in our life in sequence and, by including or consolidating all trips in with those actually considered vacations, makes it easier to determine or locate the dates of particular travel.

As Tom and Mark grew older during the later years of the 1950's, our year would include a journey to some specific location in the country or Canada. We usually retained a sufficient number of vacation days to insure a trip to Breckenridge for Christmas. We also reserved a certain number of days for use at the lake cabin during the Memorial Day, July 4th, and Labor Day holidays.

The trip distances on vacation were directly related to the salary increases I was receiving.

Until recently we still had boxes filled with items picked up along the way, each labeled as to the year the trip was made. The items became useless-- a map obtained here, chop sticks from Chinatown, a place mat from there, cheap ash trays, and half stubs of tickets for events attended. They mean nothing to anyone but us. Sorting through the many boxes at the time of their disposal flooded our minds with memories of seeing the excitement in our children's eyes when they were experiencing something for the first time. It was a time when we derived our excitement through and because of them. We also recorded many of the happy events on 35- mm colored slides. Those slides now remain with my sons and I was hopeful they would some day put them on DVDs so I could enjoy viewing events happening in those early years.

We have at one time or another been in all 50 States. Some we have vacationed in and others we may have spent only a night or two when passing through. We have been to a number of World's Fair such as Spokane and Seattle. We've been to all the National Parks in the country. We went to Expo 66 in Canada and came back by way of Quebec, Washington, DC and the Gettsburg Battlefield. We've covered Canada from one coast to the other. The family has been to Disneyland and Disney World. Kay and I have had Breakfast at Brenen's and dinner on the Mississippi River Boat out of New Orleans. We have eaten in the rotating dining room at the top of the Space Needle in Seattle. We have been at the bottom of the coal mine in the museum in Chicago, the top of the Empire Building in New York and the bottom of the Grand Canyon in the West. I'm pretty satisfied I have seen most of the important sites in this country.

During the 4-day Teachers' Conference we would go to Chicago to spend time at the Museum of Science and Industry. We stopped to see my Uncle Frank once during a Chicago visit. He was in the Veterans Hospital at Wood and had been since the end of World War One.

After Kay's death in January 1996 I traveled with my son Tom and his wife Patty to the Kennedy Space Center in November 1997 to see the lift off of the Columbia Shuttle. Patty and the shuttle pilot's wife were cousins. We received the VIP treatment when it came to tours and viewing of the actual lift off. We sat in a viewing stand about three miles across the bay from the launching pat. The ground shook like I imagine and earthquake would feel. It is amazing the amount of detail that precedes the lift off itself.

A neighborhood camping group consisting of approximately 40 in number usually made three trips a summer. The camping sites selected were such places as the Black Hills in South Dakota, Riding Mt. National Park in Canada, Itaska State Park in Minnesota, and Theodore Roosevelt National Park in North Dakota. Since these were usually three day trips we couldn't venture too far from home. The women's planning, shopping and preparation for the trip made Eisenhauer's plan for the invasion of Normandy seem pretty small in comparison.

Everyone came home tired, dirty and happy they made the trip.

My work would take me to Denver, Colorado and Billings, Montana for review and consultations. Since the work we were doing also involved the transfer of water between Canada and the United States, meetings were held with the International Joint Commission. Where possible, I would take the family along on these trips. They could shop and play during the day and when I was completed for the day we would try to find something to do in the evening. The meetings with the Canadians alternated between cities in their country and cities in our country.

We packed up on August 1st, 1974 but didn't get going until 11:30; Shark's had a sale that Kay had to stop for before we could leave town. We got to and camped at Big Timber, Montana, that night. The next morning, I met Tom Casey in the shower, and they had breakfast with us. Tom and I worked in the same office in Bismarck. We drove on to Spokane and camped in a K.O.A. Campground that night.

We spent 12 hours at Expo '74 on August 3rd, taking in all the exhibits and the various bands. Toward the end of the day, we sat and rested our tired feet in the river. We returned to our campsite late that night.

The next morning after eating breakfast, we drove on to Seattle, spent a little time there and then took the ferry to Bremerton. After spending a little time looking over the area where we had worked during the mid-1940s, we drove on to Paulsbo to see Frank and Rosemay Olsen. Kay had worked and roomed with Rosemay during those wartime years, and Frank and I were in the same 517th Regimental Combat Team. He had been wound but survived the war. It was good to see them, and we had a nice visit.

We drove around in the Olympia Mountains and in Paulsbo. It was so nice to be back in the area where we had so many pleasant memories of our younger years.

We packed up on August 6th and returned to Bremerton for a short ride around town. There were so many memories associated with the area and every time we saw a particular park or building one of us would say, "Do you remember-------? We drove on to Olympia to see a fellow employee Ted Mann but they weren't home. We got a motel on the beach at Seaside, Oregon, for the night.

We spent the next morning on the beach picking up driftwood and watching the tide come in. We got to Portland at 6 o'clock and had dinner at Art and Judy's. Judy is the sister that was born after I left high school. We spent the evening visiting. They lived in Beaverton, Oregon.

On August 8th, we spent the morning shopping with Judy in Washington Square. After lunch, we left for Salt Lake City and got as far as Boise, where we camped in a K.O.A. Campground. We got up early the next morning and arrived in Salt Lake City at 5 o'clock. Kay's sister Lorraine lived there.

As I mentioned earlier all our trips large and small are detailed in the earlier book Remembrance of Things Past and I won't bore you any further. Many of the travels Mardy and I have taken are covered in other parts of the book.

CHAPTER 23

Canadian Fishing

It doesn't seem possible that it is over 35 years ago that a couple of neighbors and I would make an annual trip to Canada for some Walleye and Northern Pike fishing. We would leave right after Merle Kenny finished work for the day and we would then drive all night arriving at Flin Flon, Canada around 7:00 A.M. just as the graveyard shift was finishing their work in the mines. One of the workers had his own plane and would fly us in to Anderson Lake.

We took turns driving on the way up to Canada so the other two might get some sleep. I took a wrong turn and no one noticed it until we were about 40 miles off course. Rather than back track we decided to take the back roads until we could tie up with the main highway again. Suddenly a vehicle behind us started flashing red lights. It was 2:00 a.m. and law enforcement was certain they had intercepted a van loaded with illegal drugs. We were traveling in one of Merle Kenny's white beat-up vans. We were told to exit the van with our hands up. Canadian law enforcement was certain they had apprehended some drug smugglers using the back roads to bring drugs into the country. The van was searched thoroughly and we were having a hard time trying to convince them we had gotten lost and were trying to find the highway leading to Flin Flon. Finally they let us go but not until they had verified some of the information we had furnished to them.

The next year Merle Kenny, Bob Dorothy and I left again for some Canadian fishing at 6:00 P.M. on August 17th, 1975. We drove to Flin Flon and then flew in to Anderson Lake with a man who worked in the mines. There was one cabin on the lake, so we pretty well had the lake to ourselves. I don't know what we would have done if one of us had gotten sick or hurt. There was no way to communicate with the outside world. Had we been told at the time that someday we would all carry cell phones that would provide instant communication with others, we would not have believed it.

The fishing was great, and we kept enough walleyes each day for eating. Merle found a walleye spot about a 1000 yards beyond where the river exists from the lake. Every cast resulted in a walleye. Never again would I have fishing success like that.

The nights were cool and the sky brilliant with stars. The moon was nearly full and night fishing would have been fairly simple. Total darkness in the Northern Hemisphere doesn't arrive until after 11 P.M. However, by sundown we were ready to put our fishing gear away for the day. Fishing can be tiring if one is pulling in large fish all day.

The next afternoon of August 25th, we began listening for the engine of the floatplane. I think we were all ready to get back to civilization. Soon the engine sound could be heard and then a small speck could be sighted in the far distance. We were as excited about going home as we were about going up to Canada. He circled the lake once and then set his glide approach. His floats touched the still water of the lake and sent small waves splashing on shore before he stopped to turn and taxi back to the dock.

We were as crammed into that plane going back as we had been coming out. It was about a 45-minute ride, and I was happy when we touch down because I could feel a bout of airsickness coming on. We ate dinner in Flin Flon and arrived back in Bismarck Tuesday, on August 26th. For record purposes, the cost of the trip was as follows:

Beer	$11.65
Gasoline	67.50
Coffee	3.00
Breakfast (Flin-Flon)	7.20
Fishing Licenses	30.00
Air Transportation	136.00
Cabin, Boat and Motor	89.00
Sales Tax @5%	4.45
Food	34.00
Total	$382.85

It was some pretty cheap entertainment when we considered we had spent less than two hundred dollars each.

Merle Kenny, Bob Dorothy, my brother Bob, Virgil, and I left on a fishing trip to Canada on August 5, 1976. The arrangements were the same as they had been the previous year. We drove as far as Flin Flon and then had a floatplane take us in to Anderson Lake. Because of the number of people, it required two shuttles. As was the case on previous flights to the lake, the plane packed and it was impossible to move for 45 minutes until we pulled up to the dock at the lake. My brother Bob told me recently about the airsickness that he was experiencing on the trip in. He kept opening tackle boxes to see where he could toss his cookies if he had to. All boxes were pretty full. About the time he didn't think he could make it much longer, the plane banked and came in for a landing. As soon as Bob got some fresh air he was all right.

After unloading all the gear and food, we put the fishing tackle in the boat and headed out into the lake. We usually spent most of our time hooking into the big Northerns. It was catch and release with the Northerns and then before going in for the evening we would catch a number of Walleyes for dinner.

As soon as we got to the location where we were going to begin our fishing, my brother hooked about a 12 pound Northern as his first fish. I took the fish off the lure, held it up for him to look at and then threw it back in the lake. I thought he was going to dive in after it. I think I convinced him we would be catching some more like that and even larger.

I usually did all the cooking on these fishing trips. Oatmeal, eggs, toast and coffee was on the breakfast menu. We would take sandwiches, fruit such as oranges, candy bars and beer in the boat for our noon lunch. In the evening the meal was primarily walleye, fried potatoes, vegetables and a dessert made from a box mixture. I made pancakes for those who wanted a change for breakfast.

Fishing and the weather were good, and when we heard the engines of that floatplane coming we were ready to return home. We arrived back in Bismarck at 10:30 A.M., August 9th.

On one of our fishing trips we encountered a number of sled dogs tethered along the shore of the lake. The owner of the dogs evidently came by occasionally and threw some fish up to them periodically. There was no evidence that water for drinking was available to them.

The following year on August 24th, Merle K. Bob D. and I left on another Canadian fishing trip at 6:00 P.M.

We drove all night so we would arrive about 7:00 A.M. The fellow that would fly us in to Anderson Lake would be coming off the night shift at the mine in Flin-Flon. The flight was about a 45-minute ride.

The lake we were on had only one cabin on it so we had the lake to ourselves. The fishing was not as good as it had been on previous trips. We caught enough walleyes for a fish fry in the evening and then began to fish for Northern Pike. They were all in the 10- pound range. Merle Kenny went scouting around on the shore and found a walleye spot where the river leaves the lake. Each cast resulted in a catch.

We returned home on August 30th at 7:30 A.M. but didn't realize at the time that this would be our last Canadian fishing trip. We did notice on this last trip the Northern were not as large and were more difficult to catch. Regulations became more complicated because local residents opposed the taking of fish by nonresidents. The fishing success was not like it was on some of the earlier trips because it was rumored that fish were being seined for sale in the United States. Limits that could be taken home were decreased and costs relating to fishing became more expensive.

As we became more involved in family activities, exciting thoughts of Canadian fishing began to diminish. We accepted the fact that our Canadian fishing trips were probably a thing of the past.

Merle Kenny and Bob Dorothy died a number of years ago. I alone cherish those wonderful memories of those carefree days of some great Canadian fishing.

CHAPTER 24

Return to Europe-1989

After returning home from service I wouldn't see any European countries again for 45 years. Members of our 517th Parachute Regimental Combat Team had planned for a number of years to return to the areas where we had fought 45 years earlier in Italy, France, Belgium and Germany.

My wife Kay was already having some major health problems and I opt not to go. She insisted I go and we arranged with a local hospital to have her hooked into a monitoring system whereby she could alert or call for help with the press of a button.

We were scheduled to leave from John F. Kennedy Airport for Brussels on October 5, 1989. I left Bismarck the day before in case I missed plane connections somewhere along the way. There was no refund if I wasn't there to board the plane when it left for Brussels. I arrived at JFK at 6:00 p.m. on October 4th and spent the night in the terminal. My sons made fun of me for years because I didn't get a motel for the night. I was unfamiliar with the large city and I was reluctant to get too far away from the terminal since this increased my chances of being unavailable at flight time. It might have been different if I was a part of a group. By staying in the terminal I knew I was at the point of departure.

I met a Polish fellow who had been visiting in New Orleans. Neither one of us could speak the other's language but we got along just fine. I told him I had attended a soccer match in a large stadium in Warsaw. My only complaint was that no matter where I sat in the stadium I was always behind a Pole. I don't know if he got the joke or not.

There were a number of homeless people in the terminal but they were kept on the lower level. Passengers with tickets could be on second level where the gates for boarding were located. This was long before all the security measures were necessary such as we have now.

Early the next morning a few familiar faces began to show up from all over the country and I felt a little better. It was like the feeling one has after a combat jump during the dark of night and you run into the first familiar face. A sense of relief sets in. We gathered at a central location (snack bar) and then left on Sebena Airlines at 7:30 P.M. Dinner and breakfast were served during the overnight flight. We arrived in Brussels at 7:00 A.M. local time. Seventy-five men and women made the trip. Jack Dunaway, who had gone over a few days earlier, welcomed us at the airport with a "picket" sign which said, "Go Home 517th, we remember you from 1944." The reverse side said, WELCOME BACK DADDY. The local Belgian people at the airport enjoyed the reception we got.

Two tour guides from American Express also met us. After we cleared customs, we were loaded on two large buses and taken to the Ramada Inn in Liege. It was a 70-minute ride from Brussels through beautiful countryside. The highway had lighting standards every

100 feet in the median for the entire distance between the two cities.

Our rooms were not ready when we arrived, so we took a walking tour around Liege. Most of us crashed into bed at 4:30 P.M. European Time. With the exception of one hour on the plane, I had been awake for 54 hours.

The streets of Liege were stacked with garbage and littered with paper. Someone told us the city was bankrupt. Prices were high. A cup of coffee was $1.40 and if you wanted a warm-up, it was a $1.40.

We walked through a large carnival area in the center of town. We were told the carnival would remain for the entire summer every year. The weather was damp, cold, and lacking in sunshine. It was typical fall weather for that part of the continent.

We left the hotel at 8:30 A.M. on October 7th and went to Pont d' Erezee where we met Mr. Leon Delvaux and Mrs. Fontaine. They served as our guides until later in the afternoon when we met Leo Carlier and his wife Francine at Trois Ponts.

We stopped in the city of Hotton at 9:30 A.M. A reception was held in the Municipal Hall. Our Colonel Boyle presented a 517th plaque to the mayor and the mayor presented an inscribed plate to the 517th

One farmer was questioning everyone to see if anyone knew a soldier named Shields. Years earlier a German tank had been knocked off the road and rolled down an embankment. Parts of the tank were dismantled and salvaged over a seven-year period. When the tank was completely removed, the remains of an American soldier were found. The Belgian had information that showed the soldier's name was Shields. He was hoping some of us could clear up the mystery that had bothered him for so many years. He was told we would follow up with the military in Washington when we returned home.

We were served a prepared lunch in Hotton and then went on to St. Jacques where we visited a 517th memorial. Leo Turco and Richard Tallakson placed a wreath and a small ceremony was conducted. Many small villages have monuments to designate where 2 or 3 men fell during the liberation of their village. The local people place flowers on special days.

One monument we visited listed 45 Belgian people who had been shelled by American artillery. Five were killed. A man standing by the plaque was 5 years old at the time. His father had just stepped out of the house to get something and was killed by the shelling. He said he understood and was not bitter because there were many Germans in the area at the time.

We then went on to Rochelinval and were 45 minutes late. All the town people were standing in the rain and waiting. A memorial was presented in honor of the Belgian patriots who had assisted us during this period in 1944. Many tears were shed. All the old veterans were proud with their medals pinned to their suits. A local honor guard was present for the ceremony.

At 3:00 P.M., we stopped at a monument placed on the side of a hill next to the highway in honor of paratroops from the 551st Battalion. A picture of the major who led the attack was on the monument. He started his attack with 790 men and four days later 110 were left. One lieutenant and two sergeants were in command.

The highlight of the day was the dedication of a memorial we had placed in the village of Wanne. It was dedicated to the Belgian people who assisted us during the war. After unveiling, flowers were placed and a history of the work connected with the monument was given.

We then returned by bus to Trois Ponts for a reception and an hour of friendly wine. We returned to the hotel in Leige after a day of cool, rainy weather.

We left the hotel the next morning at 9:00 A.M. on October 8th after a continental breakfast. The coffee was strong, but diluted with fifty- percent cream. It was a cold, Sunday morning as we headed for Henri-Chapelle American Cemetery. There are 7,989 known Americans buried there and the pylons contain the names of 450 who were never found or identified.

We held a Service at the Chapel. A wreath was placed on the altar and then Cameron Gauthier recited an opening prayer. Our Association Secretary Bill Lewis read the 40 names of our Combat Team that are resting at the Cemetery. Bob Dalrymple had a closing prayer. After the Memorial Service, we spent some time visiting individual gravesites of our buddies. Belgians who visit the cemetery on holidays and weekends with floral arrangements have adopted many graves and continue to honor the men buried there.

We had lunch in a cafeteria Leo found for us and then we traveled to the monument erected in memory of the 85 prisoners shot at Malmedy by German SS troops. A group of green army artillery personnel was captured at a crossroads. The Belgians have built a long wall with the names of those killed inscribed on plaques attached to the wall. At the end of the wall, a small altar exists.

We then went to the mayor's office in St. Vith for friendship wine. Jim Benton presented a plaque to the mayor. I was beginning to think that if we had many more receptions to attend, I should apply for my AA membership.

We then traveled to Vielsom and Parker's Cross Road. A monument has been erected near the crossroad and is maintained by the local Lions Club. A Lt. Parker and a number of stragglers held up the German advance for three hours at this point. The crossroad was named in honor of the lieutenant.

We moved to Manhay late in the afternoon for a reception hosted by the City Council. Another ceremony was held on the grass near a stone monument in front of the city office building. The reception was held in an adjacent highway maintenance building. These towns and villages were small and the ceremonies held there by returning American veterans were very important to them. It was recorded in their city records as a historic event.

We returned to the hotel at 7:00 P.M. It had been another cold and rainy day.

On Monday, October 9th, we left the hotel at 9:00 A.M. and went to the museum at Le Gleize. It contains a display of both German and American items of World War II. Out in front of the Museum stands the only German Tiger Tank left in Belgium. Sal Icontro presented a plaque for display in the museum.

We then traveled to Stavelot where we met the mayor at the bridge spanning the Ambleve River. A small ceremony was held and Charley Pugh presented a plaque to the mayor. We spent about an hour walking around Stavelot before leaving for Logbierme at 2:00 P.M.

Five men were killed at a crossroad in Logierme trying to hold a bridge. A safe in a building located upstream from the bridge was blown later during the battle. A box of jewels were suppose to have been thrown in the river from this bridge by Americans who hoped to later retrieve them. Members of the Provost Office were looking for members of our outfit who were from New York or Chicago. The job was so good; it was assumed professionals did it. The Belgians had erected a monument to the five men at the crossroad and we stopped there for a ceremony.

Another man from the village erected his own monument in a location where he, as a five-year old, had seen two unarmed Americans and three civilians killed by Germans. He told us he had a son as exchange student in Stockton, California. The son was returning home in two months. Everyone was extremely friendly and wherever we stopped there was friendship wine and high cholesterol desserts.

At 3:30 P.M. we were invited to a reception at the 3rd Regimental Chasseurs Ardennais Officers' Mess. We toured their facility, which must have been similar to one of our National Guard Units. They were considered one of the best regiments guarding the frontier in 1940. After a parting glass of wine, we left for Val D' Ambleve Restaurant in Coo.

The stop in Coo would be our Farewell Dinner in Belgium. We spent five hours over dinner. After an excellent meal, we presented gifts to our guides and thanked them for their help and assistance during our visit. One lady at the dinner did spy work for our unit during the war.

We were up at 7:00 A.M. on Tuesday, October 10th. After breakfast we boarded buses for Brussels. Later that morning we left Brussels for Nice, France on Sebena Airlines. We arrived in Nice at 1:30 P.M. and checked into the Atlantic Hotel which was located a few blocks from the beach. Years later in 2002 Mardy and I would stay at this same hotel for a few days.

The rest of the day was spent just sightseeing in town. Not much had changed since we had been there 45 years earlier. The barricades the Germans had placed on the streets fronting on the beach had all been removed. I went to look at the hotel I had stayed in a number of times while I was on leave in 1944. A large park near the beach has a river running beneath it. I hadn't remembered that; evidently it was an open stream with bridges over it when I had last seen it. It seemed strange how the years disappeared as I stood looking at familiar sights. I felt 21 years old again.

We were up at 7:00 A.M. on October 11th and after breakfast a half-hour later we loaded on buses.

We were on our way to Draguignan to visit the Rhone American Cemetery located there. Fred Brown and Mike Bulino laid a wreath at the monument in the cemetery. Forty-two men from our unit are interred in the cemetery. It is small with only 861 buried there. There are men from every State in the Union except North Dakota. There are 62 "unknown" headstones and a "wall of missing" with 293 names for those who died in action, but their remains were never found.

We went to La Motte for a ceremony and the placing of a wreath at the Airborne Memorial by John Fraser and Burton Meador. Fraser presented Mayor Rose with a 517th plaque.

We had lunch in Le Muy at 1:15 at the town hall. It was a 5-course meal and took two hours to finish. After lunch, H.G. Lawrence placed a wreath and J.K. Horne presented the mayor with a plaque.

We then went to Les Arcs where Mayor Rene Meissonnier welcomed us. Eugene Mars and James Royer placed a wreath. Col. Bill Boyle presented a plaque to the mayor.

At 5:30 P.M., we visited Chateau Ste. Roseline, which was our Regimental Command Headquarters after the jump into France. The Chateau had been built in the year 1205. It had been in the family for over 200 years. We were greeted by Baron de Rasque de Laval who took us on a tour of the winery. It was the height of the wine season and they were in the process of wine making. The Baron's father, who had been operating the winery in 1944, died in 1984. The present operator was in the French Air Force during the war. After a period of wine tasting, we returned to our hotel at 8:00 P.M. Mardy and I visited this winery on one of our trips and made the present day owner aware it had been our headquarters at the time of the invasion in World War II. We also showed him the plaque on the wall designating it as such. However, the plaque is now totally covered by climbing vines and will probably be forgotten and lost to future generations.

On Thursday, October 12th, we assembled in front of the Luceram City Hall and were welcomed by the mayor. Luceram is a small mountain village located to the northwest of Nice. We strolled to the city monument located at the south end of town where Jim Benton and Bill Westbrook placed a wreath. We then returned to a reception at the city hall where Merle Mc Morrow presented Mayor Noat with a plaque.

It was quite a coincident, that while we were in Luceram, a woman came up to us and wanted to know if Major Laval was with us. She then told us she went into labor during a German shelling on October 12th (45 years to the day). Major Laval, head of our medical unit, took care of her during a very difficult birth and had saved both her and the baby's lives. She had a letter she wanted to present to the Major. When we told her the Major had died a few years prior, the tears streamed down her face. The lady gave us a picture of her son who had been delivered on that day. He had been killed in an auto accident in 1980.

We assembled in the parking lot at l' Escarene where Mayor Cordon welcomed us. Don Pargeon and Sal Incontro placed wreaths at the War Memorial and the Mausoleum. As at all previous ceremonies, both National Anthems were played. We had lunch in the hotel at l' Escarene, which had also been a Regimental Command Post in 1944. The large bridge crossing the valley near the hotel had the center span rebuilt. The Germans had blown out a 100-section as they retreated in 1944.

We then traveled a winding road up the mountain to Col de Braus. It was the pass over the top before dropping back down toward the sea. At the top was a small restaurant called Buvette du Col de Braus. Mardy and I had lunch there on one of our trips to France.

Afterwards we walked out above the restaurant where a German bunker existed and picked up a few pieces of shrapnel

We presented the owner Antoine Migone with one of our plaques to display in his restaurant. He had been a former inmate of Buchenwald Concentration Camp. After making the presentation we spent an hour in the area looking at some of the concrete bunkers the Germans had built and also picking up pieces of shrapnel. The south end of the Maginot Line was only a few miles from where we were located and the Germans used the French guns to fire on this area.

We dropped down the curving mountain road into the town of Sospel located near sea level. We were welcomed by Mayor Gianotti in the town square where the war monument was located. Sal Incontro and James Royer laid a wreath at the base of the monument. We then went in the mayor's office for friendship wine. During the reception we were presented with medals by Jean Pierre Domerego. Freddie Scotto gave us French parachute wings and red berets.

We then took the highway through Mentone back to Nice. It was the highway Princess Grace of Monte Carlo was traveling when she was killed. Driving on the mountainside highway provides a beautiful view of Monte Carlo. We arrived at the hotel at 8:00 P.M. tired and ready for bed.

We planned to place a plaque at the entrance to the Nice Airport on Friday, October 13th. Six engineers had been killed removing about 2,500 land mines the Germans had place at the airport. Bob Dalrymple, who was in charge of the Engineer Company, gave the following remarks at the dedication of the plaque honoring the men:

Bonjour Mesdames et Monsieurs

"As we landed at the Nice Airport Tuesday afternoon, my mind was flooded with memories and thoughts of a few fateful days in September 1944.

The 596th Engineers, the Engineer Company of the 517th Parachute Infantry Regimental Combat Team, had been ordered to clear the Nice Airport of German mines and fortifications so that it could be used by allied aircraft.

The task was hazardous and, as I recall, of high priority. As Company Commander, I assigned the mission to the 3rd Platoon, which moved to the vicinity of the Airport on 15, September.

For those of you unfamiliar with the happenings, I offer a brief review of the operation. The Germans had prepared the Airport for defense against assault by land, sea, or air, and especially so from attack from the sea. There was an anti-tank wall approximately 3,000 feet long on the seaward side, which was constructed of heavy, steel-reinforced concrete. Numerous pillbox type, anti-aircraft heavy concrete gun emplacements existed (Flak Towers), all properly sited to deny avenues of approach to and on the field. Additionally, in the ground, buried two feet deep, were hundreds of anti-tank mines (Telermines), interspersed with all types of anti-personnel mines and too many mines were "booby-trapped".

The general procedure for mine clearing and demolition was to excavate, usually by hand, a Tellermine, deactivate its detonator, remove the mine from the ground and then use a number of mines as high explosives to demolish the seawall and Flak Towers.

For several days the operation proceeded as planned. The pattern of how the mines were laid had to be established, and using the mines as high explosives required experimentation to determine how much damage a given number would do when used on heavy concrete structures.

On 18 September, a truck loaded with mines was about to be unloaded so that the mines could be used to blow down a Flak Tower. For reasons unknown, the load exploded resulting in the death of the six soldiers working on the load. The cause of the tragedy has never been determined.

It is a lasting tribute to the courage and bravery of these men that they continue and completed the mission on 11 October, 45 years and two days ago.

And so with heavy hearts but great respect for these brave soldiers we here, now, dedicate this memorial plaque in their honor, and in eternal remembrance of those six men who made the ultimate sacrifice on this battlefield."

The ceremony was covered by French Television and newspapers. Bill Hudson was interviewed by Dieter Friedrich for Radio Free Europe.

We were up at 5:00 A.M. on October 14th to catch an 8:00 A.M. train to Rome. A number of fellows left us at Nice and either went to England or returned home. It was a relaxing and pleasant trainride along the seashore. Every previous day had been busy and crowded with activities. It was nice to just sit back and enjoy the scenery. We had been warned to be aware of pickpockets if we moved about the train. However, one fellow still became a victim.

We arrived in Rome at 6:00 P.M. and we were in the Fleming Hotel by 7:00 o'clock. A number of us ate at a small restaurant near the hotel and then went to bed. I could feel a cold coming on all day and I had a fever most of the night.

Sunday morning we were on our own. However, there was a tour of Rome available and many of us took it. We went to the King Victor Immanual Memorial, the Vatican, and many of the Roman ruins. The Italians were in the process of restoring many of the old ruins. Their money could be better spent correcting some of their traffic problems. No such things as parking lots or ramps existed. Anywhere an open area existed, including sidewalks, became a parking spot.

On Monday, October 16th, we traveled to the Lago Albano-Frascati area. The Pope's summer home is located in the heights above the lake. It was our staging area before leaving for Southern France in 1944. We had coffee in a small sidewalk cafe on the shore of the lake. Many memories of the five-mile run from the olive grove near Frascati to Lake Albano were refreshed. After a short swim, we would return to our pup tents, passing many Tokay grape vineyards on the way back.

After leaving the lake, we traveled to Castel Gondolfo. The city was built on the side of a cliff and seemed much higher now than it did in 1944. A number of our group walked to the top.

We had lunch at Illmanero where an Italian wedding reception was being held. We livened up the reception and I am sure the bride and groom will always remember those crazy Americans who happened to be at the same restaurant where their reception was held. After lunch, we went into Frascati to roam around. The olive grove where our tents were in 1944 is now filled with homes and streets. Before leaving the town and returning to our hotel in Rome, we presented a plaque to the mayor.

On Tuesday, October 18th, we left for Civitvecchia, Grosetto, Gavarano, and other towns north of Rome that had been a part of our lives during those few brief weeks in June 1944. We had lunch at a restaurant inside a 1500 A.D. wall that had encircled the old city. After lunch, we went up to Gavarano where a plaque was presented to the mayor. Evidently no military veterans of World War II had ever visited his village. Great excitement resulted and he had a number of city officials assembled in the City Square. It was pleasing to see how gratified they were that their city was remembered. We had a farewell dinner at the hotel when we returned that evening. We were scheduled to return to Brussels the next day.

We left Rome at 12:15 P.M. on October 18th and arrived in Brussels two hours later. We passed over the rugged mountains of Switzerland. It was a perfectly clear day and the cities of Geneva and Lausanne were easily recognized lying next to the lake. A minor incident occurred as we were making our final approach into the Brussels Airport. Another plane cut in front of us and the pilot had to give it full throttle and circle the city again. We stayed in Brussels overnight and our group was split into three parts and each group went to different hotels. Some went to the Pulmer; some to the Jolly and the group I was with went to the President Hotel. It was very nice.

We were scheduled to depart Brussels at 1:45 P.M. on October 19th. The Sibena 747 had an oil-leaking engine. The mechanics worked on it for five hours while we wandered around the terminal. They eventually removed the engine and installed a different one. By the time we arrived in New York, everyone had missed his or her connecting flight. After checking through customs, we were put up at various motels. I was with a group that was lodged in a Travelogue Hotel. It was elegant compared to the 4-star hotels we were staying in while we were in Europe. We were offered dinner when we arrived (1:00 A.M.), but it was 6:00 A.M. Belgian time.

The next morning we were given slips for breakfast and a ride to La Quadadia Airport. I caught a Northwest flight at 10:00 A.M. and arrived home Friday afternoon.

It had been a very emotional trip. We have enjoyed freedom all our lives and can't visualize what it would be like to lose it. The Belgians and French, especially the Belgians, conveyed sincere appreciation for the sacrifices that the Americans had made on their behalf. They have also conveyed to the younger generation the need to remember the sacrifices that the Americans made to insure their freedom.

CHAPTER 25

Southern France

Mardy and I left for the south of France during the latter part of September 2002. Every other time I had been back to the area where I spent warm sunny days of 1944 it had been with a group. This time just the two of us flew into Nice, rented a car and checked into the Atlantic Hotel located in the middle of the city on a very fashionable Boulevard named Victor Hugo.. It is about 3 miles from the airport. We spent two days in Nice proper visiting some of the sites I had remembered from fifty-eight years earlier. Nothing really results in drastic changes in Europe. We walked through the doorway into the Negresgo Hotel and about the only change I notice were the employees. Some of our three-day passes during wartime were spent in that hotel. We would come down to the seashore out of the Maritime Alps, bring our rations with us, and have our meals prepared by the hotel chef. The hotel was located across from the street that ran parallel with the beach.

On the sunny afternoons during a three-day pass to Nice we would sit on the promenade next to the beach and watch the girls in their bikinis. They were amazing in their ability to change from street clothes to their swimsuit using only a large towel in the process. We always prayed for a good wind during our viewing.

Another place our Unit was assigned for R & R during our 3-dy passes was the winter home of King Leopold of Belgium. It was a beautiful place with winding marble stairways, marble columns and terrazzo floors. We bunked two men to a room and the rooms were much larger than the average bedroom. Chow was prepared in an enormous kitchen and we ate on tables in what to me was the largest dining room I had ever seen.

One night a dance was arranged and held in the large ballroom. Dozens of French girls came escorted by their mothers. The mothers sat around the edge of the dance floor with their watchful eyes glued on their daughters. About midnight an air raid alarm sounded. The lights went out and two German planes came over. The alarm lasted about 20 minutes. When the lights came on, the mothers were still sitting around the dance floor but their daughters and their daughters' partners were gone. That was the last dance the Battalion was able to arrange. On this day in 2002 the place was quiet but the sight of it refreshed many unforgettable memories.

We drove to Monaco one day. It is a small free principality governed by Prince Rainer. There were many beautiful yachts anchored in the harbor in front of the casino and a cruise ship was anchored out in the harbor. Mardy and I visited the casino, watched the changing of the guard at noon and sat in the church where Prince Rainer and Grace Kelly were married. After leaving the church we strolled along the streets viewing the gifts meant to be sold to the tourists.

Monte Carlo is a beautiful place because of its cleanliness and its type of architecture. All roofing on their buildings is made of the semicircular, orange tile. Looking at the city from above on the coastal highway presents an aerial view different from any other city in the world.

Small shops are cut into the rocky terrain overlooking the seashore. Narrow stairways are cut into rock to provide access to these shops.

Before leaving Monte Carlo to go on to Mentone we drove the route used in staging the Grand Prix. My speed was no more than 20 mph.

Mentone is situated near the Italian border and is a famous seaside resort preferred by many during the winter season. We spent very little time there. We took the highway leading up into the Maritime Alps and stopped in Sospel, a small city at the lower elevation, to visit a monument the city had erected in a park to honor their World War I dead. Our destination was Col de Braus, an area that once had had a few buildings but now consisted of one family. The location is situated at about elevation 1100 feet above sea level. Much of our fighting during World War II in September and October 1944 took place in this area. The objective was Hill 1098. We had lunch in a small restaurant owned by the only family living in the town in recent years. Members of our Unit had visited this establishment on previous trips. A plaque hangs in the restaurant with the names of the men from F Company who were killed trying to take Hill 1098.

After lunch Mardy and I walked out behind the restaurant to look at a concrete structure the Germans had built as a protective fortification. We also picked up pieces of shrapnel that were lying around in great quantities in the area. Hill 1098 had been shelled repeatedly by artillery and mortars.

About mid afternoon we started down the twisting hairpin turns from the peak of the mountain toward our hotel in Nice. A restored section of the road blown out in 1944 by the Germans as a means of slowing our attack was visibly and easily identified by a change in color.

After freshening up from the day's activities, we walked down to a street restaurant for dinner. It was only a few blocks from our hotel but when we attempted to return home, we found out we were lost. We walked for two hours trying to find the hotel. Eventually someone directed us to where he thought it was located.

The next day we drove to the small city of Draguignan where a friend named Aime Leocard lived. We had a room in a small quiet hotel on a hillside overlooking the city. They served and we enjoyed a typical French breakfast consisting of boiled eggs, pastry, fruit and coffee.

Aime had been a Freedom Fighter during World War II. After the war he became a teacher. The Rhone-American Cemetery is located in this city. It is small in size containing less than 900 graves of soldiers killed during the invasion of southern France. On holidays such a Memorial Day, and July 4th Aime would have his students place American flags on each gravesite.

Aime and his lady friend had come to the Army Reunion, which was held in Oklahoma City in 1993. We met her there and on this particular trip to France she had us for lunch one day and dinner one evening. She is a professional artist and we have 3 of her paintings hanging our home that she had given to us.

One afternoon we sat in a small park located at one end of the city's parking lot in the center of town to enjoy for a moment the wonderful fall day. The leaves were beginning to gently fall and I caught one of the larger ones and brought it home. I had it framed and gave it to Mardy. It hangs in our sunroom with the caption "I'll never leaf you".

We spent a day at Saint Tropez watching windsurfers jumping the high waves. The city was a 15th century stronghold but today is a playground for the famous and extremely wealthy wintertime guests. The harbor was filled with large, expensive yachts, many from the United

States. It was the first city liberated on that coast during World War II.

We spent a day at the winery that had been the 517th command headquarters immediately after our invasion of southern France. The plaque designating it as such hangs on the outside of the building but is pretty well covered with creeping vines.

We had a hotel room west of Nice for a couple of days before we left for home. It was situated along the shoreline. Our evening dinners were at a Chinese place not too far from the hotel. By sitting on the balcony outside our room we could watch all the airline flights coming into the Nice airport just prior to sunset. In the morning when we went down to order breakfast. The lady would go down the street a short distance to get freshly made French bread.

The day finally came when we turned in our BMW undamaged. The owner of the agency walked around the car at least three times expecting that there must be some damage on a car turned in by these old people. We left for home from the Nice Airport and as Dorothy from the Wizard of Oz says, "There's no place like home"

CHAPTER 26

Europe

We departed Bismarck the afternoon of my birthday, April 22, 2004, on Northwest Airlines. After a short delay in Minneapolis we had a direct flight to London, England. The trip was titled *Collette Vacations' D-Day Tour* and there were 32 people from all over the country. The airport is many miles from downtown London and the bus ride to the city gave us an opportunity to see the English countryside.

Field sizes were small, averaging maybe ten to twenty acres in size. Some of their fields would make it difficult to turn a big Stieger four-wheel drive tractor around with tillage equipment. Their season is about three to four weeks ahead of ours and the crops appeared to be winter grains.

Our hotel was in the main part of old London two or three blocks from the Thames River where all the historical buildings and bridges are located. There seemed to be a bridge every block or so including London Bridge and the one you see in pictures all the time—Tower Bridge. St. Paul's Cathedral was across the river and some of the group went over to tour the cathedral. We went to the Globe Theater where Shakespeare presented his dramas. There was a large crowd around the theater since it was Shakespeare's birthday. Near by is a huge ferriswheel called "The Wheel" by the locals. We were told many weddings take place in the wheel. Down the street a block or so from the hotel was a large open market that covered about a square block. You could buy about any thing from apples to venison. Some of the items such as meat is cooked or prepared on site. The cheeses were all of local manufacture and were unique and very good.

Since this was an open day for us we were require to locate a restaurant on our own. Since we didn't want to take a chance on getting lost we ate in a place next to the hotel. The food was good and so was the service.

The next day on Saturday the tour proper began. The bus took us past many of the familiar sites of the city. Street traffic is terrible; I don't know how they wheel those large buses around on such narrow streets. They have many traffic circles which the French and Americans call roundabouts.

Many of the buildings are several hundred years old. These buildings are under constant repair. We went by No 10 Downing Street; the residence of the Prime Minister but it is off the main street and not accessible to the passer by. Near by was the hotel building that housed the headquarters of the Allied Command during World War II. It is a huge red brick structure.

The next stop was the war cabinet building that was set up to house the British government in case of air attack. The building was really an underground bunker of reinforced concrete. Here were limited quarters for all the members of the British Cabinel as well as situation rooms and conference rooms. There were bedrooms for Winston and Clemetine Churchill. It was in operational use from August 27, 1939 until the Japanese surrender in

1945. The Cabinet War Rooms are preserved exactly as they were during the six years of war. There are twenty-six historic rooms in the complex.

One of the main attractions in London is the changing of the guard at Buckingham Palace. This is done with much ceremony and pageantry. As the units marched away to their posts a band played a Sousa march. Their close order drill was excellent and I imagine a result of many hours of practice.

The entire area was a beautifully tended flower garden. Our walk back to the bus took us through a large park with an adjacent stream. Ducks and Pelican were abundant in the stream.

After returning to the bus we continued on to a Museum dedicated to WW II. One whole level contained displays depicting the campaign in Normandy. Specimens of combat equipment from both sides were displayed in the balance of the building.

We saw the beautiful rose garden and the church in which John Wesley spent his later years. The churches are comparably similar to those in our country, not the huge cathedrals like you see in Europe.

Our next stop was the port city of Portsmouth located on the southern coast of England directly opposite the invasion beaches in France. On the way we passed through farmland. One thing that makes the countryside so picturesque is the complete lack of fences. Trees and bushes mark out fields and farms. This was probably due to the fact boundaries were established long before steel barbed wire was invented.

Portsmouth is a British naval base that dates back many years. It is now more a museum displaying old and modern ships. Along with modern war ships are three very old ships. These old ships are: Mary Rose, flag ship of Henry VIII, Victory, flag ship used by Lord Nelson at Trafalgar and Warrior, the world's first iron-clad battle ship. More about these ships later if space permits.

The museum featured a tapestry depicting the events involved in D-Day. The tapestry is 234 feet long and about 4 feet wide. Thirty-four panels of hand-sewn cloth of different colors were completed to make a huge patch work quilt. It was sewn in the 1950s.

A large ferry took us across the Channel to Le Harve, France. It took about fours to make the crossing. We had wonderful weather so it was a smooth sailing. The temperature was in the 60s so many spent their time topside in the salt air. Meals were served on board and the difference between Europe and US is that excellent meals are served on transportation systems.

A bus picked us up at Le Harve and took us to Caen, France. We spent the afternoon in the "Peace Museum" which covered the entire period of World War II. The unique aspect of the displays was that they were composed mostly of news media items. The Fargo Forum's front page was used to cover the Normandy invasion by the Allies. Outside of the museum is a large showcase containing blocks of stone the size of cemetery markers with inscriptions promoting peace. Each stone was sponsored by a different nation. It was a fitting way to leave the museum.

By North Dakota standards, Caen is a large city consisting of approximately three hundred thousand people. Bitter fighting took place during the invasion and the city was basically destroyed. Today it is new and a prosperous city. Our stop for the night was a motel on the outskirts of Caen at the Omaha Beach Country Club. The location was quiet and peaceful and the dinner was excellent French food.

Bright and early the next morning we headed for the invasion beaches. Sixty years had erased all signs of war except for the Rommel's Spargel (Rommel's Asparagus) which is still visible at low tide. It was steel members set in the seabed off the shore and was intended to rip holes in the bottom of the invading landing craft. Explosive mines were also set on top of them. Since the invasion occurred at low tide much of the defensive obstruction was visible.

Rommel and the German Army spent the better part of three years building Fortress Europe as the coastal fortifications were called. It took less than a week for the allied forces to by-pass them.

The invasion site was a well-chosen and open sandy beach that stretched for many miles. The only cliff was Ponte du Hoc. I have often wondered what a German thought that morning when he looked out at the ocean and saw 5,000 ships coming toward the shoreline. Eight hundred of them were naval combat units and the balance was bringing troops and their equipment.

Ponte du Hoc is located between Omaha and Utah Beach. Before Omaha Beach could be cleared Ponte du Hoc had to be neutralized. This job was given to the US Army Rangers. Using ladders borrowed from the London Fire Department, the rangers scaled the cliff under enemy fire only to find the guns had moved back away from the shore. However, the rangers were able to find the guns and render them inoperable. There was plenty of evidence of combat in this area with bomb and shell craters. Pillboxes of reinforced concrete have been left as they were in 1944.

Utah and Juno Beach appear today very much as Omaha Beach. Little sign of activity today. Much different from what took place sixty years earlier. The Canadian Army landed on Juno and had a difficult time. A memorial facility was under construction at that beach.

Brigadier General Theodore Roosevelt Jr. was the first allied officer ashore. Although his unit, the Fourth Division, was located a kilometer or so off course, he made the decision to start inland from that spot. Once the Fourth started inland some of the pressure on Omaha was relieved. General Roosevelt died in his sleep of cardiac arrest in July of 1944.

Leaving the trip in Europe for a moment, I would to explain the currency we were using. In England the pound sterling still reigns. A pound is worth about $1.90. All paper bills are in pounds of various denominations. Coins are in pence similar to our pennies or cents. Rather than using multiples of five as in the US, the pence are somewhat random using two pence, five pence, ten pence, twenty pence, etc. Coins valued at one pound and two pounds are also in use. Most countries in Europe use the Euro as the official currency. This is a new currency and has some unique features. Paper bills are in Euro dollars. Coins are in Euro cents. The Euro system is quite similar to the US. Similar to the English, Euros make use of one and two dollar bills and coins. At the time we were visiting our dollar was worth 75 cents in Euros. The face or head of all Euro coins is of the same design. Each issuing country places their own unique design on the back or tail of the coins. To aid the blind each coin denomination has a different rib pattern. It is like reading Braille.

Ste.-Mere-Eglise located a few miles from the sea between Omaha and Utah beaches, was one of the first objectives of D-Day. Its capture was assigned to the US Airborne troops. An early morning drop was used to allow the paratroopers to arrive before the beach landings. Darkness and cloudy skies resulted in the troops being scattered all over Normandy. Two museums commemorate this action. One is for the 101st Airborne Division and one is for the 82nd Airborne Division. Both museums are housed in buildings shaped like a parachute. Inside are displays depicting what happened on this first day of the invasion. One of the strange things that happened was a trooper had his parachute catch on the town's church steeple. He played dead for two hours while the Germans still occupied the town. He was cut down after the 82nd occupied the town. Had the Germans realized he was still alive they would have shot him. Today a dummy hangs from the church steeple.

Memorial cemeteries are located near the main battle sites. We visited the one adjacent to Omaha Beach and one in Luxembourg. General George Patton lies in the one at Luxembourg. All cemeteries are located on land donated to the United States and these facilities are kept in immaculate condition. There are 9,387 buried at Normandy.

From here we travel to Reims located in the northeast part of France. It is one of the oldest cities in Europe having been established by the Romans some two thousand years ago. There is approximately a quarter of a million people living in the city. A stone gate constructed by the Romans in 300 A.D. remains standing today. Charlemagne used Reims as the capital of the Holy Roman Empire. Today Reims is a prosperous, vibrant city with modern buildings mixed in with the ancient.

The Reims Cathedral is one of the oldest in Europe. Joan de Arc is enshrined here. These ancient cathedrals were all built along the same lines. A Roman Cross shapes the floor plan. Depending on the Cathedral there is an altar area somewhere. Elaborate stained glass windows form the background for the altar. A tower or spire reaches skyward. This was symbolic to reaching for heaven.

A site important to WW II is located in Reims. It is a red brick school building, not a little red schoolhouse, but a large building covering the better part of a block. This building housed SHAEF during the latter stages of the war. It was here that the Germans capitulated in May of 1945 almost exactly eleven months after D-Day. Maps and situation rooms are preserved, as they were that day. Many photos of the event decorate the walls of the rooms.

The Germans had spent several hours trying to get an agreement with Eisenhower to make their surrender to the Allies only. For good reason they did not wish the surrender to involve the Russians. Very late in the evening Ike announced he was going to bed and if agreement to his terms were not reached by morning he would give them safe conduct back home. About 2:00 am in the morning, realizing they didn't have much power to negotiate terms, the Germans signed the papers. Needless to say the pictures showed the German representatives as a sad and weary group of people.

From here we continued on to Bastogne, Belgium where I had been surrounded with the 101st Airborne Division during the Battle of the Bulge. As soon as we reached Belgium the terrain changed. We were now reaching the Ardennes area, which is heavily forested and hilly.

The Bastogne Museum is very impressive and both sides in the conflict are represented. Much of the equipment is placed on mannequins making things very real in appearance.

A large memorial is built on the museum site and is in the shape of a 5-pointed star. Cut in stone around the top of the three-story structure are the names of the 50 states of the United States. A description of the events that took place there in December 1944 is depicted. Many books have been written about the Battle of the Bulge.

We stopped for the night at Luxembourg City. It is situated at the bottom of a large coulee or canyon. The motel was nice and the food was good.

The next morning we left for Remagen following the Rhine River. The terrain was quite typical of a valley through which a large river flows. Many vineyards grew along the slopes of the valley.

Between World War I and World War II Germany built a railroad bridge across the Rhine River at Remagen. The bridge was proposed by the military and was named for General Ludendorff who was Chief of Staff for the German Army during World War One.

On March 7, 1945 the US 9th Armored Division captured the bridge from the Germans. All that was left of the bridge after its capture was the two towers on either side of the river.

A museum occupies the tower on the east bank of the river. It tells a story of the bridge's capture from the German viewpoint.

We went on to Cologne, another city constructed in Roman times. The name is Latin meaning colony. The first order of business was lunch. We ate in a huge outdoor restaurant across the street from the famous Cologne Cathedral.

We were allowed some time for shopping and the most popular item was a product labeled 4711 Or Eau du Cologne. It was here that cologne originated and was spread about the world by soldiers when they returned from whatever campaign they were on.

The Cologne Cathedral is world-renowned and has many stained glass windows. Over 600 years were spent building it. The corner stone was placed August 15, 1248. It was finished in 1880. Many prominent individuals are buried within its walls.

On the way to Berlin we past many large wind power generation farms. We also detoured to Potsdam where Truman, Atlee and Stalin met to plan the post war administration of Germany. We toured the building where the meeting was held.

Our tour of Berlin took us to many landmarks. Some were famous and some were infamous. It was a drive-by and we saw the Templehof Airfield where the Berlin Airlift in 1948 took place. We saw the Reichstag bunker where Hitler ended it all. This area was flooded and filled in with dirt and seeded over. A memorial to Holocaust victims was being constructed.

We saw the Brandenburg Gate, the German version of the French Arc de Triomphe. A stature of Otto von Bismarck faces Winged Victory erected to celebrate victories that led in 1871 to the unification of Germany with Bismarck as its Chancellor and Berlin as its capital. We walked up to CheckPoint Charley. We stopped at the building where the men of the April 20, 1944 failed assignation attempt on Hitler were executed by a firing squad

Closer to the city center was an area titled "Topograph of Terror". Between 1933 and 1945, the central institutions of Nazi persecutions and terror were located on the "Prinz Albrecht" between Prinz-Albrecht-Strasse, Wilhelmstresse and Anhalter Strasse. The headquarters of the Nazi Gestapo and SS were housed here. The displays were mounted along a sunken wall and reminded me of a baseball dugout. The dungeons where people were held and tortured were well insulated to muffle the sound of those screaming before death. The secret police were authorized in 1936 and were not to be under the rule of the courts. It was here that the genocide of the Jews and the systematic persecution and murder of other parts of the population were planned.

Running between this exhibit and the sidewalk was a remnant of the Berlin Wall.

Rarely is a highway patrolman seen. Recorders are mounted in cars. They record speed and other data that reflects the driver's driving practices. These need to be turned in to have a driver's license renewed.

It takes a foreign trip to make one appreciate your home country. We were ready to return.

CHAPTER 27

Italy

On March 29, 2007 we traveled from Fargo to Bologna, Italy. We were bussed to Florence and spent 3 days in the area. Our accommodations were at Hotel Brunelleschi. We spent the first day on a walking tour of Florence. It's magnificent Cathedral with the huge dome and its vast bronze door by Ghiberti is one of the main attractions. Another must see was Micheiangelo's most famous sculpture of David at the Academy of Fine Arts. We traveled the famous Chianti wine route to the 5th century Castle Vicchiomaggio, a centuries old wine producing estate, where Leonardo DA Vinci was a guest while he painted the Mona Lisa. We had lunch and enjoyed a beautiful view of the Chianti Hills as we sampled the local wines.

The next day we traveled to northern Tuscany and the classic city of Pisa. The splendid architecture is reflected in the Field of Miracles, home to the buildings that recall Pisa's past grandeur, including the famous Leaning Tower. We climbed the famous Leaning Tower to take a few pictures from its height and then continued on to the city of Lucca, rich in art and history. The city's ancient narrow lanes still follow the original Roman street plan laid out when it was founded in 180 BC. Massive red brick walls enclose the city, making it one of the best preserved Renaissance defenses in Europe, and the remains of a Roman amphitheater can be seen as you walk along the ancient walls.

We stopped on our bus trip 80 miles south of Rome at Cassino for a sandwich and drink at the bakery and deli. From the parking lot the Montecassino Abbey could be viewed perched high up above on the mountain. The Air Force destroyed the Abbey during the Second World War. The Abbey has had a troubled history suffering from repeated attacks, pillages and natural disasters. As mentioned, the most recent loss happened when it became the site of a terrible battle with the loss of many lives. This is where Senator Bob Dole was severely wounded. The Germans saved all the artifacts and the Abbey was rebuilt in 1944 using the original plans. The initial construction by St. Benedict was completed in the year 530 AD.

We spent Palm Sunday in Rome and it seemed like everyone else in the world was there. Had I had a heart attack in the Sistine Chapel, there wouldn't have been room to fall over. The masterpieces of Genesis and Last Judgement by Michelangelo are admired much too long by everyone. One marvels at the size of St. Peter's Square and the size and beauty of St. Peter's Basilica, the largest church in the world. My first visit to the square was in the summer of 1944 while on a 48-hour pass. At that time it was not crowded and only military personnel were present.

All around the area were dozens of small shops selling every imaginable type of religious items Including rings, necklaces, good luck bracelets, etc.

We spent an entire day on what can be described as a walking tour. I felt sorry for an elderly lady (I should choose my words more carefully. I was 84 at the time.). The walking paths are cobblestones and broken concrete. She had an injured foot and was in extreme pain. She really should have stayed in the bus but I guess she came to see Italy like the rest of us.

We went up in the Coliseum and tried to visualize standing side by side with the ghosts of some of the gladiators in furious hand to hand combat. Emperor Vespasianus built the Coliseum to entertain his subjects. He also wanted to impress visitors and the general public. Being able to build such a large impressive structure showed that the government was wealthy. It essentially showed the emperor's power.

The Romans had the capability of flooding the Coliseum and staging naval battles. They also spent many Sunday afternoons and holidays watching fights to the death between lions and gladiators or gladiator against gladiator. Today Sunday afternoons are spent watching the Vikings football team try to overpower the Green Bay Packers.

We viewed the ancient remains of the Forum with the Arch of Constantine. I had to see one of the landmarks I used as a means of orienting myself during my visit to Rome during World War II---Castel Sant'Angelo sitting near the Tiber River. No one leaves Rome without sitting on the steps in front of the Trevi Fountain, Rome's largest and most famous fountain. Everyone throws coins in the fountain for good luck. As we sat there one of the street people comes to the fountain with a small net attached to a six-foot pole. He scoops up a few coins from the bottom of the pool and is gone before the police can show up.

We marvel at the dominating Court of Justice and the picturesque Tiber with its graceful bridges and more. The list of marvels is endless.

The Romans were great travelers in their day, even if they sometimes overstayed their welcome, but their favorite place lay close to home. Their summer villas and estates were outside the city. The legendary Pompeii was one such place. It was destroyed in 79 A.D. by ashes and pumice from an erupting Mt. Vesuvius burying all signs of life. The city of Pompeii lay covered until the 17th century when unearthing it began. The frescoed villas, temples, shops and street walls with still visible graffiti were well preserved ruins that gave one an idea of life lived centuries earlier. Mt. Vesuvius was smoking in 1944 when I was with the military in Naples but has been dormant since that time. We thought if it hasn't erupted since 79 AD there wasn't really too much to worry about. Except for the smoking in 1944, nothing indicates that it may become active in the near future.

At the end of the day we returned to Rome and left from the airport there to return to the familiar surroundings of home.

CHAPTER 28

CHINA

One of the most relaxing and interesting trips we took was the trip to China beginning on March 27, 2008. We placed our luggage at the check-in desk at the airport terminal in Fargo, North Dakota and the next time we saw it was in our room in Shanghai, China. By crossing the International Date Line, we lost a day. It was late in the afternoon on Friday when we landed in Shanghai. There is thirteen hours difference in time. We were met at the airport and taken to the Hua Ting Hotel & Towers. Our tour guide was Lei Liu who had graduated from college with English major and spoke very good English. He passed the appropriate test necessary to obtain the necessary license to become a tour guide. In China students begin learning English in elementary school and have to pass an English test before entering college.

Some random comments by lei on our way to the hotel were:

Seventeen million people populate Shanghai, approximately the same as Beijing.

China's population is 1.3 billion people, 22% of the world's population. China has 7% of the world's land area.

Don't drink the tap water. Locals call it "rural water".

The yuan is Chinese currency. Seven yuan equals an American dollar.

Shanghai is the commercial center of China.

Beijing is the political center of China.

Tibet is not a separate country from China. The freedom protest in Tibet is a family problem in China. The West needs to separate itself from the Tibet protest.

When walking, give way to anything stronger than you.

China has had one birth per family policy since 1978. If a family has a second birth, they pay a fine and government workers lose their jobs.

The Chinese do not own land but can own property on the land. They can purchase a condo, for example, and have a lease for 100 years.

We stayed at elegant Hau Ting Hotel & Towers. CNN in English was on twenty-four hours a day.

Saturday, March 29, 2008 was rainy and foggy and a light jacket felt good. Before leaving the hotel, we had breakfast which included almost everything in the buffet—both American and Chinese food. The number in tour group was approximately 60 who met with Mary Jane, the main Go Next tour leader, and Lei and Rocky, the Chinese tour guides. The three informed the tour group on a number of issues related to China and the tour. These comments included the following:

Recently, security at a China airport did not stop a female airplane passenger with some gasoline, so security has increased. No one is allowed any liquid in hand luggage, including toothpaste. Checked luggage in China must be locked and weigh 44 pounds or less.

Public toilets Chinese style is a "hole in the ground." Many do not include toilet paper. Chinese believe that the hole is cleaner because there is no seat.

The guides warned the group of pick pockets, vendors, peddlers, and beggars. Street vendors sell "knock-off" imitations. Stores sell more authentic products. The guides suggested that the group avoid buying from the street vendors and do not make eye contact with them.

Most people live in apartments or condos. A typical condo has two or three bedrooms and is 1000-1500 square feet.

In the larger cities, the government is promoting more public transportation. In Shanghai, only one in six families have cars. Public buses and bicycles on many streets have a special lane.

We took the bus for a stop to see the Bund, a famous street for business. It is on the Huangpu River, which flows through the city. The fog blurred our ability to see much of the street. The Bund was built in the past 15 years and shows a Western influence.

We then went to Yu Gardens, a Mandarin garden, in the oldest part of Shanghai. In the Yu Garden were the usual plants, rock formations, and buildings with pagoda roofs. We then walked through what the guide called a "Chinatown" business area with many small shops. We saw a McDonald's, a Dairy Queen, and a Starbucks. In this area, we ate the first of many typical Chinese meals. Each was served at a round table for eight or ten people. The meals consisted of a half dozen cold appetizers, usually some kind of soup, steamed bread, white rice, and several warm dishes. We had a choice of a beverage—beer, bottled water, or a soft drink, never milk. Most often for dessert was fresh fruit—watermelon, apple slices, pineapple, etc.

After lunch, we stopped at the Shanghai Museum. The museum was crowded with long lines of people waiting to get into the building. The museum had a large display of Chinese ethnic culture, Chinese furniture, ancient bronze and paintings, among other items. Of course, we exited the museum through a shop where we purchased some bookmarkers. After dinner, we attended a show, a combination of acrobatics, balance, and dance.

Sunday, March 30, (cloudy, light-jacket weather)
We drove to the Jade Buddha Temple where many people, mostly monks and nuns, participated in prayer and chanting in a number of different rooms. Buddhism is the main religion in China since Buddha came to China from India 2000 years ago. The second largest religion is Taoism and then Christianity. According to the tour guide, the Buddhist believe that, if they do the best possible, then this person goes to Nirvana, the Buddhist paradise. The monks helped others to go to Nirvana. Those who do not go to Nirvana are reincarnated. Buddhist do not kill living creatures and most monks are vegetarian. Many of the Chinese burned incense in the appropriate places on the temple grounds. In one room of the temple was a large jade Buddha brought from Burma in 1918. Tourists were not allowed to take pictures of this Buddha. In another room was a resting Buddha. Many trees and bushes had red ribbons that were placed when people donated money. On most of the doorways were high thresholds, which the Chinese believe keep out the devil and other evil spirits.

According to the guide, the Christian church is the third largest religion in China. He said that the Catholic Church in China does not answer to the Pope.

From the Buddhist temple, the group went to a silk factory. A person there discussed the process of how silk is made—from the silk worm to cocoon to thread. Of course, the factory had a store where we could buy silk products. We saw silk comforters, scarves, pajamas, ties, etc. Some of the group made several purchases.

We then drove to a Cashmere Factory where we had lunch. The tour guide called this a barbecue where we picked up the raw food we wanted, added the spices, and then gave it to the cook to prepare. Upstairs was a store selling cashmere products.

The tour guide continued to give the group information about China and Shanghai.

Shanghai does not have many historical sites as it is known more for its silk production.

Shanghai has over 4,000 high-rise buildings over 40 floors.

China has become more Western with more freedoms. The tour guide mentioned blue jeans, cigarettes, long hair, and sunglasses as Western influences. During the strict Communist period, there was no incentive and no work as everybody was treated equally. China started to be more open after President Nixon's visit in 1972. The buildings started to open. The guide talked a lot about people becoming wealthy—"rich."

The Houston Rockets is the Chinese team because Yao Ming from Shanghai plays for them. Every Chinese claims to be a cousin of Yao!

The government controls the number of cars. A car owner pays 56,000 yuan to purchase a license, a one-time requirement.

The medical system is much like that in the United States. The government has started to insure farmers who typically can't afford insurance. Chinese doctors use more herbal medicine. They try to maintain balance in the body. Now more doctors are using more Western doctors' practices.

We then went to the Shanghai airport for a flight to YiChang, located at the eastern end of the Yangtzi River. A guide from the city met us. While driving from the airport to dinner, she informed the group about the city. The current population is three million, an increase from 400,000 before 1970. The building of the dam is one reason for the increased population. We saw small canola fields and many tombs with paper flowers as decorations. We stopped at a city park where many children and adults enjoyed the facilities. Some were selling colorful kites.

We had dinner at the Imperial Court, a buffet with mostly Chinese and some American food including dessert—ice cream, cake, cookies, and fruit.

The group was then taken to a Victoria Cruise ship. A band greeted us as we boarded the ship. Before going to bed, the people on the ship were introduced to the crew and given information about the events of the next three days on and along the Yangtzi.

Monday, March 31, 2008 (a light rain in the morning, light jacket weather)

We left the boat and went to see the new dam on the Yangtzi River. The river is the third longest in the world and the longest in China with the Nile and Amazon the two longest in the world. When the dam is finished, it will provide electricity for 10% of the people in China and will be the largest hydroelectric dam in the world. On the reservoir side of the dam, the water level will be raised 65 meters to 175 meters above sea level. Because of the water level, 1.3 million people have already been relocated. Many of these moved to a higher level in the same area. Because the water level will weaken the foundation of more houses, some speculate that two million people will eventually be relocated. Thirteen cities and thousands of villages have been moved. The purpose of the dam is four fold: flood control (in 1870 floods caused the death of over 300,000 Chinese and another 300,000 in 1935), hydroelectricity (100 billion kilowatts annually), tourism, and jobs. It will also improve the waterway by covering the rapids and will pump water to dry areas. It will take 17 years to construct and will be completed later this year or early next year. The river will need continued dredging to combat the silt accumulation. The feeling is that the dam will survive an earthquake. There has been some concern about the environmental impact. The lecturer indicated that some think that the temperature and precipitation will change, e.g., the summer of 2007 was the hottest in 50 years, and the winter has been colder than normal.

On the bus back to the boat, the guide explained the Chinese "folklore" on green tea. It helps with digestion and weight control. A host will offer two cups but not the third because after two cups, the guest must know that it is time to go home.

After lunch, we went to a lecture by a medical doctor on Chinese medicine, especially acupuncture. He showed the group the different acupuncture points. A volunteer from the audience agreed to treatment followed by a massage. I visited with this person the next day and he said that he felt much better and scheduled another visit to this doctor. He evidently had some medical problem that he felt needed treatment.

Later, there was a power point presentation on the Yangtzi River. It is 3,900 miles long (from Tibet to Shanghai) and has the third largest volume of water. The river used to be dangerous because it drops too much—from 4000 meters to 40 meters. The dam will help solve this problem. Along the river is the home of 400 million people, one-third of China's population. The waterway is the path of shipping and the land on the bank provides half of the crop production in China. It is "the cradle of ancient Chinese civilization." The river flows west to east because Tibet in the west is higher than the places in the east.

The three gorges are the Xiling Gorge, the Wu Gorge, and the Qutang Gorge. The Xiling Gorge is called the Gateway to Hell because it is dangerous for boats.

I haven't talked much about the food we were being served at the various locations where we ate. This is the menu for dinner tonight. This is also a typical menu for a Chinese meal.

Soup (crabmeat and vegetable soup)

Appetizers (spicy chicken, cucumbers with garlic, beef with coriander, and steamed pork dumplings)

Salad (tomato and basil salad)

Main courses (King Pao chicken, spareribs with cumin, Hungarian beef, mushrooms and baby bok-choy, ma po tofu, and vegetable fried rice)

Deserts (apple pie and fruit platter)

Tuesday, April 1, 2008 (started cloudy and foggy and then sunny)

Last night, the ship cruised to Wu Shan, a city of 70,000 people. The group then transferred to a smaller boat for a cruise down the Lesser Gorges. "Lesser" here means that the river is not as wide; it does not mean that the mountains are lower. There is always some doubt about being able to take this trip because of the weather. There was no wind, probably because of the high hills and mountains on both sides of the river. We cruised the Daning River to see the Lesser Gorges. We immediately went under the Dragon Bridge, which will be destroyed later this year because of the water level with the cruise ships and other boats being unable to go under it. The bridge was built in 1987.

On the sides of the mountains, the Chinese grow wheat, canola, and soybeans. When the water level raises in the reservoir side of the dam, the Chinese will take the good soil to higher ground. Some temples have been moved uphill with every brick marked so that the temple remains exactly as it was on the lower level.

We saw Rhesus monkeys and hanging coffins. The hanging coffins were in caves on the hillside and were placed there more than 2000 years ago. They were high on the cliffs so that they were closer to heaven. They were also in difficult places so that others could not reach them. We saw many villages on the way. One of the guides mentioned the schools in the villages and said that elementary and middle schools are free in China. Those going to high school and college pay tuition.

We transferred to a sampan to go further down the Lesser Gorges. Along the bank were musicians and other entertainers. "Trackers" used to pull the boats down the river and were naked as they were in and out of the river.

Wednesday, April 2, 2008 (cloudy, light-jacket weather)

The cruise ship docked in Feng Du, population 760,000. Beggars and vendors lined the path we took to the bus, which took us to "Ghost City," built during the Han Dynasty. Mardy and I walked up approximately 600 steps to the top but most of the others took the chair lift. However, we rode the lift down. "Ghost City" replicates Hell and the different kinds of punishment people suffered because of their sin. There were "templelike" structures with statues of demons. According to the guide the philosophy and the statues of Ghost City are Buddha with a lot of folklore added.

As in other places already seen during this tour, the thresholds over the doorways are high to stop the demons. Also, women stepped over the threshold starting with their left foot and men with their right foot. If they used the opposite foot, they took the risk of a gender change. Also, in front of one of the "temples" was a ball, which if someone could stand on it for three seconds and face the "temple" without falling meant he or she did not have a guilty conscience.

After lunch on the boat, we went to the captain's bridge for a brief explanation of his job. Mardy took over as pilot briefly. And then, as for most days, we watched the happenings on the shoreline.

In the late afternoon, we went to a Q and A session with Campbell Hur, one of the program leaders for the cruise ship. Individuals in the group asked questions about China, and Campbell responded. Some of the random comments as are follows:

Chinese farmers use water buffalo to plow the ground.

Chinese don't eat as much meat or drink as much milk as Americans.

China has one time zone. Normal business hours are 8:30-5:30.

China has a welfare system. Health insurance and retirement benefits, especially for those in the city, are similar to those in the United States. This system is about 20 years old.

Approximately, 73,000 belong to the Communist Party. The voting system is much different than it is in the United States. Those in one government unit vote for those in the next higher unit. Campbell has never voted and did not seem upset about not voting.

Chinese are not allowed to own guns.

Most hospitals are public, not private. Doctors are usually paid by how much medicine they sell.

The birth law has created an imbalance between genders. There are 117 men to every 100 women. The penalty for a second birth is 1200 yuan, but the penalty varies throughout the country. Campbell said that soon there will be shortage of laborers (to me this seems impossible). If both mother and father are one-child families, they may be permitted to have a second birth. Someone asked about abortion as the main method of birth control, and he mentioned that he has an aunt who was pregnant a second time and who was pressured to have an abortion. He really never said that abortion was the main method of birth control.

China is a socialist country even though people have a lot of freedom. The media are censored, but people have the freedom of speech.

Most Chinese consider Tibet and Taiwan as part of China. Campbell definitely favors the current China policy regarding Tibet.

Chinese think that most foreigners, especially those from the United States, as rich.

In China, 56% of the people are farmers. In the 1980's 80% of the people were farmers. Campbell talked about his background on the farm. His parents still farm, and he envisions returning to the countryside when he retires. His wife grew up in the city, and she is not as anxious to move back. Campbell had a power point presentation about his home on the farm, the crops and the animals, and his current family, which consists of his wife and son.

Thursday, April 3 (cloudy, light-jacket weather)

The cruise ship docked at Chong Qing, which is in the most populated province in China, 33 million people. On the way to the bus Mardy was "helped" by two men, not a particularly good experience.

The tour group visited the General Stillwell Museum. Stillwell was the American military officer in charge of the United States' forces in China during World War II. He had lived in China between World War I and II and could speak both Chinese and French. John Majors, a member of the tour group, gave a brief speech on General Stillwell who had the ear of Chang-Kei-Shek and Madame Chang-Kei-Shek. Part of the museum is formerly the headquarters for Stillwell during the war. The museum also contained Chinese paintings, all for sale. The tour guide talked extensively about the relationship between China and Japan. Because Japan bombed Chong Qing during the war, residents of the city painted their houses black to make them less visible to bombers. Still the relationship between the two countries is sour. The guide said that one gas station in Chong Qing refuses to sell gas to anyone owning a Japanese-made car.

Chong Qing's weather during the summer is extremely hot, sometimes as high a 125 degrees with 90% humidity. The guide said that people sometimes attend an all-night movie theater to avoid the heat.

We stopped at a square with the Great Hall of the People, a very impressive building and a cultural center for concerts, etc.

As in all of the places we saw in China, Chong Qing is highly polluted. Chong Qing may be more than other places with its 28,000 industries.

We took a flight from Chong Qing to Xi'an. On the way to the Grand New World Hotel in Xi'an, we stopped at the city wall. It is almost 14 kilometers long and 30-40 meters high and wide enough for three chariots to be driven side by side. We stayed at the Grand New World Hotel for two nights.

Like every city we have been to, Xi'an has much activity—a lot of people, bicycles, cars, and buses. Six million live in Xi'an. The guide called cities of one million "small." People walk through traffic almost daring vehicles to hit them. One of the guides during this trip said that jaywalkers in China are often referred to as "organ donors."

Friday, April 4, 2008 (cloudy, light-jacket weather)
Today is Tomb-Sweeping Day in China, the equivalent to Memorial Day in the United States. On this day, the Chinese put new dirt of their relative's graves or take their remains to the mountains.

The bus stopped at the Qinn Fu Temple, built in 709 A.D. Near the temple, people were doing Tai Chi—an exercise, not a religious ritual. This area is like a city park rather than a religious place. During the Cultural Revolution, it was severely damaged. Also here was the Wild Goose Temple. During a period of hunger, a group of people noticed a flock of geese. One fell dead and was buried here.

We then went to the Jade Factory. The guide said, "There is a price for gold, but jade is priceless in China." Jade comes in different colors, but green is the best. Soft jade is translucent and is the most expensive. We saw a nondescript piece of jewelry worth two million yuan, approximately $300,000. Hard jade is opaque and is less valuable and will be part of the Olympic medals. Jade symbolizes happiness and love. The dragon symbolizes power and good fortune.

We stopped at a counter in the Jade Factory for tea. The server commented on my long ear lobes. In China, long ear lobs symbolize greater happiness and she mentioned that Buddha had long ear lobes.

We then drove to the tomb of the First Emperor of China and the terra-cotta figures. A farmer digging a well for irrigation in 1974 discovered this tomb by accident. He pulled some ceramic pieces and then contacted the appropriate government agency regarding antiquity. The tomb consists of three pits with the first pit having 6,000 larger than life-sized military figures, the second with over 1,000, and the third with 68. More pits are still being discovered. These figures were in pieces with archeologists putting them together. In one pit were two chariots with four horses. One of the chariots and horses was in approximately 200,000 pieces and was pieced together. When looking at it, one cannot tell that it was broken.

Over 700,000 people started to put the tomb together 2200 years ago and were killed upon completion so that no one would know where it was. The workers took forty years to complete the tomb with the Emperor dying before completion. The tomb was plundered and burned during an intense wartime in China. Currently, buildings are over each pit, and the visitors look down onto the pits. After viewing the first pit, the group ate at the restaurant on the grounds. This area of China is noted for a preference for noodles over rice, and at the restaurant two cooks were preparing noodles which the customers ate immediately. Also, some in our tour group drank a shot of snake wine. I was one of them. A real snake—dead, of course—occupied much of the container. At the end of this visit, we went to the bookstore where we saw a video about the terra-cotta figures and purchased a book and post cards.

The tomb and terra cotta figures have been called the Eighth Wonder of the World.

On the return to the hotel, the tour guide talked about aspects of China. In China if one is caught with 50 grams of a drug, he may receive the death penalty. If one has a gun in possession, he may be sentenced to three to twenty years in prison. Joining the army in China is competitive, as upon completing the term of service, the government will find of job for the service person. The guide commented on "paddy cap" drivers, like a rickshaw but with three wheels.

During this evening, the group went to a dinner theater. During dinner, an eight-piece orchestra, consisting of all women, played. Four women played string instruments (two guitar-like instruments and two 2-string instruments), two percussion instruments, one flute, and one horn with no fingering. It is difficult to describe accurately these instruments. The meal was a fairly typical Chinese meal with hot rice wine. The performance was a re-enactment of the music and dance of the Tang Dynasty approximately 2000 years ago. The performers wore colorful costume with a lot of bright reds and yellows. The movement was graceful at times and warlike at other times. The marquee advertised this performance as "An Authentic Tang Dynasty Cultural Presentation."

Saturday, April 5, 2008 (cloudy with light-weather jacket)

First this morning, we flew to Beijing. Lei reminded us again not to put any liquid, even toothpaste, in our checked luggage and to lock it.

Lei told us about Beijing on the way to the Hutong section. Mountains surround Beijing on three sides, thus trapping the pollution. Only the south is open and flat, so not much agriculture is produced near the city. Lei had trouble with the microphone, so he laughingly commented, "This was made in Japan." Beijing at one time had an extensive wall, but it was torn down so that the bricks could be used for "toilets." The Ming Dynasty built the wall 600 years ago.

We stopped at the Hutong section and boarded a cart (rickshaw?) pedaled by a native. The Hutong is three to five hundred years old and must not be destroyed. The buildings can be reconstructed only in the ancient style. They cannot change the outside but can decorate the inside as they wish. Many were repairing the buildings and encouraged to finish them before the Olympics. The owner also owns the land, the only place in China where they can. We rode through the narrow streets and with a courtyard and occupied by an extended family. We stopped at one of the quadrangles, four separate buildings The entire group went into the living area and drank tea made by the son. The son's parents are in their nineties and live in one of the buildings. He was a retired cook and owns a condo elsewhere in Beijing. He devotes much of his time to caring for his parents. Ten members of the family live in this quadrangle. The wife of the son, the host, is a teacher at a middle school. Their son is a college student and is typical of the young people who do not want to return to live in the Hutong section. Most of the houses have a shower, but many do not have a toilet. Public toilets are available throughout the section.

After the tour of the Hutong, we went to the Drum Tower, built in 1272 and used initially to tell the people when it was seven in the morning and seven in the evening. When the drums were beaten, the doors to the wall were closed. If someone was outside, that person waited twelve hours before being able to go on the other side of the wall. Five men came in to give us a demonstration of beating the drum.

We then went to a tea party. The host explained some techniques and customs of making and drinking tea. She poured tea in a certain way, both inside and outside of the teapot. She used cups, which changed colors, when she added a hot liquid. She showed how to hold the cup—thumb and index finger on the top with the middle finger on the bottom. The color of the tea is important with the black tea increasing memory. When drinking the tea, one takes three sips, the first signifying happiness, the second a long life, and the third good fortune.

We then went to the Capitol Hotel.

Sunday, April 6, 2008 (cloudy and cool)
We first visited the Temple of Heaven, a religious temple for Taoist, and built in 1420 during the Ming Dynasty and now used only for tourist and locals for their entertainment. The main temple has no nails. It was built with wooden pegs to give it more flexibility in case of an earthquake. The main temple is surrounding by many buildings all with pagoda roofs. The temple was built so that the Chinese could pray for a good harvest. In the corridor and outside of the corridor people were singing and playing cards, "checkers," stringed instruments and harmonicas, dancing, and doing Tai Chi.

We then went to the Silk and Carpet Factory. We were guided through the carpet factory and given an explanation of carpet making from silk. Making the carpet is very intricate work with the women having to take a break every 30 minutes and working only five or six hours a day. Depending on the number of knots, a two by three-foot carpet can cost anywhere from $500 to $8,000. The tour guide said that only women make the carpets because the "men do not have the patience." Most of the carpets are made in the homes as a "hobby business." According to Rocky, one of the tour guides, carpet making with silk is a dying art because after five years the maker loses her eyesight.

Contained in this factory was an art gallery of embroidery art, again all of them for sale for upward to $50,000.

For lunch we shared a room with whom Lei said was a wedding party even though a one-month baby girl was the center of attention.

In the afternoon, we walked through Tiananmen Square, the largest in the world as it can accommodate 1,000,000 people. Also in the square is an obelisk to honor the Chinese heroes and a mausoleum for Mao. The mausoleum was not open during this day. To the side of the square was the Museum of History and Revolution with an Olympic sign on its front. The sign had a countdown to the opening of the Olympic Games. On the last day in Beijing, another couple stood in line to view the body of Mao.

Before the trip, one fellow suggested that his wife not wear her "Free Tibet" tee shirt in Tiananmen Square. He did not want his mother and father to spend any of his inheritance bailing her from a jail in China!)

As the group walked across Tiananmen Square, Lei talked about the Chinese flag and the army soldiers who were there. It was obvious that Lei, even though he is not a member of the Communist Party, gave the group the government line. Like Campbell on the cruise ship, he said that the Tibetan problem was a family squabble and that the West should stay out of it. He then talked about the Last Emperor. Lei talked favorably of the overthrow of the dynasty and the repatriation of the Last Emperor, who in his later years became a gardener, like a common person. Lei said that Mao is considered a national hero, "Seventy percent of what Mao did was correct, and 30% was wrong. Mao's main error was the Cultural Revolution."

Across the widest street in Beijing is a building with a picture of Mao, a picture that is changed every year. On one left side of the picture are the words in Chinese translated as "Long Life of the Peoples Republic of China." On the right side are the words "Long Life to All Peoples of the World." This building lies almost at the entrance of The Forbidden City.

We walked into the Forbidden City with its many buildings and 9,999 rooms, one short of the 10,000 rooms in Heaven. The City took fifteen years to build with 1,000,000 workers and covers 250 acres. In The Forbidden City are a business section and a housing section for the Emperor and his many concubines. One emperor had up to 3,000 concubines. The eunuchs would put the names of the concubines in a basket and draw out the one to be used. The concubine would then prepare herself for the emperor. Many times the concubine would bribe the eunuch so that she would be selected, become pregnant, and hopefully have a male child. If the emperor selected this child to be his successor, the mother would have a favorable position. Lei said, "Many emperors died young, maybe because of too many concubines."

As we entered The Forbidden City, on the balcony of one the buildings was an "emperor" type individual dressed in yellow. In the old times, only the emperor wore yellow. If anyone other than emperor wore yellow, they risked being killed.

For a few years, Starbucks had a business in The Forbidden City. Lei pointed out to the group its location. People in Beijing criticized Starbucks being there, so it closed.

On the corners of the buildings are statues of animals. The number of animals signifies the importance of the building. Nine is a lucky number for the Chinese, so if the building has nine animal statues, that building is important. Lesser important buildings have fewer statues. I don't remember seeing any building with fewer than three statues.

The last section of The Forbidden City the group saw was a garden with many flowers, trees, and rock formations. Lei said that the gardens are built with harmony in mind. The elements to achieve harmony in the garden are the following and are in the order of importance: water, stone, trees and plants, and buildings.

We returned to the hotel and had a typical Chinese dinner in the hotel.

Monday, April 7 (cloudy and cool)
One never really knows if the sun shined in Beijing when we were there because of the pollution haze.

Lei (our tour guide) majored in English in college and has a company of tour guides whom hire out to travel agencies like Go Next. He laughed when I suggested that he was a CEO. We visited about the Chinese alphabet with its thousands of characters. He said that Chinese learn the characters one at a time. He already is teaching his ten-month old daughter some of the characters. He has software for his computer which has a Standard English board and which he uses to type the Chinese characters. He said that the average income for people in Beijing is $3,000 to $5,000 a year.

Peking University, one of the best in China, cost about $3,000 a year.

On the way to the Ming Tomb, Lei described the Cultural Revolution, a counter-revolution from 1966 to 1976. The main people involved were the Red Guard, mostly college and high school students. They believed that they must destroy Old China before New China will occur. Professionals, e.g., teachers, were forced into menial job, such as cleaning hog pens. Most believe it was led by Mao even though they were unsure. Mao died in 1976, and his wife and the Gang of Four replaced him. Chinese called the Gang of Four evil.

The Ming Tomb is a graveyard for the Ming Dynasty, who ruled during the Golden Age of China. They believe that they would have a similar life after death. They sacrificed concubines for the next life. Thirteen emperors are buried in separate tombs. Only one tomb, that of the thirteenth emperor, has been excavated. The Red Guard during the Cultural Revolution destroyed most of the treasure from this tomb.

The road to the Memorial Building is lined with trees and statues. The Memorial Building of the tomb is made of sandalwood with large support poles and beams. The main memorial is to Cheng Zu, the third emperor of the Ming Dynasty. Inside the Memorial Building were displays of gold, silver, and jade pieces and some crowns and clothing taken from the thirteenth tomb. The government is trying to decide if it wants to excavate the tomb of Cheng Zu.

We ate lunch at The Friendship Restaurant, a combination of restaurant and cloisonné factory. Cloisonné is enamel work in which a metal surface is decorated with thin copper wire and then painted.

After lunch, the tour group went to the Great Wall. The Wall is approximately 4000 miles long running east and west in Northern China. The Wall was built beginning 500 BC and continued until the Ming Dynasty.

Its purpose was to keep warlike tribes, such as those from Manchuria, away from Southern China. The wall is wide enough for six horses with frequent towers. The towers were used to signal the nearby community when the enemies came.

Lei led the group to a starting point to the Wall, and Mardy and I walked perhaps a mile. The brick and stone used to construct the wall are steep and uneven. Some places are steep enough so that we held onto the railing to keep from falling. As usual, the vendors did not help as they sometimes stepped in front of us trying to sell their product. We expended a lot of energy in this walk.

On the return trip to the hotel, we drove by The Bird Nest, the Olympic stadium for 90,000 spectators, but the dense smog clouded a clear view of it. Both The Bird Cage and the adjacent aquatic center are unique. The tour group did not have the opportunity to tour the Olympic area. We took pictures of The Bird Nest from the moving tour bus; pictures, which are blurred because of the haze, caused by the pollution.

At home after the tour, I read that Beijing is the most polluted city in the world. Lei said that all industries will be closed for two weeks before the Olympics and that the cars will be restricted. A car with an odd number as the last number on its license plate will be allowed to drive on odd numbered days and an even number on even numbered days.

That evening was the farewell dinner featuring Peking duck. The duck was sliced in front of the table. The slices were put in a bun or a pancake along with raw cucumber and onion and a thickened soy sauce. The remainder of the meal was much the same as the other Chinese meals we were served.

Tuesday, April 8, 2008 (cloudy)

We packed our luggage the evening before and watched some CNN. Occasionally the screen would go dark and it was obvious news about the protests over Tibet were being blacked out. Everyone was aware of what was happening as well as the Chinese.

The next morning we were bussed to the beautiful Beijing Airport. The airport opens six months before the 2008 Summer Olympics are held. It is the world's largest airport building and took 4 years to construct. By 2012 the airport it is expected to handle 90 million passenger per year. There are beautiful young girls at every doorway and many other locations to answer questions or help in any other way they can. They have so many people in their country that I imagine they try to keep them employed any way they can. After clearing customs, which was quick and easily accomplished, we began the long trip home.

Chapter 29

Australia, New Zealand and Fiji

This chapter probably was not meant to be. I put the chapter heading in early during the summer and intended to fill in content after returning from the trip. We were scheduled to meet a group in Los Angeles on October 1 2010 and leave for Melbourne Tullamarine Airport. We set up a flight with United Airlines to get us to LA to catch the group leaving from there at 11:20 PM aboard a Qantas Airbus A380-800. Duration of the flight was to be 15 hours and 35 minutes.

We would continue the remainder of the tour using Qantas from Melbourne to Alice Springs, from Ayers Rock to Cairns, from Cairns to Sidney Kingsford Smith Airport, from Sidney to Christchurch International Airport. We would have then flown Queenstown, New Zealand to Auckland, from Auckland to Nadi, Fiji and then from Nadi to Los Angeles on October 26, 2010.

The brochure and other material explaining what we would see made us sorry we had to cancel after being a point where all we had to do was board a plane. All the preliminary requirements had been accomplished.

Why did we cancel? About two weeks before the scheduled departure date I got an abdominal obstruction. I had had 4 similar occurrences since my colon cancer surgery in February 1981. Although it had never required surgery to correct the problem, it did require a hospital stay. We didn't want to be out the country even if we corrected the problem before the departure date. Then I developed flu-like symptoms. I am not fully recovered from that and final doctor's appointment is tomorrow morning, September 23rd, seven days prior to what would have been our departure day. Thank goodness we had A Travel Protection Plan.

CHAPTER 30

Conclusion

There is so much more that could have been covered had I expanded on events that took place in my life. My wife Mardy kept stressing that I should convey my feelings as they related to happenings and how they affected me at the time. I would have to list the years 1941 and 1981 as the two most difficult years in my life. I had just finished high school in 1941. I didn't know what I wanted to do. College was not even given a thought since it wasn't financially possible. My high school girl friend would have two years of schooling left before graduating. I was almost certain she would meet others during those two final years of schooling she had remaining.

My parents were separated with divorce being considered. The war clouds were building and that added to the uncertainty as to what course or direction should be taken. There was no one I felt I could turn to for guidance. Although it is almost 70 years since all those feelings, frustrations, fears, and concerns were experienced, they can be just as real today if I leave myself dwell on them.

The year 1981 was also difficult but by that time I could more easily cope with problems than I could at age 18. My wife Kay had a series of medical problems beginning about 20 years earlier. Toward the end of 1980 Kay's creatine levels became so high during the last part of 1980 that she was placed on dialysis. It was determined she was experiencing kidney failure. Her name was placed on a list but chances of receiving a donated organ were slim because of her age. In the meantime she was placed on dialysis twice a week to keep her alive. I had retired from my work in December 1980 to be able to insure she could meet the hospital schedule for her visits. Because of the limited number of dialysis machines, Kay had to be in the hospital by 5:30 A.M. This was because she lived in town and could be on the machine during the time those living in the outlying areas were driving into the hospital. She was usually done by 9:30.

In March 1981 the family obtained a franchise and started selling supplies to business firms to insure they were in compliance with OSHA requirements. Monthly quotas and yearly goals were established. The stress of trying to operate the business and take care of Kay was beginning to have an effect on my health. Early in 1982 I suffered a heart attack and passed it off as a bout with the flu. My youngest son returned from California early in 1983 and acquired the business. He moved the operation from Bismarck to Fargo, North Dakota. I was so happy to be rid of that operation. He has turned it into a very successful and profitable business.

Kay received a kidney transplant in March 1983 because she was willing to test a new anti-rejection drug for the University of Minnesota. Otherwise she was considered ineligible because of her age. We began to travel. Her health continued to worsen and as indicated in an earlier chapter her life became a series of clinic visits and hospital stays. Life wasn't enjoyable for her since she really wasn't ever free of pain.

I would like to conclude by listing some of the more memorable and enjoyable periods in my life.

My Early School Years

How exciting it was to start school. Learning the alphabet, making new life-long friends and learning to read opened up a whole new world for me in my early years. Concluding my three years of high school with a successful basketball team made for some remarkable memories.

My Military Years

The 3-year army career with the US Paratroops provided me with travel I would never have found possible on my own. Here again I met men that became very close to not only during our service time together but also continued long after active duty and up to the time of their deaths. We formed an Association to maintain that closeness through reunions and a web site on the Internet. I had the privilege and honor of being selected twice to serve as President of that Association. The military was instrumental in my being able to attend college, which resulted in a much more satisfying, and fulfilling life.

My First Marriage

The young 14-year old girl I thought about so much in my early teen-age years eventually became my wife after I returned from military service. We were only six months shy of spending 50 happy years together. Although she was plagued with poor health during a large part of those years, I give her credit for not only providing me with a happy marriage but was instrumental in raising two fine sons.

My College Years

Again we were able to meet a large number of people who would become life-long friends. Although many are no longer around or able to associate with us, the memories of our times with them remains. The benefits of the college education have greatly improved my life not only financially but also socially. It was a great three years.

My Sons' Development

That Saturday morning, April 2, 1949 seems like such a short time ago. More than six decades have passed since I was called out of Lab at the university to give consent to surgery. It was one of the most frightening moments in my life. Why when giving birth for so many women was simple did my wife need what could be life threatening surgery to accomplish the task? I was told that after 30 hour of labor our first born son may die if not taken by C-Section. What a relief and happy moment when I was told everything was just fine. Today Tom is married, successful and leads a happy life.

On February 8, 1952 my second Mark was born by the same procedure. However, this time some of the fear was not present but concern for a healthy baby was hoped for and received. He is so much different from Tom. They each have taken separate paths in their developing years and it has been enjoyable for Kay and me to observe that.

My Productive Years

My years in Engineering were satisfying and enjoyable. I spent 31 years with the same organization and was stationed in the same location. I could have applied for openings all over the world but we wanted to give our sons the opportunity to attend one high school, live in one city and make life-long friends. I loved the work and the people I worked with.

Second Marriage

I had a second opportunity that many do not get. After 5 years I met my first wife's best friend and discovered a person can love more than once. It may not be the same type of love as that first love but I have found happiness and contentment by being with a person that I find intelligent, funny, and spirited. We have now been married almost ten years. We have traveled England, Europe, China, and almost Australia, New Zealand and the Fiji Island. We will continue to travel as long as we are able.

We have shared many pleasant moments at home and at the lake in Minnesota. Our toast with a glass of wine is "100". We both know what it means. May it happen. If I don't make it I will be satisfied with what I was dealt in life.

About The Author

Merle W. Mc Morrow was born in Hankinson North Dakota on April 22, 1923. He spent his 12 years of schooling in Breckenridge, Minnesota. At the age of 18 he went to Puget Sound Navy Yard in Bremerton, Washington to work on ships returning for repair after being damaged by the Japanese bombing of Pearl Harbor, Hawaii on December 7, 1941.

In December 1942 he returned to Breckenridge to enlist in the U.S. Army Air Corps. However, before he could obtain a draft release from the Draft Board in Bremerton, the Air Corps closed their enlistment program at midnight on December 15, 1942. He then volunteered for the US Army Paratroops at the age of nineteen. He saw action in Italy, France, Belgium, Luxembourg and Germany. He returned home Christmas Day 1945.

He married Kathryn Jonietz on June 12,1946 in Glendale, California. Returning home to Minnesota he enrolled in Civil Engineering in October 1946 at North Dakota State University and graduated in August 1949. He accepted a position with the United States Government on September 12, 1949. He retired on December 30, 1980.

His wife died on January 8, 1996 just six months short of their 50th wedding anniversary. They have two sons; Thomas, born on April 2, 1949, lives on Lake Minnetonka in Wayzata, Minnesota and Mark, born on February 8, 1952, lives in Fargo, North Dakota.

On December 9, 2000, Merle married Margaret Chapman, a former Bismarck resident and long-time neighbor. The author is active with his military unit assisting with reunions and was editor of the Unit's newspaper for four years. He was President of the Unit's Association in 1999-2001 and again in 2009-2011.

He and his wife travel as well as being involved in charity work and volunteer work with the Fargo Police Department and Habitat for Humanity.